DISCOVER FRONTPAGE 97

FrontPage Explorer Toolbar Buttons

- Open the New FrontPage Web dialog box, so you can add more pages to the existing web or create an entirely new one.
- Open the Open FrontPage Web dialog box, so you can open an existing web on the Web server you are currently working on or on another Web server.
- Open the Find in FrontPage Web dialog box, so you can search for text in any of the pages in the web.
- Open the Spelling dialog box, so you can check the spelling of any pages in the web.
- Display Hyperlink view.
- Display Folder view.
- This button is only active in Folder view. A typical up-one-level command, which selects the parent directory of the selected one.
- Display images in Hyperlink view (has no effect in Folder view).
- Include repeated links in Hyperlink view, multiple links from a Web page to another object (has no effect in Folder view).
- Include internal links in Hyperlink view, links from one part of a Web page to another (has no effect in Folder view).
- Open the FrontPage Editor, where you'll create and edit Web pages.
- Open To Do List, which you'll use to keep track of tasks you must complete in your web.
- Open the Image Editor, in which you can create images for your Web pages.
- Cancel an operation, such as opening a document in the FrontPage Editor or recalculating links.
- Open the FrontPage Help system. Click the button, then click something you want information about.
- A *busy* indicator. When FrontPage Explorer is busy doing something, this icon is animated.

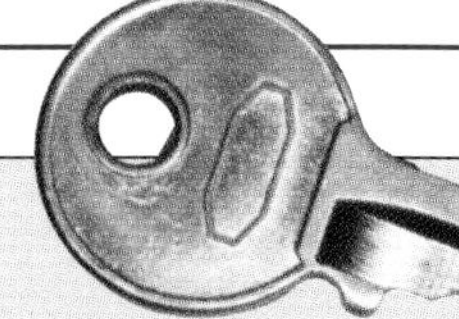

The Web Page Icons

You'll see these icons in your Web pages

This means that there's a piece of JavaScript embedded into this Web page.

This represents a piece of VBScript embedded into the page.

This represents a file that's been embedded into the Web page (using the <EMBED> HTML tag). It's intended to be displayed or played by a browser plug-in.

This represents a Java applet, embedded into the Web page using the <APPLET> HTML tag.

This represents a piece of HTML code that the Editor can't recognize.

This represents a <!-- --> HTML tag, an HTML comment line.

This represents a bookmark.

This represents an image that is embedded into the document but cannot be displayed by FrontPage because it's not in your web.

This represents an ActiveX control.

For more information about IDG Books call **1-800-762-2974.**

ISBN 0-7645-3085-2

DISCOVER FRONTPAGE™ 97

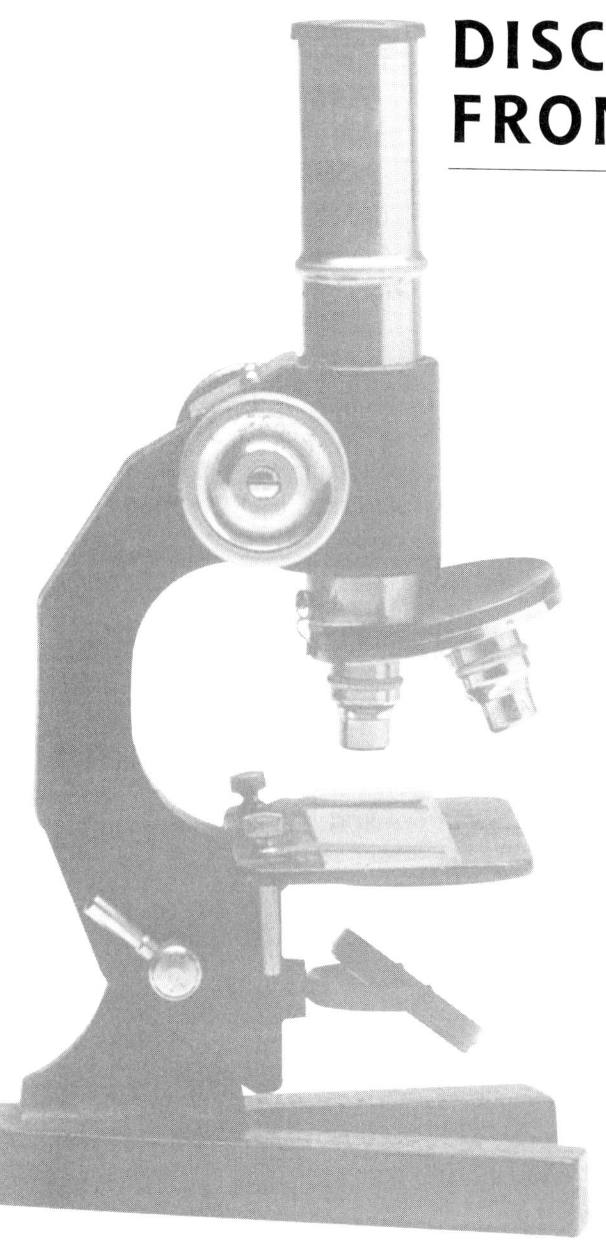

DISCOVER FRONTPAGE™ 97

BY PETER KENT

IDG BOOKS WORLDWIDE, INC.

AN INTERNATIONAL
DATA GROUP COMPANY

FOSTER CITY, CA • CHICAGO, IL •
INDIANAPOLIS, IN • SOUTHLAKE, TX

Discover FrontPage™ 97

Published by
IDG Books Worldwide, Inc.
An International Data Group Company
919 E. Hillsdale Blvd., Suite 400
Foster City, CA 94404

`http://www.idgbooks.com` (IDG Books Worldwide Web site)

Library of Congress Catalog Card No.: 96-70133

ISBN: 1-7645-3085-2

Printed in the United States of America

10 9 8 7 6 5 4 3 2 1

1B/RU/QT/ZX/FC

Distributed in the United States by IDG Books Worldwide, Inc.

Distributed by Macmillan Canada for Canada; by Contemporanea de Ediciones for Venezuela; by Distribuidora Cuspide for Argentina; by CITEC for Brazil; by Ediciones ZETA S.C.R. Ltda. for Peru; by Editorial Limusa SA for Mexico; by Transworld Publishers Limited in the United Kingdom and Europe; by Academic Bookshop for Egypt; by Levant Distributors S.A.R.L. for Lebanon; by Al Jassim for Saudi Arabia; by Simron Pty. Ltd. for South Africa; by Pustak Mahal for India; by The Computer Bookshop for India; by Toppan Company Ltd. for Japan; by Addison Wesley Publishing Company for Korea; by Longman Singapore Publishers Ltd. for Singapore, Malaysia, Thailand, and Indonesia; by Unalis Corporation for Taiwan; by WS Computer Publishing Company, Inc. for the Philippines; by WoodsLane Pty. Ltd. for Australia; by WoodsLane Enterprises Ltd. for New Zealand. Authorized Sales Agent: Anthony Rudkin Associates for the Middle East and North Africa.

For general information on IDG Books Worldwide's books in the U.S., please call our Consumer Customer Service department at 800-762-2974. For reseller information, including discounts and premium sales, please call our Reseller Customer Service department at 800-434-3422.

For information on where to purchase IDG Books Worldwide's books outside the U.S., please contact our International Sales department at 415-655-3172 or fax 415-655-3295.

For information on foreign language translations, please contact our Foreign & Subsidiary Rights department at 415-655-3021 or fax 415-655-3281.

For sales inquiries and special prices for bulk quantities, please contact our Sales department at 415-655-3200 or write to the address above.

For information on using IDG Books Worldwide's books in the classroom or for ordering examination copies, please contact our Educational Sales department at 800-434-2086 or fax 817-251-8174.

For press review copies, author interviews, or other publicity information, please contact our Public Relations department at 415-655-3000 or fax 415-655-3299.

For authorization to photocopy items for corporate, personal, or educational use, please contact Copyright Clearance Center, 222 Rosewood Drive, Danvers, MA 01923, or fax 508-750-4470.

ABOUT IDG BOOKS WORLDWIDE

Welcome to the world of IDG Books Worldwide.

IDG Books Worldwide, Inc., is a subsidiary of International Data Group, the world's largest publisher of computer-related information and the leading global provider of information services on information technology. IDG was founded more than 25 years ago and now employs more than 8,500 people worldwide. IDG publishes more than 275 computer publications in over 75 countries (see listing below). More than 60 million people read one or more IDG publications each month.

Launched in 1990, IDG Books Worldwide is today the #1 publisher of best-selling computer books in the United States. We are proud to have received eight awards from the Computer Press Association in recognition of editorial excellence and three from *Computer Currents'* First Annual Readers' Choice Awards. Our best-selling *...For Dummies®* series has more than 30 million copies in print with translations in 30 languages. IDG Books Worldwide, through a joint venture with IDG's Hi-Tech Beijing, became the first U.S. publisher to publish a computer book in the People's Republic of China. In record time, IDG Books Worldwide has become the first choice for millions of readers around the world who want to learn how to better manage their businesses.

Our mission is simple: Every one of our books is designed to bring extra value and skill-building instructions to the reader. Our books are written by experts who understand and care about our readers. The knowledge base of our editorial staff comes from years of experience in publishing, education, and journalism — experience we use to produce books for the '90s. In short, we care about books, so we attract the best people. We devote special attention to details such as audience, interior design, use of icons, and illustrations. And because we use an efficient process of authoring, editing, and desktop publishing our books electronically, we can spend more time ensuring superior content and spend less time on the technicalities of making books.

You can count on our commitment to deliver high-quality books at competitive prices on topics you want to read about. At IDG Books Worldwide, we continue in the IDG tradition of delivering quality for more than 25 years. You'll find no better book on a subject than one from IDG Books Worldwide.

John Kilcullen
CEO
IDG Books Worldwide, Inc.

Eighth Annual Computer Press Awards 1992

Ninth Annual Computer Press Awards 1993

X WINNER

Tenth Annual Computer Press Awards 1994

Eleventh Annual Computer Press Awards 1995

IDG Books Worldwide, Inc., is a subsidiary of International Data Group, the world's largest publisher of computer-related information and the leading global provider of information services on information technology. International Data Group publishes over 275 computer publications in over 75 countries. Sixty million people read one or more International Data Group publications each month. International Data Group's publications include: **ARGENTINA:** Buyer's Guide, Computerworld Argentina, PC World Argentina; **AUSTRALIA:** Australian Macworld, Australian PC World, Australian Reseller News, Computerworld, IT Casebook, Network World, Publish, Webmaster; **AUSTRIA:** Computerwelt Osterreich, Networks Austria, PC Tip Austria; **BANGLADESH:** PC World Bangladesh; **BELARUS:** PC World Belarus; **BELGIUM:** Data News; **BRAZIL:** Annuário de Informática, Computerworld, Connections, Macworld, PC Player, PC World, Publish, Reseller News, Supergamepower; **BULGARIA:** Computerworld Bulgaria, Network World Bulgaria, PC & MacWorld Bulgaria; **CANADA:** CIO Canada, Client/Server World, ComputerWorld Canada, InfoWorld Canada, NetworkWorld Canada, WebWorld; **CHILE:** Computerworld Chile, PC World Chile; **COLOMBIA:** Computerworld Colombia, PC World Colombia; **COSTA RICA:** PC World Centro America; **THE CZECH AND SLOVAK REPUBLICS:** Computerworld Czechoslovakia, Macworld Czech Republic, PC World Czechoslovakia; **DENMARK:** Communications World Danmark, Computerworld Danmark, Macworld Danmark, PC World Danmark, Techworld Denmark; **DOMINICAN REPUBLIC:** PC World Republica Dominicana; **ECUADOR:** PC World Ecuador; **EGYPT:** Computerworld Middle East, PC World Middle East; **EL SALVADOR:** PC World Centro America; **FINLAND:** MikroPC, Tietoverkko, Tietoviikko; **FRANCE:** Distributique, Hebdo, Info PC, Le Monde Informatique, Macworld, Reseaux & Telecoms, WebMaster France; **GERMANY:** Computer Partner, Computerwoche, Computerwoche Extra, Computerwoche FOCUS, Global Online, Macwelt, PC Welt; **GREECE:** Amiga Computing, GamePro Greece, Multimedia World; **GUATEMALA:** PC World Centro America; **HONDURAS:** PC World Centro America; **HONG KONG:** Computerworld Hong Kong, PC World Hong Kong, Publish in Asia; **HUNGARY:** ABCD CD-ROM, Computerworld Szamitastechnika, Internetto online Magazine, PC World Hungary, PC-X Magazin Hungary; **ICELAND:** Tolvuheimur PC World Island; **INDIA:** Information Communications World, Information Systems Computerworld, PC World India, Publish in Asia; **INDONESIA:** InfoKomputer PC World, Komputek Computerworld, Publish in Asia; **IRELAND:** ComputerScope, PC Live!; **ISRAEL:** Macworld Israel, People & Computers/Computerworld; **ITALY:** Computerworld Italia, Macworld Italia, Networking Italia, PC World Italia; **JAPAN:** DTP World, Macworld Japan, Nikkei Personal Computing, OS/2 World Japan, SunWorld Japan, Windows NT World, Windows World Japan; **KENYA:** PC World East African; **KOREA:** Hi-Tech Information, Macworld Korea, PC World Korea; **MACEDONIA:** PC World Macedonia; **MALAYSIA:** Computerworld Malaysia, PC World Malaysia, Publish in Asia; **MALTA:** PC World Malta; **MEXICO:** Computerworld Mexico, PC World Mexico; **MYANMAR:** PC World Myanmar; **NETHERLANDS:** Computer! Totaal, LAN Internetworking Magazine, LAN World Buyers Guide, Macworld Netherlands, Net, WebWereld; **NEW ZEALAND:** Absolute Beginners Guide and Plain & Simple Series, Computer Buyer, Computer Industry Directory, Computerworld New Zealand, MTB, Network World, PC World New Zealand; **NICARAGUA:** PC World Centro America; **NORWAY:** Computerworld Norge, CW Rapport, Datamagasinet, Financial Rapport, Kursguide Norge, Macworld Norge, Multimediaworld Norge, PC World Ekspress Norge, PC World Nettverk, PC World Norge, PC World ProduktGuide Norge; **PAKISTAN:** Computerworld Pakistan; **PANAMA:** PC World Panama; **PEOPLE'S REPUBLIC OF CHINA:** China Computer Users, China Computerworld, China InfoWorld, China Telecom World Weekly, Computer & Communication, Electronic Design China, Electronics Today, Electronics Weekly, Game Software, PC World China, Popular Computer Week, Software Weekly, Software World, Telecom World; **PERU:** Computerworld Peru, PC World Profesional Peru, PC World SoHo Peru; **PHILIPPINES:** Click!, Computerworld Philippines, PC World Philippines, Publish in Asia; **POLAND:** Computerworld Poland, Computerworld Special Report Poland, Cyber, Macworld Poland, Networld Poland, PC World Komputer; **PORTUGAL:** Cerebro/PC World, Computerworld/Correio Informático, Dealer World Portugal, Mac*In/PC*In Portugal, Multimedia World; **PUERTO RICO:** PC World Puerto Rico; **ROMANIA:** Computerworld Romania, PC World Romania, Telecom Romania; **RUSSIA:** Computerworld Russia, Mir PK, Publish, Seti; **SINGAPORE:** Computerworld Singapore, PC World Singapore, Publish in Asia; **SLOVENIA:** Monitor; **SOUTH AFRICA:** Computing SA, Network World SA, Software World SA; **SPAIN:** Communicaciones World España, Computerworld España, Dealer World España, Macworld España, PC World España; **SRI LANKA:** Infolink PC World; **SWEDEN:** CAP&Design, Computer Sweden, Corporate Computing Sweden, Internetworld Sweden, it.branschen, Macworld Sweden, MaxiData Sweden, MikroDatorn, Nätverk & Kommunikation, PC World Sweden, PCaktiv, Windows World Sweden; **SWITZERLAND:** Computerworld Schweiz, Macworld Schweiz, PCtip; **TAIWAN:** Computerworld Taiwan, Macworld Taiwan, NEW ViSiON/Publish, PC World Taiwan, Windows World Taiwan; **THAILAND:** Publish in Asia, Thai Computerworld; **TURKEY:** Computerworld Turkiye, Macworld Turkiye, Network World Turkiye, PC World Turkiye; **UKRAINE:** Computerworld Kiev, Multimedia World Ukraine, PC World Ukraine; **UNITED KINGDOM:** Acorn User UK, Amiga Action UK, Amiga Computing UK, Apple Talk UK, Computing, Macworld, Parents and Computers UK, PC Advisor, PC Home, PSX Pro, The WEB; **UNITED STATES:** Cable in the Classroom, CIO Magazine, Computerworld, DOS World, Federal Computer Week, GamePro Magazine, InfoWorld, I-Way, Macworld, Network World, PC Games, PC World, Publish, Video Event, THE WEB Magazine, and WebMaster; online webzines: JavaWorld, NetscapeWorld, and SunWorld Online; **URUGUAY:** InfoWorld Uruguay; **VENEZUELA:** Computerworld Venezuela, PC World Venezuela; and **VIETNAM:** PC World Vietnam.

2/14/97

Welcome to the Discover Series

Do you want to discover the best and most efficient ways to use your computer and learn about technology? Books in the Discover series teach you the essentials of technology with a friendly, confident approach. You'll find a Discover book on almost any subject — from the Internet to intranets, from Web design and programming to the business programs that make your life easier.

We've provided valuable, real-world examples that help you relate to topics faster. Discover books begin by introducing you to the main features of programs, so you start by doing something *immediately*. The focus is to teach you how to perform tasks that are useful and meaningful in your day-to-day work. You might create a document or graphic, explore your computer, surf the Web, or write a program. Whatever the task, you learn the most commonly used features, and focus on the best tips and techniques for doing your work. You'll get results quickly, and discover the best ways to use software and technology in your everyday life.

You may find the following elements and features in this book:

Discovery Central: This tearout card is a handy quick reference to important tasks or ideas covered in the book.

Quick Tour: The Quick Tour gets you started working with the book right away.

Real-Life Vignettes: Throughout the book you'll see one-page scenarios illustrating a real-life application of a topic covered.

Goals: Each chapter opens with a list of goals you can achieve by reading the chapter.

Side Trips: These asides include additional information about alternative or advanced ways to approach the topic covered.

Bonuses: Timesaving tips and more advanced techniques are covered in each chapter.

Discovery Center: This guide illustrates key procedures covered throughout the book.

Visual Index: You'll find real-world documents in the Visual Index, with page numbers pointing you to where you should turn to achieve the effects shown.

Throughout the book, you'll also notice some special icons and formatting:

A Feature Focus icon highlights new features in the software's latest release, and points out significant differences between it and the previous version.

Web Paths refer you to Web sites that provide additional information about the topic.

Tips offer timesaving shortcuts, expert advice, quick techniques, or brief reminders.

The X-Ref icon refers you to other chapters or sections for more information.

Pull Quotes emphasize important ideas that are covered in the chapter.

Notes provide additional information or highlight special points of interest about a topic.

The Caution icon alerts you to potential problems you should watch out for.

The Discover series delivers interesting, insightful, and inspiring information about technology to help you learn faster and retain more. So the next time you want to find answers to your technology questions, reach for a Discover book. We hope the entertaining, easy-to-read style puts you at ease and makes learning fun.

Credits

ACQUISITIONS EDITOR
Ellen Camm

DEVELOPMENT EDITOR
Kay Keppler

TECHNICAL EDITOR
Mary Meyers

COPY EDITOR
Felicity O'Meara
Larisa North

PRODUCTION COORDINATOR
Susan Parini

QUALITY CONTROL SPECIALIST
Mick Arellano

GRAPHICS AND PRODUCTION SPECIALISTS
Laura Carpenter
Jude Levinson
Ed Penslien
Christopher Pimentel
Dina F Quan
Andreas F. Schueller

PROOFREADERS
Desne Border
Andrew Davis
Stacey Lynn
Candace Ward
Anne Weinberger

INDEXER
Lori Lathrop

BOOK DESIGN
Seventeenth Street Studios
Phyllis Beaty
Kurt Krames

About the Author

Peter Kent has been testing and installing software and hardware, training users, and writing computer books and documentation for 15 years. He's the author of *Discover Microsoft Windows NT Workstation* (IDG Books Worldwide), the best-selling *Complete Idiot's Guide to the Internet* (Que), and around 30 other computer- and Internet-related books. His work has appeared in a variety of publications, from *The Manchester Guardian* to *Internet World*, *Windows User*, and the *Dallas Times Herald*. His books have been translated into more than a dozen languages.

Peter spent about ten years selling his technical writing services to anyone who would pay, but now mostly sits at home in monkish isolation writing computer books. Well, not quite monkish; he lives with his wife and two boys in Denver, Colorado, 50 minutes from the nearest ski slopes (which he plans to visit far more often once he slows down and writes fewer books). He can be reached at `idg1@arundel.com`.

FOR NICHOLAS

PREFACE

Welcome to *Discover FrontPage 97*. This book provides step-by-step instructions for using FrontPage 97 to create attractive and sophisticated Web sites. If you've created Web pages by working with HTML, you'll find that FrontPage is an exceptional shortcut. What might have taken hours or even days in "the old days" may now only take minutes. If you've never created Web pages before, you'll discover that using FrontPage is much like working with a word processor.

Either way, you'll need a little help to get up to speed as quickly as possible. That's where this book comes in. It will help you learn everything you need to know about FrontPage quickly and efficiently. In a few days, you'll be creating collections of Web pages that would have required the skills of a programmer in days past. You'll create forms that collect information from users and save them in a form you can use to import the data into a database program. You'll create discussion groups that make your Web sites interactive; users can leave messages for you or for other users, then return later to read responses. The complicated series of Web pages required for a discussion group can be created in five minutes or less with the help of FrontPage. Without FrontPage it may take you hours or longer.

Here are just a few of the things you'll learn in *Discover FrontPage 97*:

* What the FrontPage server extensions can do for you, and how to find a Web server that has them installed
* What FrontPage *webs* are, and how to create and manage them
* How to work "live" online, modifying your Web pages stored at a site that may be thousands of miles away
* How to create Web pages within your web
* How to create hyperlinks between pages
* Working with images: inserting them into your documents and making them work as links
* Embedding multimedia — sounds, video, animations, and more — into your Web pages
* Using the FrontPage WebBots to automate useful functions: inserting data from one page into another, swapping images automatically at a particular time and date, and much more
* How to insert Java applets into your documents, and how to work with JavaScript and VBScript

- Creating tables — using different dimensions, background images, colors, border sizes, and so on
- How to create framed documents and use targeted windows
- How to work with forms of many kinds: feedback forms, search forms, discussion groups, survey forms, and so on
- How to define who can edit your Web pages, so that other members of your department or workgroup can collaborate on a Web site
- Creating private Web sites that only authorized users may view; or creating Web sites that anyone can view as long as they register first

In addition to the standard Discover series icons, you'll also find the following icon:

The Server Extensions icon indicates features that work only on FrontPage-enabled servers.

Discover FrontPage 97 is a down-to-earth guide to making the best use of FrontPage 97. Turn to the first chapter . . . and get started.

Acknowledgments

Thanks to Kay Keppler and Felicity O'Meara, this book's development editor and copy editor, who made this the smoothest editorial process of my career. Thanks also to Digiserve, the Web-hosting company with the misfortune to be hosting my domain, who had to put up with me creating and deleting fake webs just to see what would happen.

CONTENTS AT A GLANCE

PART THREE—ADVANCED WEB AUTHORING

CONTENTS

FRONTPAGE 97 QUICK TOUR

PRACTICE USING THESE SKILLS

Opening FrontPage and Creating a Web

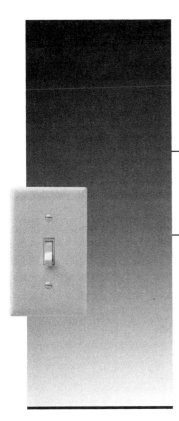

This procedure assumes that you have installed FrontPage and a Web server. By default the FrontPage installation program will install the FrontPage Personal Web Server for you.

1. Open FrontPage 97: select Start → Programs → Microsoft FrontPage. If this is the first time you've started FrontPage you'll see a message saying "FrontPage will now try to determine your machine's hostname and TCP/IP address. This may take several minutes."
2. Click OK and FrontPage begins checking for information related to your computer's connection to the web server.
3. In a few moments you'll see another dialog box providing your hostname. This is the host computer storing your webs. For instance, "localhost" means that the computer you are currently working with is storing your webs.

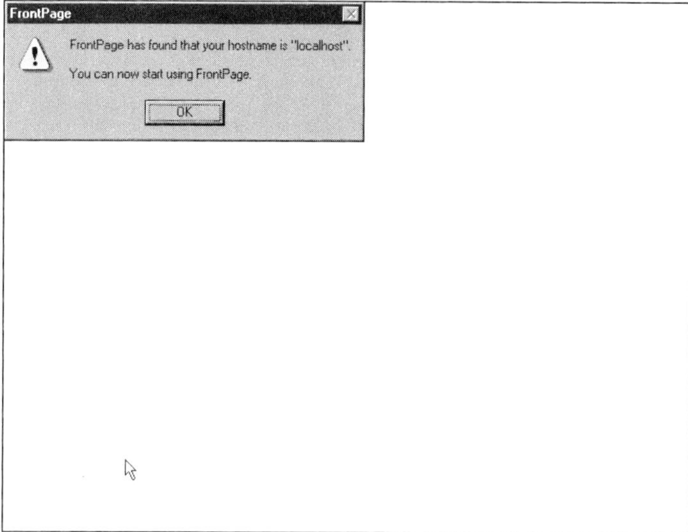

4. Click OK and you'll see the Getting Started With Microsoft FrontPage dialog box.

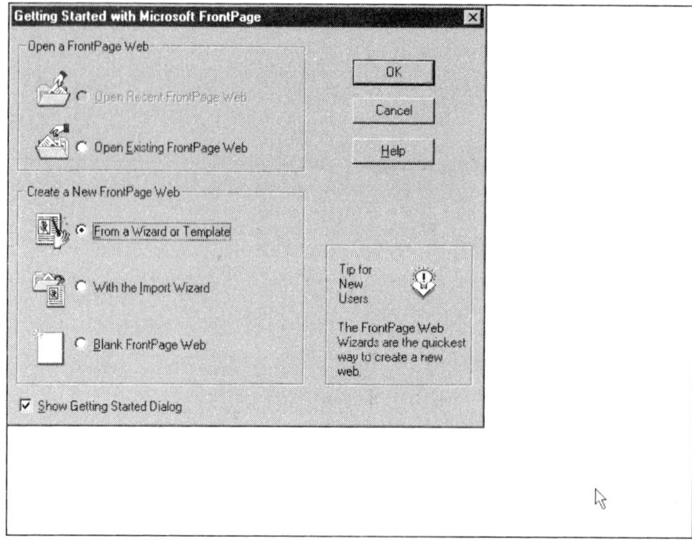

5. Click the *From a Wizard or Template* option button, then click OK.

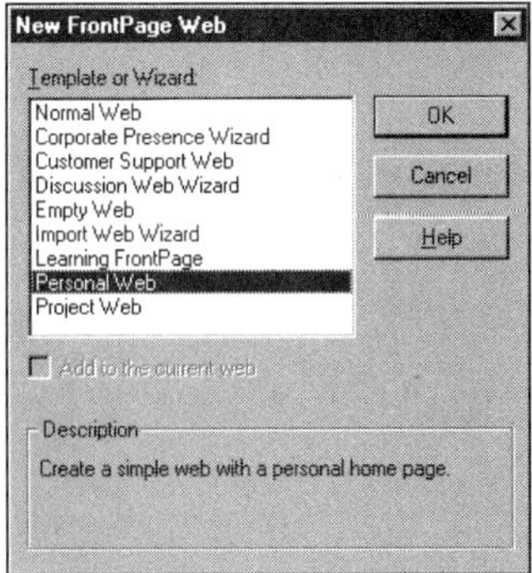

6. Click on Personal Web in the list box, then click OK.

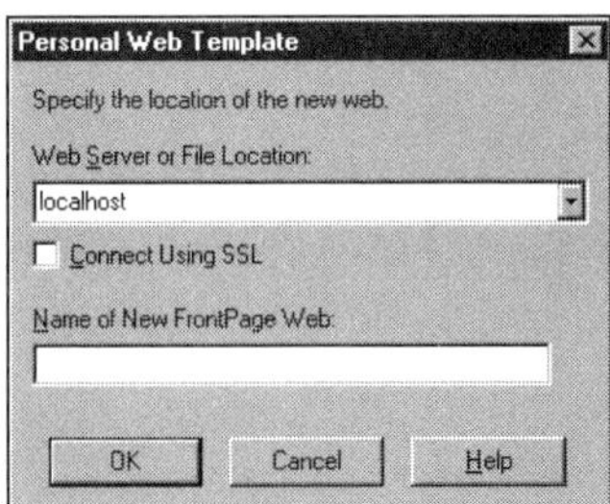

7. In the *Name of New FrontPage Web* text box, type a name for your web: "Personal" or "My Web," for instance. Click OK and FrontPage begins creating the web, then prompts you for your account information.

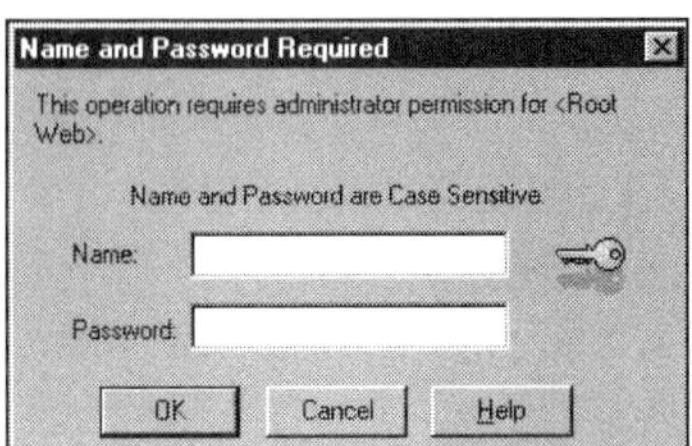

8. Type the account *Name* and *Password* that you were given by your system administrator, or that you entered when installing FrontPage, then click OK. (Type the information with the correct case; PeterKent is not the same as peterkent or PETERKENT.) FrontPage displays the web in the FrontPage Explorer window.

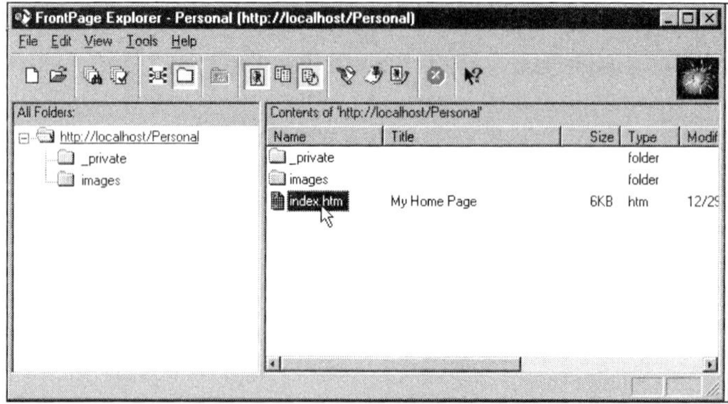

9. Double-click on index.htm in the right pane to open FrontPage Editor, then use the scroll bar to move down and view the document. You can use FrontPage Editor's word-processing features to modify the text.

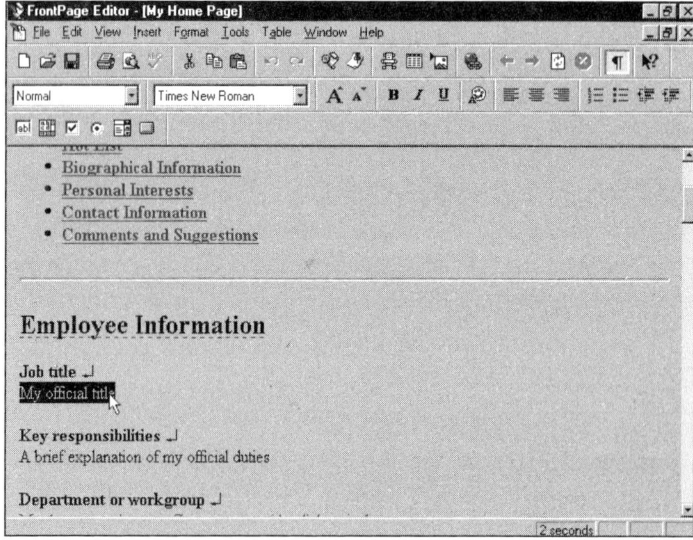

10. Select **File** → **Exit** to close the Editor. If prompted to save your work, click Yes.

11. If you would like to delete the web you've just created, view the FrontPage Explorer window and then select **File** → **Delete FrontPage Web**.

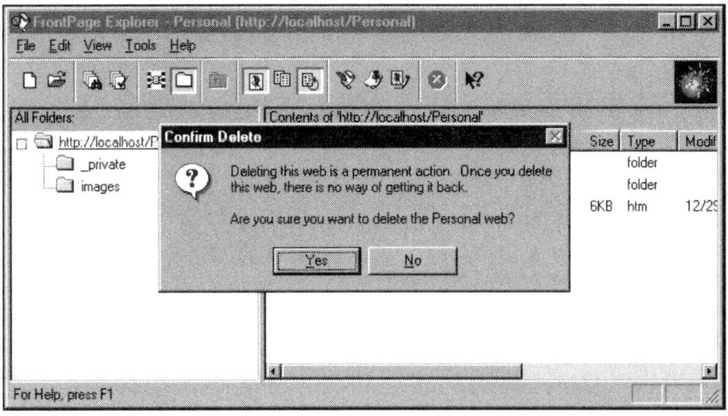

12. Click Yes and FrontPage removes the web.

Now that you're familiar with this basic procedure, let's get started!

PART ONE

WORKING WITH WEBS

THIS PART CONTAINS THE FOLLOWING CHAPTERS

Microsoft FrontPage is not your average Web-authoring tool. In fact, authoring is just one of its many features. Think of FrontPage as a complete Web-site management tool. In Part One, you'll begin by learning how to create and view a FrontPage web.

ROACH PATROL

Cartoonist Gary Larson, famous for his "Far Side" comic strip, once drew a panel in which several bums — one of which was a giant insect — were sitting in the gutter. The human-sized bug lamented that he had once had it all — great job, nice car, and so on — until one day, someone looked at him and said "Hey! He's just a big cockroach!"

The Internet, too, sometimes can be incoherence dressed in credible clothing. A sharply designed Web page may look authoritative, but logic and reason (and some help from Usenet) help us to separate the electronic wheat and chaff.

Urban legends, stories with little historical accuracy that have made their way through American (and worldwide) folklore, have found new life on the Internet. Their success is due largely to several factors. First, people often consider the Internet a reliable source of information. We often think — or want to think — that the people on the other end of the ether have all their facts in front of them. While this may be the case, it might be wise to get a second opinion, especially if you rely on the Internet for more than entertainment.

Fortunately for us, the Internet does a wonderful job of policing itself. Duty-minded netizens have established sites that report the best of the worst, including urban myths, conspiracies, and anticonspiracies.

The Urban Legends Archive (http://www.urbanlegends.com/) contains a fantastic collection of modern myths. Sorted in categories ranging from "innocent" topics (Animals and Disney) to those on the seedier side (Drugs and Sex), this site also contains archived messages from alt.folklore.urban, the Usenet newsgroup where such stories are put to the test daily. Examples of archived legends include the story about the charred remains of a scuba diver found in the forest (the amazing thing is how he "arrived" there), and Craig Shergold's brain tumor (hold onto your business cards).

Hundreds of sites exist to let the public know about conspiracies and government coverups. JFK's assassination, the Whitewater scandal, and perhaps the Internet's favorite coverup, UFOs and alien visitation, are all paid great tribute on the Web. In response to such sites, Net users with alternate views often develop sites with the sole purpose of refuting the original site's claims. To find a complete index of conspiracy sites, go to http://www.yahoo.com and search for "conspiracy." And to contribute to the collection yourself, enter your favorite conspiracy at the Encyclopedia of Conspiracies Homepage (http://www.cruzio.com/~blackops/), where you can achieve the dubious honor of helping society determine whether "the truth is out there."

CHAPTER ONE

UNDERSTANDING FRONTPAGE

IN THIS CHAPTER YOU LEARN THESE KEY SKILLS

FrontPage is *not* simply a Web-page authoring tool . . . and therein lies a problem. Although FrontPage is a fantastic tool, one that makes creating a Web site incredibly easy, it can at first glance appear a little confusing, because it simply doesn't work like most of the other HTML tools that people are used to. I've had people tell me that they got a little lost when they started working with FrontPage, that they didn't really understand what was going on. So we're going to start by learning what FrontPage is and what it can do for you. In this chapter I'm going to explain a few basic terms and ideas you should understand before you can get started.

TIP **HTML means HyperText Markup Language, and refers to the special coding used to create Web pages. FrontPage creates the pages for you, so you don't need to understand HTML to use FrontPage.**

Understanding Web Sites, Webs, and Servers

Before I explain what FrontPage is and what it can do for you, let me start by explaining several important concepts. First, the term *Web server.* A Web server is a system that is used to run a Web site. When a Web browser tries to view a document at a particular Web site, the Web server is the system that makes the document available. The browser sends a message asking for a particular document, and the server sends it back.

The term *Web server* often means the entire Web server package: the server software and the computer on which that software is running. You may also hear the term used to refer to only the software; after all, a computer that is working as a Web server may be carrying out other tasks as well.

Another term you need to understand is *Web site.* This is a collection of associated Web pages. A company may set up a Web site, for instance, and all the pages placed on the World Wide Web by that company may be thought of as that company's Web site. Or a company may have several Web sites: the manufacturing department may have one, sales may have another, human resources yet another. Of course all these sites may be linked together . . . so where does one site end and another begin? Perhaps we could think of a Web site as a collection of associated Web pages managed by the same Web server. That's the definition I plan to use, anyway.

A Web server may manage one or more Web sites. For instance, there are many companies that *host* Web sites. A Web-hosting company (termed *Web presence providers* by Microsoft) enables other firms and individuals to set up Web sites using the company's Web servers (for a fee, of course). So a single Web server may have a Web site owned by a software company, another owned by a professional association, another by an association of horse lovers, and so on. One server, many sites. When I use the term *Web host,* I'm referring to a computer that is hosting Web sites in this manner.

So where does FrontPage fit in? FrontPage is a suite of programs used to create and manage Web sites. FrontPage is not a Web server. (It does contain a simple personal Web server, which I'll discuss in a moment, but it's not a full-blown Web server.) Its tools are used to set up a Web site and to create the documents contained by that site.

That may not sound like much, but FrontPage is far more than a fancy HTML editor. Here are the FrontPage components:

FrontPage Explorer — A program that gives you an overview of your Web site, showing how each document is linked to the rest of the site. It contains lots of useful tools, such as a system for checking for broken links.

FrontPage Editor — The actual HTML editor, far more powerful than most HTML editors. This one helps you add tables, frames, and forms and contains a

number of useful little *bots*: utilities that help you carry out complicated functions such as automatically inserting graphics and documents on a particular date, or handling form input.

Templates and Wizards — Useful items that help you create simple Web pages, such as FAQ or glossary pages, or much more complicated systems such as discussion groups or entire corporate Web sites.

Image Library — A library of graphics for use in your Web pages as backgrounds, headers, bullets, and so on.

FrontPage To Do List — A simple reminder tool that can be linked to your Web pages to help you remember to carry out tasks.

FrontPage TCP/IP Test — A little program that checks your TCP/IP connection and provides useful information about your system's hostname and URL (Uniform Resource Locator, the Web address).

FrontPage Personal Web Server — A very simple Web server, suitable, perhaps, for use in a small corporate workgroup connected to a LAN. It's really not a full-blown Web server; in other words, it's not really suitable for hosting Web sites on the World Wide Web. As you'll see, though, you generally must be running a server in order to work with FrontPage, so if you don't already have one, you can use this. (By the way, just to confuse things a little, the full name of this Web server is the Microsoft FrontPage Personal Web Server. You'll see in a moment why that name is confusing.)

FrontPage Server Extensions — Special utilities that work alongside the Web server to provide services to your Web pages. For instance, you can use the extensions to handle form input, automatically taking information from a form and placing it in another Web page or a text file.

Server Administrator — A simple program for managing FrontPage settings on the server. You may be using the Frontpage Personal Web Server or another, more powerful server, but in either case the server administrator is used to manage the FrontPage server extensions and to set permissions for the Web site, that is, to enable you to decide who may modify or read documents at that Web site.

FrontPage 97 comes with a Bonus Pack, containing these additional components (which you don't need in order to work with FrontPage, though they can be useful):

Microsoft Image Composer — A program that helps you create and edit images for use on your Web site. It comes with a collection of clip art and photos, too.

Microsoft Personal Web Server — A more advanced Web server than the FrontPage Personal Web Server. While the FrontPage Personal Web Server provides few administrative functions, the Microsoft Personal Web Server allows you more control over a Web site, provides FTP access, and has faster performance.

TIP **Do not install the Microsoft Personal Web Server unless you plan to publish your Web site on your own computer. If all you plan to do is create a Web site on your computer and then transfer it to another computer, use the FrontPage Personal Web Server — it's far easier to work with, and is, at the time of writing, more stable. In other words, using the Microsoft Personal Web Server may lead to unnecessary problems for you! The FrontPage Personal Web Server is installed for you by default by the FrontPage installation program, so there's no need to install the Microsoft Personal Web Server from the Bonus Pack.**

Internet Explorer — Microsoft's Web browser.
WebPost — A utility that helps you transfer your Web pages from your hard disk to a non-FrontPage Web server on another system.

Understanding FrontPage's Modus Operandi

Before you can work with FrontPage you should understand the manner in which FrontPage operates; this is where the confusion lies for new FrontPage users. With most other Web products you open a Web page and start editing it. That doesn't happen with FrontPage. You open the FrontPage Explorer and have to then create or open a *web*. But what's a web?

I've already explained the term *Web site*. But Microsoft uses another term, *web*, which is not the same thing. A *web*, in FrontPage-speak, is a single collection of Web pages that has been created in FrontPage Explorer. You can work on one web at a time in FrontPage. In the same way that a word-processing program can open a document, Explorer can open a web. Just as a word-processing document may contain many pages and images, so too a FrontPage Explorer web can contain many pages and images (and links, and forms, and so on).

A *web* may, in fact, be exactly the same as a *Web site*; in many cases it probably is. But it doesn't have to be. For instance, you may choose to create several webs for your company: one for human resources, one for documentation, one for sales, and so on. You can then allow different people around the company to work on these separate webs. When someone opens a web in FrontPage, all he or she can see and work on is that one collection of Web pages. The person working on the human resources web can't modify the pages in the sales web, for instance. However, you can have links from pages in one web to pages in the others; in fact, you'd probably want to do that, wouldn't you? Then, when someone comes to your Web site and uses a browser to view your Web pages, all the webs appear as one single system to that person — a single Web site.

So it's important to understand that when FrontPage refers to a *web* it doesn't mean a Web site. It's talking about a single collection of Web pages. FrontPage doesn't really care what you do with your webs; they can be linked together to form a single Web site, if you wish, or you may create a single Web site in a single web. To return to the word processor analogy . . . a word processor regards a document as a collection of pages, but doesn't care if that document is part of a larger collection. It's the same for FrontPage and its webs. You can see an example of a web in Figure 1.1.

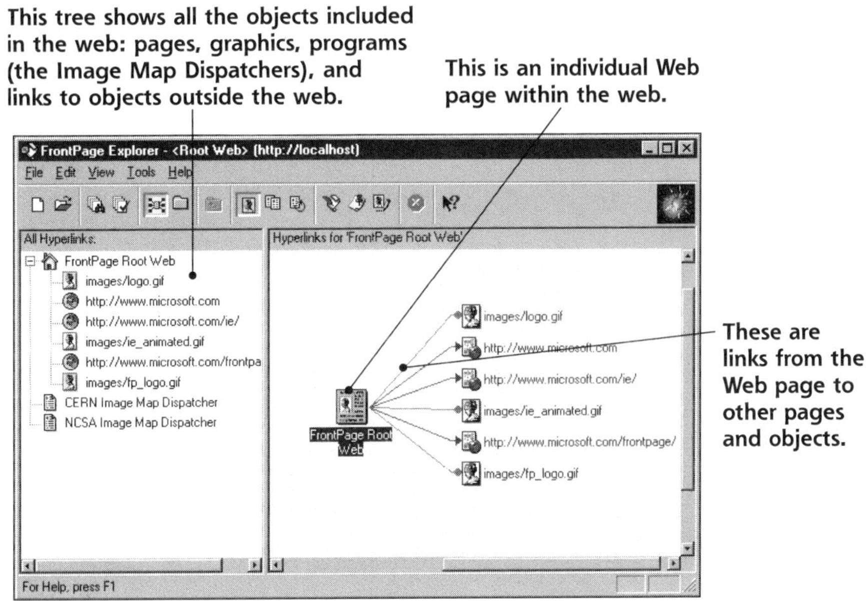

Figure 1-1 A FrontPage web, shown in FrontPage Explorer

Avoiding Server Problems

Another area of confusion is the role of the Web server. With most Web-authoring products it doesn't matter to the author which server will be used to host the Web site, or whether the server is running while the author creates pages. But FrontPage is different, for two reasons:

- In order to use FrontPage you must be using a Web server. FrontPage calls for Web pages in a way that is similar to the method used by Web browsers to request Web pages, so a server must be running.
- The type of server you are using affects what features you can use in your Web pages.

The first issue is not a problem, for a couple of reasons. First, as you've already seen, FrontPage comes with a server, the FrontPage Personal Web Server. When you open a web in FrontPage Explorer this Web server opens automatically, and away you go; you can forget the server is there (it's minimized, and you don't need to do anything to it).

You can also be running another server on your computer. The FrontPage Bonus Pack contains the more advanced Microsoft Personal Web Server. (The FrontPage Personal Web Server is really intended to be run with minimal management. The Microsoft Personal Web Server provides easier access to configuration controls, and has better performance.) Or perhaps you've got another server, from a different source. If so, you'll have to configure the server to use the FrontPage Server Extensions (I'll talk about that later in this chapter, in the section "Why You Need the Server Extensions"), then start the server before you start FrontPage.

Remote Web Management

Or you can use a server on another computer. One of the really nice things about FrontPage is that you can work on a Web site at a distance; you can edit a Web site live.

For instance, just before I began writing this book I started work on a new Web site. Now, I have this site hosted on a system owned by a company called Digiserve (`http://www.digiserve.com/`). But my domain is actually `http://www.arundel.com/`. Digiserve has Web servers in several places around the world, currently in southern England, in Washington, D.C., and in Singapore. My `http://www.arundel.com/` domain is physically located on a computer in Washington. But I live in Denver, Colorado. So I log on to the Internet and use FrontPage to work on my Web site on the Digiserve server in Washington. I could do the same if the site were in England or Singapore — distance is no concern.

Let me be clear about this: I'm not making changes to Web pages on my computer, then transferring them to Washington (though I could do this if I wished; see "Author Here, Publish There," later in this chapter). Rather, I'm editing my Web site live. When I sit in my office in Denver and modify a Web page, it's a computer file in Washington that is being changed, and the changes are instantly *published* — that is, anyone viewing that page immediately after I save a change will see what I've done. In order to manage this, the server you want to work with has to be set up to work with FrontPage. That's okay, though, as many Web-hosting companies now work with FrontPage.

TIP **Not all FrontPage-enabled servers allow live editing. In some cases you must create the web on your own computer, then transfer it to the server. See "Finding a FrontPage-Compatible Web Host" later in this chapter for more information.**

You need a server, then, before you can use FrontPage. Here, to summarize, are your choices:

1. **The simplest thing to do** — Use the FrontPage Personal Web Server on your own computer. If you don't have another server set up, FrontPage will start this server for you.
2. **Next easiest** — Use the Microsoft Personal Web Server from the bonus pack. There's no need to do so, though, unless you want to make your work available to others through that server. If all you want to do is create the Web pages, then transfer them to another server somewhere, you can stick with the FrontPage Personal Web Server.
3. **And the next** — Find a Web server on another computer that is FrontPage enabled, and edit live on that system. (See "Finding a FrontPage-Compatible Web Host" later in this chapter.)
4. **The most complicated** — Set up a Web server, other than the Microsoft Personal Web Server, on your own computer, and set it up to run with FrontPage. (See "Setting Up Your Own Server" later in this chapter.)

Your choice depends on what you are trying to achieve, of course. If you plan to create a Web site on your hard disk, then transfer it to another Web server later, use option 1. If you are setting up a simple Web site on a LAN that's available to everyone in your department, for instance, option 1 may be okay, though 2 would be better. If you want to make a Web site available on the World Wide Web, and want to manage your own Web server, use option 2 or 4 — preferably option 4. Or perhaps your company has a Web server on a machine somewhere, and you want to edit live on that system; option 3 is the one you'll be using.

If you don't plan to run your own Web server, publishing your Web pages on your own computer, *don't* install the Microsoft Personal Web Server. You'll run into fewer headaches if you use the FrontPage Personal Web Server instead.

In this book I'll explain these procedures:

* How to create a web on your own computer, using the FrontPage Personal Web Server (see Chapter 2).
* How to transfer a web from your own computer to another FrontPage-enabled Web server (see Chapters 3 and 17).
* How to transfer a web from your own computer to a Web server that is *not* FrontPage-enabled (see Chapter 17).

* How to work on a web that's on another computer somewhere else on the Internet or your corporate intranet, being hosted by a FrontPage-enabled Web server (see Chapter 2).

I won't be talking in detail about setting up Web servers in this book; that's way beyond the scope of the book and is not necessary for most users.

TIP **The FrontPage installation program encourages you to install the Microsoft Personal Web Server, so there's a good chance that you installed that one rather than the FrontPage Personal Web Server. If you haven't yet installed FrontPage, and you don't plan to set up your own Web server for other people to connect and view your work (rather, you plan to publish your Web site on another computer's Web server), I'd recommend that you install the FrontPage Personal Web Server, not the Microsoft Personal Web Server.**

Author Here, Publish There

You don't have to create the Web site in the same place you publish it. I didn't originally *create* the `http://www.arundel.com/` Web site live.

My connection to the Internet is just too slow to make it worthwhile. Rather, I created the site on my own computer, then transferred it to Digiserve; now, when I *modify* the site, I work live.

If you have a fast connection to the Internet or are working with a remote server on a corporate intranet, you may find that you can work live right from the start. If you have a slow connection you'll probably want to do the same thing I did: create the site on your computer (using the FrontPage Personal Web Server to manage the web during its creation), transfer it to the computer on which it will finally reside when it's finished, and then make the day-to-day modifications online. There are several ways to transfer webs — I'll explain these in Chapter 17.

Why You Need the Server Extensions

FrontPage's server extensions are one of its great strengths. The extensions make it far more than just another HTML-editing tool. They enable you to do complicated things very quickly and easily, such as create a discussion group or place information submitted in a form into a Web page or text file.

The server extensions work in conjunction with the server. The FrontPage Personal Web Server and Microsoft Personal Web Server have these extensions built in. But if you are working with another server, the extensions must be manually installed — that's no problem for most Web authors, as all the dirty work is done by some kindly system administrator working behind the scenes (and installing the extensions is not terribly complicated anyway). Extension kits are available for a number of popular Web servers, on various operating systems.

These extensions are important. Their presence — or absence — has a bearing on a decision you must make: whether to use a FrontPage-enabled host (one that has the server extensions installed) or a non-FrontPage-enabled host (one without the server extensions).

NON-FRONTPAGE HOSTING

You don't *have* to use a FrontPage-enabled Web server to publish Web sites created in FrontPage. You can, if you wish, use FrontPage to create Web pages, and then transfer them to a non-FrontPage-enabled host. For instance, suppose you already have a Web site hosted by a company that has not set up its server to work with FrontPage. You can use FrontPage to edit the files on your computer, then transfer them to the Web host. However, you should be aware that there are certain things that you can't do if you work this way. If you are working with a non-FrontPage-enabled Web server, you won't be able to use any FrontPage tools that work with the server extensions. Or rather, you'll be able to use them, but the pages won't work correctly once you place them on the server.

I've used the icon shown at left to indicate areas in the book that discuss subjects that are dependent on the FrontPage Server Extensions. For instance, a number of the form utilities simply won't work unless the Web server has the extensions available — where I discuss those utilities, you'll see this icon.

WHAT YOU CAN'T DO

So what can't you do, then, if the server extensions are not present? FrontPage has a number of *bots* (also known as *Web bots*), little utilities that carry out particular functions for you. The bots write scripts into your Web pages, but these scripts work only if the FrontPage Server Extensions are present. That's OK while you're working on your own computer, using the FrontPage Personal Web Server, because that server has the extensions built in. But if the extensions are not present at the Web server to which you transfer your pages, those scripts won't work. There are also a few things related to images, permissions, and remote administration that you can't do, as well. Here are a few examples of things you cannot do unless the server extensions are present:

- Edit your web directly on a remote server
- Set access controls to allow particular authors to modify pages, or to limit access to particular readers (see Chapter 17)
- Automatically take information a user has entered into a form and place it on a confirmation page (see Chapter 15)
- Create a discussion group on your Web site (see Chapter 15)
- Create a search engine that readers can use to search for information at your Web site (see Chapter 16)

- Create a registration page in which readers can register a user ID and password (see Chapter 15)
- Use FrontPage-format image maps (though you can still create image maps that will work with other servers — see Chapter 8)
- Save information, entered by a user into a form, to a Web page or text file (see Chapter 13)

Actually I haven't been quite fair to non-FrontPage servers; you *can* do all these things, if you know how to create CGI scripts! CGI stands for common gateway interface, a widely used scripting system on the World Wide Web. It's used to add a degree of interaction to Web pages. If you know a lot about CGI, you can write your own scripts that run on a server and work with your Web pages. The beauty of FrontPage, though, is that it has a number of special FrontPage scripts already written for you — but you can use them only if you are working with a FrontPage-enabled Web server.

TIP **Many Web-hosting companies provide libraries of CGI scripts that you can use. It's still easier to use FrontPage's bots wherever possible, but if you find a particular CGI script that you want to work with, you can do so, even if you create your pages with FrontPage and even if you are working with a FrontPage-enabled server. See Chapter 15 for more information.**

Finding a FrontPage-Compatible Web Host

So what do you do if you want to use the fancy FrontPage tools provided by the bots and scripts? You need to make sure that the Web server that will be administering your completed Web site has the FrontPage server extensions installed. So if you are going to be putting the Web site on someone else's computer, under the control of someone else's Web server, you'd better find out, before you start creating your Web site, if that server has the server extensions installed. If it doesn't, you have two options. You can still create a Web site and use that server, but you'll have to avoid using the features that require the server extensions. Or you can find another Web server.

If you'd like to find a company that will host your Web site, and you want a FrontPage-enabled site, go to the Microsoft FrontPage Web site for more information. Scores of companies are currently listed there, with more being added all the time. Don't pay too much money for the hosting service, though. The company hosting my Web site charges a $25 setup fee, and that's it . . . no monthly charges for the privilege of using FrontPage at the site. I've seen another Web-hosting company charge $150 a month for that privilege, on top of their normal hosting fees, which is totally ridiculous — so shop around.

The main FrontPage Web page is currently `http://www.microsoft.com/frontpage/`**, and you can find information about Web hosts that work with FrontPage at** `http://www.microsoft.com/frontpage/wpp/list/` **(though this second URL tends to move!).**

When you find a company to host your site, ask these questions:

Can I edit live? In other words, can you work directly on your Web site, modifying the pages and instantly publishing them, or must you make changes on your system and then transfer them?

Is the host a manual-restart host? Some Web servers are what's known as *manual-restart servers*. When you create a new web, FrontPage writes information to the server's configuration file. In order for this information to be used by the server — and for you to begin working on the new web — a manual-restart server must be restarted. That's not too much of a problem in most cases, because few users will want to create completely new webs very often; rather, they'll be working on a single web that encompasses their entire Web site, or perhaps creating new webs just occasionally.

If it is a manual-restart host, is it configured to let me create new webs online? Or do I have to ask it to create a web for me? If it's a manual-restart server, there are two ways to create new webs. You can create the web, and then wait until the system administrator restarts the system, perhaps at a predefined time each night or each week. Once the system is restarted, you can add pages to your web. (Meanwhile, you can work on your web on your own computer, and then, after the system's been restarted, transfer it to the host.) Or you may have to ask the system administrator to create the web for you. He or she will create the web and restart the system, and then the web is available to you to work on.

BONUS

Setting Up Your Own Server

If you plan to set up your own server and make it FrontPage-enabled, you have to install the server first and then install the server extensions. FrontPage has some of these extensions already built in: for O'Reilly WebSite 1.1 (Windows NT and Windows 95), Netscape Communications Server v1.12 (Windows NT), and Netscape Commerce Server (Windows NT).

Other server extensions are available, but you'll have to look for them. You'll find detailed information on the subject in the area of the FrontPage Web site that explains to Web-hosting companies how to set up their servers. Go to `http://www.microsoft.com/frontpage/wpp.htm` or, if that page is no longer there, try `http://www.microsoft.com/frontpage`. There are kits available for these servers, on a variety of operating systems: Microsoft Internet Information Server (IIS), NCSA, CERN, Apache, Netscape Commerce Server, Netscape Communications Server, and Open Market Web Servers.

I haven't provided information in this book about how to add server extensions to these servers; see the online documentation and the information in the server-extension kits.

Summary

I hope this chapter hasn't left you thinking that working with FrontPage is complicated; it's really not. It's just that before you start you need to understand how FrontPage works and make a few basic decisions. Get too far working with FrontPage before you make these decisions, and you may regret it — you may end up creating all sorts of neat things in your Web pages, only to discover that they won't work on the server you picked!

So, just to prove that this stuff really isn't complicated, here's a quick summary:

* A *Web server* is a system (software and hardware) that administers a Web site, sending Web pages to browsers that request them.
* A *Web site* is a collection of related Web pages, administered by the same Web server.
* A *web* is a single collection of Web pages that has been created in FrontPage Explorer. You can work on one web at a time in FrontPage.

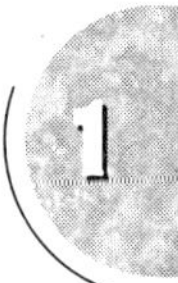

- A web may contain an entire Web site, or it may be just one part of a larger Web site.
- When FrontPage is running it needs a Web server running, too. You can use the FrontPage Personal Web server, which comes with FrontPage.

- If the server that will be used to publish your Web site does not have the FrontPage server extensions installed, a variety of FrontPage features will not work.
- You can create your web on your own computer, then transfer it to the computer that has the Web server you will be using to publish your Web site.
- You can work remotely, modifying a FrontPage web on a computer elsewhere on the World Wide Web or your corporate Intranet.

Now that you understand all this, we're ready to get started working with FrontPage. We won't be beginning by opening a Web page, as most HTML tools do. Rather, in the following chapter, we'll begin by opening a web, a FrontPage document.

CHAPTER TWO

CREATING AND VIEWING WEBS

IN THIS CHAPTER YOU LEARN THESE KEY SKILLS

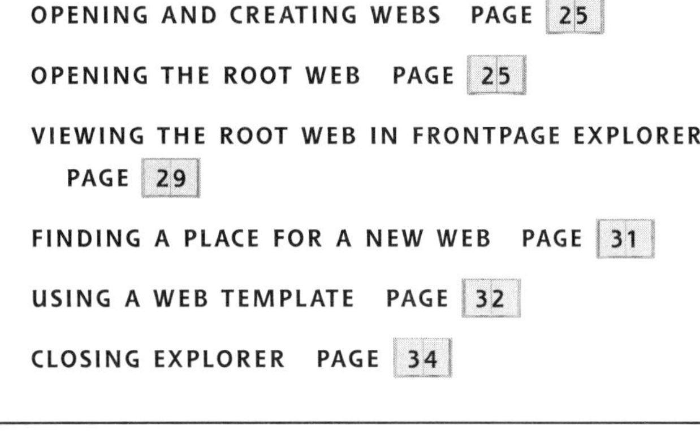

In this chapter we'll take a look at a FrontPage web and how it's structured. We'll also take a look at how to create an entire Web site very quickly, using one of FrontPage's wizards.

We'll begin by opening FrontPage Explorer. Follow this procedure:

1. If you plan to work on a web on another computer somewhere on the Internet or on an intranet, make sure that your Internet or intranet connection is running. (If you're going to begin by working on a web on your own hard disk, you don't need to worry about this.)
2. Select Start → Programs → Microsoft FrontPage. If this is the first time you've started FrontPage you'll see a message saying "FrontPage will now try to determine your machine's hostname and TCP/IP address. This may take several minutes."
3. Click the OK button and FrontPage begins checking for information related to your computer's TCP/IP connection to the Internet or corporate intranet.

TCP/IP means *Transmission Control Protocol/Internet Protocol*, and refers to the network protocol used by the Internet, intranets, and the World Wide Web. The FrontPage Personal Web Server, or whatever server you happen to be using, uses TCP/IP to send Web pages and information about the web to FrontPage Explorer.

4. In a few moments you'll see another dialog box, providing your hostname. In Figure 2-1 you can see that FrontPage has found the hostname to be localhost. In this example I'm using the FrontPage Personal Web Server. My computer is not really connected to a network — the Personal Web Server is simply acting as if it were, and has assigned the name localhost to my computer. You may see your computer's network name here, extracted from your operating system's network information.

If you get an error message at this point, there's a problem with your connection to the network or to the Web server you've installed. Talk with the network system administrator, or, if you are setting up the server yourself, check the documentation. If you're using the FrontPage Personal Web Server, you probably won't run into problems. If you chose the Microsoft Personal Web Server, you might — so in this case you may want to install the FrontPage Personal Web Server and use that. It's installed automatically if you choose not to install the Microsoft Personal Web Server during the installation program.

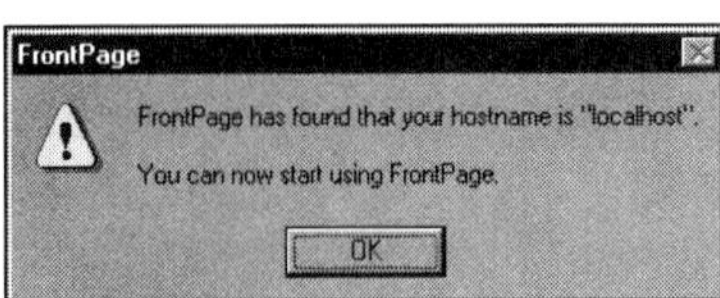

Figure 2-1 FrontPage has found your hostname, so you're ready to begin.

5. Click OK and you'll see the dialog box in Figure 2-2.

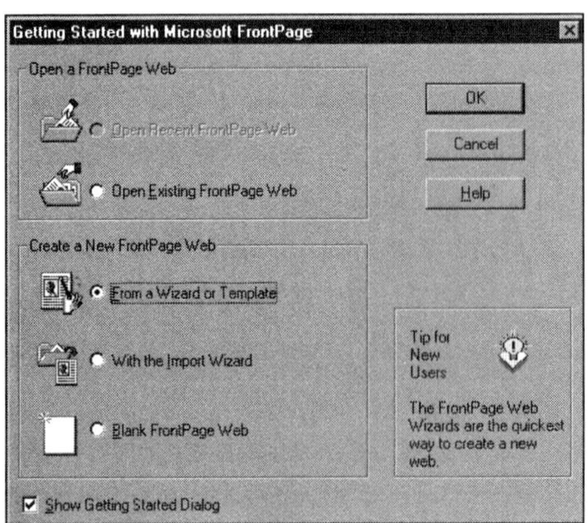

Figure 2-2 You can now open or create a web.

This dialog box lets you open an existing web or create a new one.

Opening and Creating Webs

The Getting Started with Microsoft FrontPage dialog box provides a number of ways for you to get started.

Open Recent FrontPage Web — The first time you open FrontPage, this option is disabled. In subsequent sessions the label will show Open "`http://hostname`" with the hostname of the Web server holding the last web you worked on.

Open Existing FrontPage Web — This option lets you select a web to open on your local server or on another server somewhere on the intranet or Internet.

From a Wizard or Template — This helps you start a new web using one of FrontPage's wizards or templates (we'll see an example later in this chapter, under "Using a Web Template").

With the Import Wizard — Choosing this option creates a new web from your existing, non-FrontPage Web pages (see "Importing Existing Webs," later in this chapter).

Blank FrontPage Web — This option creates a new web, with a single blank page.

TIP **You don't need to have this dialog box open each time you start Explorer. You can open a web from within Explorer by choosing File → Open FrontPage Web; create a new one using File → New → FrontPage Web; or import a web using File → Import. If you clear the Show Getting Started Dialog check box, this dialog box won't appear anymore. If you decide later that you want it, select Tools → Options, click the General tab, and click the Show Getting Started Dialog check box.**

Before you create a web, take a look at Appendix A. This lists the web templates and wizards (the Web *page* templates and wizards, too). See if anything in the list sounds like the type of web you want to create; you can use the template or wizard, then modify the web that's created.

Opening the Root Web

We'll begin by looking at a *root web*. You already have one of these created for you, either on your own computer (if you are using the FrontPage Personal Web Server) or on a remote computer (if you have arranged with someone to set up a FrontPage directory for you on a remote computer, somewhere on the World Wide Web, or on an intranet).

Follow this procedure:

1. Click the Open Existing FrontPage Web option button, then click OK. You'll see the dialog box shown in Figure 2-3.
2. If you are using the FrontPage Personal Web Server, you should see the name of the host (localhost) in the Web Server or File Location box. If you want to open a web on a remote computer, enter the URL into this box. If you are not sure what this should be, ask the administrator of the Web server to which you want to connect.

Each time you connect to a Web server, that server's name is added to the Web Server or File Location drop-down list box. You can then select the name from the list. Doing so automatically clicks the List Webs button for you.

3. Click List Webs, and a list of webs at the selected site appears in the FrontPage Webs list box (see Figure 2-3). This may take a little while if you are connecting to a server on the Internet or intranet, and if that server is not connected or functioning you may get an error message rather than a list of webs.

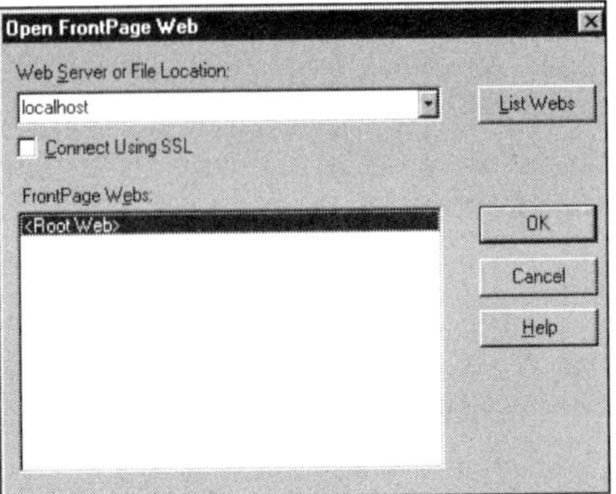

Figure 2-3 Select the host you want to work with, then click List Webs.

4. In the illustration you can see <Root Web>. Select this.
5. If you want to connect to the Web server using the *Secure Sockets Layer,* click Connect Using SSL. This is a system by which information transmitted across the network or Internet is encrypted first, so it can't be intercepted. Ask your system administrator if you can use this feature.
6. Click OK and you'll see the dialog box in Figure 2-4.
7. Type your account name in the top text box (this is case sensitive, by the way; *Pkent* is not the same as *pkent*), and in the lower box type your password.

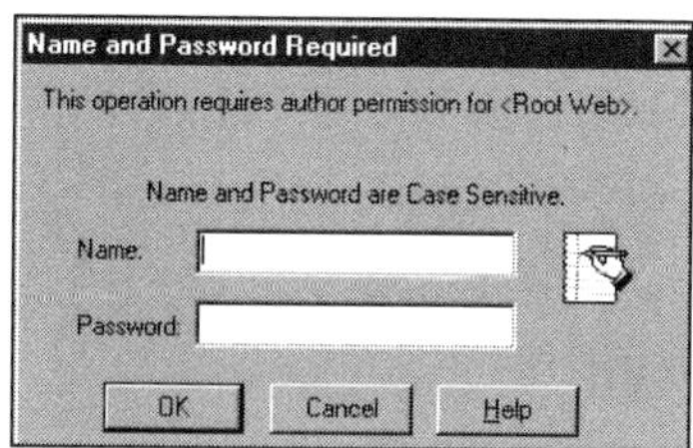

Figure 2-4 Enter your account name and password.

What **account name and password, you ask? The account name and password you entered into the FrontPage setup program. (Of course, if someone else installed the program, you'll have to get the information from that person.) Or, if you're opening a web on another computer — on a Web server owned by a Web-hosting company, for instance, or a corporate server administered by someone else — it will be the account name and password specified on that server for that particular web, an account name and password that you requested or that was assigned by the system administrator.**

8. Click OK, and FrontPage begins to load the web. Again, if this web is on another server somewhere, it may take a little while to load.

Inside the Root Web

The root web is a sort of base directory. For instance, when someone types `http://www.arundel.com/` into a browser and presses Enter, the browser sends a message to the Web server that administers the `www.arundel.com` domain (one of the Digiserve Web servers). The Web server then looks in the `www.arundel.com` root web, finds the file named index.htm, and sends that file to the browser.

If you are working with the Personal Web Server on your computer's hard disk, where's the root web? It's the `C:\FrontPage Webs\Content\` directory (unless you chose a different disk drive or directory when you installed FrontPage, of course). If you look inside that directory using Windows Explorer or some other file-management tool (see Figure 2-5), you'll see a file called **index.htm** (that's the *home page* or *main page* for the root web) and a file called **#haccess.ctl** (that's a file used by FrontPage to control access to the web). There are a couple of .html files, too: **postinfo.html** and **_vti_inf.html**. These are configuration files used by FrontPage to determine whether non-FrontPage programs — such as Microsoft FrontPad — may be used to edit webs held by this server and to manage the server extensions.

TIP

By default, Windows Explorer is set up so that it doesn't show file extensions of many common file types, so you may not see some of the extensions for the files I've named; instead, you'll see only the file

names. You can modify this setting in Windows Explorer by selecting View → Options and clearing the check box labeled *Hide MS-DOS file extensions for file types that are registered.*

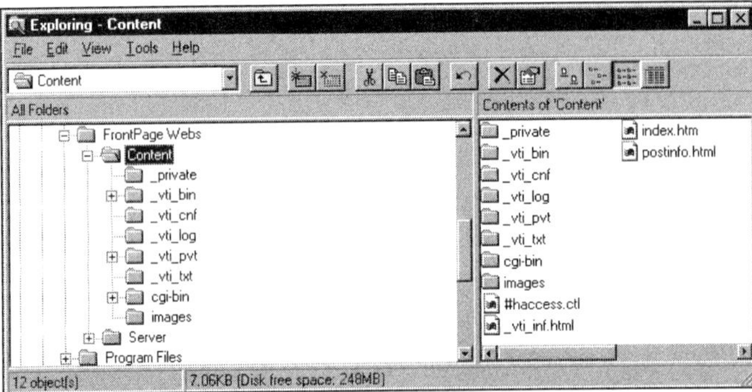

Figure 2-5 The \Content\ directory, shown in Windows Explorer

TIP **I don't much like the term *home page*. It originally meant the page that appears when you open your browser, or when you use the browser's Home command. Now it has a common second meaning, the main page at a Web site. I personally prefer the term *main page*.**

You'll find a variety of subdirectories, too. There's the **images** directory, where FrontPage stores image files you add to your Web pages. There are several directories with names beginning with **_vti_**; these contain files required by the FrontPage server extensions. Then there's a directory called **cgi-bin**. This contains files used to work with CGI scripts — including special programs that enable you to work with CERN and NCSA format image maps (see Chapter 8). And there's a directory called **_private**; this is used to store information created by bots, such as information entered into a form by a user. These are the default root web directories, though the web may contain others, too, such as a directory designed to store messages created in a discussion group if you've created such a system. There may eventually be additional directories, if you create new webs, because each time you create a web, that web is placed in a subdirectory of the root web. You'll learn more about that later in this chapter, under "Finding a Place for a New Web."

If you are working on a remote server, where is the root web? Wherever the system administrator decided to put it. It doesn't much matter to you, because you'll simply use the URL given to you by the administrator. For instance, although I use the `http://www.arundel.com/` URL to access my root web, the root web is actually in a directory called **/opt2/web/guide/arundel/**. However, `http://www.arundel.com/` is *mapped* to that directory, so the Web server knows where to look.

TIP You can create a new root web, somewhere else on your hard drive, by publishing the current root web to a directory. See Chapter 17.

Viewing the Root Web in FrontPage Explorer

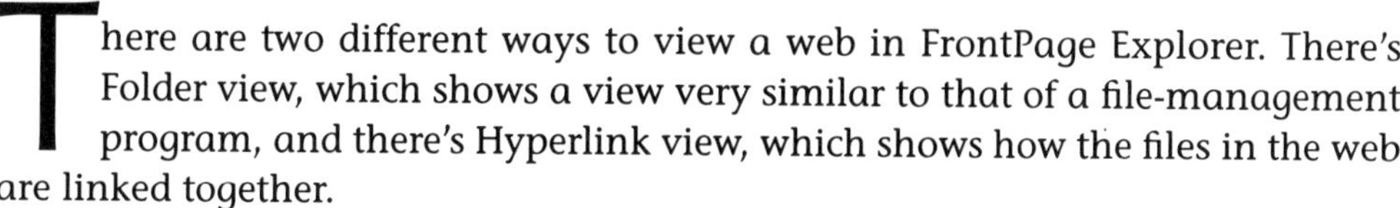

There are two different ways to view a web in FrontPage Explorer. There's Folder view, which shows a view very similar to that of a file-management program, and there's Hyperlink view, which shows how the files in the web are linked together.

Folder View

Figure 2-6 shows you what your root web looks like when displayed in the FrontPage Explorer window. The illustration shows Folder view. You can display this view by clicking the Folder View button on the toolbar, or by selecting View → Folder View . In Folder view you can see the folders — the directories — that are part of your web. Where are the _vti_* directories? Explorer doesn't show them, because these are administrative directories that you shouldn't be modifying.

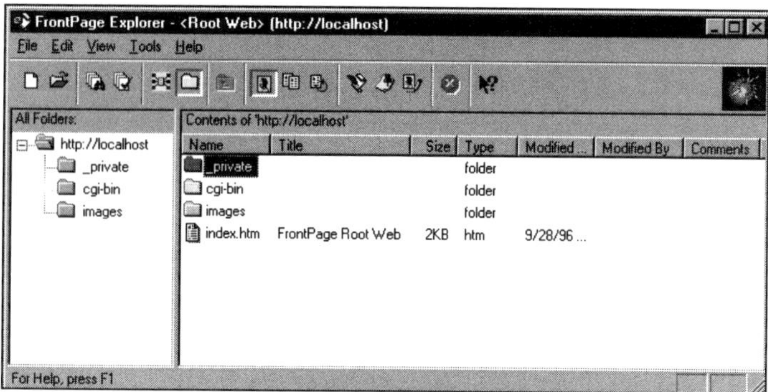

Figure 2-6 The root web, shown in FrontPage Explorer

In the left pane you can see a directory tree. The top directory is the root-web directory; in this case `http://localhost` really means `C:\FrontPage Webs\Content\`, or whatever directory you specified when installing FrontPage. Below that directory are shown the subdirectories. You can close or open this tree by clicking the little – or + icon next to the top directory.

In the right pane you can see the contents of the selected folder; I've selected the `http://localhost`, so you can see a list of the subdirectories and two files, **center.gif** and **index.htm**. Where are the other files, **#haccess.ctl, postinfo.html,** and

_vti_inf.html? Again, these are files that you wouldn't normally work with while creating a web, so FrontPage has hidden them from view.

You can click the other directory folders in the left pane (or double-click one in the right pane) to see the contents of that directory. When you begin the **_private** directory is empty, but the **cgi-bin** directory contains two *.exe files (the Image Map Dispatcher files), and the **images** directory contains several image files.

Hyperlink View

There's another way to view your web. While Folder view shows you the physical structure of the directory tree in your web, Hyperlink view shows you how your files are linked together in your web using hyperlinks.

To use Hyperlink view, click the Hyperlink View toolbar button, or choose View → Hyperlink View. Explorer will now look like the example in Figure 2-6. This view provides a sort of hierarchical link tree, showing you the pages in the web, and the links from the pages to other things.

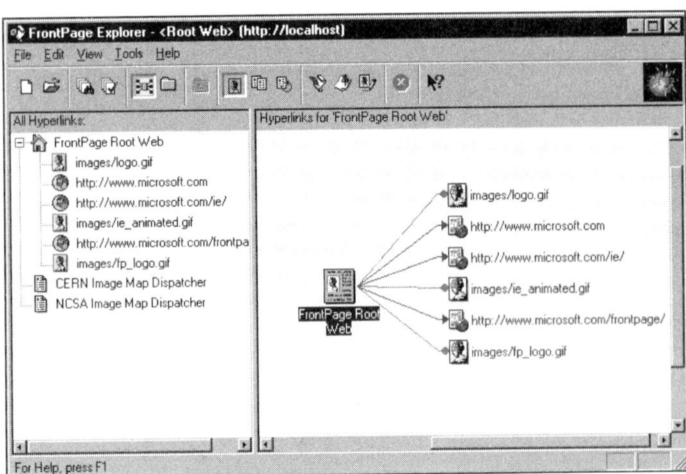

Figure 2-7 Explorer's Hyperlink view

Now, at the top of the left pane, you can see a picture of a house. This represents the home-page document (the main page). As you can see, the title is FrontPage Root Web. This text is actually the HTML title of the document (the text between the <TITLE> and </TITLE> tags for those of you who understand HTML... you don't need to understand HTML to use FrontPage, though).

Next to the house symbol is a – icon. Click this and you'll notice that the little globe symbol disappears and is replaced by a + symbol. When you click the – icon you are collapsing the link tree so you can't see the links, and when you click the + you are opening the link tree, so you can see them. You're probably familiar with this system; it's used in Windows Explorer and many other file-management programs.

TIP **Rather than single-clicking either the little – or + icon, you can double-click the entire name to open or collapse the tree.**

So what's the Globe symbol? This represents a link to something outside this web, something elsewhere on the World Wide Web or on your intranet. It could be another Web document, a Telnet site, FTP site, and so on. (If FrontPage figures out that the URL pointing to this item ends in .jpg or .gif, it knows it's a picture, and uses a different symbol — you'll see more symbols in Chapter 3.)

The little Document icon generally represents documents, Web pages. It can also represent programs — in this case the two document icons represent the programs used to work with image maps if you decide not to use FrontPage-style image maps (see Chapter 8).

Now look in the right pane. The large Document icon in the middle represents the page highlighted in the left pane. You can see lines running to Documents with a Globe symbols; these are links to other items on the Web. And there are lines running to Picture icons; these are images embedded within the document.

Finding a Place for a New Web

Now that you've learned about the root web, you can move on and find out how to create your own web. But where will you place your web? You have several choices. You can modify the root web, and make that your own web. You can create a web below the root web, in a subdirectory of the root web. Or you can create a brand new root web in a different directory somewhere. Your choice depends on where the web is now, and where it will be when you finish.

For instance, suppose you are working live; you have a web set up on a remote server, perhaps at a Web-hosting company — that's what I've done with my `http://www.arundel.com/` Web site. So, when I begin creating my Web site, I need to work in the root web. Why? Because the index.htm document in the root web is the one that the server will send to any browser that uses the `http://www.arundel.com/` URL.

What if I want to set up a subdirectory of `http://www.arundel.com/`? Perhaps I want to set up a site for my newsletter, Internet Publicity News, and call it `http://www.arundel.com/IPN/`. Well, then I'd create a new web, and call it *IPN*. This web will automatically be placed inside a subdirectory of the root web. The IPN web will have an index.htm file, too, and it's this file that the server will send if anyone uses the `http://www.arundel.com/IPN/` URL.

You may have several root webs. For instance, I've got `http://www.arundel.com/`, and I have `http://www.freelanceconnection.com/`. These could both be mapped to the same directory, a single root web. Or they could each have their own root web directory, so that when I select one of these URLs I'm shown one root web, and if I select the other URL I get a different root web.

If you are working on a corporate intranet you could be in the same situation, with different root webs on different servers or even on the same server. What if you are working on your own computer, and transferring files to the server when you've finished? If you are only working with one Web site, you may want to modify the root web. On the other hand, you can create a new web and do your work in that — I personally believe that it's better to leave the root web clean and place new webs within the root web in this situation. If you are creating several Web sites, you'll have to create new webs for each, anyway. Finally, you can take an existing Web site you've created using some other HTML authoring tool, and convert it into a new FrontPage web. You'll see how to do that in this chapter's Bonus section, "Importing Existing Webs." For now, let's move on and see how to create new webs.

Using a Web Template

To create a new web, follow this procedure:

1. Select **File** → **New** → **FrontPage Web**, or click the New toolbar button, and you'll see the New Web dialog box (shown in Figure 2-8).

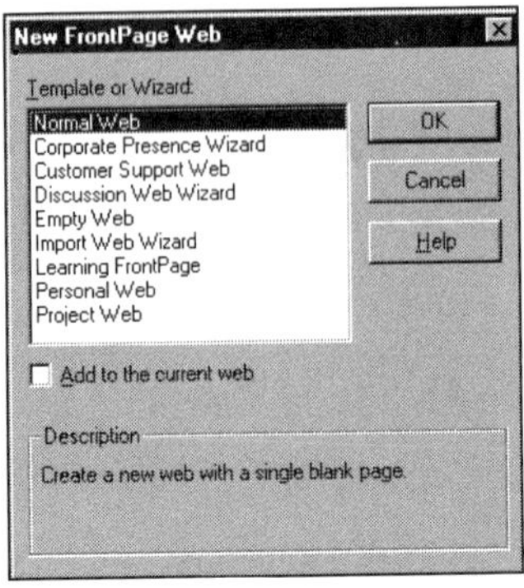

Figure 2-8 Here's where you select a new web, from a list of wizards and templates.

2. You can choose from the list of templates and wizards. As an example, I'm going to create a Customer Support Web template. (In FrontPage, a *template* is a simple copy of an existing sample web; a *wizard* creates a web to your specifications by asking you a series of questions.) Click Customer Support Web.

3. If you want to add the new web to the existing web — to the root web if that's still open — click the Add to the Current Web check box. If you want to place the web somewhere *outside* the current web, leave the check box unchecked.

TIP **If you select the Add to the Current Web check box, you're not really creating a new web. Rather, you are modifying the existing web by adding files and folders to it. I recommend that you don't use this option to experiment with. Rather, create a new web within the root web; you can always delete it later.**

4. Click OK. If you checked the Add to the Current Web check box, FrontPage begins adding the files and folders held in the template to the current web — you'll see a dialog box asking if you want to replace the index.htm file with the new one from the template. If you didn't check this check box, you'll see the dialog box in Figure 2-9.

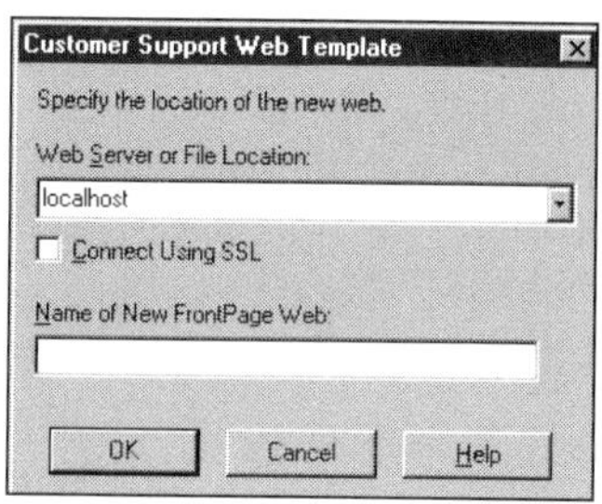

Figure 2-9 This box lets you tell FrontPage where you want to place the web.

5. Type a hostname or select it from the Web Server or File Location box. This tells FrontPage on which Web server you want to create the web. (It will become a subweb of the root web.) In the illustration I've selected localhost, which means the web will be placed on my computer's hard disk.

6. Type the web's name into the Name of New FrontPage Web text box. For instance, you might call it Customer. Not only will this be the name of the web, but it will also be the name of the directory in which the web is stored. You can't use spaces in this name, and in fact you should limit yourself to creating only names that are acceptable to the computer on which the Web server is running. You can check with the system administrator to find out what characters are unacceptable if you wish, but if you simply limit yourself to using nothing more than letters and numbers in your names you should be okay.

TIP **If you are working with a remote Web server and that server requires a restart before you can use your new web, you may want to experiment by creating a new web on your hard disk rather than on the remote server.**

7. Click the OK button. You may see a dialog box asking you to enter your account name and password. Do so and click OK.

8. FrontPage now begins creating your new web — it may take a little while. If you're using a remote server that requires restarting, you won't be able to use the web right away, of course; in fact, depending on the version of the server extensions installed on the server, you may even see an error message (HTTP error 501) telling you that FrontPage is unable to process your request. FrontPage created your web, then tried to open it, but because the server has not been reset it's unable to do that, so you get an error message. You'll probably also see a message telling you to restart the server.

   Ask the system administrator to restart the server. The administrator may have to add some information to a configuration file, so he needs to know that you've created a new web, and what it's called. (The latest version of the FrontPage server extensions should handle this automatically, but if your system administrator is still using earlier extensions, he or she will have to make the changes by hand.) In the meantime you can close the message and dialog boxes and work on another web. Later you'll select File → New → FrontPage Web to open the web you created. But note that the web will appear in the list of webs even if the server hasn't been restarted. If you try to open it before the server has been restarted, you'll get an error message (HTTP Error 501) telling you that the FrontPage Extensions cannot open the web.

9. FrontPage now displays the new web in FrontPage Explorer (if the server doesn't need resetting, that is).

Where is the new web placed? In a subdirectory of the root-web directory. So, for instance, if you are working on your hard disk, and created a web called Customer, then it's in **C:\FrontPage Webs\Content\Customer**. (Remember, the \Content\ directory is the root-web directory.)

TIP **Note that if you open the root web in FrontPage Explorer, you won't see the new web — FrontPage doesn't regard this new web as part of the root web. You will, however, see the new web's directory as a subdirectory of the root web's directory in Windows Explorer.**

Closing Explorer

You can quickly close Explorer using the normal Windows commands for closing an application; choose File → Exit, press Alt+F4, double-click the Control menu, and so on. Explorer will close. However, the FrontPage Personal Web Server won't close. You can switch to that program and close it in the normal way.

You can close the current web, without closing Explorer itself, by selecting File → Close FrontPage Web.

BONUS

Importing Existing Webs

You've seen how to create a web using a template, but what about your existing Web site? Have you been creating Web sites for a while, and have just switched to FrontPage? Do you want to take your existing Web sites and convert them to FrontPage webs, so you can use the power of FrontPage to continue working with them? If so, here's how:

1. If you are viewing the Getting Started with Microsoft FrontPage dialog box (Figure 2-2), click the With the Import Wizard option button, then click OK. If you are already in FrontPage Explorer, select File → New → FrontPage Web, click Import Web Wizard in the Template or Wizard list, then click OK.

2. You'll see a dialog box asking for the Web server where you want to place the new web, and the name you plan to give your web. (This box is the same as that in Figure 2-9.) Select the server, type a name, and click OK. You'll see the Import Web Wizard (Figure 2-10).

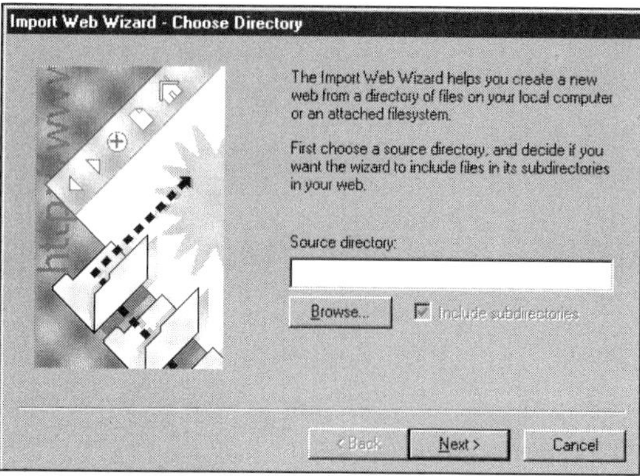

Figure 2-10 The Import Web Wizard

3. You may next see a box into which you must enter your account name and password (see Figure 2-4). Do so and click OK.

4. Click Browse and find the directory in which your current Web site files are stored.

5. If you want to include subdirectories within that directory, make sure the Include Subdirectories check box is selected.

6. Click Next and a list of all the files in your Web site is shown (Figure 2-11). You can remove some if you wish, by clicking the name and clicking Exclude. (Clicking Refresh grabs a new file list, including all the ones you've excluded.)

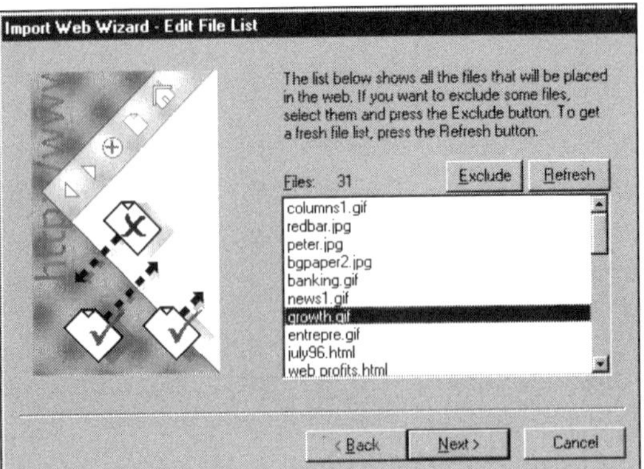

Figure 2-11 Remove any of the files you don't want.

7. Click Next, then click Finish, and FrontPage imports your files and creates a new web, then displays the new web if it can (if the server doesn't have to be reset, that is).

This procedure creates a new web from the existing files. You can also import files into an existing web. Open the web and then use the **File** → **Import** command.

Summary

If you've used other Web-authoring tools, you may be wondering why all this is so complicated. Don't worry; it'll be well worth it. As I've mentioned before, FrontPage is not an HTML authoring program. It's a Web site–management program. It's not designed simply to help you get your words into Web page format. Rather, it's designed to do that and lots more, from examining your site for broken links, to creating very complicated forms and scripts automatically. In order to do all this, it needs a certain structure within which it can work. It needs the right sort of server, as we discussed in the previous chapter. And it needs to keep tight control of how and where you create your webs.

At first you'll find this a little strange. Before, you simply created directories on your hard disk and placed your Web pages inside, transferred them to your Web site using FTP, and so on. And that's what FrontPage is doing for you, really — it's just taking some of the decisions and procedures out of your hands.

One of FrontPage's most important features is its ability to create webs and Web pages using templates and wizards. You've just seen how to create brand new webs using the web templates and wizards. What may not be so clear is how you can use templates and wizards to add more things to your web. There are basically two ways to do this:

* Use the Add to the Current Web check box, as you saw earlier in this chapter, to add the contents of a web template or wizard to your web.
* Use the File → New command in the FrontPage Editor (see Chapter 4) to choose from dozens of templates and wizards to create single pages or groups of pages.

2

As you continue through this book you'll see how to get these templates and wizards to work for you.

CHAPTER THREE

WORKING WITH FRONTPAGE EXPLORER

IN THIS CHAPTER YOU LEARN THESE KEY SKILLS

3

In this chapter we're going to see in more detail how to work in FrontPage Explorer — how to view your webs in Hyperlink and Folder view, and what sort of information these views provide. You'll see what the Explorer toolbar can do for you, as well as the different mouse pointers that appear now and again; then you'll learn a few more web-manipulation techniques, from copying webs to merging them, from deleting them to renaming them.

Working in Hyperlink View

Let's begin by taking a closer look at Explorer. I'm going to use the Customer web that I created in the last chapter as an example. The Customer web is larger and more complex than the root, so there's more to see this time. Begin by clicking the Hyperlink View toolbar button to open Hyperlink view, then click a few + icons to open up the link tree. In Figure 3-1 you can see what this web looks like.

You'll find lots of different icons representing all sorts of different things in Hyperlink view. Refer to Table 3-1 for a description of the Hyperlink view icons (though not all are present in the Customer web).

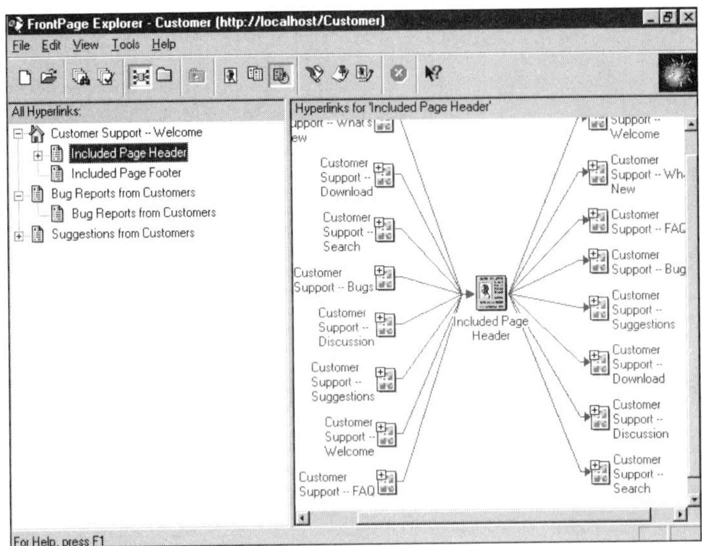

Figure 3-1 The Customer web, in Hyperlink view

TABLE 3-1 Explorer's Hyperlink View Icons

Icon	Meaning
	Represents the home page/main page, the index.htm file. The doorway is red when the tree below the page can be expanded, blue when it can be collapsed.
	Click here to expand a portion of the tree.
	Click here to collapse a portion of the tree.
	A page in your web, or a program such as the CGI programs used to administer NCSA and CERN imagemaps.
	This indicates a document with a broken link. In other words, a document has linked to another item in your web, but the item doesn't exist, or the link information has been incorrectly entered.
	The globe represents a link from one of your pages to something out on the Internet or intranet: another Web page, or an FTP, Gopher, WAIS, or Telnet site. It may also represent a file:// URL, which is a link to a file of some kind on a hard disk.
	This represents an image. These are shown in Hyperlink view only if the View → Hyperlinks to Images menu option has been chosen or the Hyperlinks to Image toolbar button has been clicked.

Icon	Meaning
	This represents a *mailto:* link, a link that automatically opens a browser's Email program and inserts an e-mail address.
	The red triangle indicates that the Web page contains some kind of web bot error. Right-click the document, then choose Properties. Under the Errors tab of the dialog box that opens, you'll see an explanation.
	These icons, along with some of the previous icons, appear in the right pane:
	This represents the item you clicked in the left pane. Although the icon is a document, it can represent anything: an image, a mailto: link, a Web page elsewhere on the Internet or intranet, an FTP site, and so on.
	This is a document within your web that either links to, or is linked from, the one you selected in the left pane.
	Also a document within your web, linked to or from the object you selected in the left pane. The little + sign in the corner means that this document has links of its own. You can click the + to open up more of the view — to see what is linked to or from that page.
	After clicking the + sign, the icon changes to one with a – sign. Click the – to collapse that part of the view.new item.
	An item outside your web, on the World Wide Web or intranet. This could be anything — a Web page, an image, a mailto: link, a newsgroup, or whatever. The name of the object should make this obvious, but you can also point at the object and hold the pointer over it for a moment to display a label telling you what the object is.
	A picture, either embedded in the document (an internal image) or linked to the document yet still within your web (an external image). Pictures are shown only if the **View** → **Hyperlinks to Images** command has been selected or the Hyperlinks to Image toolbar button has been clicked.
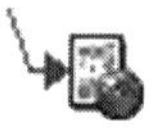	Notice the little arrow at the end of this line; that means the line represents a link.
	Notice the little blob at the end of this line; that means that the line isn't a link. It represents an included or embedded item — an embedded image or included Web page. (Note, however, that these blobs are only used to show an item that has been embedded into the item selected in the left pane. If you select the embedded item itself in the left pane, you'll see that the lines from the documents in which it is embedded are shown with arrows, not blobs.)

3

TIP **A broken link to an object is indicated by a broken line from the Web page to the object.**

TIP **You can link your own webs together. So the items shown as being elsewhere, outside your web, may be in another of your own webs.**

Play around in Hyperlink view, clicking the – and + signs, selecting items in the right pane, and you'll see how it works. Also, try this: right-click an item in the right pane that *isn't* in the center, and in the pop-up menu you'll see the Move To Center command. Choose this and the item moves into the middle position.

Here's another thing to try. Click a few of the + icons, until you've opened up a complicated structure that won't all fit within the pane. Now point to a blank space in the right pane somewhere, press and hold the mouse button, and move the mouse. You'll notice that the mouse pointer changes to a hand, and that you can move the link framework around in the pane, both horizontally and, if necessary, vertically.

Repeated and Internal Links

There are a couple of commands that enable you to view, or remove from view, two particular types of links: *repeated* links and *internal* links. By *repeated* links I'm referring to the case in which a document links to the same document more than once. In the Customer web you can find a case of this: the Customer Support — What's New page has several links to the Customer Support — Download page. So click the Customer Support — What's New page in the left pane, then click the Repeated Hyperlinks toolbar button (or choose View → Repeated Hyperlinks. You'll notice extra links appear in both the left and right panes.

Internal links are links from one part of a Web page to another part of the same page. You can find an example of this in the Customer Support FAQ document, which contains a list of questions near the top of the document, linked to the answers lower down in the same document. Click the Customer Support FAQ in the left pane, then click the Hyperlinks Inside Page toolbar button (or choose View → Hyperlinks Inside Page), and again, more links will appear.

TIP **Here's a fun little bug for you. The internal links will show the + sign on them in the right pane. Click the + sign and another list of internally linked documents appears. Click it again and another list appears. You can go on doing this all day, or until your computer runs out of memory.**

Using Folder View

We've seen Folder view already, but there are a few things I'd like to tell you about this view. Click the Folder View toolbar button to display this view. As you've seen before, this functions like a typical file-management program, such as Windows Explorer... with a few twists. First, you have some special columns in the right pane:

Title The document title; the text between the HTML <TITLE> and </TITLE> tags. You'll see how to enter a document title in Chapter 4. If the item is not an HTML document (so it doesn't have a title), then the path and filename appear here.

Type The type, as shown by the file extension; a .jpg file, .gif file, .htm file, and so on.

Modified By The person who last modified the file. FrontPage allows you to keep track of who can, and does, work on the web, as you'll see in Chapter 17.

Comments Comments that you've added to a file. Right-click a filename in this list and choose Properties from the pop-up menu. Then click the Summary tab, and you'll see a Comments box into which you can type any notes you wish.

Here's another thing you should try: right-click a filename in this list, then choose Show Hyperlinks (see Figure 3-2). FrontPage changes to Hyperlink view and places the selected file in the middle of the right pane.

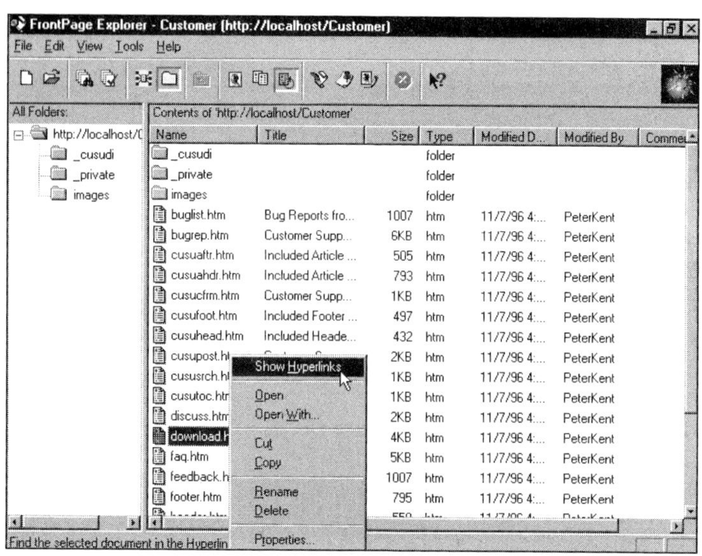

Figure 3-2 You can change from Folder view to Hyperlink view and put the selected file in the middle of the right pane.

By the way, Folder view shows only files held in the web itself. There are no entries for documents outside the web that are linked to or from the web; Folder view simply shows you the web's folders and files.

The FrontPage Explorer Toolbar

Let's take a quick look at the toolbar. You've already seen some of these buttons in action, and we'll be covering some others later. You can refer to Table 3-2 for a summary of their uses.

TABLE 3-2 The Explorer Toolbar Buttons

Button	Purpose
	Opens the New FrontPage Web dialog box, so you can add more pages to the existing web or create an entirely new one.
	Opens the Open FrontPage Web dialog box, so you can open an existing web on the Web server you are currently working on or on another Web server.
	Opens the Find in FrontPage Web dialog box, so you can search for text in any of the pages in the web. See Chapter 6.
	Opens the Spelling dialog box, so you can check the spelling of any pages in the web. See Chapter 6.
	Displays Hyperlink view.
	Displays Folder view.
	Only active in Folder view. A typical up-one-level command, which selects the parent directory of the selected one.
	Displays images in Hyperlink view (has no effect in Folder view).
	Includes repeated links in Hyperlink view, multiple links from a Web page to another object (has no effect in Folder view).
	Includes internal links in Hyperlink view, links from one part of a Web page to another (has no effect in Folder view).
	Opens the FrontPage Editor, where you'll create and edit Web pages (see Chapter 4).
	Opens the To Do List, which you'll use to keep track of tasks you must complete in your web (see Chapter 17).

Button	Purpose
	Opens the Image Editor, in which you can create images for your web pages.
	Cancels an operation, such as opening a document in the FrontPage Editor or recalculating links.
	Opens the FrontPage Help system. Click the button, then click something you want information about.
	A *busy* indicator. When FrontPage Explorer is busy doing something, this icon is animated.

3

The Explorer Mouse Pointers

There are several special mouse pointers used in FrontPage Explorer and in operations that begin in Explorer and end in the FrontPage Editor. Table 3-3 summarizes these, and we'll look at them closer later.

TABLE 3-3 The Explorer Mouse Pointers

Pointer	Purpose
	Point at the large border between the panes, or at the borders between column headings, and this pointer appears. Press and hold the button and drag the border.
	This pointer appears when you point at an item, press and hold the mouse pointer, and begin dragging the item. The pointer won't change until you are somewhere over FrontPage Editor. (See Chapter 4.)
	This pointer indicates that you have dragged the iem from FrontPage Explorer and are now holding the item over the FrontPage Editor window. If you release the mouse button over the document, you either create a link inside the document (a link to the item you dragged) or, if the FrontPage Editor window is empty, load the document into the window. If you release the button over the status bar, toolbars, or menu bar, the document you dragged is opened. (See Chapter 4.)
	This is the pointer that appears when you are dragging the right pane of the Hyperlink view around, as we saw earlier in this chapter.

More Web Manipulation

You've now seen how to open the root web, how to create a new web, and how to add pages to an existing web using the New Web dialog box. Table 3-4 is a quick rundown of a few more web-manipulation techniques:

TABLE 3-4 More Web Manipulation

To do this . . .	Carry out this procedure
To copy a web	Open the web you want to copy, then select File → Publish FrontPage Web. In the dialog box that appears enter the name of the host where you want to place the copy, and provide a name for the new web. Clear all the check boxes in the dialog box, and click OK. See Chapter 17 for more information about this command.
To merge webs	Use File → Publish FrontPage Web again. Check the Add to an Existing FrontPage Web check box, and enter the name of an existing web. All the pages in the first web are copied to the second web. (The original web remains intact.)
To rename a web	Open the web, then choose Tools → Web Settings. Click the Configuration tab, then type a new name into the Web Name box. When you click Apply or OK, FrontPage will rename the web. However, note that if you are renaming a web on a remote manual-restart server, you won't be able to use the web until the server has been restarted; contact your system administrator.
To close a web	Select File → Close FrontPage Web or File → Exit (which closes FrontPage Explorer at the same time, of course). You can also click the X button in the top right of the Explorer window, or press Alt+F4. Or simply open another web, and the current web closes automatically.
To open a web	Use any of the methods we've looked at so far (File → New → Open FrontPage Web or File → Open FrontPage Web). Or select a recently used web from the bottom of the File menu.
To delete a web	Open the web, then select File → Delete FrontPage Web. You'll see a confirmation box warning you that once the web's gone, it's gone — there's no retrieving it (unless you have backups, of course). Note, however, that you cannot delete a root web from within FrontPage Explorer.

The Web Title (also shown in the Web Settings dialog box) is, by default, the same as the Web Name. You can, if you wish, use a different title. This simply allows you to use one directory name (the Web Name), but a different "project" name in FrontPage (the Web Title). The Web Title appears in the FrontPage Title bar and the Open Web dialog box, for instance (though the directory name — the Web Name — is shown in both places, too).

***Don't* rename a directory through Windows Explorer or any other file-management program. If you do so you'll confuse FrontPage; all the links being managed by FrontPage will be broken. Rename only from within FrontPage Explorer.**

3

BONUS

Adding Non-FrontPage Pages

In Chapter 2, I showed you how to create a new web by importing an existing Web site, pages created by another Web-authoring tool. But you can also merge an existing Web site into a web you've already created, by importing the pages from your hard disk into the web. When you do this, copies of the pages are made and placed into your web's directories. Here's what to do:

1. Open your web and select File → Import. The Import File to FrontPage Web dialog box opens.
2. Click Add File or Add Folder, then find the file (or directory folder containing the files) that you want. You can select multiple files (hold the Ctrl key down while you click each) or a single directory.
3. When you click the OK button in the Add File or Browse For Folder dialog box the files are added to the list box in the Import File to FrontPage Web box (see Figure 3-3).
4. You can now click Add File or Add Folder again to select more files or folders.
5. You can postpone the operation by clicking Close. This doesn't clear the list box; it simply closes it. You can return later (during the current session) and complete the import operation.

6. You can modify the names with which the files will be imported or move them into different directories if you wish. Click a file in the list, then click Edit URL. You'll see a dialog box showing the directory name and filename. Modify these and click OK to close the Edit URL box (Figure 3-3).

7. Click OK and the files are imported.

Where are the files placed? If you selected individual files, they're placed in the main directory of the web into which they're being imported. If you selected a folder, the folder is re-created within the web, and the directory's contents are re-created inside. Of course, if you modified a file's information in the Edit URL box — removing the directory name, for instance — the file will be placed wherever you specified.

If you had a Web site with several subdirectories, this structure will be maintained, so the Web site will still work within the FrontPage web. The directory structure is re-created, so all links should still work.

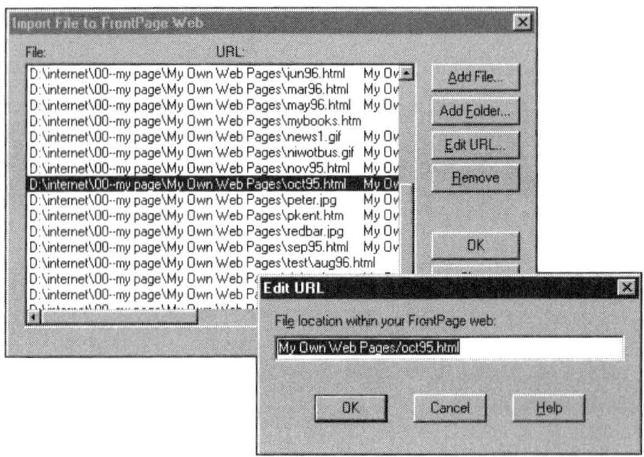

Figure 3-3 The Import File to FrontPage Web dialog box and the Edit URL box

Summary

Well, finally, we're through the web stuff, and ready to start creating Web pages. This may seem back to front. With other tools you'd create the Web pages, then create the Web site by adding links. The Web site would grow as you added Web pages. FrontPage does it differently, partly because the templates and wizards enable you to create an entire web in a few minutes and then go in and modify the web. So with FrontPage you create the web — your basic structure — and *then* you start modifying and adding pages.

You've now learned how to manipulate webs, from creating them to deleting them, copying them to merging them. One thing you haven't seen yet: how to open individual pages and work in them, or create new pages. That's what we'll be doing next.

PART TWO

WORKING WITH PAGES

THIS PART CONTAINS THE FOLLOWING CHAPTERS

First you create a FrontPage web, then you add pages — individual documents — to the web. In Part Two, you'll learn how to do everything from mundane word-processing tasks to adding pictures and creating links between pages. You'll even learn about embedding multimedia objects and working with FrontPage's wonderful WebBots.

BUILDING A SOLD-OUT SHOW

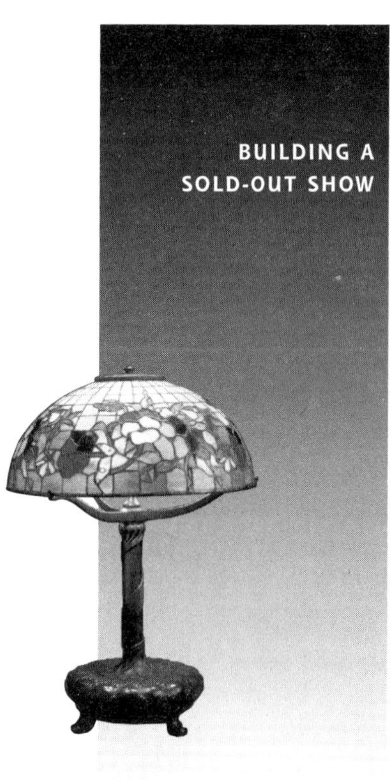

"The play's the thing," Hamlet said, "Wherein I'll catch the conscience of the king." The subsequent production was a success because Hamlet knew the message he wanted to convey, but more important, he knew his audience. Unlike Hamlet's play, the point of your Web site is probably not to extract a confession from a murderer. In a way, though, your site is a performance, and if it doesn't reach the audience you want, don't expect a curtain call.

So who are these millions of people who use the World Wide Web, anyway? How old are they? How much do they earn? Do they have particular political leanings? What are their concerns about the present and future of the Web? Fortunately, someone anticipated the need for this information, and it's readily available to you.

Several times every year, the Graphics, Visualization, and Usability Center (GVU) at Georgia Tech University publishes data about the users of the World Wide Web. Current and past survey results are available at http://www.cc.gatech.edu/gvu/user_surveys/.

GVU shows an unbelievable amount of information about Web users. For example, do you know what percentage of Web surfers are women? Does your site have a visitor registration feature? If so, can you trust the data that your visitors are entering into your system? Why would they lie about it? Does your site obtain information about users without their knowledge? If your visitors knew that, how many would return to your site? Find out the answers to these questions and more at the GVU site.

Terms such as *average*, of course, can be misunderstood. If the average score on a chemistry test is 75, one might mistakenly expect many of the test scores to be between 70 and 80. But if half the students get a 50 and the other half get perfect scores, that also leads to an average of 75. So if the average age of your site's visitors is 24, don't necessarily assume that most of them are in their twenties. Fortunately, GVU lists much more specific data than just the average for any category, making such errors less likely.

Now, granted — unless you want to appeal to everyone, it's probably not wise to think of your Web visitors as the exact average of GVU's data. A Web site that publishes results of chromosomal research will cater to a different crowd from, say, a site that enshrines Gilligan. No one knows your site's content better than you do, but the facts about the people who access that content may not be so easy to determine. The importance of GVU's data is that it can show you the entire range of users who might visit your pages. From there, it's up to you to determine how to bring them in.

CHAPTER FOUR

PREPARING A WEB PAGE

IN THIS CHAPTER YOU LEARN THESE KEY SKILLS

In this chapter you're going to begin working with your Web pages. You'll see how to open pages from Explorer, or how to open the Editor and then open a page — perhaps a page on your hard disk (but outside your web) or even a page borrowed from elsewhere on the World Wide Web or corporate intranet. Then you'll see how to set up the page's properties: the background and text colors, the background sounds, and even a few strange things such as the base URL, the default target frame, and META tags.

Opening Web Pages from Explorer

I'm going to assume that you've created the web you want to work in, and you're now ready to start creating or modifying pages. Perhaps you've imported an existing Web site or created a new web using a wizard or template. Or maybe you've created a blank web, and you want to start from scratch.

TIP **There are two ways to start from scratch. Select Normal Web from the New FrontPage Web dialog box. This contains a _private directory, an images directory, and one file, a blank index.htm file. Or select Empty Web. This contains the directories but doesn't have the index.htm file.**

You can use these methods to open the Editor and open Web pages:

* Click the Show FrontPage Editor toolbar button. The Editor opens, showing a blank page.
* Select Tools → Show FrontPage Editor. The Editor opens, showing a blank page.
* Double-click a file in the right pane (whether in Hyperlink or Folder view) — the Editor will open and display that file.

In Explorer — and a number of dialog boxes throughout FrontPage — although you can see both the filename and the document title, you must click or double-click the *filename*, not the document title.

* Right-click a file (right or left pane, doesn't matter which), and select Open.
* Click a file and select Edit → Open.
* Click a file and press Ctrl+O.
* If the Editor is already open, drag a file from the Explorer onto the Editor. If there's no file open in the Editor, drop the file anywhere. If another file is open, drop it onto any part of the window except the workspace. (Dropping it into the workspace creates a link to the file; you'll learn about links in Chapter 7.)
* Right-click a file and select Open With. You'll see a dialog box from which you can select a program to open the file; for instance, you could open a Web page in Notepad, or a GIF file in Image Composer. (The editors you can use are set in the Configure Editors pane of the Options dialog box — select Tools → Options.
* Click a file and select Edit → Open With.

TIP **As you'll see in Chapter 6, you can also use the Insert → File command to merge an existing Web page with the one in the FrontPage Editor.**

Which file should you open? If you are modifying your root web or a web created from a template or wizard, you'll probably want to begin by modifying the main page.

Your Home or Main Page

The main, or home, page is represented in the Hyperlink view as a house. What makes this the main page? How does FrontPage know it's the main page? Because it's called index.htm. (On your hard disk it's index.htm; if you are working on a remote server, the system administrator may have set things up to use index.html, instead.)

All Web servers can be set up to provide a default file to any browser coming to the site without naming a file. So if a user provides a URL with only the host name portion, the server sends the default file from the root directory. If the user provides a URL with both host and directory name, but still no filename, the server sends the default file from the specified directory. This default file is sometimes known as the *welcome* file (or the *home-page file*, or the *index file*, or the *directory index file* — whatever).

Different servers use different default filenames. In fact, servers can be configured to use various names. The default name may be welcome.html, or default.html, index.html, index.htm, and so on.

FrontPage regards the index.htm or index.html file as the main or home page. So when you open a web, it looks for index.htm or index.html and gives it the house icon. In fact you can test this very quickly. Use Windows Explorer to modify the index.htm filename (to !index.htm, for instance), then open the web in FrontPage Explorer. The house icon will have gone, and the renamed file is now treated like any other page in your web. (You can rename files in the Folder view — click a file, press F2, type a new name, and press Enter.

TIP **If you are planning to transfer your Web site to a non-FrontPage-enabled Web server, ask the system administrator what filename you must use as the welcome-file name, then change the name before transferring the web. FrontPage-enabled servers are already set up to use index.htm or index.html. If you are using a FrontPage-enabled server, FrontPage will automatically modify the filename for you. That is, FrontPage uses index.htm as the "home page" filename, but if the server to which you are moving the web is using index.html, the filename will be modified during the transfer process.**

Of course you're going to want to edit this page, to add your information. If you created a new web using the Normal template, the page is empty. In the case of the root web it contains a little information: a FrontPage logo image, a link to the Microsoft Web site, and a little text. You can either delete all this stuff and replace it with your own, or simply rename this file and create a new one. In Figure 4-1 you can see the default root home page in the FrontPage Editor.

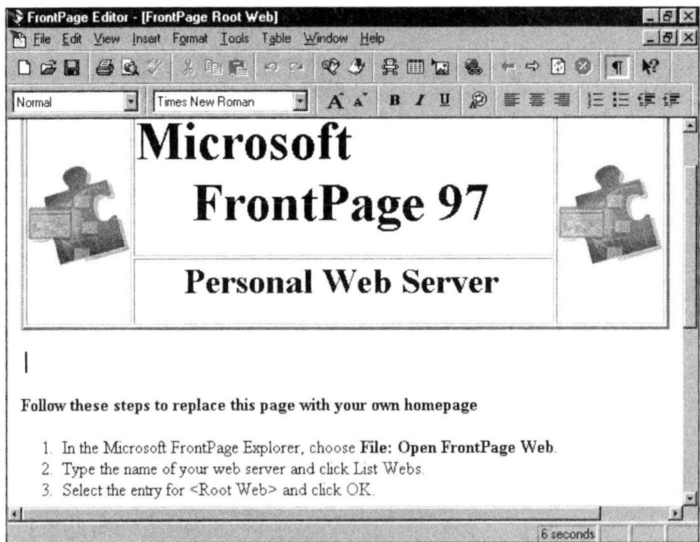

Figure 4-1 The FrontPage Editor window, displaying the root web's index.htm file

Opening Web Pages from Within the Editor

You're not restricted to opening pages from FrontPage Explorer, nor only those within your own web. Once the Editor is open you can open pages from your web from within the Editor. And you can open other pages, too. You can open pages from other webs, pages that you created using other HTML authoring tools, and even "snarf" pages from somewhere else on the World Wide Web or corporate intranet. Use one of the following methods.

Opening a Page from Your Web

1. Select File → Open or click the Open toolbar button. The Open File dialog box opens (Figure 4-2).

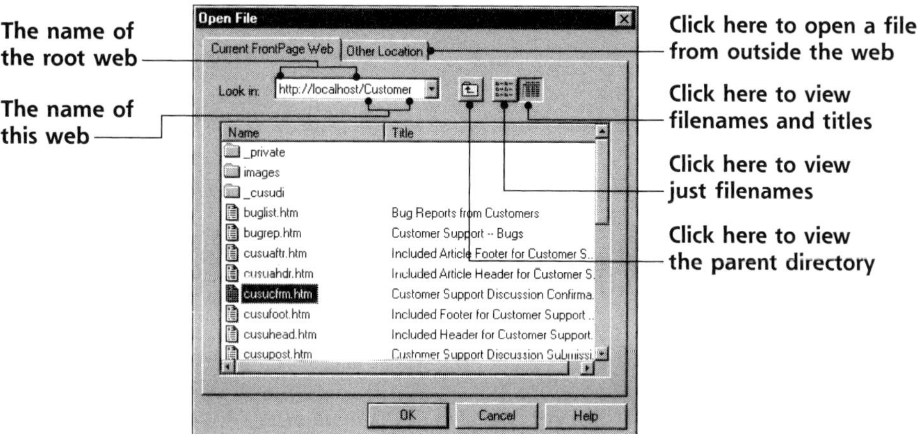

Figure 4-2 The Open File dialog box

2. This pane displays the files held in your web. Double-click a folder to open it if necessary.

3. Double-click a file to select it. That file will be opened in the Editor.

You can also open pages that you've opened in previous sessions by selecting from the bottom of the File menu.

Opening a Page on Your Hard Disk or LAN

1. Select File → Open or click the Open toolbar button. The Open File dialog box opens.

2. Click the Other Location tab (Figure 4-3).

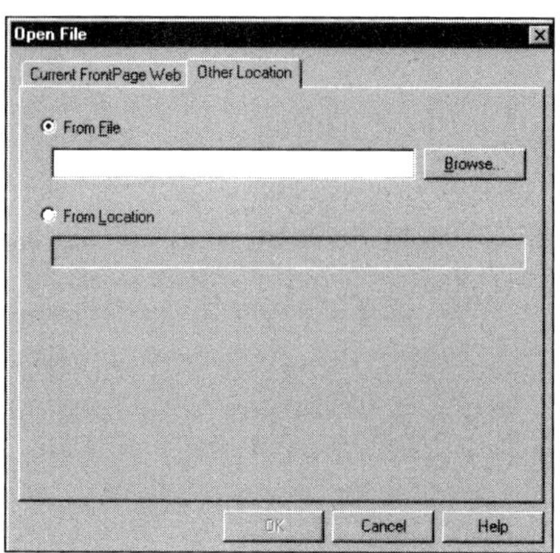

Figure 4-3 The Other Location pane enables you to open a file from your hard disk, LAN, intranet, or the Internet.

3. Click Browse and find the file you want to open. This may be any file on your hard disk, including files stored in other webs. It could also be on other computers on your network, of course (use Network Neighborhood).
4. When you've found the file you want, double-click it to place it into the Open File dialog box.
5. Click OK and the file is opened in the Editor.

Snarfing Web Pages

Here's another way to import a page into your web. You can copy it — *snarf* it, as Microsoft used to call it (though they seem to have dropped the term; did it sound too close to *filch* or *snatch*, perhaps?). In other words, you can grab it from elsewhere on your corporate intranet or from the World Wide Web. In the Other Location pane of the Open File dialog box (Figure 4-3) click the From Location option button and then type the URL of the page you want to borrow, then click OK. FrontPage loads a copy of that page into the Editor (assuming you have your network or Internet connection up and running, of course).

It almost goes without saying that you don't necessarily own what you snarf from the World Wide Web, or even from a corporate intranet. I'll say it anyway: Just because you can snarf something doesn't mean you have the right to use it. Copyright law protects the rights of Web authors, so before you use something you've found, make sure you have permission to do so.

When you snarf things, you'll often end up with a strange-looking document, with lots of odd little icons, such as these:

This means that there's a piece of JavaScript embedded into this Web page. See Chapter 9.

This is a piece of VBScript. See Chapter 9.

This represents a file that's been embedded into the Web page (using the <EMBED> HTML tag). It's intended to be displayed or played by a browser plug-in. See Chapter 9.

This represents a Java applet, embedded into the Web page using the <APPLET> HTML tag. See Chapter 9.

This represents a piece of HTML code that the Editor can't recognize. See Chapter 5.

This is a <!— —> HTML tag, an HTML comment line. See Chapter 6.

This represents a bookmark. See Chapter 7.

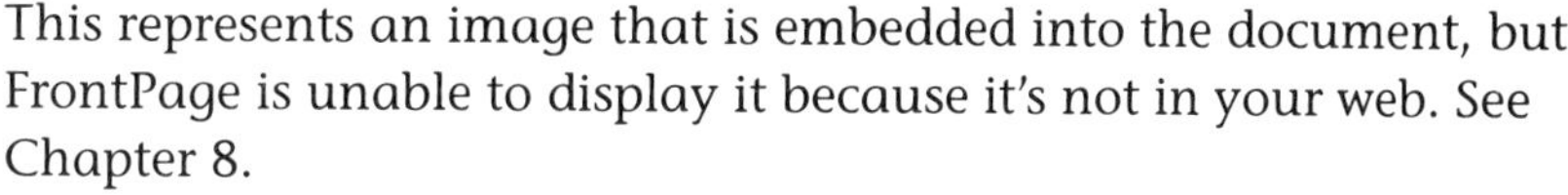

This represents an image that is embedded into the document, but FrontPage is unable to display it because it's not in your web. See Chapter 8.

This represents an ActiveX control. See Chapter 9.

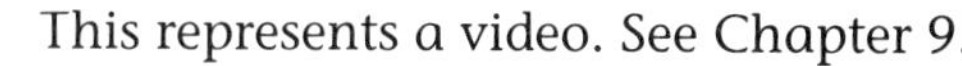

This represents a video. See Chapter 9.

By the way, if you use the MS Internet Explorer Web browser, there's another way to snarf a file. You'll find an Edit button on the Internet Explorer toolbar. Click that and FrontPage Editor opens, with the document that is currently shown in the Internet Explorer window loaded.

Opening a Template or Wizard

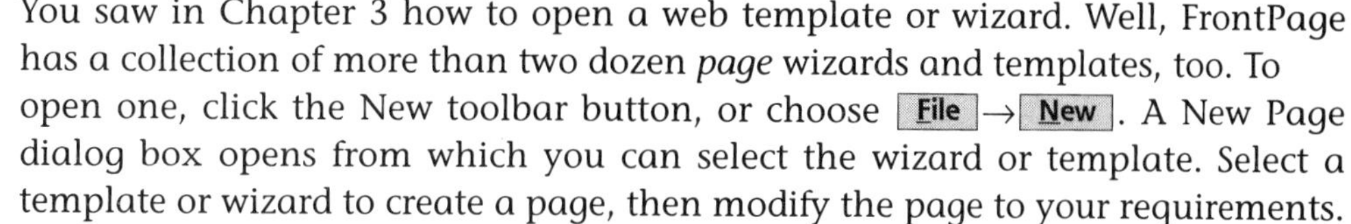

You saw in Chapter 3 how to open a web template or wizard. Well, FrontPage has a collection of more than two dozen *page* wizards and templates, too. To open one, click the New toolbar button, or choose File→New. A New Page dialog box opens from which you can select the wizard or template. Select a template or wizard to create a page, then modify the page to your requirements.

Customizing the Editor Window

The Editor window has *dozens* of toolbar buttons — not just the ones that you can see when you first open the Editor, but three additional toolbars full of buttons as well. Open the View menu and select the toolbars you want to view:

* **Standard** — The buttons on the top row.
* **Format** — The text and paragraph format buttons on the second row (see Chapter 5).
* **Image** — Image-editing buttons. This toolbar appears automatically when you click an image (see Chapter 8).
* **Forms** — A toolbar used for creating forms (see Chapter 13).
* **Advanced** — A toolbar that opens the dialog boxes used for adding HTML tags, ActiveX components, JavaScript and VBScript scripts, and links to databases, and for embedding Java applets and files handled by plug-ins. See Chapters 9 and 10.

TIP **You can drag the toolbars off the window edge and into the work area, creating toolboxes. You can also drag each bar around within the main toolbar block, to take up less room. If you are using VGA mode you may have to do that in order to see all the tools.**

Setting Page Properties

One of the first things you'll want to do is configure the page's properties. These are things that define the overall look of the document and how it works, as you'll see right now.

Select **File** → **Page Properties** or right-click anywhere in the document and choose **Page Properties**. The box shown in Figure 4-4 opens.

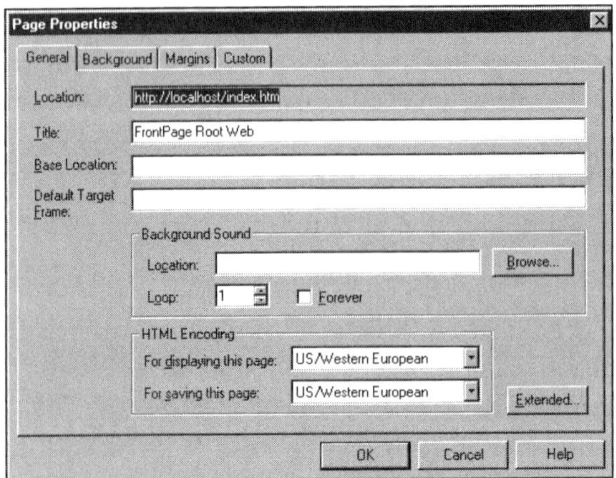

Figure 4-4 The Page Properties dialog box

Let's look at the panes one by one.

The General Pane

These are the things you'll see in the General pane:

Location The hostname, path, and filename of the document.

Title This is the document title, the text that appears between <TITLE> and </TITLE> tags in the HTML document. The title is displayed in a browser's title bar when it opens the document. It's also used in history lists and bookmark or favorites lists. And it's used by many Web indexing and cataloging programs to figure out what your page is about. So use clear, understandable titles. The title is also displayed next to icons in FrontPage Explorer, and in many FrontPage dialog boxes, to help you choose documents, such as when creating links.

Base Location The base URL for this page. (Don't know what that is? It takes a little explanation, so see "The Base URL," later in this chapter.)

Default Target Frame The frame that should be used by default if this is part of a frameset. (Sorry, another one that takes a lot of explanation! See "The Default Target Frame," later in this chapter.)

SIDE TRIP

HTML?

FrontPage insulates you from the HTML tags. Many users understand a little — or a lot — about HTML tags, though many new FrontPage users don't. That's okay, they don't need to. I'll be mentioning HTML tags now and then, to help people who *do* understand HTML understand what FrontPage is doing for them. For those of you who don't understand HTML, all you need to know for now is that a Web page is actually a text document with special codes (*tags*) that describe each element. (If you want to see what I mean, open a document and then choose View → HTML.) We'll discuss HTML tags more in Chapter 10.

Background Sound Location If you want to play a background sound when this page is displayed, use the Browse button to find the sound. You can use .wav, .mid, .aif, .aiff, aifc, .au, and .snd sound files.

Loop You can define whether you want the sound to play just once (make sure 1 appears in the box). Or play it as many times as you wish — enter another number into the box, or click the Forever check box.

HTML Encoding These drop-down list boxes define how the page is displayed or saved — which character system should be used. The vast majority of World Wide Web pages are using the US/Western European character coding. In fact, the systems required to work with different character codes have only recently appeared in Web browsers. In most cases you can leave this setting as it is.

Extended You'll see the Extended button in most dialog boxes. You can click here and see a dialog box into which you can type extra attributes for the HTML tag that FrontPage is creating for you. You'll be able to do this only if you understand HTML coding! See Chapter 10 for more information.

THE BASE URL

Now for that base URL stuff. Before I can explain a base URL, I'd better explain the concept of relative and absolute URLs. (Skip down a couple of paragraphs if you already know about this!) An *absolute* URL is one that is complete; it provides all the information needed to find the file that it references, regardless of how the URL is used. For instance, `http://www.arundel.com/images/undercon.gif` is an absolute URL. You can type it into a Web browser and press Enter, and, assuming all the necessary Internet connections are working (and the undercon.gif file actually exists), the browser will find the file.

Now look at this: `/images/undercon.gif`. This is a relative URL. It's known as relative because it provides the browser with enough information to find the undercon.gif file *relative to the document position.* So if this image file is embedded into the document, or if there's a link in the document to this image, the browser can find the image even though the URL does not contain the full URL. The browser simply looks for the file in the images directory, which it knows must be a subdirectory of the directory in which the current document is held.

What if that document is moved, though? If, for instance, someone makes a copy of the document on his hard disk, or sends it in e-mail to someone? The relative links won't work anymore, because they won't make sense. That's where the base URL comes in. It helps a browser figure out where the document came from, so it can grab files that are referenced within the document using relative URLs. All you need to do is tell the browser (using this base URL) where the original document used to be, and the browser can figure out where the referenced items are held. So, if you wish to use this, simply type the full URL of the document, or the directory in which the document is held (if you use just the directory, make sure you end with a trailing /).

TIP **You can quickly copy this information from the Location text box. But remember, if you plan to move this web to another server when it's finished, you need to enter the final URL, the URL of the document once the web has been transferred.**

THE DEFAULT TARGET FRAME

You don't need to worry about the default target frame unless you are creating a document that will be used within a frameset (we'll look at frames in Chapter 12).

When a user clicks on a link in a document that is held in a frame, the browser has to figure out what to do. (You'll see how to create links in Chapter 7.) Does the browser remove all the frames and display the referenced document by itself? Display the document in the same frame? Display the document in one of the other frames . . . and if so, which?

The link contains information that tells the browser what to do. It can tell the browser which frame to use and which document to place in the frame. Or it can tell the browser which document, and not mention which frame. What will the browser do? It'll look for the *default target frame.* So if you are setting up a frame system in which you want to set up most links to display the specified documents in one of the frames, you can enter that frame name in the Default Target Frame box, rather than in each and every link that you create. See Chapter 12 for more information about targets.

The Background Pane

Click the Background tab to see the information in Figure 4-5.

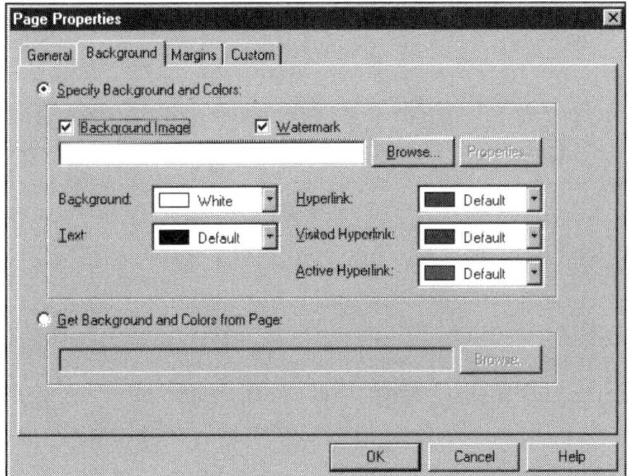

Figure 4-5 The Background pane in the Page Properties dialog box

This is where you'll specify what the background and the text should look like. Here's what you can do:

Specify Background and Colors Select this option button if you want to specify the background pattern, background color, and text color for this page.

Background Image Click this check box if you want to specify the background image. Then click Browse to find the image. I'll show you this in more detail under "Selecting Your Background Pattern," later in this chapter.

Properties If the image you selected is in your web, you can click Properties and modify the image's properties. (See Chapter 8 for information about image properties. Note also that you may not be able to modify these properties until you leave this dialog box, save the file, and return.)

Watermark A watermark is a background that remains static while a Web page can scroll over it. (This is an Internet Explorer browser feature, not yet in wide use in other browsers. That's okay, though; if a browser can't use a watermark, it just treats it like a normal background.)

Background Select a background color for the page from this drop-down list box. Of course if you've defined an opaque image this color won't appear; it'll be blocked by the image.

Text The color of normal text on your page, text that does not contain a link.

Hyperlink The color of text that contains a link.

Visited Hyperlink Most browsers these days change the color of links that lead to documents the user has already seen. This is the color that will be used.

Active Hyperlink The color that link text changes to when you click the link and hold the mouse button down. You'll notice that most browsers these days change the text color momentarily when the user clicks a link.

Get Background and Colors from Page The quickest way to add a special background image, background color, and text colors is to copy them from another document, using it as a sort of "style" document. That way you can set up just one document the way you want the others to appear, then copy the settings from that document to the others. Click this option button, then use Browse to select the "template" document that you've set up. If you ever change the document containing the styles, the settings in this one will change too.

SIDE TRIP

Be Careful with Color!

Changing text and background colors is a double-edged sword. On the one hand, you can create very attractive pages, if you do it right. On the other hand, you can also make pages that appear very attractive on some systems and quite ugly on others.

These color drop-down list boxes have a Custom entry at the bottom; select this and a box opens in which you can create your own colors. Should you do so? Probably not. You can create any color you want, but there's a good chance that it will be a dithered color, a color made up using dots of different colors. Remember that few World Wide Web users are working with more than 256 colors, so if you have your video mode set up to work with more, *change your video mode!* Millions of Web users are still working with a 16-color video mode, too, so you may want to restrict yourself to the basic 16-color palette (the colors in the drop-down list box).

If you create pages that look good with 16 colors, they should look the same with 256 colors or more. Create a page using 256 colors, and it may look completely different (and very ugly) with 16 colors.

Also, please, please, *please* be sensible with your background and text color matches. Test them to see if the text is legible. All the time I find documents that are almost completely unreadable thanks to a bad mix of text color and background color or image. Check what the final document looks like in various different browsers and, if possible, on different video setups (different screens, resolutions, and numbers of colors).

SELECTING YOUR BACKGROUND PATTERN

FrontPage has lots of clip art you can use, including a number of special background images. Here's how to use them:

1. Click the Background Image check box.
2. Click Browse and the Select Background Image box opens.
3. Click the Clip Art tab.
4. Select Backgrounds from the Category drop-down list box. You'll see a collection of background images (Figure 4-6).

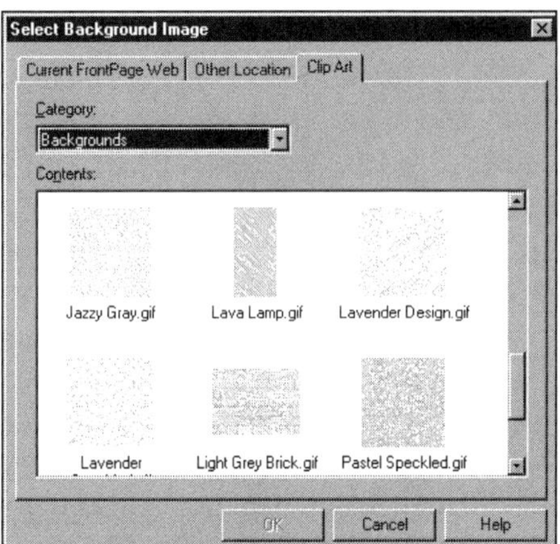

Figure 4-6 FrontPage has a small collection of background images.

5. Click the image you want, and click OK.

You'll also see that the Clip Art pane allows you to open a variety of other image types: animations, bullets, buttons, icons, lines, and logos (Microsoft logos, of course). We'll see how to use these in Chapter 8.

The Margins Pane

Click the Margins tab to set up the page margins. Note that this feature is not currently supported by many browsers — it's an Internet Explorer feature. You can set a top margin and a left margin, and they define, in browsers that use the feature, how much space should appear between the top or left side of the page and the text.

The margins are set using pixels, the smallest dot on a computer screen. For instance, a computer that is using VGA mode is using a resolution of 640 × 480; that is, 640 columns of pixels (dots) by 480 rows of pixels. Of course, not everyone is using VGA mode. Many users are working with 800 × 600, 1024 × 768, or even higher resolutions, so setting a margin is not absolute; it all depends on what video resolution will be used to display the page.

The Custom Pane

Click the Custom tab to see the information in Figure 4-7. What is all this, you ask? This is where you set the *META tags.* META tags are placed at the top of a Web page and provide information about the document, information that may be read by browsers, servers, and other programs.

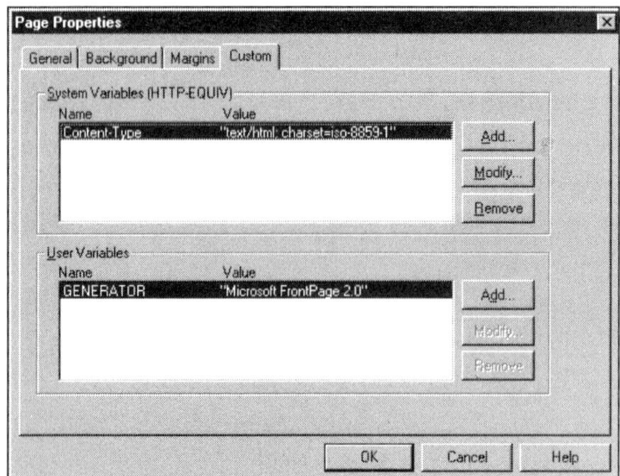

Figure 4-7 The Custom pane

You'll find that FrontPage automatically enters a couple of META tags for you. There's the **Content-Type** tag and the **GENERATOR** tag. The first states what character set is being used in this document, and the second states what HTML authoring tool was used to create the document (**Microsoft FrontPage**).

FrontPage doesn't provide much direct help with these tags. It assumes that you know what you want to enter. All it provides are dialog boxes into which you can type the information.

There are two categories of META tags: the HTTP-EQUIV= tags (or system-variable tags) and the NAME= tags (or user-variable tags). The HTTP-EQUIV= tags contain system information that the Web server can include in the header when sending information to the browser, telling the browser important information that it feels the browser must know — the expiration date of the document, for instance, or a file to load using client pull (see "Bonus" later in this chapter for more about client pull). The NAME= tags contain document information that may, in some cases, be extracted by a program, such as the information used by the search engines.

Entering these tags is much the same for both types of tag. Click the appropriate Add button. In the dialog box that opens (see Figure 4-8; this dialog box appears after clicking Add in the User Variables section, the lower Add button) type the attribute name in the first text box (the text that appears after HTTP-EQUIV= or NAME=). Then type the text that appears after CONTENTS= in the Value box. For instance, if entering the KEYWORDS, type **KEYWORDS** into the top text box and all the keywords you want to use into the lower text box. Click OK and FrontPage creates the tag for you.

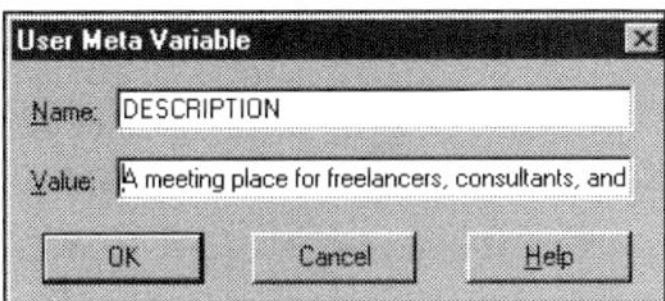

Figure 4-8 Entering a new META tag

BONUS

Those Wacky META Tags!

You didn't think I'd leave you with no more META tag information, did you? Well, I'm not providing a detailed lesson on META tags, but I will give you an idea of what they can do for you.

You might, for instance, want to use the DESCRIPTION and KEYWORDS tags, because these are used by those other programs I mentioned earlier, programs used by World Wide Web search engines to build their listings. These programs view Web pages and often look in the META tags for information about the page. So the DESCRIPTION and KEYWORDS tags can help get your page listed in the right places.

The DESCRIPTION tag is a simple description of the contents of the document. For instance, the DESCRIPTION META tag might look something like this:

```
<META NAME="DESCRIPTION" CONTENT="A meeting place for freelancers,
  consultants, and contractors of all kinds.">
```

The KEYWORDS tag contains keywords that are used by search engines to categorize the site so it can be found by people searching for those keywords. In other words, you need to think about the words that your intended audience is likely to type into a search engine to find you, then put those words into the KEYWORDS tag. For instance, a Web site for freelancers might use this KEYWORDS tag:

```
<META NAME="KEYWORDS" CONTENT="freelancers, freelancers,
  freelancers, freelancers, freelancers, freelancers, freelancer,
  freelancer, freelancer, freelancer, freelancer, freelancer,
  freelance, freelance, freelance, freelance, freelance,
  freelance, contract, contract, contract, contract, contract,
  contractor, contractor, contractor, contractor, contractor,
  contractor, consult, consult, consult, consult, consult,
  consult, consultant, consultant, consultant, consultant,
  consultant, consultant, consultants, consultants, consultants,
  consultants, consultants, consultants, consulting, consulting,
  consulting, consulting, consulting, consulting">
```

Why have I repeated each word six times? To improve the hit rate on a search. Does this really help? I'm not sure, though a lot of people do it, and it depends on the search engine that's looking at the Web page. You'll often find documents with keywords repeated scores of times (if you happen to be looking at the document's META tags, that is), but I do know that doing this can be counterproductive, as some search engines will ignore keywords that have been repeated too many times. I limit my entries to six repetitions each, which should avoid this problem.

Another META tag that you may want to use is the AUTHOR tag, which contains your name and e-mail address. For instance:

```
<META NAME="AUTHOR" CONTENT="Peter Kent: pkent@arundel.com">
```

Other tags are more advanced, allowing you to take advantage of a feature called *Client Pull*, for instance, a system that enables you to tell the browser to grab another file from the server after a particular time has passed. And remember, the information that appears after CONTENT= goes into the Value text box in FrontPage's Meta Variable dialog box.

I've given you a few common META tags. There are others, but we're really getting away from the scope of this book. Refer to an up-to-date HTML reference for more information.

Summary

You've got the page open, you've made sure its properties are correctly configured and now . . . the next step, of course, is content. It's time to begin adding the text and images to your page.

You could, of course, skip all this page-configuration stuff and come back to it later. But don't forget it, especially if you plan to put your site on the World Wide Web. In particular, using sensible page titles is very important, and using the correct META tags can be very helpful in getting your pages listed properly in the Web search engines.

You may also want to spend a little while creating a style document or a series of them. That way you can use the Get Background and Colors from Page text box to configure your pages in a few seconds, rather than setting each page up individually.

CHAPTER FIVE

WORKING WITH TEXT IN THE FRONTPAGE EDITOR

IN THIS CHAPTER YOU LEARN THESE KEY SKILLS

5

In this chapter we'll begin working in your Web pages, creating and modifying them by using FrontPage's text features. The FrontPage Editor looks remarkably like a word processor . . . which is probably because it *is* a word processor. It's a word processor with extra features to create not paper documents, but hypertext documents.

TIP **Note that you can open multiple Web pages in the Editor. You can use the Window menu to move between these documents (the open documents are listed at the bottom of the menu), or press Ctrl+Shift+F6 to move to the next document in the Window list (or Ctrl+F6 to move to the previous document).**

Using the FrontPage Word Processor

I'm not going to waste your time explaining how to use a word processor. You already know how to type and how to format paragraphs and fonts. I'll simply point out the word-processing tools and explain the differences between working with FrontPage and working with a word processor. In Table 5-1 you can see a quick rundown of the word-processing toolbar buttons.

TABLE 5-1 FrontPage Editor's Word-Processing Toolbar Buttons

Button	Purpose
	Open a blank document.
	Open an existing document (see Chapter 4).
	Save the document. You must have a web open in the Explorer in order to use this button.
	Print the document.
	Spell check the document.
	Cut: Remove the selected object and place it in the Clipboard.
	Copy: Place a copy of the selected object in the Clipboard.
	Paste: Place a copy of the object in the Clipboard into the document at the cursor position.
	Undo the last operation.
	Redo the last operation.
¶	Show formatting characters (new-paragraph characters, form and table grids, and bookmark or reference anchors).
 Normal	Select a paragraph style (see "Using Styles and Fonts," later in this chapter).
 Times New Roman	Select a font (see "Using Styles and Fonts," later in this chapter).
A	Increase the size of the selected text.
A	Decrease the size of the selected text.
B	Bold the selected text.
I	Italicize the selected text.
U	Underline the selected text.

Button	Purpose
	Modify the color of the selected text.
	Left justify the paragraph.
	Center the paragraph.
	Right justify the paragraph.
	Create a numbered list.
	Create a bulleted list.
	Move the paragraph's left margin further to the left.
	Move the paragraph's left margin to the right.
	Place a table in your document (see Chapter 11).
	Place an image in your document (see Chapter 8).

You'll find that working with the FrontPage Editor really is like working with a word processor. You type the same way, move around with the keyboard and mouse in the same way, select text in the same way . . . it's only when you come to place images, tables, frames, and so on, that things work differently.

TIP **To remove formatting that you've applied to text, select the text and then select Format → Remove Formatting, or press Ctrl+Spacebar. This removes formats applied to characters, not to paragraphs.**

You can also format text and paragraphs using the Format → Font and Format → Paragraph commands. The Font dialog box, under the Font tab, has a couple more options, enabling you to create strike-through and typewriter text. And, as you can see in Figure 5-1, it also allows you to format a variety of different characters, from blinking text to superscript and subscript.

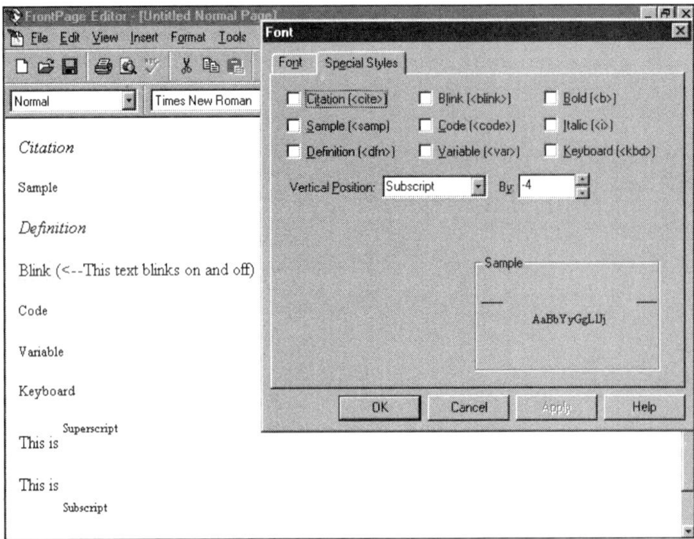

Figure 5-1 More font formats are available in the Font dialog box.

Using Styles and Fonts

The paragraph styles and the fonts work in the same manner as with a word processor, but your choices are different. First, you have a fairly limited choice of paragraph styles, and you can't create your own. Why? Because the styles provided are standard styles that are recognized by browsers. In fact it's important to understand that when you select a style, you are not really defining how that style will appear in your document. You can see in Table 5-2 (included for those of you who are familiar with HTML) that when you assign a style to a paragraph, certain tags are used to define the style in the HTML document. When a browser reads your Web page, it looks at these tags and then displays the text accordingly. And that's not necessarily the same way that FrontPage Editor or your browser displays them. In most cases it's similar, but it may vary slightly, and some browsers allow users total control over styles — so the manner in which your document is displayed in one browser may be completely different in another. So what's shown in Figure 5-2 is how FrontPage Editor displays the styles, not how every browser shows them.

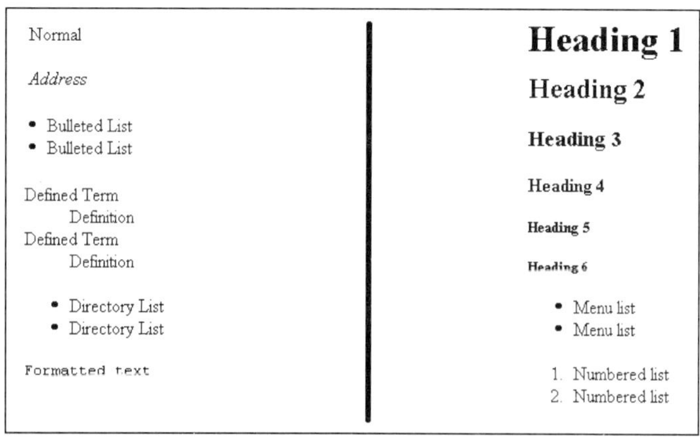

Figure 5-2 The FrontPage Editor paragraph styles

TABLE 5-2 The Paragraph Styles

Style Name	HTML tag used
Normal	<p></p>
Address	<address></address>
Bulleted List	<ul></ul>; <li> before each item in list
Defined Term	<dl> at the top of the definition list, </dl> at the bottom; <dt></dt> for each defined term
Definition	<dd></dd>
Directory List	<dir></dir>; <li> before each item in list
Formatted Text	<pre></pre>
Heading 1	<h1></h1>
Heading 2	<h2></h2>
Heading 3	<h3></h3>
Heading 4	<h4></h4>
Heading 5	<h5></h5>
Heading 6	<h6></h6>
Menu List	<menu></menu>; <li> before each item in list
Numbered List	<ol></ol>; <li> before each item in list

The styles may take a little getting used to. For instance, some of them are sort of active styles that change automatically. Select Defined Term, type a word, press Enter, and the style is automatically modified to the Definition style, indented a little. (Unfortunately, the drop-down list box may show Normal, but it's actually using the Definition style, which you can see in the HTML code if you select View → HTML.) Type a definition and press Enter, and the style changes back to Defined Term so that you can type another entry. The Heading styles also automatically change back to the Normal style when you press Enter.

TIP **You can, in general, only type single spaces; HTML doesn't accept double spaces, so you can't use spaces to line up text (you'll even find that the Tab key doesn't work correctly in the FrontPage Editor). If you really need double spaces you can use the Formatted paragraph style, which *will* accept multiple spaces (and in which the Tab key works, too). Generally, though, you'll use tables to line up text; see Chapter 11.**

Now, about fonts. You can select whatever font you want to use from the fonts drop-down list box. This shows all the fonts installed on your system. By default Times New Roman is shown, but you can pick another if you wish. Should you do so? Probably not, at least not at this stage in the game. Most browsers currently in use do not support different fonts, so you'll be defining a font that most browsers can't display.

By the way, although Times New Roman is shown by default, the text in the document is actually *not* being set to Times New Roman. This would, perhaps, be more accurate if it showed Default Font or something similar. The font used for text defined as Times New Roman will be the one defined for the browser as its default font. Pick another font, though, and the Editor will use the <font face=></font> tag pair to modify the font — though as I've stated, most browsers currently ignore this pair.

SIDE TRIP

WHAT ABOUT OTHER TAGS?

If you are familiar with HTML, you'll know that there are a lot of tags that FrontPage hasn't provided. There's no direct way to use the <blockquote></blockquote> tag pair, for instance. But there is an indirect way. Simply select Insert → HTML Markup, type the first tag of the pair and click OK; type the text you want to format into the document; select Insert → HTML again; type the second tag; and click OK. You'll see the little Question Mark icon where you placed the tags. We'll look at this technique in more detail in Chapter 10.

By the way, HTML allows mixing of styles. Unlike in a word processor, in which text can be only one style at a time, HTML actually lets you apply two or more styles at once, which is a little confusing sometimes. For instance, you might create a bulleted list, then, while the cursor is still on a line with a bullet, select a heading. Now the text is both bulleted *and* uses the heading style you select.

To make sure you have cleared a style out before selecting another, either press Enter twice (if creating a list) or press Enter once and then select the Normal style.

Saving and Exporting Files

When you are ready to save your work, you'll find that you have three ways to do so:

* Save in the current web
* Save as a template
* Save as a file outside the web

Here's how this works. Click the Save toolbar button, or select File → Save. You'll see the dialog box shown in Figure 5-3. The first text box shows the document's title. Did you enter a title into the Page Properties dialog box (Chapter 4)? If not, FrontPage will pick a title for you, by grabbing the first line of text on the page. You can change it if you wish.

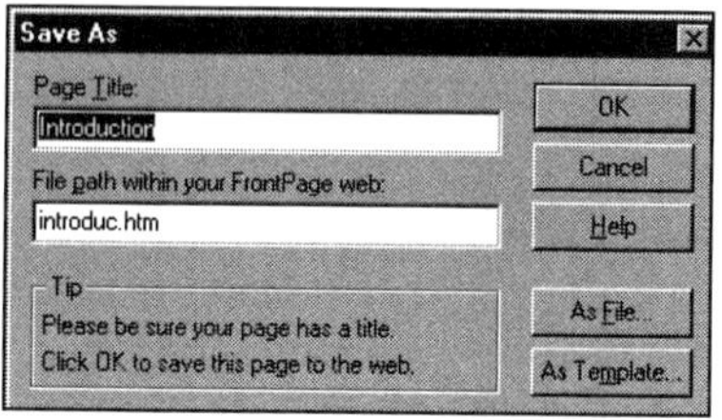

Figure 5-3 The Save As dialog box

The second text box shows the URL within the web. Initially it shows only the filename (based on the first word that you typed into the page). But you can also define where you want to place the page — in which directory folder. Simply precede the filename with the folder name and a forward slash (/).

TIP **Want to create new folders within your web? In FrontPage Explorer click the folder in which you want to create a new folder, select File → New → Folder, type a new folder name, and press Enter. The server you are working with must have the FrontPage 97 server extensions (not the old FrontPage Version 1 extensions) in order for this to work, so if you get an error message, talk with your system administrator.**

Click OK and the file is saved to your web . . . if you have a web open, that is. If you don't, you'll see an error message and have to either open a web or save the file outside the web. Also, if you have inserted images into your document (see Chapter 8), you'll get the box shown in Figure 5-4. Click Yes (or Yes to All, so you don't have to answer the question for every image in the document), and FrontPage saves a copy of the image in your web. You may want to precede the filename with **images/** to place the picture in the image directory (your document will be properly modified so that it knows where to get the image).

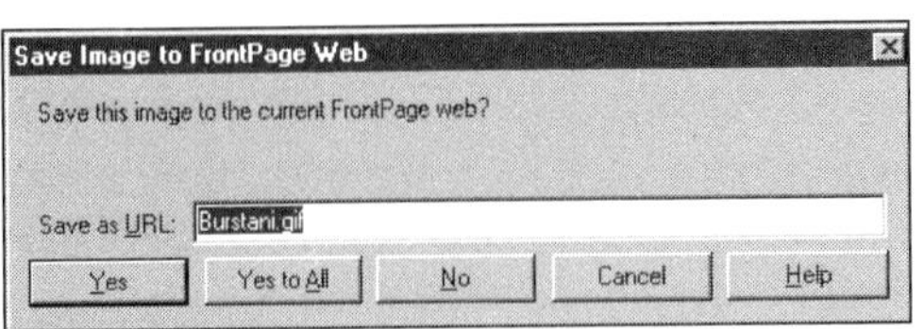

Figure 5-4 FrontPage wants you to confirm that it should save the image file.

Once you've saved the file using File→Save or clicked the Save toolbar button, the document is simply saved over the existing file, in the manner normal for a Windows application. To save elsewhere, use File→Save As.

Exporting Pages

You can also export web pages when you save them; that is, you can save them outside your web. If you are in a corporate workgroup and want to pass a Web page to someone else, for instance, this is how you'd do it:

1. Select File→Save As. The Save As dialog box opens.
2. Click As File. A typical Windows Save As dialog box opens.
3. Find the directory into which you want to save the file.
4. Type a name into the File Name text box.
5. Click OK.

TIP **There are a couple more ways to export files. You can click a file in FrontPage Explorer, then select File→Export. Or you can simply copy the file using a file-management program such as Windows Explorer.**

Creating Templates

To save a file as a template — so you can select it within the New Page dialog box (using File→New) — click the As Template button in the Save As dialog box. You'll see the dialog box shown in Figure 5-5. Provide a document title, a document name, and, if you wish, a description of the template. (The description is the text that appears in the Description box at the bottom of the New Page dialog box.) Then click OK.

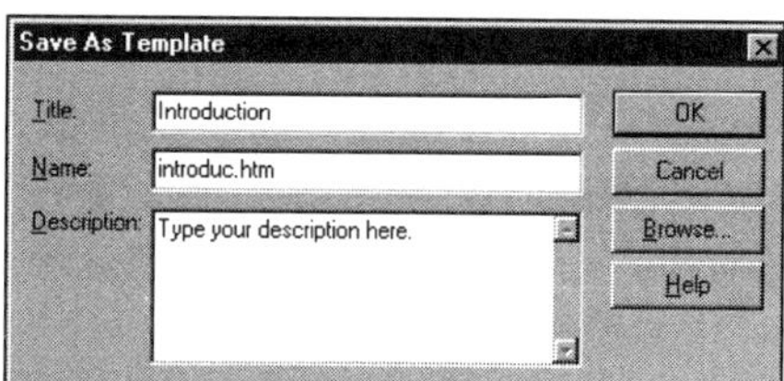

Figure 5-5 Save a file as a template, so you can copy it later.

In effect you've just created a file that will be copied each time you select it from the New Page dialog box, a great way to quickly duplicate page formats that you use frequently.

Creating a template is easy, but how about creating wizards? More complicated, unfortunately. You'll need the FrontPage Development Kit, plus programming skills. Search the `http://www.microsoft.com/frontpage/` **site for more information.**

Deleting Pages

Now and then you'll need to remove pages from your web. You might want to start by exporting or copying the page into an archive directory, so you can always get it back if you need it. (After years of losing data, thanks to software bugs and "user error," I've become paranoid about losing data and tend to back up my backups!) Then simply click the document in FrontPage Explorer and press the Delete key (or choose **Edit** → **Delete**; or right-click the document and choose Delete from the pop-up menu).

Viewing and Editing the Source

Would you like to see the HTML document that FrontPage has created for you? Remember, when you add or modify text within the FrontPage Editor, FrontPage is working in the background to create the HTML file for you. Web browsers read HTML files, so that's what has to be created when you are building a Web site.

You can see what FrontPage has done by selecting **View** → **HTML**. You'll see a window like that shown in Figure 5-6. You'll see that there are four colors used in this window: purple (HTML tags), blue (the attribute names within tags), green (the attribute values), and black (the text that is visible to someone reading the Web page). (If you can't see the colors, check the Show Color Coding check box.)

```
View or Edit HTML
<!DOCTYPE HTML PUBLIC "-//IETF//DTD HTML//EN">
<html>

<head>
<meta http-equiv="Content-Type"
content="text/html; charset=iso-8859-1">
<meta name="GENERATOR" content="Microsoft FrontPage 2.0">
<title>FrontPage Root Web</title>
</head>

<body bgcolor="#FFFFFF" bgproperties="fixed">

<p align="center">   </p>
<div align="center"><center>

<table border="3">
    <tr>
        <td rowspan="2"><img src="images/logo.gif" width="95"
        height="89"></td>
        <td><p align="center"><font size="7"><strong>Microsoft FrontPage
        97</strong></font> </p>
        </td>
        <td rowspan="2"><img src="images/logo.gif" width="95"
        height="89"></td>
    </tr>
    <tr>
        <td><p align="center"><font size="6"><strong>Personal Web

Original  Current  Show Color Coding   OK   Cancel   Help
View or edit the current HTML
```

Figure 5-6 Viewing the HTML source; you can edit it, too.

You'll also notice two option buttons, Original and Current. If you click Original, you'll see the text in the saved document. Click Current, and you'll see all the document, including changes you've made since you last saved.

You can copy text from this window if you wish. Simply use the mouse to highlight the text you want, then press Ctrl+C. Move to the program in which you want to paste the text, then press Ctrl+V.

If you understand HTML you can also edit the source in this window, adding your own HTML tags or modifying existing ones. (The tags you add or modify may not be understood by FrontPage, of course, in which case you'll see the little Question Mark icons when you view the changes in the Editor.) When you've made your changes, simply click OK and they're added to the document.

Pasting into FrontPage Editor

You can cut or copy text from another application and paste it into FrontPage. When you do so, FrontPage takes a quick look and decides whether it needs to convert any of the text. If it's all plain text, there's no problem. It simply pastes it into the document. If the text is formatted in some way, though — with colored text, quotation marks, different fonts, and so on — it will convert the text, adding all the necessary HTML tags to make the text look correct inside the document.

Paste text in Times New Roman and the editor leaves the text as the default. Use any other font, though, and the editor adds the <font face=> tag to define the typestyle.

A good way to see this at work is to copy text from the View or Edit HTML window (View → HTML), then paste it into the FrontPage Editor. FrontPage converts the text so that it looks just the way it appears in the View or Edit HTML window; because it contains all those HTML tags, it has to add lots of special codes so that it's able to display the tags in the window (these tags are normally invisible to the user, after all). It also has to add tags to convert text colors, so the correct colors are shown in the FrontPage Editor, too.

You can also paste images into your FrontPage Editor window. Sometimes the images come in well, sometimes they don't! (If you have trouble pasting an image, copy it into a graphics program and then save it and insert it into the document using the techniques we'll discuss in Chapter 8.) A temporary file is created when you do this, and then when you save the file, you have the option of naming the image file and defining where you want it placed.

BONUS

Picking Features and Previewing Documents

5

Here's a problem you'll run into while working with Web documents. You are not creating documents the way you want them to appear. Rather, you are providing a set of instructions to browsers, telling them how the document should be displayed. When you use a word processor to create a letter, manual, or book, what you see is what you get — you define how the document looks, and the end user (the reader) has no way to modify it. But Web pages are different. In order to read them, the user needs a special program (a browser) to display the document. So when you create the document and define how things will look, you're actually providing a set of instructions to the browser, telling it how to display the document. There are two problems with that, though:

1. The browser may ignore your instructions.

2. The browser may not understand your instructions.

You may think the document will be displayed using the default font, Times New Roman. But a browser displaying your document may have a different default font. You may specify the font to be something else. But the browser may not understand the HTML tag used to define fonts, or perhaps doesn't have the font you want.

You might specify a background image. But the browser may be set to override all background images and colors. You may select text colors . . . but the browser may be set to ignore those, too.

HTML is evolving very quickly, so some features in FrontPage create HTML tags that some browsers won't be able to use. You can use a marquee, for instance (see Chapter 9), but most browsers currently in use can't work with it. You can use a watermark (Chapter 4), but again, most browsers can't use it. Luckily, in most cases browsers ignore tags they don't understand. For instance, most browsers that don't work with marquees and watermarks simply display marquees as static text, and watermarks as scrollable background images.

Another important example. At the time of writing, a significant portion of browsers, perhaps 30 or 40 percent, cannot display the fonts defined by the <font face=> tag. Netscape 2 can't, and perhaps some of the Netscape 3 betas can't either. Netscape 3 and later can, as can Internet Explorer 3 and later. But many people are still using old browsers.

So it's a good idea to check what your document looks like in as many browsers as possible. First, find out what everyone is using. Go to some of the web statistics sites for that information.

Web Browser Agent Statistics `http://www.xmission.com/~snowhare/statistics/browsers.html`

WWW Statistics `http://blueridge.infomkt.ibm.com/knudsen/stats/current.html`

EWS Browser Statistics `http://www.cen.uiuc.edu/bstats/latest.html`

Browser Watch `http://browserwatch.iworld.com/stats.html`

Yahoo! Browser Usage Statistics `http://www.yahoo.com/Computers_and_Internet/Internet/World_Wide_Web/Browsers/Browser_Usage_Statistics/`

Currently about 95 percent of users are working with Netscape 3, Netscape 3 betas, Netscape 2 and its betas, and Internet Explorer 2 and 3.

When you've decided which browsers you want to test, load a copy of each on your hard disk. You can then view your document by selecting File → Preview in Browser. (Remember to save your work in the Editor before previewing.) You'll see the dialog box shown in Figure 5-7. Click the browser you want to view, then click the Window size you want to check, and then click Preview to view the document in the browser. (The 640 × 480 window size is the full VGA screen size. It's a good idea to check a document using this size, as many, many users are still working with the VGA video mode.)

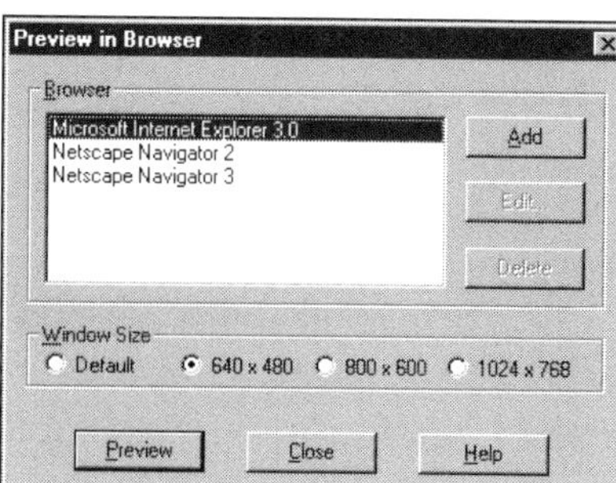

Figure 5-7 Check to see what your page looks like in various browsers.

 You can also click the Preview in Browser button to open the document in a browser — the last one selected in the Preview in Browser dialog box is opened. By the way, if you've recently previewed the document in the browser you'll see the *old* version. Click the browser's Reload button (or, in the case of Internet Explorer, the Refresh button). Leave the browser open, and you can simply save your work in FrontPage, switch to the browser, and click the Reload button to preview your work. And finally, one more quick way to preview a document: simply drag it from FrontPage Explorer and drop it onto your browser. (This works with recent versions of both Internet Explorer and Netscape Navigator.)

TIP **Don't feel that you have to use all the latest cool features provided by FrontPage. If most users can't see the feature, or if the feature actually causes problems in many browsers, avoid it!**

5

Summary

If you know how to use a word processor, you already know how to use many of FrontPage's features. You can start creating a document immediately, typing or modifying your text, and formatting the text and paragraphs. There are a few differences, though, as you've seen in this chapter, and we'll be looking at a few more differences in the next chapter, too. I'll explain how to create horizontal lines and how to insert special characters. I'll also show you how to add your *comments*, text that is embedded into the HTML document but not visible to the user; how to create lists with bullets, numbers, and letters; how to print your documents; and a few more ways to work with text in your Web pages.

CHAPTER SIX

MORE TEXT FORMATTING

IN THIS CHAPTER YOU LEARN THESE KEY SKILLS

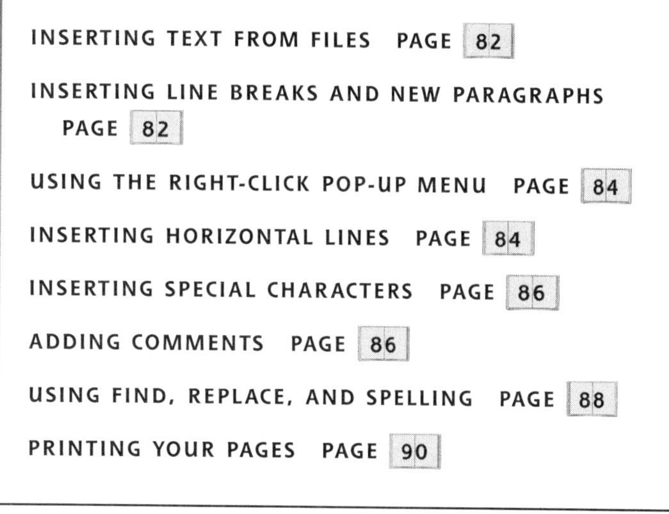

In the preceding chapter you saw how to add text to your documents, and in this chapter we're going to continue with that theme. In most cases the heart of a Web site is text. For all the hype about graphics and Java and animations and other types of Web candy, when you look closely you'll find that the most common use of a Web page is to provide information, and that information is provided in the form of text. There's nothing wrong with that, either. Text is a pretty good way to transfer information from one person to another. It's fast and cheap, for a start.

In this chapter we'll carry on learning how to manipulate text in your Web pages, starting with inserting text into a page from an existing file, and going on to formatting text into lists.

Inserting Text from Files

Do you have text already written, text that you want to simply insert directly into a Web page? You can copy and paste it from the program in which it was created, of course, but if you have large documents it may be quicker to insert the documents directly into the Web page.

You can do this by selecting Insert→File. You'll see a typical File Open dialog box, in which you can find the file you want to insert. You can insert any of these file types:

.doc Word for DOS, Word for Windows, and Word for the Macintosh files, and WordPerfect files.

.htm and .html HTML files. The HTML tags will be incorporated into the current Web page, so you are, in effect, merging the two Web pages.

.htt HyperText Template files.

.htx and .asp Reprocessed HTML, files created by programs that create Web pages on the fly, such as search engines creating Web pages in response to a search query.

.mcw Microsoft Word 4 to 5.1 for the Macintosh.

.rtf Rich Text Format, a file format that most Windows word processors (and even some Macintosh word processors) can create.

.txt Simple text files, in ASCII or ISO Latin 1 format.

.wpd WordPerfect 6 files.

.wps Microsoft Works for Windows files.

.wri Windows Write files.

.xls, .xlw Microsoft Excel files.

When you insert a file, FrontPage converts the file, adding all the HTML tags required to display it correctly.

Inserting Line Breaks and New Paragraphs

Web pages don't handle lines of text in the normal word-processing way. In a word processor you can put as many blank lines as you want into a document page. Not, generally speaking, into an HTML Web page, though. In fact, many HTML-authoring tools don't let you enter blank lines. Why? Because HTML itself doesn't recognize blank lines created by pressing the Enter or Return key twice. Browsers ignore excess spaces and line breaks. (By excess, I mean more than one at a time!)

However, if you place a blank line in your text using FrontPage Editor, the blank line is placed into the HTML file. FrontPage has to place a special code into the file, the ` ` code, which tells the browser to enter a blank line.

There are also two ways to end a line in HTML. There's the <p> tag. That identifies the end of a paragraph and is entered into the text by pressing Enter. There's also a line-break tag, <br>, which means that the following text is moved down to the next line, but is still regarded as part of the preceding paragraph (paragraph formatting will apply to it, for instance). That is entered into the text either by pressing Shift+Enter, or by selecting Insert → Break and clicking OK in the Break Properties dialog box (see Figure 6-1).

TIP **If you've turned on Format Marks (select View → Format Marks, or click the Show/Hide toolbar button), you'll see the symbol representing a line break.**

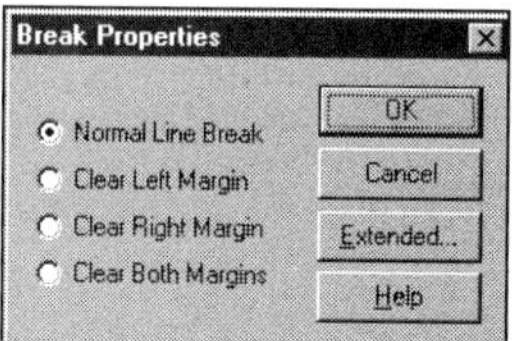

Figure 6-1 The Break Properties dialog box

You'll notice in Figure 6-1 that there are other options in this dialog box. You can define *where* the next line should be placed if there's an image in the way. These options often (usually, perhaps) make little difference. But now and then you'll run into an alignment problem in which they can be useful.

For instance, let's say you have an image and you've set the properties such that the text is aligned with the image at the left, the text wrapping down the right side of the image. If you insert a normal line break, the text moves down one line and continues — the image is still on the left side of the text. But if you'd rather have the next line of text placed underneath the image, you can open the Break Properties dialog box and use the Clear Left Margin option. That means, in effect, "move down until the left margin is clear of images."

So these are the different line-break options:

Clear Left Margin Move down until the left margin is clear of images.

Clear Right Margin Move down until the right margin is clear of images.

Clear Both Margins Move down until both margins are clear of images.

Using the Right-Click Pop-Up Menu

Don't forget to right-click. Throughout FrontPage you'll find useful right-click pop-up menus. In FrontPage Editor these provide quick access to various Properties dialog boxes and the Clipboard commands (Cut, Copy, and Paste).

Wherever you right-click within the work area, you'll see the **Page Properties** option; select this to open the Page Properties dialog box, which we looked at in Chapter 4. You'll also see other options, depending on what you click. Click a picture to see **Image Properties**; on a line to see **Horizontal Line Properties**; on text to see **Paragraph Properties** and **Font Properties**; on a form to see **Form Properties**; on a WebBot to see **WebBot Component Properties**; and so on.

Inserting Horizontal Lines

You've probably seen the horizontal lines used in many Web pages to separate blocks of information from each other. FrontPage actually provides two ways for you to insert horizontal lines. You can get the Editor to insert an HTML horizontal-line tag (the <HR> tag), or you can insert an image file.

Here's how to work with the normal horizontal-line tag:

1. Select **Insert** → **Horizontal Line**. The horizontal line is placed into the document. If the line looks the way you want it, you can stop now. Otherwise, continue to the next step.
2. Double-click the line, or right-click and select **Horizontal Line Properties**. The box in Figure 6-2 opens.

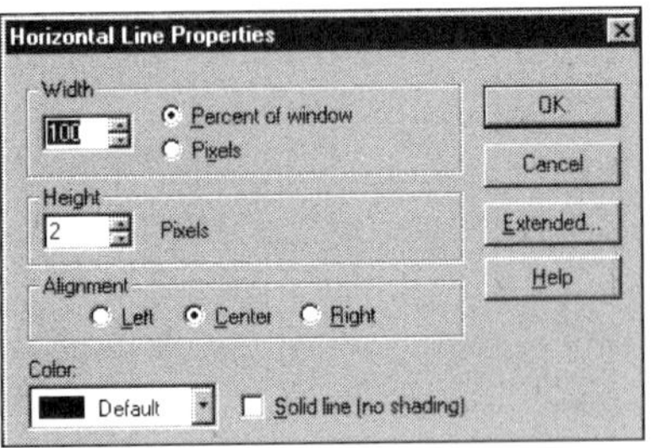

Figure 6-2 The Horizontal Line Properties dialog box

3. Define how wide the line should be. You can set it to fill a certain percentage of the browser window, or a pixel size. The percentage is probably the best way to adjust the line; if you adjust the pixel size you don't know how much of the window the line will cross, as it will be dependent on the screen resolution on which the browser window is displayed.

4. Pick a pixel size for the height of the line. Yes, what it actually looks like will depend on the screen resolution, but there's not much you can do about that (except to test your document in several different video resolutions).
5. Select the line alignment: Right, Center, or Left.
6. Select a color for the line from the drop-down list box.
7. If you want a solid line, click the Solid Line (No Shading) check box.
8. Click OK, and your line is modified.

The other way to create a line is to use one of the lines provided for you in the clip art library. You'll learn how to use this in Chapter 8, but here are a few specifics related to using the horizontal lines:

* The horizontal lines are in the Image dialog box (Insert → Image), under the Clip Art tab. Select Lines from the Category drop-down list box.
* After inserting the line into the document, right-click it and select Image Properties. Don't double-click, or you'll open the file in the Image Composer program that comes with the Bonus Pack, or whatever other image editor you've set up as the default (see Chapter 17).
* Under the Appearance tab in the Image Properties dialog box you can adjust the line's width, height, alignment; modify the amount of space around the line (between the line and the text); and even place a border around the line.

Figure 6-3 shows a few examples of the types of horizontal lines you can create.

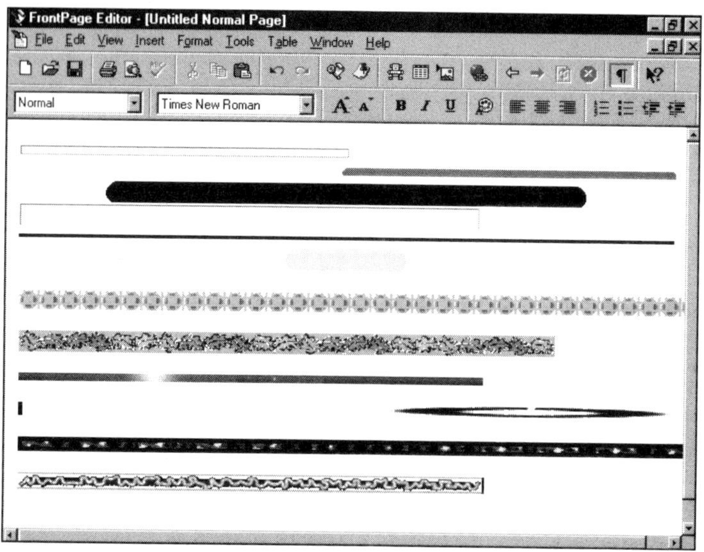

Figure 6-3 All sorts of horizontal lines — the six at the top are created with tags, the six below with images

Inserting Special Characters

Putting special characters into a Web page used to be a little tricky. Remember, Web pages are stored as text files, so the file can't store any character other than those in the normal text character set. Most browsers these days can work with files that use the ISO Latin 1 character set, which is a sort of extension of the well-known ASCII (American Standard Code for Information Interchange) character set. The ISO Latin 1 set (also known as ISO 8859) contains a number of special characters that are not present in the ASCII character set — the copyright symbol ©, the registered trademark ® symbol, and so on.

However, there are still some common symbols that ISO Latin 1 doesn't handle. To get around that problem, browsers were programmed to identify codes and convert them to special characters. For instance, if a browser sees `™` in the Web page it knows that it's supposed to display the little ® trademark symbol.

To enter a special character or symbol into your text, select **Insert** → **Symbol**. You'll see the dialog box in Figure 6-4. Click the symbol you want, then click Insert. Click the next symbol, then Insert, and so on. When you've finished, click Close.

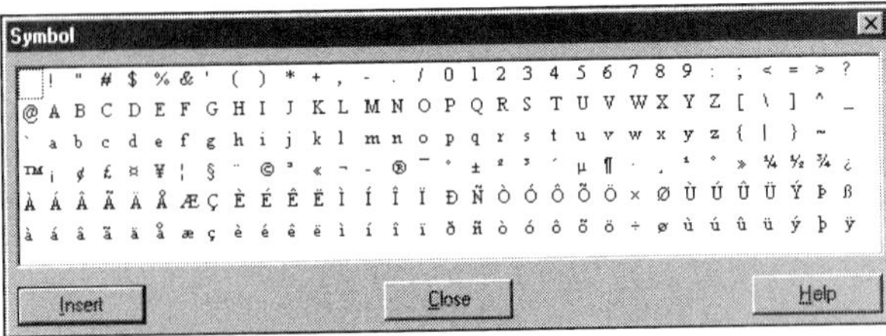

Figure 6-4 The Symbol dialog box

If you use these symbols, it's a good idea to check what they look like in several browsers, as some browsers don't do a very good job of displaying them (though more recently browsers have been doing quite well). See Chapter 5 for information on previewing your work.

Adding Comments

You can add hidden comments to your documents if you wish — comments that are visible to you but are not shown when the document is displayed in the browser. You can create comments that remind you of things that you need to do to a document, or how you created a particular feature. If you work as part of a group, comments are a useful way for group members to let others know what they've done, and what needs to be done, to a document. There are actually two ways to add comments to your documents. You can create HTML comments or FrontPage comments.

FrontPage comments

The quickest way to add a comment to your document is to select **Insert** → **Comment**. The dialog box shown in Figure 6-5 opens. Simply type your comment and click OK. The text is inserted into your document — it's colored purple and preceded by the word *Comment*. But you'll find that when you view the document in a browser (see Chapter 5), the text is invisible. So you can leave these comments as long as you want, even after you've published your Web pages.

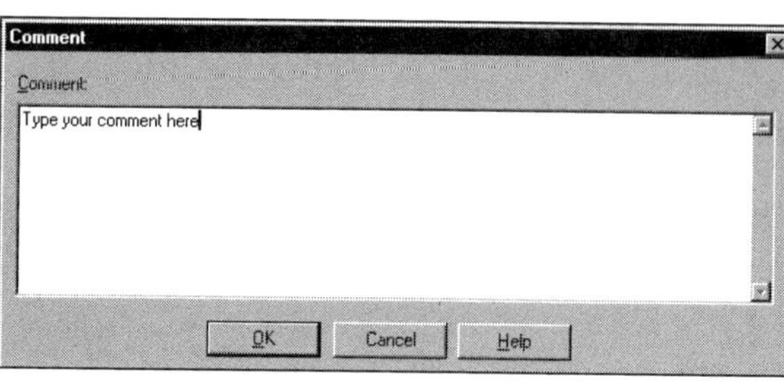

Figure 6-5 Type a comment and click OK.

Although comments are not visible in the browser window, virtually all browsers have a command that allows the reader to view the source HTML document. So your comments may be read by others.

HTML Comments

If you really want to enter normal HTML comments, you can do so (though as you'll see in a moment, there's really not much point). HTML comments are placed inside a <!– –> tag, like this: <!–This is a normal HTML comment–>. When a browser sees the <!– and –> bits, it knows it's a comment, so it hides the tag and the text within the tag.

You can create a comment tag by selecting **Insert** → **HTML Markup**. When the HTML Markup dialog box opens, type the entire tag, beginning with <!–, including your comment text, and ending with –>. Then click OK. An Exclamation Point icon is placed into the document to show you where the comment is.

But why bother? Why not use the FrontPage comment and be able to see the actual comment text within the FrontPage Editor? Both forms of comment will work the same in a browser: both will be omitted from the document in the browser window. In fact, here's what the HTML comment tag actually looks like in the HTML file:

```
<p><!–webbot bot="HTMLMarkup" startspan –><!–This is a normal HTML
  comment–><!–webbot bot="HTMLMarkup" endspan –></p>
```

It's actually enclosed in a special pair of webbot comment tags. On the other hand, if you create a FrontPage comment, here's what it looks like:

```
<p><!-webbot bot="PurpleText"
preview="This is a FrontPage Comment" -></p>
```

Using Find, Replace, and Spelling

FrontPage contains a few more tools that you'll be familiar with from your word processor, although they work slightly differently. You can search for a particular word or phrase, search for a word or phrase and replace it, or spell check your work.

Finding Text

If you want to find a word or phrase within the document you are viewing in FrontPage Editor, select Edit → Find. You'll see a Find dialog box similar to those found in thousands of word processors and text editors. Type the text you want to search for, click Match Whole Word Only or Match Case if appropriate, select from Up and Down, then click Find Next.

Suppose you want to find a particular Web page you created a while back, and you can't remember what you named it. Or you want to find a particular piece of text but don't remember which file you placed it in. You can use FrontPage's webwide search tool to search all the documents in your web — or just a selected few.

In Explorer select Tools → Find and you'll see the dialog box in Figure 6-6. This works like a normal Find dialog box, except that you can choose to search all the documents in your web, or just the ones selected in the FrontPage Explorer window. Click OK and away it goes, searching your web.

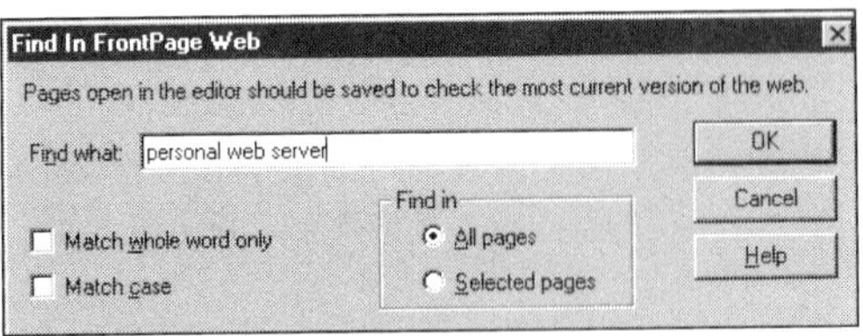

Figure 6-6 FrontPage Explorer helps you search your entire web.

TIP **To switch from FrontPage Editor to FrontPage Explorer, use the normal Windows task-switching tools, or click the Show FrontPage Explorer toolbar button.**

When it has found your text, FrontPage displays the dialog box shown in Figure 6-7. You can now double-click an entry in the list (or click it and click Edit Page) to open the FrontPage Editor and load the document; the text you searched for will be highlighted. You'll find the Find dialog box is already open, so you can search through the document for subsequent occurrences.

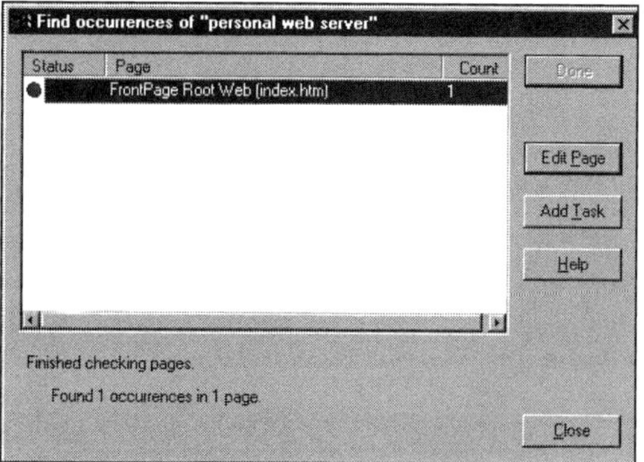

Figure 6-7 FrontPage finds your text and shows you where it is.

You can also click the Add Task button; click this if you want to add a reminder about this page to the ToDo program, which we'll look at in Chapter 17. And the Status column shows you whether the item has been added to the To Do program (yellow) or not (red).

Replacing Text

Replacing text works in a similar manner. To use the normal Find and Replace tool in the Editor, select **Edit** → **Replace**. But to replace text webwide, go to FrontPage Explorer and select **Tools** → **Replace**. Type your text, both the text you are searching for and the text you want to replace it with, then click OK. You'll see a dialog box similar to that in Figure 6-7. Again, you can click Edit Page (to open the Editor, display the document, and open the Replace dialog box) or Add Task (to add the entry to the To Do list).

TIP **Be careful when replacing text or using the spell checker to replace text. If you replace text that has a hyperlink set on it (see Chapter 7), the hyperlink is removed. Also, the Find, Replace, and Spell Check features do not work on any text but the text that users can see on the page; they ignore text in the page title, in comments, in URLs used in links, and so on. In particular, be very careful about using the Replace All button in the Replace dialog box, as it may break links without your realizing it.**

Spell Checking

If you've spent any time on the World Wide Web, you may have come away with the idea that there's a World Wide Rule: Don't spell check your documents. Well, there isn't. In fact, I wish you *would* spell check your documents, as there are enough spelling mistakes on the Web to last us for generations; we don't need more.

Again, there are two ways to check spelling. You can check a document's spelling from within FrontPage Editor, in the same way you'd check spelling in your word processor. Click the Check Spelling toolbar button to get started, or select Tools → Spelling. By the way, if you've *included* a file in the current page (I'll explain in Chapter 10 how to include files), the text in the included file is not spell checked; you'll have to do that separately. And it doesn't check the text in dialog boxes, such as the title you entered into the Page Properties dialog box, for instance.

But you may want to wait and check the document's spelling later, just before you publish your web. You can check spelling in all documents at once, using FrontPage Explorer. In Explorer select Tools → Spelling and you'll see the dialog box in Figure 6-8. You can choose to search all the documents in your web or just the ones selected in the FrontPage Explorer window. Notice also the Add Pages with Misspellings to the To Do List check box. Click this if you want to automatically add a reminder to fix misspellings to the To Do program.

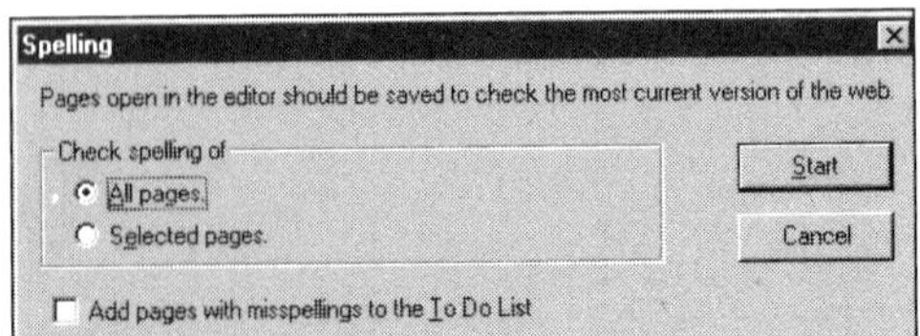

Figure 6-8 Select Tools → Spelling in the Explorer, and you can spell check all your documents at once.

When you click Start, FrontPage looks for mistakes in each page and shows you a list of results. You can click Edit Page to edit a particular error — the page will be opened and the error shown.

Printing Your Pages

What I'm about to say may be deemed heresy in some quarters, but here goes anyway. Sometimes, hypertext can be a bit of a nuisance. Having created many hypertext systems, I've found that there's a significant problem with them. Complex hypertext systems are often very difficult to review for errors. The problem is that there's generally no top or bottom, no first page or last page, so it's difficult to ensure that all the information has been read and confirmed. Sure, you can spell check, but what about checking grammar, or checking technical accuracy? How do you get other people in your organization to read the pages and make sure that what's been written in them is correct?

For this reason it's often useful to print your web pages, particularly if you want to have other people review your work — and sign the review, to confirm that the pages contain the correct information. There are three print-related commands: Page Setup, Print Preview, and Print. These work in the same way as they do in most Windows word processors, so I won't go into detail, beyond pointing out the commands:

To set up the page headers, footers, and margins File → Page Setup.

To see a print preview File → Print Preview.

To print the page File → Print or click the Print toolbar button.

Unfortunately you can't print from FrontPage Explorer, so you can only print one document at a time. This is a real weakness, it seems to me, so perhaps multipage printing will be added to FrontPage later.

BONUS

Bullets and Numbering

You can quickly create bullet lists and numbered lists using the Bulleted List and Numbered List toolbar buttons. Simply press Enter to begin a new line, click the button, then begin typing. Each time you press Enter, the text moves to the next line and a new bullet or number is added to the beginning of the line. Press Enter twice to finish the list and start working with the Normal style again.

There are a number of things you can modify on your lists. You can select the type of bullet or the type of numbering, or even use letters instead of numbers. You can also choose from a few different types of lists and define which number or letter the list should begin with.

You can begin creating your list by setting up these properties: select Format → Bullets and Numbering, set up the properties, click OK, and then begin typing your list. Or you can modify an existing list. Right-click in the list and select List Item Properties if you want to modify the single item that you clicked, or List Properties if you want to modify the entire list.

In Figure 6-9 you can see the Bulleted tab of the List Properties dialog box. As you can see, you can select from one of three different types of bullet lists: black circles, empty circles, or black squares. (Or click the one without bullets to remove a bullet list, returning the text to Normal style.)

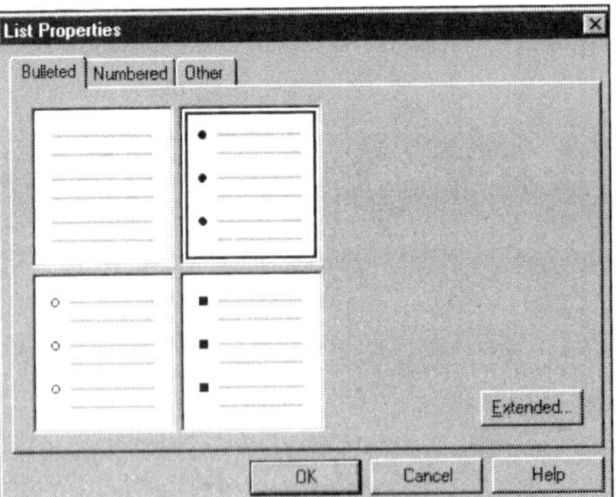

Figure 6-9 Pick your bullets here.

If you want a Numbered list, click the Numbered tab. As you can see in Figure 6-10, you have five "numbered" list choices, including two lists in which uppercase or lowercase letters are used instead of numbers. You can also select, in the Start At incrementer, the starting number or letter. (You must use numbers, even if your list will use letters, to specify the first entry in the list.)

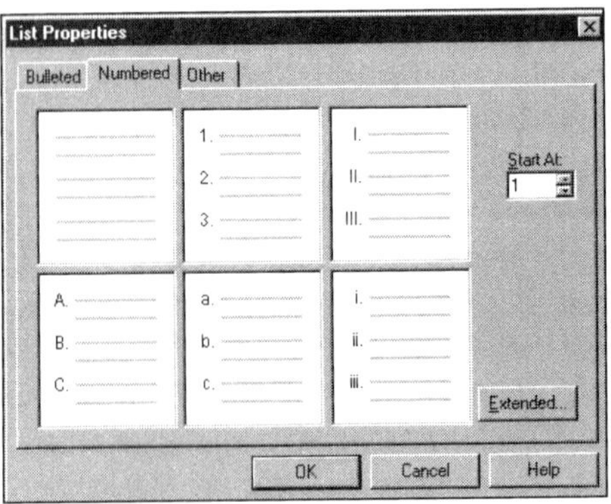

Figure 6-10 Numbers sometimes means letters; pick your numbering or lettering scheme.

Finally, click the Other tab to select a different type of list. You can create a Definition list, Directory list, or Menu list. This is the same as selecting these list types from the style drop-down list box. Also, note that this pane is not present in the dialog box unless you create the list and then right-click in the list and select **List Properties**.

You can also use bullet pictures, in the same way that you can use images as horizontal lines (see "Inserting Horizontal Lines," earlier in this chapter). The Clip Art pane in the Image dialog box contains a Bullets category. However, if you use these you'll have to create the lists manually — that is, you won't be able to use the Bulleted List or Numbered List styles.

Summary

We've finished word processing. You've learned how to work with FrontPage to get your text into your documents, how to use all the normal word-processing features, with the slight variations that the FrontPage Editor presents. In this chapter and the previous you've seen how to use styles and fonts, how to save and export files, how to insert text from files and print your work, how to create lists, and more.

But what have you produced? The features we've looked at enable you to create pages, Web pages even — but isolated Web pages. Using these features you can create pages that are online pages but not hypertext pages. In the next chapter we'll start learning about hypertext, about the way in which you can link documents — both to other documents in your web and to documents elsewhere on the World Wide Web or corporate intranet.

6

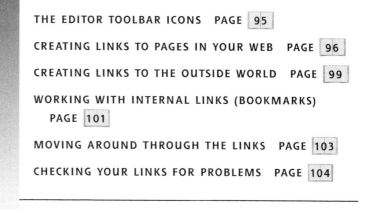

CHAPTER SEVEN

CREATING HYPERTEXT LINKS

IN THIS CHAPTER YOU LEARN THESE KEY SKILLS

Finally, we reach the hypertext portion of the book. You've seen how to create webs, and how to create pages within webs, and now it's time to see how to link the pages together. In this chapter you'll learn about hypertext, about linking documents within your web, and creating links to documents outside the web, too.

The Editor Toolbar Icons

In Chapter 5's Table 5-1 you saw most of the toolbar buttons, the ones related to the word processing functions of FrontPage Editor. Table 7-1 shows you some of the others, this time buttons that are related to the hypertext functions and that carry out a few advanced page-creation functions (such as the placing of images and tables).

TABLE 7-1 The FrontPage Editor's Hypertext Toolbar Buttons

Button	Purpose
	Open the FrontPage Explorer.
	Open the To Do List (see Chapter 17).
	Insert a WebBot (see Chapter 10). These carry out a variety of special functions.
	Insert a table into the document. (See Chapter 11.)
	Insert an image into the document. (See Chapter 8.)
	Create or edit a link
	Go back to the previous document traveled to through the links.
	Go forward to the document you've just come back from.
	Reload the document — that is, display the last saved copy of the document.
	Stop the current operation.

Creating Links to Pages in Your Web

There are two ways to create links to other pages in your web. You can create a link to an existing page, or you can create a link and a new page at the same time. We'll start with the former method.

A Link to an Existing Page

Let's say you have several pages created already, and you want to link them. For instance, you want to link from your main page, the index.htm file, to the other pages. Here's how to create a link:

1. Select the text on which you want to place the link. That is, the text that the user will have to click to activate the link.

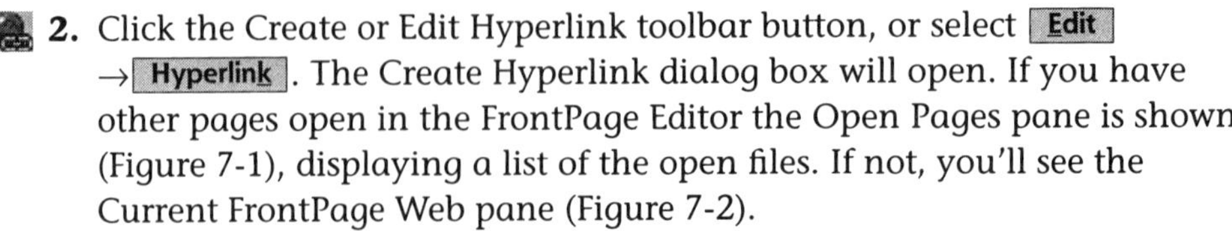

2. Click the Create or Edit Hyperlink toolbar button, or select Edit → Hyperlink. The Create Hyperlink dialog box will open. If you have other pages open in the FrontPage Editor the Open Pages pane is shown (Figure 7-1), displaying a list of the open files. If not, you'll see the Current FrontPage Web pane (Figure 7-2).

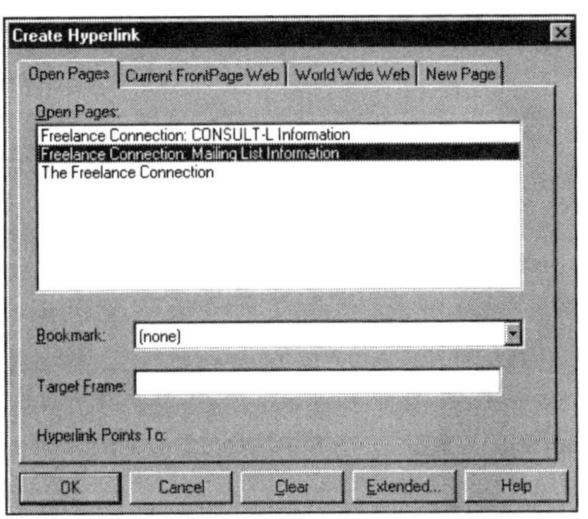

Figure 7-1 You can link to one of the other open documents if you wish, from the Open Pages pane . . .

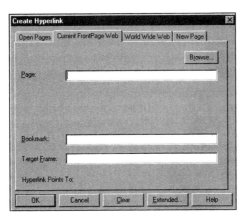

Figure 7-2 . . . or you can open any file from the web in the Current FrontPage Web pane.

3. To link to one of the open pages, simply click the page in the Open Pages pane and then click OK. (Look at the bottom of the Open Pages pane and you'll see the Hyperlink Points To line. This shows the filename of the selected page.)

TIP **Don't worry about the Bookmark and Target Frame boxes for now. We'll discuss the Bookmark box later in this chapter, under "Working With Internal Links (Bookmarks)." And you'll learn more about the Target Frame box in the chapter about frames, Chapter 12.**

4. To link to a page that is in the current web, though not open in the Editor, click Browse in the Current FrontPage Web pane, and select the file you want to link to from the Current Web dialog box (Figure 7-3).
5. Click OK, and you've created your link.

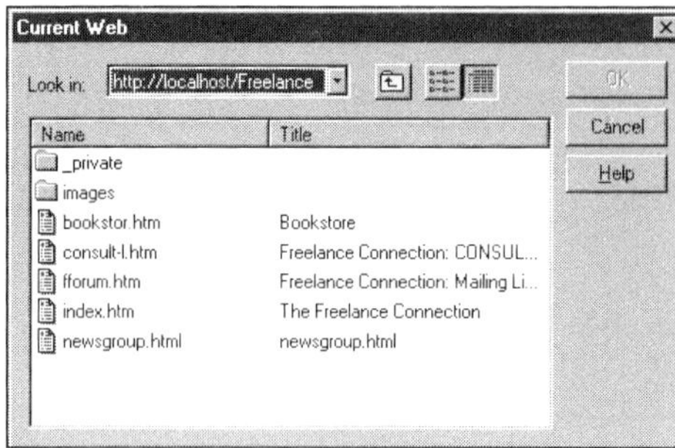

Figure 7-3 Pick the page you want to link to.

Modifying and Removing Links

If you want to modify a link, simply click inside the link text, open the Create Hyperlink dialog box (you can right-click and select **Hyperlink Properties** if you wish), and select a different file. But how about clearing a link, removing the link from the text?

Click inside the text, then open the Create Hyperlink dialog box. The appropriate pane is shown, depending on the type of link you've created. Simply click the Clear button, then click OK. You'll see that the text has changed back to normal — no color or underline.

Creating a New Page When You Link

You can create a link to a page that doesn't yet exist, if you wish. Here's how:

1. Select the text on which you want to place the link.
2. Click the Create or Edit Hyperlink toolbar button, or select **Edit** → **Hyperlink**. The Create Hyperlink dialog box will open.
3. Click the New Page tab. You'll see the information in Figure 7-4.
4. The Page Title box already contains text; this is the text that you highlighted in the document. Replace this text, if you wish to use a different document title for the page that you're about to create.
5. The Page URL box also contains text, a suggested filename. Replace this with the filename you want to use. Also, you may include a directory name, if you want to save the file in a directory other than the main web directory. But make sure you use a forward slash after the directory name, not a backward slash: ***directory/filename.htm***.
6. Ignore the Target Frame box for now; we'll cover that in Chapter 12.

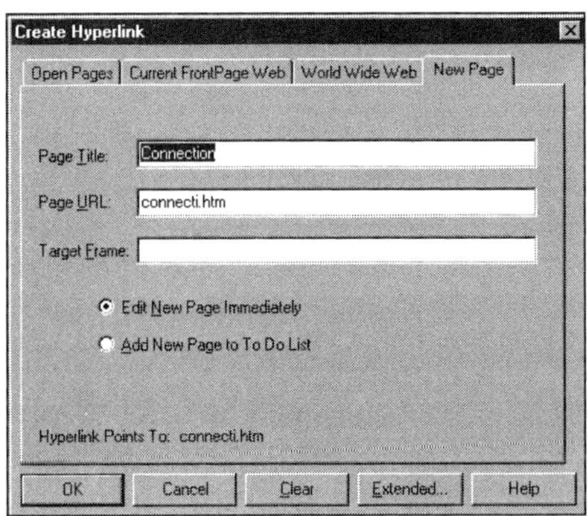

Figure 7-4 Create a link and a new page at the same time.

7. If you want to open the page you are about to create in the Editor right away, leave Edit New Page Immediately selected.
8. If you don't want to create the page right now, but want to be reminded to create it later, select Add New Page to To Do List. You'll learn more about the To Do List in Chapter 17.
9. Click OK and the New Page dialog box opens, the one you saw in Chapter 4 when learning about creating pages.
10. Select a page template or wizard, and click OK.
11. If you chose Edit New Page Immediately the new page appears in the Editor, ready for editing (though not yet saved; save it as normal). If you chose Add New Page to To Do List, FrontPage will save the file and return you to the document in which you created the link.

So you've created your link; what does it look like? Well, if you're reading this book you surely know what a link in a Web page looks like. It's colored and underlined text, and when you point at the link in a Web browser the mouse pointer changes to show a little hand icon (not in FrontPage Editor, though). Remember, you can modify the link colors using the Page Properties dialog box (see Chapter 4).

Creating Links to the Outside World

You'll probably want to link to other resources on the World Wide Web or corporate intranet. To do that you'll click the World Wide Web tab in the Create Hyperlink dialog box. This time you'll see the information in Figure 7-5.

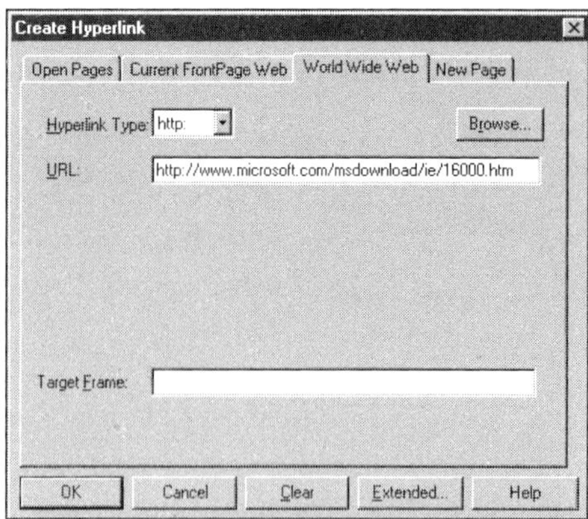

Figure 7-5 Enter a URL, or click Browse to open your browser.

You have to tell FrontPage what document (or other object) you want to link to. You do this by providing a URL, a Web address. So you need to know the address of the document you plan to link to. For instance, to link to Microsoft's FrontPage Web Page you'd have to enter this address: `http://www.microsoft.com/frontpage/`.

You can select a URL type from the Hyperlink Type drop-down list box if you wish (you'll learn more about URL types in "URL types for the newbie," later in this chapter), then type the rest of the URL into the URL text box. Or simply type the full URL you need into the box.

You can also go looking for the page you want to link to. Click Browse and your Web browser opens. (Which browser, you ask? You have several? Whichever one is associated with the .htm file type in Windows 95.) Open the page you want to link to; use the history list, bookmarks or Favorites list, search for the page, or whatever. Then, when you've found the page you want to link to, simply use the Alt+Tab method to switch back to FrontPage Editor. (In other words, press and hold Alt, then press Tab until you see the FrontPage Editor icon selected, then release both keys.) The URL of the page currently displayed in the browser is placed into the URL box in the Create Hyperlink dialog box. Click OK and you've created your link.

Using the browser works well, as long as you only have one browser window open. If you have two or more open, FrontPage may pick up the wrong URL.

Linking Your Webs

How about linking multiple webs? For instance, remember the example I mentioned back in Chapter 1, of someone creating several webs: one for the manufacturing department, one for the sales department, one for human resources, and so on. How do you link these webs?

Well, as far as FrontPage is concerned, if it's outside the current web, it's just the same as any other World Wide Web link. You'll have to go to the World Wide Web tab and enter the URL of the page to which you want to link in the other web.

TIP **Now and then you may want the link *text* to contain the URL that the link itself uses. For instance, the link text in the Web page says `http://www.idgbooks.com/`, and that's the page that is displayed when the user clicks on the link, too. Creating a link like this is very simple. Just type the URL into the page. When you finish the URL (when you type a space, or a period, comma, or other punctuation followed by a space), FrontPage will create the link for you. If FrontPage creates a link from text that you don't want to be a link, simply press Alt+Z and the linking is removed. This works with other kinds of links, too: e-mail addresses, gopher links, ftp links, and so on. And if the URL begins with an identifier such as www, ftp, or gopher, you can even drop the beginning; for instance, type www.idgbooks.com rather than `http://www.idgbooks.com/` to create a link.**

Working with Internal Links (Bookmarks)

You've probably seen documents with links that take you from one part of the document to another. For instance, a group of links at the top of the page link down to various different sections of the page. How's that done? By creating what FrontPage calls *bookmarks* (though you'll typically hear them referred to as targets or anchors by Web authors).

Creating such a link is a two-step process. First you must create the bookmark or target. Then you create the link to the target. As you'll see, you can also use this system to link across documents; that is, you can create a link on a piece of text in one document and have it link not to the top of another document but down to a bookmark within the document somewhere.

7

Creating the Bookmark

To create a bookmark, place the cursor at the beginning of the line you want to bookmark — that is, the line to which you want to be able to link. Then select Edit → Bookmark. The Bookmark dialog box opens (see Figure 7-6). Type a name for the bookmark into the top text box and click OK. And that's it, you've just created a bookmark.

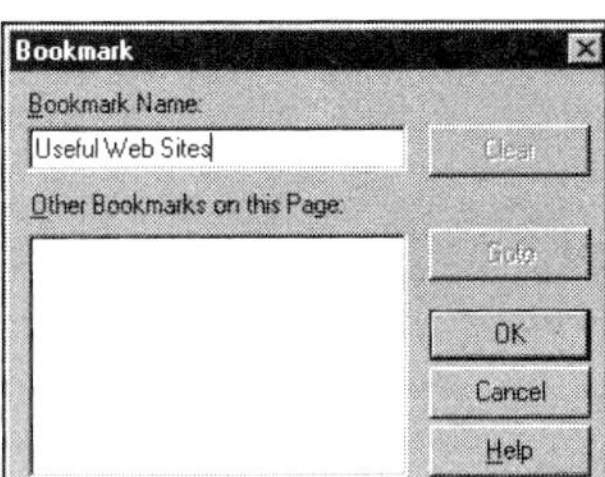

Figure 7-6 The Bookmark dialog box

You'll see the Flag icon in the document, showing you where the bookmark is. You can right-click the icon and select **Bookmark Properties** to get back to the dialog box, where you can clear (remove) the bookmark or rename it.

You can also create the link using existing text. Simply highlight the text you want to link to, then select **Edit** → **Bookmark**. You'll find that the text you selected is already shown in the text box. Simply click OK and the bookmark will be set. However, this time you won't see the Flag icon, but you will notice that the text is underlined with a blue dashed line.

TIP **Not only can you use the Bookmark dialog box to create these targets so you can build links to them, but you can also use it like a typical word processor's bookmark system. Open the dialog box, click an entry, and click Goto to go to a particular line.**

Creating the Link — within the Document

Okay, so you've got your bookmark created. Now how do you link to it? You've already seen how to create links to other documents, and the procedure is very similar:

1. Select the text on which you want to place the link.
2. Click the Create or Edit Hyperlink toolbar button, or select **Edit** → **Hyperlink**. The Create Hyperlink dialog box will open.
3. Click the Open Pages tab; make sure the current document is selected in the Open Pages list.
4. Click inside the Bookmark box. The Bookmark drop-down list box opens (Figure 7-7).
5. Click the bookmark you want to link to.
6. Click OK.

That's it, a link from one part of the document to another. Preview your document (Chapter 5) and test your links.

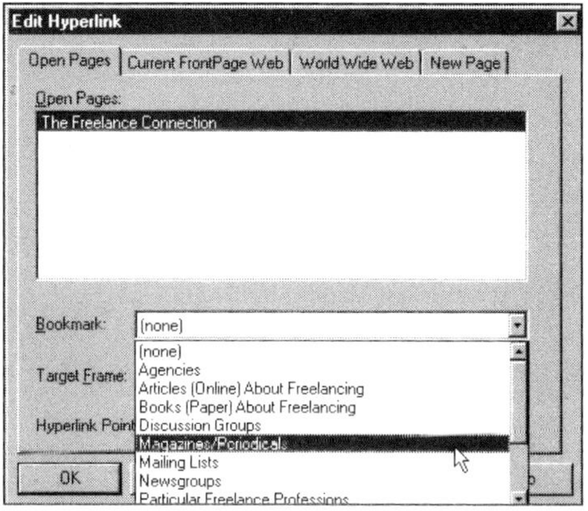

Figure 7-7 Select the bookmark you want to link to.

Creating the Link — to Other Documents

What about creating links from one document to another, but linking to a bookmark within the document, not the document itself? That's easy, though there are a couple of things to look out for.

Link to another open document If the other document is open in the Editor, simply select the document in the Open Pages pane and select the bookmark from the Bookmark drop-down list box.

Link to a closed web document If the page is not open, FrontPage can't provide a list of bookmarks in the Current FrontPage Web pane. You can either type the name of the bookmark into the Bookmark text box (if you know it), or open the other document and then use the Open Pages pane.

Link to a page on the World Wide Web Again, FrontPage can't list bookmarks for you if you're using the World Wide Web pane. However, in some cases you may find that the URL you've got from your browser already has a bookmark included. If there's a filename in the URL followed by # and more text, that's a bookmark (for instance, **index.htm# Discussion Groups**). If you know the bookmark you want to use, you can type ***#bookmarkname***.

Moving Around Through the Links

You've probably noticed by now that you can't use a link in the Editor in the same way that you use it in a browser; that is, you can't click a link to follow the link. However, you can follow the link using the Ctrl key. Simply hold down the Ctrl key — when you move the pointer over a link you'll notice that the pointer changes to the Right-Pointing Arrow icon. Click the link and the document that is referenced by the link is displayed in the Editor.

If you click a link to a bookmark in the same document, the line on which the bookmark sits is moved to the top of the Editor. And if you click a link to a document outside you web, FrontPage will attempt to load that document, whether it's somewhere on your hard disk or out on the World Wide Web. You can actually move around on the World Wide Web like this.

TIP **You can also follow links by clicking inside a link and selecting Tools → Follow Hyperlink.**

If you follow links around in this manner, you're using the Editor like a browser. And you can use browser commands to move back and forward through the pages you open this way:

- **Back to the previous document** Click Back or select Tools → Back.
- **Forward to the next document** Click Forward or select Tools → Forward.
- **Use the "history" list** Open the Windows menu and select a page to view it.
- **Stop loading a page** Click Stop or press Esc.
- **Reload a document** Click Refresh or select Tools → Refresh. (Microsoft uses the term *Refresh* to mean what every other browser manufacturer calls Reload.)

Checking Your Links for Problems

Now we're going to see a little magic at work. We're going to get FrontPage to check all our links, to make sure they're working correctly. There are actually three separate procedures that are related to checking hyperlinks (though the final one is really misnamed):

- Verify internal hyperlinks — Makes sure that all the links within your web are working properly.
- Verify external hyperlinks — Makes sure that links from your web to the outside are working correctly.
- Recalculate hyperlinks — Updates search indexes, the display of new pages, and so on. This is not simply a hyperlink-checking procedure; personally, I think it's misnamed.

Checking Internal Links

To check all the internal links in your web, select **Tools** → **Verify Hyperlink** in FrontPage Explorer. FrontPage quickly looks at all the internal links, then displays the Verify Hyperlinks dialog box (Figure 7-8). This box shows you two things: internal links that are not working properly (either the target document is no longer in your web, or the link has been misspelled), and external links.

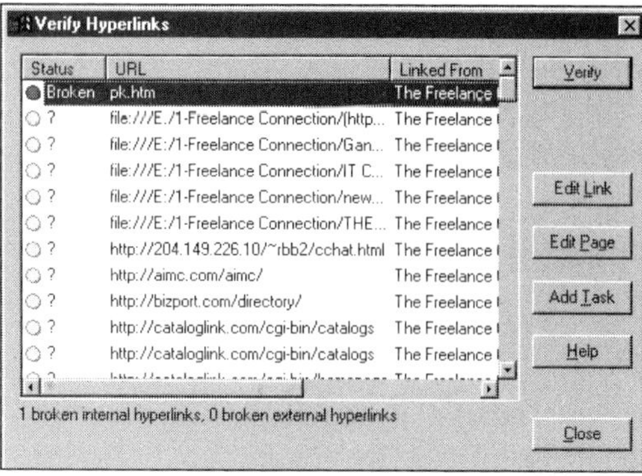

Figure 7-8 The Verify Hyperlinks dialog box shows you broken and external links.

In Figure 7-8 you can see that the first link is broken. The others, the ones with ? next to them, are external links (see "Checking External Links," later in this chapter). To fix a broken link, click the link in the list, then click Edit Link. The dialog box in Figure 7-9 opens. You can now type the correct URL into the With box, and choose either the Change All Pages With This Hyperlink or Select Pages to Change option button, and click OK.

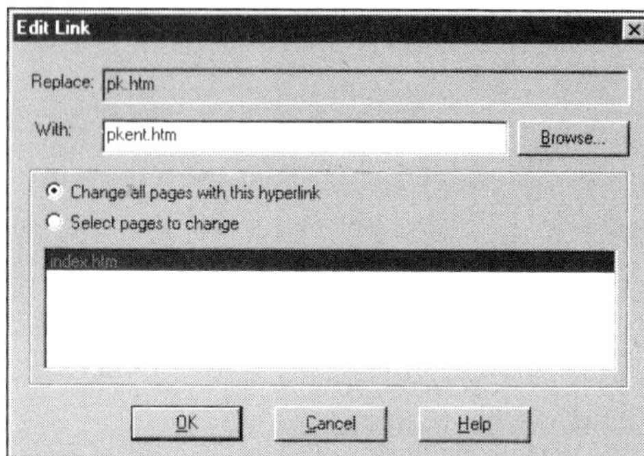

Figure 7-9 Quickly fix broken links, in one or all pages.

If you prefer you can go to the link in the document; click the link in the list, and then click Edit Page. FrontPage Editor opens, the document is loaded, and the broken link is highlighted.

TIP **Want to fix it later? Click Add Task and an entry is placed in the To Do List. See Chapter 17.**

Checking External Links

How about those external links you see in the Verify Hyperlinks box? FrontPage doesn't automatically check those, because it can take a while. In order to check them you must click the Verify button. FrontPage begins checking all the links. After a while you'll see one of these icons next to each entry:

(red) ● Broken The link is broken; FrontPage was unable to connect to the specified Web page.

(green) ● OK The link is good.

(yellow) ○ ? The link has not been checked.

Just because a link is broken right now, that doesn't mean it'll be broken tomorrow. The site's Web server may have been out of service when FrontPage checked, for instance.

This verification procedure can take a long time, so you may want to set it to do its work during lunch or at night. Once it's finished, though, you can use the same procedures you used for the broken internal links: click Edit Link to modify the link in all or selected pages, Edit Page to go to the page that contains the broken link, or Add Task to add an entry to the To Do List.

By the way, if you use Edit Link you'll notice that the URL from your open Web browser is placed into the With text box. So you can use your Web browser to move around on the Web or intranet and search for the correct URL, then press Alt+Tab to switch back to FrontPage and automatically enter that URL.

Recalculating Hyperlinks

Recalculating hyperlinks is very different from verifying them. It's actually a sort of refresh command. I really don't think this is a good name for the procedure; it should have been called something like *web refresh* or *web update*.

When you select **Tools** → **Recalculate Hyperlink** FrontPage goes through the web checking that everything's up to date. It ensures that the Explorer is correctly displaying all the pages, for instance, including new ones created in the current session. It also updates pages that are dependent on the WebBots, which you'll learn about in Chapter 10. The WebBots may be used to insert one page into another, or to search your web. The information used to do this — the index used by the search WebBot, for instance — will be updated. It's a good idea to do a Recalculate Hyperlinks procedure whenever you make major changes to your Web site, such as adding or deleting pages, or inserting a lot of new text.

BONUS

URL Types for the Newbie

Confused by all those URL types in the Create Hyperlink dialog box? Here's what they all mean:

http:// The basic HyperText Transfer Protocol URL, used when referring to Web pages or other items stored at a Web site.

https:// Similar to HTTP, but this one refers to a *secure* Web server.

mailto: Use this if you want to create a link that, when the user clicks on it, opens a mail program. For instance, a link with **mailto:pkent@arundel.com** will, when clicked, open the user's mail program and place the e-mail address into the To line.

news: A link to a newsgroup. The user's browser will try to retrieve the newsgroup headers from the user's news server.

telnet: A telnet site. The browser will attempt to open a telnet program and connect to the telnet site.

wais: A Wide Area Information Server. Most browsers don't currently work with the wais: URL.

gopher:// A Gopher menu. For instance, **gopher://wiretap.spies.com**.

ftp:// An FTP site, a sort of file library. For instance, **ftp://ftp.microsoft.com**.

file:// A file on your hard disk.

Note that while most URLs have a double forward slash after the URL type (ftp://, for instance), some don't (news:, for instance).

7

Summary

We spent only a few paragraphs learning about checking links, but that's one of the great strengths of FrontPage. Imagine building a site with hundreds of links — many sites have that many, or many more. How do you know all those links are still good? How do you know if your Web site users are being frustrated by clicking dead links? One way to figure it all out is to use FrontPage's Verify Hyperlinks command. Simply leave it to do its work for an hour or two, then come back and go through the broken links one by one, fixing them.

Creating hyperlinks is really quite easy. Checking them, as you've seen, is easy too. And once you've learned out how to do both these tasks, you're well on the way to creating a Web site.

CHAPTER EIGHT

PLACING IMAGES INTO YOUR PAGES

IN THIS CHAPTER YOU LEARN THESE KEY SKILLS

What would the Web be without images, eh? A lot faster, that's what! Still, you'll almost certainly want to use images in your pages. If possible, though, restrain yourself and try not to overdo it. All those graphics take time to transmit, and can really slow down your pages. In this chapter we'll see how to place images in your documents.

Use a number of small images spread around your page to give it a little visual variety. And reuse images throughout your web. Once an image has transferred the first time, it's taken from the user's browser's cache the next time it's used, so it'll appear very quickly.

Placing Images in Documents

You can use images from four different sources:

* Images stored within your FrontPage web
* Images from the FrontPage Clip Art library

* Images stored elsewhere on your hard disk
* Images snarfed from the World Wide Web or intranet

Let's see how to use each of these.

Images from Your FrontPage Web

Here's how to place an image from your web:

1. Place the cursor where you want your image.
2. Click the Insert Image toolbar button, or select Insert → Image. The Image dialog box opens.
3. Click the Current FrontPage Web tab. You'll see the pane in Figure 8-1.

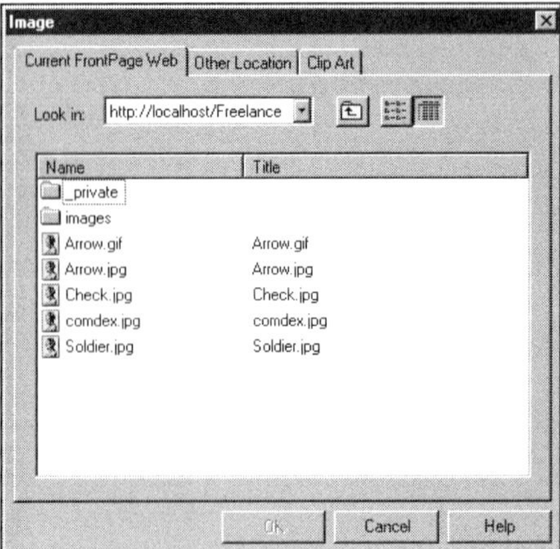

Figure 8-1 The Current FrontPage Web pane

4. Click the image you want to use in the large list box. (Note that images are often stored in the \images\ directory.)
5. Click OK.

Images from the FrontPage Clip Art Library

To use an image from the FrontPage clip art library, click the Clip Art tab in the Image dialog box. You'll see the pane in Figure 8-2.

There are several categories of clip art you can select from. Click the Category box and the list box opens up:

* Animations — These are what's known as GIF89a images. That's a special file format that holds multiple images, along with instructions on how to display them (the order and frequency). By displaying each internal image one after another, the image appears to be animated.

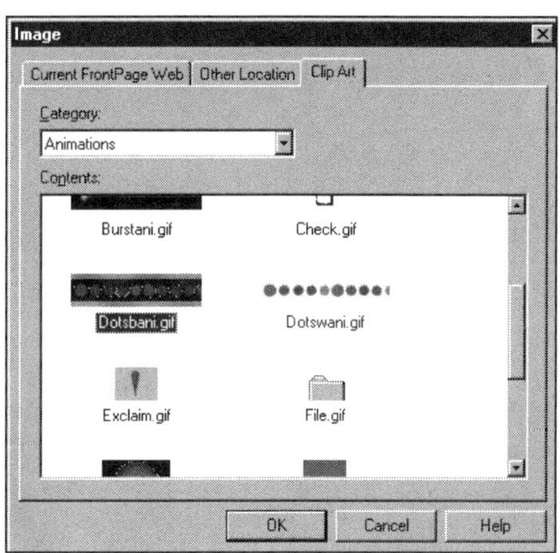

Figure 8-2 The Clip Art pane

- Backgrounds — Background images. See Chapter 4.
- Bullets — Small images that are useful for bulleted lists. Almost all are less than 1Kbyte; some are even around 100 bytes.
- Buttons — Various button images; you can place links on these images if you wish.
- Icons — Various small icons: folder, CD-ROM, floppy disk, handshake, target, and so on.
- Lines — A number of lines you may want to use as dividing lines, in place of the normal <HR> horizontal-line tag (see Chapter 6).
- Logos — A few Microsoft logos.

Want to play around with GIF89a images, perhaps create some yourself? Take a look at Alchemy Mindworks' GIF Construction Set (`http://www.mindworkshop.com/alchemy/alchemy.html`) **and the GIF animation on the WWW site** (`http://www.reiworld.com/royalef/gifanim.htm`).

Click the image you want to use and click OK to place it into your document.

By the way, you can add to this library of clip art if you wish. Look in the \Program Files\Microsoft FrontPage\clipart\ directory and you'll find that each category has a subdirectory. Simply place your art into the appropriate subcategory and it's added to the lists in the Image dialog box. You can even create your own directories, and they'll appear in the Category drop-down list box.

Images Stored Elsewhere on Your Hard Disk

To use an image stored elsewhere on your hard disk, click the Other Location tab to see the pane in Figure 8-3. Use the Browse button to find the image you want, then click the OK button.

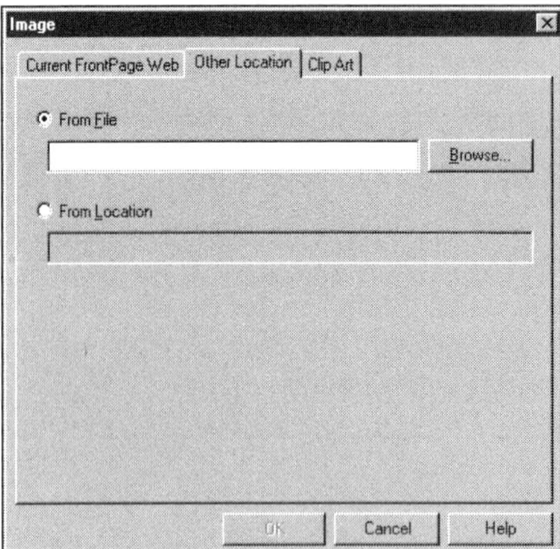

Figure 8-3 Use this pane to grab images from your hard disk or the Web.

If you've installed Microsoft Image Composer, part of the FrontPage Bonus Pack, you'll find hundreds of images and photographs you can use. They're in the \Multimedia Files\Graphics\ and \Multimedia Files\Photos\ directories. In particular look in the \Multimedia Files\Graphics\Web\ directory. However, note that all of these images in are in the Image Composer .mic format and cannot be opened in FrontPage. You'll need to open them in Image Composer, then save them as .gif or .jpg files, and then open them in FrontPage.

Images Snarfed from the World Wide Web or Intranet

In the same way that you can borrow Web pages from the World Wide Web or intranet and import them into your webs (see Chapter 4), you can also import images you've found in the outside world. You'll use the Other Location tab again, but this time type the URL of the image into the From Location text box.

How do you find an image's URL? Well, that depends on your Web browser. Open your browser and find the image you want, then try these procedures:

If you are using Netscape 3 or 3.01 — Right-click the image and select Copy Image Location.

If your version of Netscape doesn't have the Copy Image Location **command** — Right-click the image and select View This Image. It appears in the browser window by itself. Highlight the URL in the text box at the top of the browser, then press Ctrl+C.

If you are using Internet Explorer — Right-click an image and select Properties. You'll see the image's URL, which you can highlight (try it; it's not in a text box, but you can still highlight it), then copy using Ctrl+C.

Once you've got the URL using one of these three methods, you can paste it into the From Location text box in FrontPage Editor's Image dialog box (click in the box and then press Ctrl+V). When you click OK in this dialog box, FrontPage loads the image into your page from the World Wide Web or intranet. You're really creating a reference to the image on the Web or the intranet, rather than placing it in your web; see "Saving Your Images", below.

Use this method with most browsers — You can use this method with Internet Explorer or Netscape Navigator. Right-click the image and then select Save Picture As or Save Image As, or something similar. Save the image to your hard disk, then use the previous method (see "Images Stored Elsewhere on Your Hard Disk," above) to insert it into the document.

Don't save images into your web directories on your hard disk. They won't be properly registered, so they won't appear in the file list when you try to insert them into your documents.

The first three methods may not work well. Sometimes when FrontPage tries to retrieve the file it's unable to do so. If you run into this problem, the easiest thing to do is to use the last method: save the image on the hard disk. Or you can close the FrontPage Personal Web Server and then try transferring the image.

Remember copyright law! You can't simply use any image that takes your fancy. Make sure you have permission to use an image before you do so.

Drag 'n' Drop, Cut 'n' Paste

You can also drag images from Windows Explorer or some other file-management program and drop them into your document. Or use the Windows Clipboard: copy the image to the Clipboard in another program, switch to your FrontPage Editor document, and press Ctrl+V to paste the image.

Try to drag an image that is not one of the types that FrontPage can handle, though, and you'll see a dialog box asking if you want to insert the image as HTML, RTF, or text. In other words, FrontPage won't recognize it.

Saving Your Images

When you save the document after inserting an image, FrontPage may ask you whether you want to save the image into the web; if the image is from the FrontPage Clip Art library, or from somewhere else on your hard disk, it presents a dialog box asking if you want to save the files (see Figure 8-4). Click Yes (or Yes to All, so you don't have to answer the question for every image in the document), and FrontPage saves a copy of the image in your web. You may want to precede the filename with **images/** to place the picture in the image directory (your document will be properly modified so that it knows where to get the image).

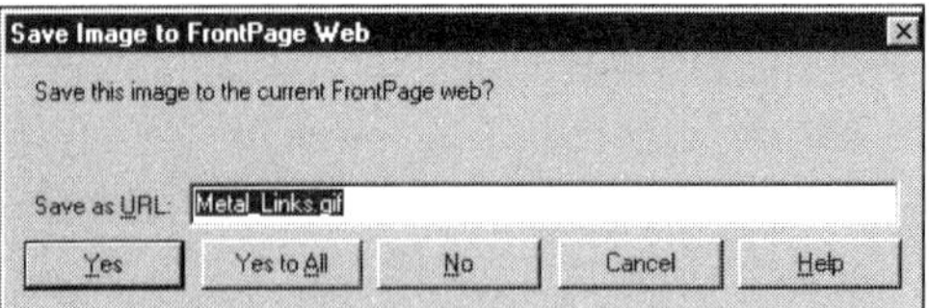

Figure 8-4 When you save your file, FrontPage asks if you want to save images.

If the image is already in your web, FrontPage doesn't bother asking if you want to save it; after all, there's no need — it's already there. And note that if you inserted the image by entering the URL of a file elsewhere on the Web or intranet, you're simply creating a reference to the image. The image will *not* be saved in your web. So if the image is moved or deleted at the other site, you'll find a hole in your Web page. However, if you modify the image type in the Properties dialog box (see "Modifying Image Type," later in this chapter), you'll force FrontPage to save the image in your web. Or you can use the last method I described for grabbing an image from outside; use your browser to save the image on your hard disk, then use the From File text box (in the Other Location pane of the Image dialog box) to insert the image into your document.

Setting the Image Properties

Now that you've got your image, what can you do with it? Well, you can set its properties. You can modify all sorts of image-related things:

- The file format in which the image will be saved.
- Alternative representations — text and an image that may be displayed in place of the image you're modifying.
- A hyperlink can be placed on the image.
- The image size.
- The image alignment.
- You can place borders around the image.

Right-click the image, then select **Image Properties**. You'll see the dialog box in Figure 8-5.

TIP **The Video tab is related to videos that you've inserted into your file. See Chapter 9.**

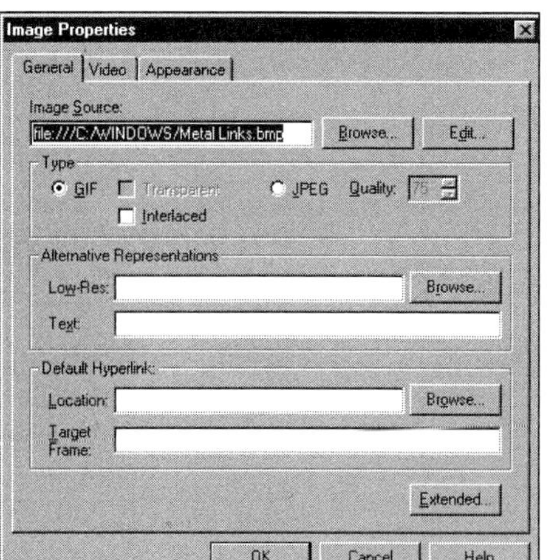

Figure 8-5 The Image Properties dialog box

Modifying Image Type

In the Image Source box you can see the URL of the image. Remember, if you've snarfed an image from the Web or intranet, the URL will show the original URL of the image; it hasn't been saved in your web. If you used some clip art from FrontPage's library, or another file from your hard disk, the URL is the original URL, too; when you save the file you'll be able to save the image to your web.

You can pick a different image, if you like, using the Browse button, or click Edit to open the image editor that you've defined in FrontPage Explorer's Properties dialog box and modify the image. If you've installed Microsoft Image Composer, which comes in the FrontPage Bonus Pack, that program is defined as the editor.

TIP **You can also open an image in the editor by double-clicking the image.**

You can tell FrontPage to save the file in a particular format. You can use GIF or JPEG. These are the two most common image formats used in Web pages. The GIF format allows you to interlace the file or make it transparent. While the JPEG format doesn't allow this, it does enable you to save images with more colors (256 or more colors) and also allows you to choose how much to compress the file. (The file is saved with the .jpg extension, not .jpeg, but both extensions are common on the Web for the Joint Photographic Expert Group image type.)

So, here are your image-type options:

GIF Graphics Interchange Format; FrontPage automatically picks this image type if the image you've inserted is already in GIF format, or if it contains fewer than 256 colors.

Transparent A transparent image is one that allows the background color to show through the blank parts of the image. In other words, the document background becomes the image background. This may be ghosted. If you want to make an image transparent, close this dialog box, click the Make Transparent toolbar button, and then click the image. (For more information about the Image toolbar see "The Image Toolbar," later in this chapter.) When you reopen the dialog box you'll see that the Transparent check box is now enabled; you can clear it to make the image nontransparent.

Interlaced You've probably seen interlaced images on the Web. The image is transferred bit by bit, so the image is displayed whole but fuzzy. As the transfer continues, the image gets sharper. This check box is selected if the image you inserted is an interlaced image, or you can use it to convert a noninterlaced image to an interlaced image or vice versa.

JPEG Joint Photographic Expert Group format; FrontPage automatically picks this image type if the image you've inserted is already in JPEG format, or if it contains more than 256 colors.

Quality This refers to the amount that the image is compressed. The higher the number you select here, the less it's compressed and the higher the image quality. The lower the number, the more it's compressed and the lower the quality.

TIP **If you modify the file format, you force a save. If you snarfed the image from the Web, so you only have a reference to the image rather than the actual image, modifying the file format will make FrontPage save the image file (it'll ask you for confirmation first) the next time you save your document.**

By the way, if the image is a .gif animation (a GIF89a image) it's fixed — you won't be able to make any modifications to the Type settings.

Alternative Representations

The Alternative Representations area lets you tell the browser displaying your Web page what to display in place of the image at certain times. There are two things you can use:

Low-Res Some browsers can display a low-res image. This is a small image — often a low-resolution image of the real image — that is shown while the main image is transferred. The idea is that an alternative image can quickly be displayed, acting as a placeholder to show the user what's coming; and then the full image, a much larger file, can be displayed when the entire thing has been transferred.

Text This is the Alt text, text that is displayed in place of the image if the viewing browser is unable to display images (if it's simply a nongraphics browser, or if the user has turned off images). The Alt text is displayed in a box in place of the image. Also, in Internet Explorer, the Alt text is displayed whenever the user points at the image and holds the mouse pointer there for a moment; the text is shown in a small pop-up box, even if the image *is* present.

Placing a Hyperlink on the Image

You can turn an image into a link very easily, by entering the URL of the page you want to link to in the Default Hyperlink: Location box. Click the Browse button to see the Create Hyperlink dialog box. You'll create the hyperlink in the same way you learned in Chapter 7.

TIP **Forget the Target Frame box for now; you'll learn about that in Chapter 12.**

Now, why is this called the *default* hyperlink? Because if you create an image with various *hot spots* — that is, an image with more than one hyperlink — the default hyperlink is the link that is activated when the user clicks on part of the image that does not have a hot spot defined. You'll see how to place hot spots on images under "Creating Image Maps," later in this chapter.

Alignment, Sizes, Margins, and Borders

Click the Appearance tab to see the information in Figure 8-6. You can set four different things here: the image alignment, border thickness, image margin or spacing, and image size.

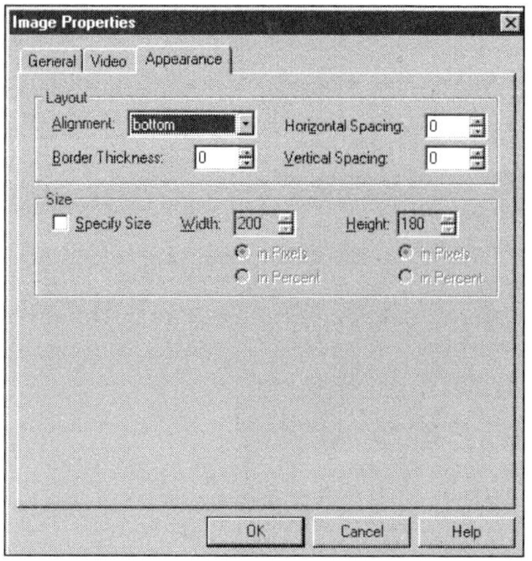

Figure 8-6 Here's where you set image size, alignment, borders, and spacing.

SETTING ALIGNMENT

Open the Alignment drop-down list box, and you're in for a surprise. What is all this stuff? These options define how the image is to be aligned with the other items, if any, on the same line. This is what these options mean:

bottom The image is aligned with the bottom of the line. (Not the bottom of the text, but the line's baseline, the line upon which the characters sit.)

middle The image is aligned with the middle of the text's baseline.

top The image is aligned with the top of the tallest item on the line — that might be an image or text.

absbottom The bottom of the image is aligned with the absolute bottom of the text; for instance, if the line has a subscript character dropping below the line, the image is aligned with the bottom of that character. Note, however, that FrontPage Editor may not display this setting correctly.

absmiddle The image is aligned with the middle of the line, allowing for different size characters and other images on the line.

texttop The image is aligned with the top of the tallest piece of text on the line. (In theory, anyway; in Internet Explorer the texttop option works the same as the top option does. It works correctly in Netscape, though.)

baseline This is the same as the bottom option. (Why have two with the same purpose? These are all the names of the HTML attributes used to align images, and HTML has two that do the same thing.)

left The image is moved all the way to the left margin, with the text to its right. The text is then wrapped down the right side of the image.

right The image is moved all the way to the right margin, with the text to its left. The text is then wrapped down the left side of the image.

Play with these options a little and you'll see how they work. Note that most of them don't cause text to be wrapped around the image. Only the last two, left and right, do that. In all other cases the options cause a single line to be positioned along the image, with subsequent lines in the same paragraph starting below the image. Also, remember that you can use the Insert → Break command to adjust the way that text wraps down an image; see Chapter 6.

Aligning things in columns is tricky. The best way to do it is by using tables; see Chapter 11.

BORDERS AND MARGINS

You can place borders around images, and also define how much space should be left around the image, between the image and the text. Note, however, that the margin you enter may not be displayed properly in some browsers (Internet Explorer tends to display *way* too much space), and some (such as Internet Explorer) won't display the border either. (Netscape Navigator seems to handle both the border and the margin correctly.)

Border Thickness Enter the number of pixels used for the border. Remember, the size of the line will depend on the video resolution and monitor size that the user is working with.

Horizontal Spacing The distance from the top or bottom of the image to the text, in pixels.

Vertical Spacing The distance from the left or right sides of the image to the text — again, in pixels.

TIP **You can color the border if you wish. You need to highlight the image — don't click it; instead, you should drag the mouse pointer across it, from one side to the other. The image will change color. Then click the Text Color button (the same one you'd use to color text) and pick your color. If you've made the entire image a link, though, the border will be the Hyperlink color (see Chapter 4).**

SIZING AN IMAGE

When you insert an image, FrontPage automatically enters its size into the HTML tags. HTML doesn't require an image size to be specified. But if you do specify an image size, before the browser loads the image it assigns a space for the image; the user sees a box with the image's alternative text inside it. It's a good idea to do this, because if you don't, as the images are loaded the text on the page jumps around a little, as it has to be moved to make way for the image.

You don't need to modify the size settings; as you can see in Figure 8-6, they're already there for you. However, you may want to modify the settings if you want to modify the size of the image; you can tell the browser to display the image smaller or larger, scaling it proportionally or nonproportionally. Simply click the Specify Size check box and then enter the numbers you want to use. Note that you can also size the image by absolute pixel size or by percentage of the page. You'll need to experiment a little to get an idea of the way that you can use these two different scaling methods.

There's an easier way to scale an image. Click an image and you'll see little black boxes, handles, on each corner and each side. Point at one of these and the mouse pointer changes to a two-headed arrow. Drag the handle in or out to reduce or enlarge the image. (This may not work well if the image is very large, in which case you can use the settings in the dialog box to reduce the image, and then use the drag method.)

You can also quickly move an image by dragging it. Click in the middle of the image and hold the button down for a few moments. Then, still holding the button down, drag the image to where you want it and release the button.

Linking to External Images

You may want to link to external images now and again. By external I don't mean outside of the web, I mean outside the page. The images we've looked at so far are *internal* or *inline* images. They were placed into the document using the <img> tag. When the browser displays the document, it places the images referenced by <img> tags inside the document.

But Web authors often link to large images. Rather than loading lots of large images, you can place small images, which load quickly, then link from the small images to the larger, *external* images. Museums and art galleries often do this, so the user can quickly view the contents of a display and then load only the full images that he or she wants.

How, then, do you create a link to an external image? You already know how. You do it in exactly the same way that you saw in Chapter 7. Instead of linking to a .htm or .html file, though, you link to one of your .gif or .jpg files. When the user clicks on the link, the original file is removed and replaced by the image file.

Unfortunately, FrontPage doesn't make creating these sorts of links quite as straightforward as it should. If you want to link to an image at your Web site (rather than linking to an image at another site — in which case you'd enter a URL on the World Wide Web pane of the Create Hyperlink dialog box), you must import the files into your web first, and then use the Create Hyperlink box — click Browse on the Current FrontPage Web pane — to link to the files. For more information on importing files, see Chapter 3.

The Image Toolbar

In a moment you'll learn how to place hot spots onto images. If you've done this before, with tools other than FrontPage, you may be pleasantly surprised; it's very simple. First, though, let's just see the image toolbar. This toolbar is displayed whenever you click an image, or if you select **View** → **Image Toolbar**. Table 8-1 explains these buttons.

TABLE 8-1 The Image Toolbar

Button	Purpose
[select icon]	Select an image hot spot.
[rectangle icon]	Draw a rectangular hot spot on an image.
[circle icon]	Draw a circular hot spot on an image.
[polygon icon]	Draw an irregular hot spot on an image.
[highlight icon]	Temporarily blank the picture, so the hot spots are clearly visible.
[transparent icon]	Make an image transparent, so the background can be seen through the blank areas.

Creating Image Maps

An image map is a picture with hot spots on it. In other words, there are links hidden on the image. When you click one part of the image a particular document is loaded, when you click a different part another document is loaded, and so on. You've already seen how to make the entire image a hyperlink (see "Placing a Hyperlink on the Image," earlier in this chapter). That's quite simple. But creating image maps is a little more complicated.

First, decide whether you want *server-side* or *client-side* image maps, or both. Server-side image maps work by sending the server the coordinates of the mouse-click when the user clicks on an image. A special CGI (Common Gateway Interface) script running at the server then figures out what hot spot has been clicked upon and what document to send.

With client-side image maps, all the information is encoded into the HTML file, so the browser figures out what to do when the user clicks on a hot spot. There's no need to run a CGI script at the server. This is a much more efficient way to handle image maps — much faster — but it has the disadvantage that some browsers won't work with client-side image maps. (However, probably 95 percent of users are working with browsers that do handle them.)

Then you must consider whether your pages will be placed at a Web server with the FrontPage server extensions installed. If so, you don't need to configure FrontPage to create image maps. By default, FrontPage will create image maps designed to work with the server extensions, and it'll create both server-side and client-side image maps — the ideal situation. However, if you are going to use a non-FrontPage-enabled server, you must go to the FrontPage Explorer and select **Tools** → **Web Spelling**, then click the Advanced tab (see Figure 8-7).

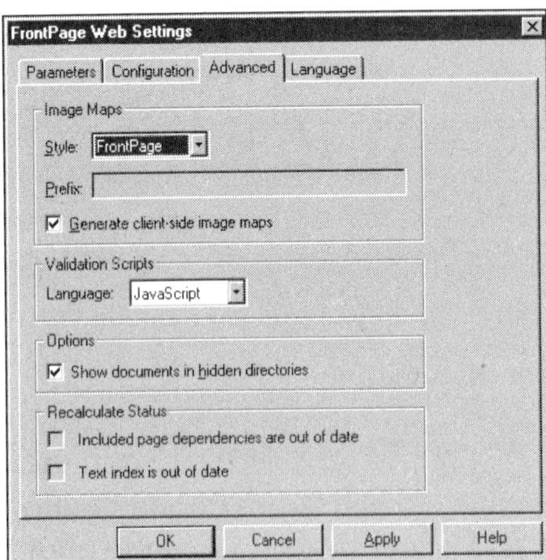

Figure 8-7 Here's where you select the image-map type.

If you want to create server-side image maps, select the type of server you'll be using from the Style drop-down list box. Discuss this with the server administrator. If you don't want server-side image maps, select None. Don't modify the Prefix. This will show which program will be used, when running your web through your FrontPage Personal Web Server, to make the image maps work.

Finally, there's the Generate Client-Side Image Maps check box. If you clear this, client-side image maps are *not* created, so you'll generally want to keep this checked. Close this dialog box, then return to FrontPage Editor.

TIP **If you are using a non-FrontPage server, you'll have to install the image map files that are created at the server. FrontPage stores map files in the _vti_map\ directory. Ask your server's system administrator where to put these. If you are using a FrontPage-enabled server, you don't need to worry about configuring image maps; FrontPage will handle everything for you.**

To create an image map, click one of the three drawing buttons on the toolbar: Rectangle (to draw a rectangle or square), Circle (to draw a circle), or Polygon (to draw an irregular shape). Then draw the shape on your image. Click the image and drag the pointer. If you're creating a rectangle, square, or circle, when you release the mouse button the Create Hyperlink box opens. (See Chapter 7 for information on using this dialog box).

If you're creating an irregular shape — perhaps around a country or state on a map, for instance — when you drag you draw a straight line. Each time you click you finish the line and start another. To finish — and open the Create Hyperlink dialog box — click twice in the same spot or press Esc.

TIP **To remove a hot spot, click it and then press Delete. To view all your hot spots, without the clutter of the image below, click the Highlight Hot Spots button.**

BONUS

Automatically Adding and Removing an Image

It's time to use a WebBot. I've mentioned them now and then, and in fact we used one earlier, in Chapter 6; the comments are actually controlled by a WebBot, though it's not obvious. But now I'd like to show you one of the WebBots that can be chosen from the Insert WebBot Component dialog box.

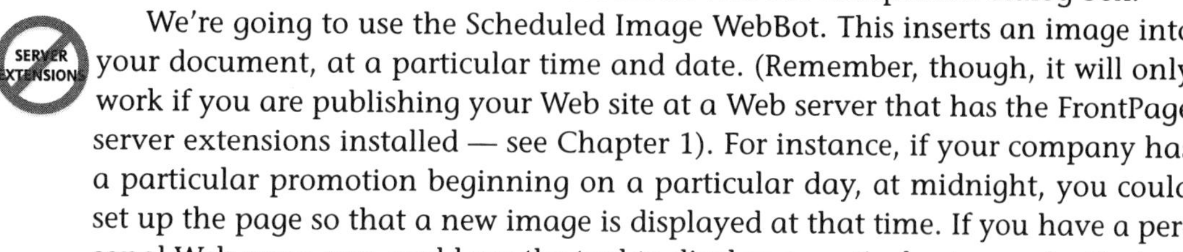

We're going to use the Scheduled Image WebBot. This inserts an image into your document, at a particular time and date. (Remember, though, it will only work if you are publishing your Web site at a Web server that has the FrontPage server extensions installed — see Chapter 1). For instance, if your company has a particular promotion beginning on a particular day, at midnight, you could set up the page so that a new image is displayed at that time. If you have a personal Web page, you could use the tool to display a particular image for the holidays, another on your kid's birthday, and so on. Here's how it works:

1. Place the cursor where you want the image.
2. Select **Insert** → **WebBot Component**. The Insert WebBot Component dialog box opens.
3. Select Scheduled Image and click OK. The dialog box in Figure 8-8 opens.

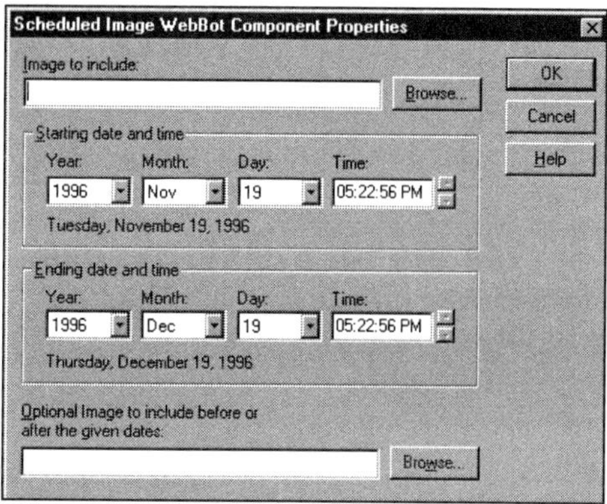

Figure 8-8 Tell FrontPage when to display an image.

4. Click the first Browse button to select the image you want to display at the scheduled time and date. You can only select an image already in your web.
5. Enter the Starting Date and Time, to schedule when the image will begin appearing in your page.
6. Enter the Ending Date and Time, to schedule when the image will be removed from your page.
7. If you wish you can click the second Browse button to select an image that will be displayed before the scheduled image is placed in the document, and after it is removed.

8. Click OK, and a Broken Picture icon will be displayed in place of the image, or perhaps the image itself if the Starting Date and Time has already passed.

You can quickly modify a WebBot. Point at the image and the mouse pointer changes to the Robot icon. Double-click the image, or right-click and select **WebBot Component Properties**.

Summary

Putting images in Web pages is fun. I personally think that it's one of the things that's made Web authoring so popular; you get to *play* with all these pictures, and goof around with the manner in which they work; add hot spots here, align text there, create borders, and so on.

The danger is that you'll get carried away and add too many pictures, and too many large pictures. Remember that most people are using fairly slow connections to the Internet. The Internet is not TV, and it's not magazine publishing. Consider your users and work with images carefully.

CHAPTER NINE

MULTIMEDIA IN YOUR WEB PAGES

IN THIS CHAPTER YOU LEARN THESE KEY SKILLS

You've got text, you've got pictures, what else is there? The World Wide Web's a multimedia system, and FrontPage will help you insert things that move and make sounds, and a lot more besides. In this chapter we're going to look at how to insert a variety of objects into your Web pages: scrolling text, video, sounds, connections to databases, and even programs.

However, in some cases you won't learn all you need to know in order to use these features. For instance, FrontPage will help you insert a Java application, or a JavaScript, into your Web pages; but it won't really help you actually create the application or script. To do that you need the skills of a programmer and a bookful of information.

Before you start, take a look at Table 9-1. This shows the advanced toolbar buttons, most of which we'll be using in this chapter.

TABLE 9-1 The Advanced Toolbar Buttons

Button	Purpose
	Insert your own HTML tag (see Chapter 10).
	Insert an ActiveX control.
	Start the Database Connector Wizard.
	Insert a Java applet.
	Insert a plug-in.
	Insert a JavaScript or VBScript.

Scrolling Text — Marquees

Internet Explorer supports a feature called *marquees*. A marquee, for those of you not used to the common U.S. meaning of the word, is a canopy over an entrance to a building — often with some kind of large banner. (In much of the rest of the English-speaking world it's more often used to mean a large tent.) A Web-page marquee is a text banner that contains moving text.

At the time of writing the only popular browser supporting the feature is Internet Explorer. Netscape Navigator (currently Version 3.01) does not display marquees properly. That's not necessarily a problem, though, as it still displays the text in the banner; it just shows it as static text.

Here's how to create a marquee. In this example the marquee will also contain a link. If you don't want your marquee to link to anything, simply omit the first couple of steps.

1. Type the text you want to appear in the marquee. You'll probably want to put this text on a line by itself (though you don't have to).
2. Place a link on the text in the normal way; see Chapter 7.
3. Format the text: pick a color and size, for instance. Make sure you've got the text format you want *before* placing the marquee, because once you've created the marquee you can't modify the text format.
4. With the text highlighted, select Insert → Marquee. The dialog box shown in Figure 9-1 opens.

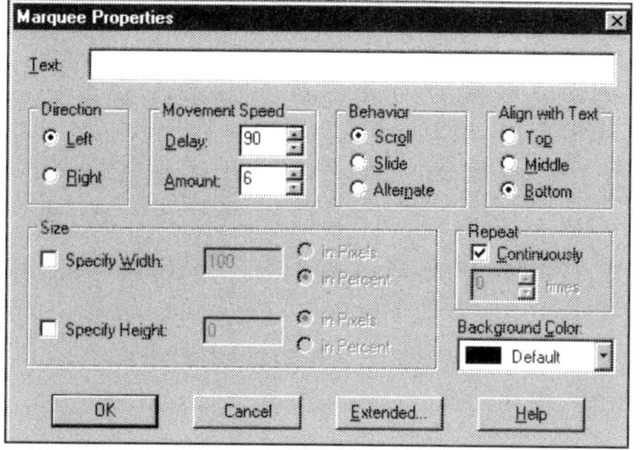

Figure 9-1 The Marquee Properties dialog box

5. Select the direction of movement: Left (meaning from the right to the left), or Right (from the left to the right).

6. Set the movement "speed." The text actually moves in jumps. The Delay setting is the number of milliseconds between jumps, and the Amount setting is the number of pixels jumped each time. So the smaller both numbers the smoother the scrolling will be. But a small Delay combined with a large Amount will create a faster scroll.

7. Set the behavior. Select Scroll to make the text scroll onto the marquee at one end and off at the other. Select Slide to have the text scroll on at one end, but stop when it gets to the other end. And select Alternate to scroll back and forth across the marquee.

8. If you've placed the marquee on the same line as other text or objects, select the alignment: Top to align with the top of the text, Middle to align with the middle, and Bottom to align with the bottom.

9. Specify the size of the marquee. For instance, you might want to specify Width to a particular Percent, so it always takes up a set proportion of the browser window.

10. By default the marquee is set to continue scrolling continuously. But you may prefer to just run it a few times and then stop. If so, clear the Continuously check box and type a number into the Times box. (Also, note that if you use the Slide setting, it only runs once, even if you have Continuously selected.)

11. Pick a Background Color. Make sure you pick something that will work well with the text color you picked. (If the browser can't display a marquee, it won't display the background color.)

12. Click OK and the marquee is created.

Adding Video

Another Internet Explorer feature is the dynsrc= attribute in the <img> tag. When you insert an image into your Web page, FrontPage uses the <img src=> tag. But Internet Explorer also recognizes another tag, the <img dynsrc=>. This lets the Web author insert a video file into the Web page.

I'll explain how to do this — it's very easy — but actually I don't recommend it! Why? Because most users are not using Internet Explorer. If you insert a video using this method, at best most browsers will be able to see just a static picture, not a moving video. And at worst they may see a blank box.

TIP **There's another reason not to insert video in your pages, using this method or any other. Most users don't like them! They're a nuisance, because they're so big and take so long to transfer. (Seven to ten seconds may be 1/2MB in size, for instance.) If you really have to have video at your site, you should probably give users the choice of whether or not to view it. See "Lots More File Formats," later in this chapter.**

Now that I've warned you, here's how the feature works. Simply select Insert → Video and pick the .avi video file you want to use (that's the Video for Windows video file format). The dialog box you'll see works in the same way as the boxes used to insert images do, letting you pick an .avi file from within your web, from a directory on your hard disk, or by entering a URL.

When you've placed the video, a box appears in your document. You can size this box in the same way you size an image: by dragging the handles around the image. To set video properties, right-click the box and select Image Properties. The box shown in Figure 9-2 will open.

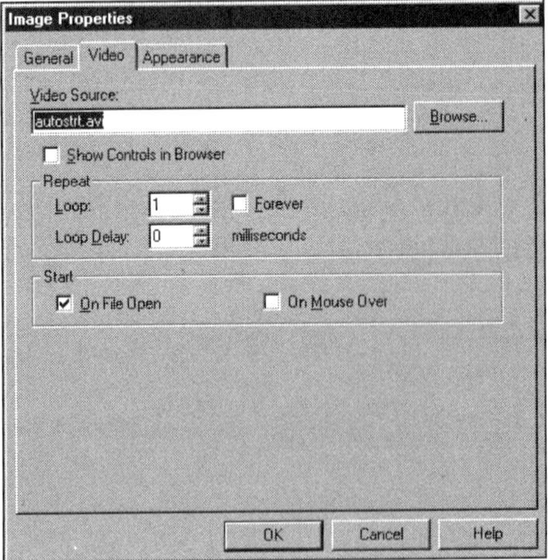

Figure 9-2 The Video pane in the Image Properties dialog box

Here's what you can set in this dialog box:

Video Source You can modify the .avi file you selected here.

Show Controls in Browser Check this to add a stop button and a slider to the video box inside the browser.

Loop This tells the browser how often to play the video. By default the video will play once.

Forever Check this to make the video play over and over.

Loop Delay If playing the file more than once, you can pause between runs by entering a number in here; enter 1,000 for 1 second, for instance. (Internet Explorer currently ignores this value, though.)

On File Open Check this if you want the video to play when the Web page loads. Actually it'll play automatically if you don't check this box, too, unless you do check the next box.

On Mouse Over Check this if you don't want the video to play until the user points at it with the mouse.

When you've inserted your video, you won't see it within FrontPage Editor. You'll have to preview the video in the browser (see Chapter 5).

Using Background Sounds

Would you like to insert a background sound? I explained how to do this in Chapter 4. You can add the sound in the General pane of the Page Properties dialog box. Or add a sound later, by selecting Insert → Background Sound. You can use sounds in a variety of file formats: .wav, .mid, .aif, .aiff, aifc, .au, and .snd.

Whichever method you use, FrontPage inserts the <bgsound src=> tag into the head of the page. To modify the information — to control how many times the sound plays — do so in the Page Properties box. Note, however, that currently only Internet Explorer plays these background sounds; Netscape Navigator will not.

Lots More File Formats

You'll remember that in Chapter 8 we discussed internal and external images. You saw how to place images into Web pages using the <img> tag. These are called inline images because the browser places them inside the document. You also saw how to work with external images, images that are loaded into the browser when the user clicks on a link. The link is a normal hyperlink (see Chapter 7), the only difference being that rather than referencing an .htm or .html file, it references a .gif or .jpg file.

Well, you can link to any file type you want. You could link, for instance, to an .avi, a Video for Windows file. When the user clicks the link, the file will be transferred to his or her computer and played in whatever program the browser uses to play video. Or link to Adobe Acrobat hypertext files, or Word for Windows word-processing files, or PowerPoint slide show files, or chemical modeling files, or whatever is useful or appropriate at your site.

TIP **The problem with using different file types from those that a browser can handle is that many users may not have the appropriate viewer or plug-in applications loaded. Think carefully before you force a user to install a special program before working at your site.**

As with linking to image files, though, you must first import the files into your web (see Chapter 3). Then use the Create Hyperlink box — click Browse on the Current FrontPage Web pane — to link to the files.

Embedding Files — Plug-Ins

FrontPage helps you insert *plug-ins* into your Web page. What does that mean, exactly? Unfortunately the term plug-in is being widely used for two different meanings, so I'll begin by explaining these terms.

The most widely understood meaning of *plug-in* is a program that is "plugged in" to a Web browser. As you've just seen, you can connect lots of different types of data to a Web page. Video, sounds, animations, documents of every kind (from spreadsheets to word processing documents, chemical models to slide shows), and so on. How does a browser handle all this stuff?

Some files are handled directly by the browser. That is, when the browser receives a file it can play or display it automatically. Most browsers these days can handle .htm, .html, .txt, .gif, .xbm, .jpg, and .wav files, and quite a few more. But the file types that browsers can handle directly are merely a fraction of the thousands of different types available. So what happens when a browser receives a file type it can't play or display? Until recently the browser would have had to start a special program, an external viewer or helper. The file would then be sent to that program and played or displayed by the program.

Then, late in 1995, came plug-ins. A plug-in is really an internal viewer or helper. It's a program that handles file types the browser cannot, but it appears to be working within the browser window itself. The browser window may change a little, to display controls for instance, but the plug-in doesn't open another window when it starts, it simply modifies the browser window temporarily.

OK, so that's one meaning of the term plug-in: a program, an internal viewer. The other meaning is an unusual file type that has been embedded into a Web page using the <embed> tag. This tag names a file, which the browser then tries to insert into the Web page at the point at which the tag appears. What if the file type is one that the browser can't directly handle, though? It uses a plug-in program to display or play it. The confusion between the two terms lies in the fact that a plug-in program is not intended purely for use by the <embed> tag. It can be used whenever a file type cannot be handled by the browser. As you saw, under "Lots More File Formats" earlier in this chapter, you can link to external files. These files will be handled by the plug-in program, too.

Here, then, is how you embed a file into your Web page:

1. Select **Insert** → **Other Components** → **Plug-In**, or click the Insert Plug-In toolbar button. The Plug-in Properties dialog box opens (Figure 9-3).

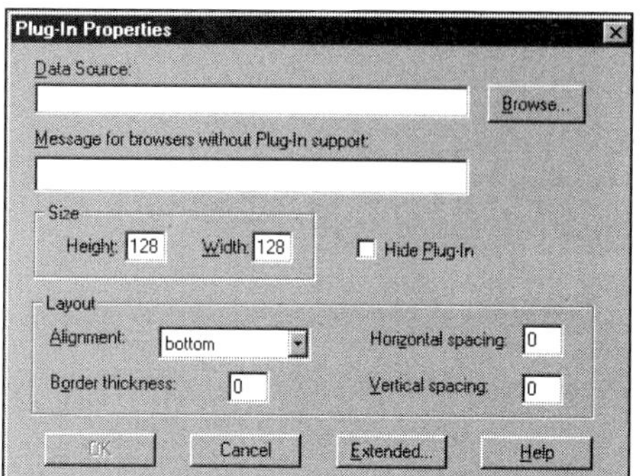

Figure 9-3 The Plug-in Properties dialog box

2. Click Browse to find the file you want to use, then return to the Plug-in Properties dialog box.
3. Type a message into the second text box. This information will be displayed if the browser cannot work with the <embed> tag. You might inform the user what plug-in program is required to use the plug-in file, and include a URL to the site where the program may be found.

TIP **You can include HTML in the Message for Browsers Without Plug-in Support text box. For instance, enter the URL like this: <a href="http://*put_url_here*/">Get the Plug-in Here</A>.**

4. Modify the size if you wish.
5. Click Hide Plug-in if you want the plug-in to be invisible; if it's playing a sound, for instance.
6. Specify the alignment. The alignment options are the same as the ones you saw for image alignment in Chapter 8.
7. Specify the border, if any, and spacing.

8. Click OK. The plug-in file will be represented in your page by the Plug icon.

Here's a great place to find plug-in programs: `http://browserwatch.iworld.com/plug-in.html`

Database Connections

FrontPage provides a way for you to connect your Web pages to a database. In other words, your users can come to your Web site, fill in a form, and search a database. The results are then displayed on another Web page.

FrontPage provides tools that enable you to connect to the database, but you'll still need much more knowledge and information about doing so than you'll find here! This database stuff is very complicated, and unless you already understand IDC Parameters, If-Then Conditional Sections, Else Conditional Sections, ODBC, SQL queries, and *plenty* more, you've got a lot to learn, a lot more than I have space to cover in this book. However, here's a quick outline of how FrontPage connects to a database.

First, you need to create a Database Results page. Select Database Results from the New Page dialog box. Then you must set up this page, entering the appropriate database fields. You'll find the dialog boxes that construct these fields on the Edit → Database submenu.

When you've finished the Database Results page, run the Database Connector wizard. You can start this by selecting Database Connector Wizard in the New Page dialog box, or by clicking the Database Connector Wizard toolbar button. Then follow the steps in the wizard. (You won't be able to follow these steps unless you really know what you are doing, though.)

Note also that you'll require the Microsoft Internet Information Server, Microsoft's new Web server that's bundled with Windows NT 4, or the Microsoft Personal Web Server, in order to make all this stuff run.

Inserting Programs

If you haven't been living in a cave in Indonesia for the past year, you've heard of Java. Well, you've probably heard of Java even if you have been living in an Indonesian cave, of course, but I'm talking specifically about Java the programming language. Although they were not originally designed for use on the World Wide Web, currently Java programs — known as Java *applets* — are mainly being embedded into World Wide Web pages. A Java applet can be written once, then used on multiple operating systems: Windows of various flavors, UNIX in even more numerous flavors, and the Macintosh. As long as the user has a Java interpreter (and the interpreter is up to date), the Java applet will run.

Where does one find a Java interpreter? Both Internet Explorer and Netscape Navigator are Java interpreters, so if the user has a recent version of one of these browsers, the Java applet will run.

But there's more to Web programming than Java. The other big players are JavaScript (Java's little brother), VBScript (Visual Basic Script, a Microsoft competitor to JavaScript, relatively little used for the moment — though rapidly gaining ground), and ActiveX (also from Microsoft). If you know how to write these programs, or if you know someone who does, you can insert them into your Web pages. I'm not going to attempt to teach you these programming languages; I don't have the required 5,000 pages available. But I will show you quickly how to put them into your pages.

Java

To insert a Java applet into your page, begin by importing the .class java file, and any other associated files, into your web (see Chapter 3 for information about importing). Then place the cursor where you want the applet in FrontPage Editor and click the Insert Java Applet toolbar button, or select **Insert** → **Other Components** → **Java Applet**. The dialog box shown in Figure 9-4 opens.

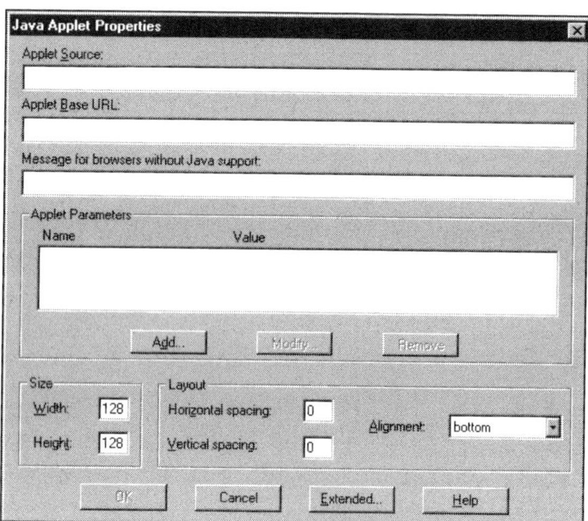

Figure 9-4 Set up your Java Applet here.

Here's the information you'll enter:

Applet Source Type the name of the Java file here. It may be something like calculator.class or data.class. *Only* include the filename, not the directory name, even if you placed the file in a subdirectory of the directory in which the Web page you are working in is sitting.

Applet Base URL If the applet is not in the same directory as the HTML document, enter the URL here. You can use a relative URL if you wish. For instance, if the applet is in a subdirectory called java, simply type the word *java* into this text box.

Message for Browsers Without Java Support Type the message you want non-Java browsers to see. It's displayed if the browser simply isn't capable of using Java, or if Java has been turned off.

Applet Parameters Parameters are instructions explaining how the applet should work. A parameter has a name and, in most cases, an associated value. If you wrote the Java applet, you know what the parameters are. If you don't, ask the programmer or refer to the documentation. Click Add to add each parameter.

Size and Layout You can modify the applet size and layout here. These are the same settings you've seen before, when inserting images (see Chapter 8).

When you've finished, click OK and the applet is placed into the document. You won't see it, though; in its place you'll see the large J icon. You'll have to preview the page (after saving it) to view the applet working. Remember to make sure that the browser has Java turned on.

JavaScript and VBScript

JavaScript and VBScript are *scripting languages*. Rather than creating a program file and embedding it into your page, you actually write the script — the program — directly into the HTML document. Now, the term *scripting language* sounds somehow friendlier than *programming language*, and you may have heard all the hype about how easy working with these scripting languages is. But don't be fooled. They actually *are* programming languages, and are by no means simple for the nonprogrammer.

However, I'll show you how to insert a simple script — a JavaScript — into your document.

Click the Insert Script toolbar button, or select Insert → Script. The dialog box you see in Figure 9-5 will open. Begin by selecting the script you want to write: VBScript (which currently only runs in Internet Explorer), or JavaScript (which currently runs in both Internet Explorer and Netscape Navigator, with varying degrees of success). In theory you can also select Other and type the name of another scripting language . . . but right now there are no others.

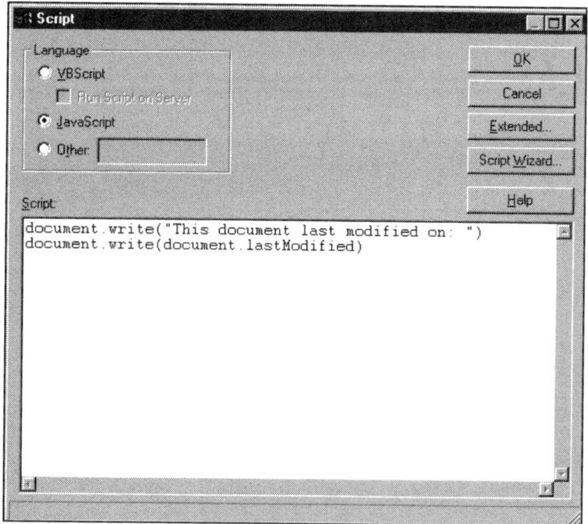

Figure 9-5 Inserting scripts is easy — if you know how to write scripts, of course.

You can write an *inline* script directly into the large Script box. An inline script is one that runs when the browser reads it. So the script is placed into your page at the point you clicked the cursor before opening this dialog box, and is executed when the browser reaches that point in the page. (I'll explain the other type of script, an event script, in a moment.)

So, here's a quick example you can use:

1. Place the cursor in your document, then click the Insert Script toolbar button.
2. Click the JavaScript option button.
3. Click inside the Script box.
4. Type this:

```
document.write("This document last modified on: ")
document.write(document.lastModified)
```

5. Click OK. A little J icon is placed in your document to represent the script.
6. Save the document, then preview it. Your browser will show something like this:

```
This document last modified on: Wed June 25 21:20:28 1997
```

You can also click the Script Wizard button in the Script dialog box to get FrontPage to help you write the script, if you're writing an *event* script, one that is carried out when a particular event occurs (such as the page opening or closing, someone passing the mouse pointer over a link, and so on). The box shown in Figure 9-6 opens. You can select a link in the left pane, then select an action in the right pane, and use the Insert Action button to actually create the script. But this is not a real wizard; it doesn't lead you through the process at all, and unless you really understand JavaScript this dialog box won't be any use to you.

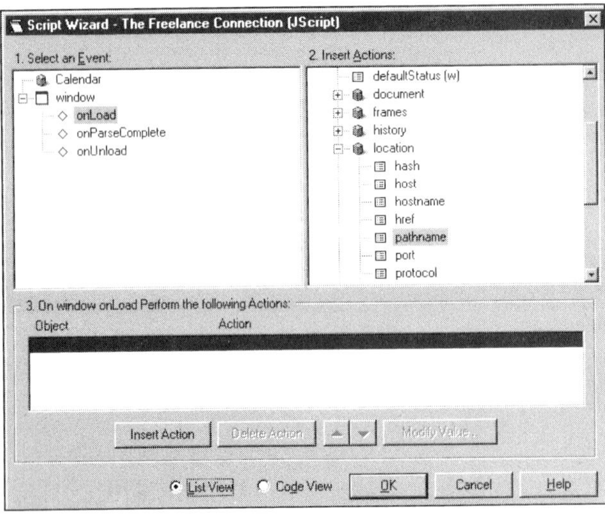

Figure 9-6 A wizard that isn't really a wizard isn't much help unless you understand JavaScript.

TIP **You can also right-click on a form element and select Script Wizard to create a script associated with that form component. You'll learn about creating forms in Chapter 13.**

ActiveX

ActiveX is Microsoft's answer to Java. With ActiveX you can place various controls into your Web pages, then write programs to use the controls (in theory any programming language can use ActiveX controls). The user's computer must have the controls installed in order to use the ActiveX program; if the browser finds that an ActiveX control referenced by a page is not installed it offers to get the control from an ActiveX Web site.

At the time of writing, ActiveX was supported by Internet Explorer, but not by Netscape Navigator — though Netscape Communications has said that it will add ActiveX support.

You place ActiveX controls into a document using the <object> tag. To get FrontPage to help you insert an ActiveX control, click the Insert ActiveX Control toolbar button, or select Insert → Other Components → Active X Control. The ActiveX Control Properties dialog box opens, which is very handy if you understand how to work with ActiveX, completely useless if you don't! You can plug other people's Java applets into your pages quite easily. You can even write fairly simple JavaScripts and VBScripts if you spend a few hours with a book on those subjects. But I'm not going to get into this ActiveX stuff because it's way out of the scope of this book.

By the way, when you insert an ActiveX control into the document, you see the Broken Picture icon in FrontPage Editor.

Go to http://www.microsoft.com/activex/ **for more information about ActiveX.**

BONUS

To Program or Not to Program . . .

These programming languages are all very nice, but should you use them? All of them have serious drawbacks right now. The major problem is one of compatibility. For instance, if you create JavaScripts using the very latest JavaScript commands, about 50 percent of Web users will run into problems. About that many users (at the time of writing), were working with Internet Explorer or with beta versions of Netscape Navigator 3 or earlier. And Netscape Navigator 3.01 has the most up-to-date JavaScript. You can use fairly simple JavaScripts and generally — though not always — avoid trouble. Get into anything sophisticated and you're asking for trouble.

How about ActiveX? Currently somewhere between 10 and 15 percent of Web users are working with an ActiveX-compatible Web browser. So the vast majority are not! And Java? Again, compatibility problems. With hundreds of different browsers in use, each handling Java slightly differently (if at all), problems can arise.

Consider also the cost. Writing programs is complicated, which is why programmers are paid so much. Does your Web site really need all this fancy stuff to serve its purpose? In most cases probably not, so save the time and money. Don't be misled by computer magazines and computer journalists, whose job it is to write about cool new technologies and make them sound fun and important. Adding programs to your Web site is not a guarantee of success, though it is a guarantee of expense and headaches.

Summary

Adding sounds, video, marquees, and other such media types is not only easy, it's fun. Unfortunately, the benefit of these things is greatly exaggerated by the media. You must have lots of visual and audio goodies on your Web site, or people simply won't come back, we're constantly told in the computer press. It's simply not true. Forget *cool* and think *useful.* If your Web site is not useful, you're going to have to spend an awful lot of time and money making it cool. But what for? If it doesn't serve its purpose, but people just come to see the sights, what benefit are you gaining?

Remember that most Web users are working with modems running at 28800 bps or even 14400 bps. And the Number One complaint from Web users is related to slow download times. (Of course, if you are developing a site for your corporate intranet, this is less of an issue.) People don't want cool, they want fast and useful. So use the fancy stuff judiciously.

CHAPTER TEN

TWEAKING YOUR PAGES — WEBBOTS AND HTML

10

IN THIS CHAPTER YOU LEARN THESE KEY SKILLS

You've got your text, you've got your pictures, you've got your multimedia. In this chapter you'll see how to tweak it all a little, using a few handy little WebBots and HTML entered directly into the source document. We'll look at these WebBots:

* The Include WebBot — Insert one HTML document into another.
* The Scheduled Include WebBot — Insert one HTML document into another at a specified time and date.
* The Timestamp WebBot — Insert information showing when the document was last saved.
* The Substitution WebBot — Insert the document author's name, the document description, and document URL.

* The Table of Contents WebBot — Create a table of contents of your entire web.

We'll also be taking a quick look at how to work with HTML directly; if you want to use tags or HTML attributes that FrontPage does not support.

We looked at the Scheduled Image WebBot — which is very similar to the Scheduled Include WebBot — in Chapter 8.

Note that almost all the WebBots discussed in this chapter will only work if you are using a server with the FrontPage server extensions installed. They all rely on special WebBot scripts that are included in the server extensions. The exception is that modifications to the file's HTML tags created by using the HTML Markup WebBot will work regardless of where you place the document.

Inserting a Web Page into Another (Include)

The Include WebBot provides a way to take one Web page and insert it into another. Why would you want to do that? Perhaps you have a header or footer you want to use in all your pages. The header or footer is exactly the same in all pages, so the easiest thing to do would be to create a single file containing the information you want to place in these headers and footers, and then include the file in each document. Then, when you want to change all those items, you simply change one file and all your documents are automatically updated. You may want to store these pages in the _private directory. That way users can't view the included file by itself, only in its included location.

The _private directory cannot be directly accessed by Web browsers, so it's a good place to store things that you don't want users to find.

Including a page takes just a few seconds. Here's what to do:

1. Place the cursor where you want the included information.
2.  Click the Insert WebBot Component toolbar button, or select Insert → WebBot Component. The dialog box shown in Figure 10-1 opens.

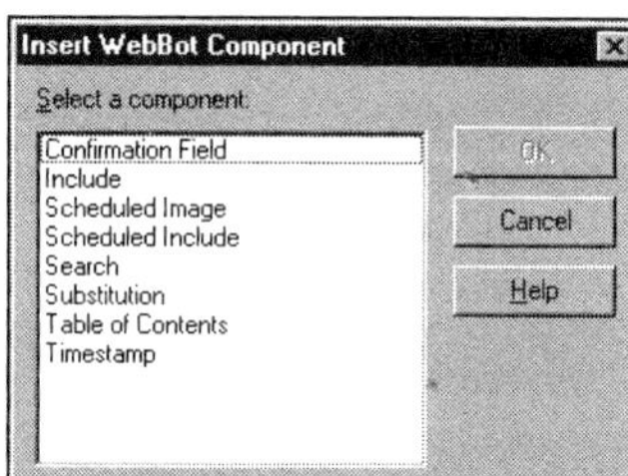

Figure 10-1 Select the WebBot you want to work with here.

3. Click Include in the list of WebBots, and then click OK. The box in Figure 10-2 opens.

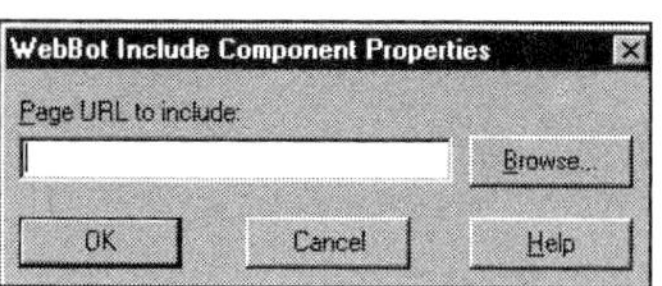

Figure 10-2 Pick the file you want to include.

4. Click Browse and find the file you want to include.

5. Click OK. The file is placed into your document at the cursor point. The included information will appear to be normal information, as if you'd put it there yourself directly. But if you point at it, the Robot mouse pointer appears. And if you double-click it, the dialog box shown in Figure 10-2 opens again.

TIP **This WebBot is designed to include files that are present in your web, not files outside the web. It appears to be possible to fool the bot by modifying the tag in the View or Edit HTML window, entering a URL in place of the filename in the <!—webbot bot="Include"> tag. The information from the file you specify will be pulled into FrontPage Editor . . . but it won't be included in the document when viewed in a browser.**

Automatically Inserting Pages (Scheduled Include)

SERVER EXTENSIONS

In Chapter 8 you saw how to schedule the insertion of an image at a particular time. You can do the same thing with a file. For instance, you could have a press release automatically inserted into a document at a time that corresponds with a product launch, or insert a message about a day's scheduled events.

I won't go into detail about this procedure; it's the same as the procedure described in Chapter 8, except that you select an .htm or .html file instead of an image, of course.

Inserting a Page-Update Date (Timestamp)

In Chapter 9 I showed you how JavaScript can be used to display a timestamp, the date that the document was last updated. The problem with using JavaScript, though, is that the script won't work if the user is not working with a JavaScript-enabled browser, or if the user has turned off the browser's JavaScript capability.

Instead you could use the Timestamp WebBot. Select Timestamp in the Insert WebBot Component dialog box, and the box shown in Figure 10-3 opens.

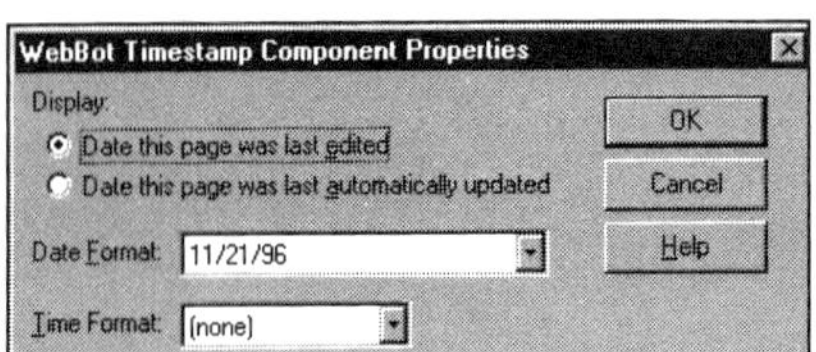

Figure 10-3 Add an automatic timestamp.

You have two types of timestamps available:

Date this page was last edited The date the page was last saved.

Date this page was last automatically updated Either the date the page was last saved, or the date that the page was modified because an included file changed, if later.

Pick a date format from the drop-down list box. If you wish you can also specify a format for the time the page was modified, using the Time Format drop-down list box.

Inserting Document Information (Substitution)

Don't be confused by the name of this WebBot. The name and the WebBot's dialog box seem to imply that you're substituting one thing for another. In fact, this bot works in the same way that the other ones do; the bot simply gets the information you specify and inserts it in the document at the bot position. (In other words, it substitutes the specified information for the bot.) This doesn't seem very logical, but nonetheless you have to select the Substitution entry from the Insert WebBot Component dialog box. The box shown in Figure 10-4 opens.

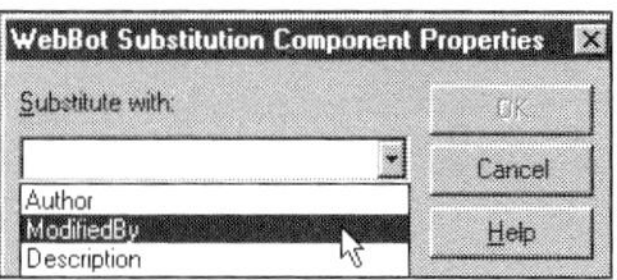

Figure 10-4 Pick the data you want to insert.

Simply select the information you want to insert from the drop-down list box, then click OK.

Where does all this information come from? Right-click the document in FrontPage Explorer, then select **Properties**. Click the Summary tab, and you'll see the information shown in Figure 10-5. As you can see, there are Created By and Modified By names; they may be the same, but as you'll see in Chapter 17 you can create different accounts to enable multiple authors to work on the same web, so the Modified By name may be different.

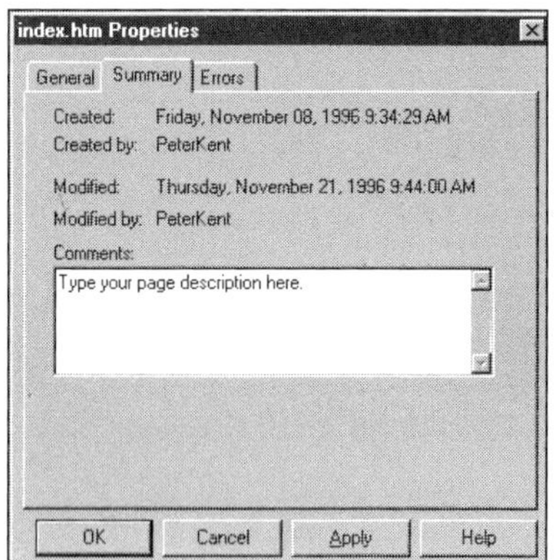

Figure 10-5 Type a comment here to be used as the description.

The WebBot Author is, of course, the Created By name. And the WebBot Description refers to the comments that you can enter into the Properties dialog box. The URL is, of course, the URL that describes the file location. (That's shown in the Properties dialog box's General tab.)

TIP **You must write the Comment *before* you insert the Description WebBot.**

You can create your own data for the Substitution WebBot, too, by creating "parameters" in the Web Settings dialog box (go to FrontPage Explorer, select **Tools** → **Web Settings**, and click the Parameters tab — see Chapter 17). For instance, you could create a parameter called Address, containing your company's address. Then wherever you need to use the address in a document you insert it using the Substitution WebBot. So if the address changes, you only have to change it in one place.

Creating a Table of Contents

You may want to create a brand new document to hold this WebBot. The Table of Contents WebBot quickly creates a table of contents to help users find their way around. What exactly is a table of contents in the world of hypertext? one might wonder. Really it's a sort of hierarchical link table, showing you the way that documents are linked together. After all, hypertext is not like a book. Books have a direction, front to back, so a table of contents can follow that direction. Hypertext has multiple directions, links here and there, so pages can, if you wish, appear more than once in your table of contents.

Select Table of Contents from the Insert WebBot Component dialog box, and the box shown in Figure 10-6 opens.

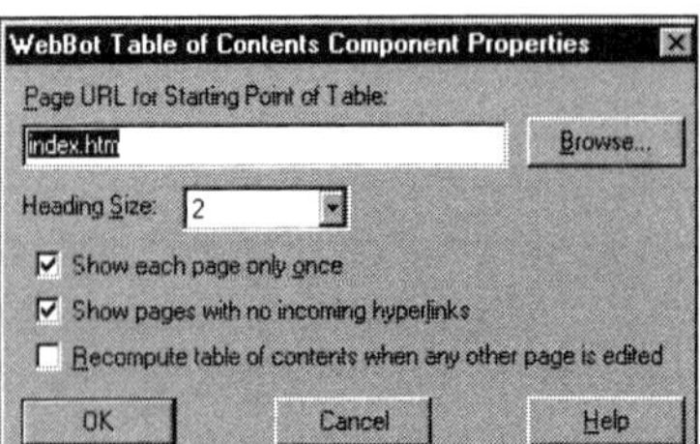

Figure 10-6 Quickly create a table of contents page to help your site users find their way around.

Here's what you can set in this dialog box:

Page URL for Starting Point of Table Click Browse to find the page you want to begin with, or simply leave index.htm shown. The table of contents will be created by following links down from this page.

Heading Size This defines the heading paragraph style to be used for the entry at the top of the table of contents (entries within the table are in a bullet list).

Show each page only once If you check this, a page is shown only once in the table even if it has multiple links from different pages. Clearing this box can create quite complicated tables. The document will be shown for each incoming link, even if a single page links to the document multiple times.

Show pages with no incoming hyperlinks Check this to include pages that are not linked to from any other pages.

Recompute table of contents when any other page is edited You should probably leave this turned off. If you select it each time you save a page, FrontPage recalculates the table of contents. That will slow down your work. Instead you can simply open and save the table of contents file to update it, or use the Tools → Recalculate Hyperlinks command in FrontPage Editor.

Click OK and FrontPage will place what appears to be a generic table of contents into the page. It won't display the actual table of contents until you save the file and then preview the document (see Chapter 5). In the Web browser you'll see something like Figure 10-7. As you can see, this is a cascading table, with documents indented below the ones they're linked from.

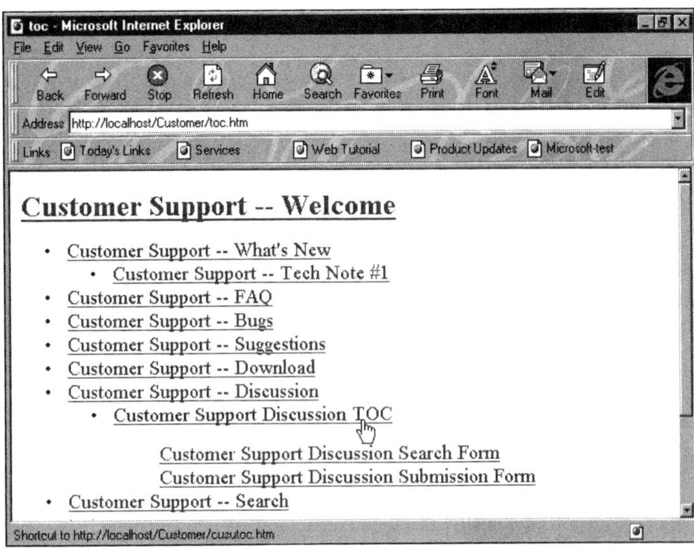

Figure 10-7 Your final table of contents

Working with HTML

Another bot we've looked at, in Chapters 5 and 6, is the HTML Markup WebBot. You won't find this in the Insert WebBot Component dialog box in FrontPage 97, though it was there in earlier versions. To use it you must select **Insert** → **HTML Markup**. Once you've created the HTML tag you'll see the Question Mark icon in your document. When you point at it you see the usual Robot mouse pointer; double-click to open the HTML Markup box again.

But there are actually four ways to insert your own HTML tags (if you understand how to do so, that is) into your document:

* The HTML Markup WebBot: select **Insert** → **HTML Markup** or click the Insert HTML toolbar button.
* Click an Extended button in a dialog box — this button is present in many dialog boxes throughout FrontPage Editor.

- Select View → HTML, make changes directly to the HTML, then click OK.
- Edit the document in another HTML editor. For instance, right-click a file in FrontPage Explorer, select Open With, then select an editor (such as notepad.exe).

TIP **Define the editors you want to use with your HTML files in FrontPage Explorer. Select Tools → Options, then click the Configure Editors tab.**

Why add your own HTML tags or attributes, though? Because FrontPage doesn't support all the possible options. No HTML authoring program does (though FrontPage seems to do a better job than most). And as more tags and attributes appear all the time, new ones will be created by the powers that be *after* FrontPage is released; there's no way for FrontPage to keep up. Note, however, that it's not always a good idea to use unusual or brand new tags or attributes. If they're that unusual, there's a good chance that many browsers won't yet work with them.

Let's see a quick example of how you can enter a special attribute using the Extended button. In this example I'm going to show you how to insert a message that opens in a dialog box when the user opens the Web page. I'll use JavaScript to do this.

1. Select File → Page Properties to open the Page Properties dialog box.
2. In the General pane click the Extended button.
3. Notice that the tag that you are about to modify is identified just above the large text box. In this case it's the <BODY> tag.
4. Click Add and the Name/Value Pair dialog box opens. See Figure 10-8.

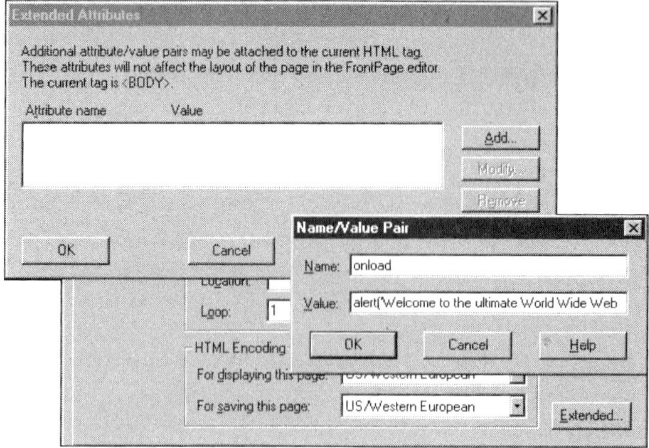

Figure 10-8 Here's where you add attributes to the tag.

5. In the Name text box type the name of the attribute you want to add to the tag; in this case type **onload**.
6. In the Value box type the attribute value. In this case type the instruction that is to be carried out when the Web page loads: **alert ('Welcome to the ultimate World Wide Web Gerbil Site')**. (Replace the message between the ' and ' symbols with whatever message you want to use.)
7. Click OK to close the Name/Pair Value box.
8. Click OK twice more to return all the way to your document.
9. Save the document and preview in a browser. If the browser can work with JavaScript, and if JavaScript is turned on in the browser, you'll see a message box open and display your message.

10

If you want to work with HTML, well, you'll have to learn HTML! That's a big subject, one that we're not covering in this book. But there are about 5 million HTML books available at your local bookstore, so go buy one if you really want to know more. (You don't need to, though; you can simply stick with what FrontPage provides, which is most of what you can do with HTML anyway.)

One note of caution, though. After modifying the page's HTML, save the file and then reopen and check to see if FrontPage has changed what you've done. There are some things it doesn't like, so it may convert things you've done to a form it prefers. For instance, when you insert a background sound (Chapter 4) the tag is placed near the top of the document. If you move the <bgsound src=> tag to the bottom of the document (so the sound plays after the text has loaded), FrontPage will simply move it back to the top.

And FrontPage won't check the validity of your additions, either. If you enter a special attribute, for instance, FrontPage will simply assume you know what you're doing (you do, don't you?) and accept your changes without checking that they're correct.

BONUS

The World's Fastest HTML Lesson

There are hundreds of different HTML tags and attributes, but here's a very quick explanation of how HTML works. When a Web browser loads a document, it reads the document before displaying it. It knows that much of the text in the file is not intended for display; rather, it contains instructions telling the browser how to display the rest of the information.

The browser looks through the document for < and > symbols. It knows that these symbols enclose special instructions. For instance, `<h1>` means "the following text is Heading 1, so format it in the way you normally show a Heading 1."

The instructions between < and > symbols are known as *tags*. Tags are in most cases, though not all, found in pairs. So `<h1>` is followed by the heading text itself and then the `</h1>` tag. This second tag means "that's it — we've finished the Heading 1 text." Notice that the second tag has a / symbol (a slash) immediately after the < symbol. That means it's an ending tag.

Tags are often more complicated than these simple heading tags. They sometimes contain special instructions, called *attributes*. Here's an example:

```
<hr size="4" noshade width="80%" color="#FF0000">
```

This is the tag used to create a horizontal line. A simple `<hr>` is enough to create a basic horizontal line, but the extra information inside the tag — the tag attributes — modifies the line. In most cases the attribute name is followed by = and the attribute value (the value is enclosed in quotes). In some cases, such as `noshade` in this example, simply an attribute name is enough.

size="4" This makes a line that is 4 pixels thick.

noshade This creates a solid line instead of a shaded line.

width="80%" This tells the browser to make the line take up 80 percent of the width of the window.

color="#FF0000" This tells the browser to make the line red; #FF0000 is the hexadecimal code used to identify red.

Now and again, take a look at the HTML source files for your documents (select View → HTML). You'll see these tags at work, and in most cases you'll probably be able to figure out exactly what they are doing.

Summary

The WebBots you've seen in this chapter are very handy. In particular, the Table of Contents and the Include WebBots are especially useful. These are the sorts of things that make creating a useful and attractive Web site easy. But you ain't seen nothin' yet. You probably noticed that we skipped two WebBots: the Search and Confirmation WebBots. FrontPage's real power comes into play when you start creating forms. You'll find out about these two bots, and the wizards that make working with forms quite simple, in Chapters 13 to 16.

As for working with HTML, it's a useful skill, though not one that you really must have. FrontPage provides enough power to create great-looking pages without your needing to understand all those funky little codes. If you're new to Web authoring, just be happy you didn't start a couple of years ago when there was only one way to create Web pages: by directly writing HTML.

PART THREE

ADVANCED WEB AUTHORING

THIS PART CONTAINS THE FOLLOWING CHAPTERS

Time for a few fancy tricks. Does your Web site need framed documents? Do you want to use tables in your pages? Or how about a discussion group, feedback form, guest book, or registration form? You'll learn about these things and more in Part Three.

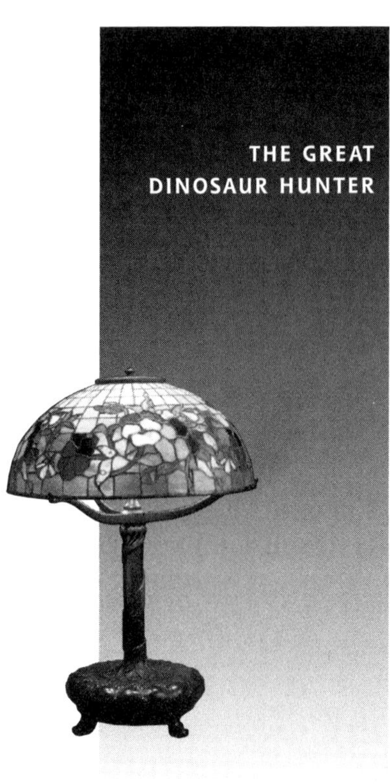

Rapid technological progress, like dessert, is often accompanied by those who warn against its overuse. In his blockbuster *Jurassic Park,* for example, Michael Crichton suggests that just because we can create a dinosaur doesn't mean we should.

Vincent Flanders agrees and has devoted an entire Web site to hunting big beasts. Flanders is an HTML instructor and the webmaster for a Bakersfield, California, Internet service provider, Lightspeed Net. But what's making him famous is a Web site in which he critiques misguided use of HTML and poor overall Web site development.

His site is found at http://www.webpagesthatsuck.com, and as you might expect, it's daintily called Web Pages That Suck. What he lacks in subtlety, however, Flanders makes up for with blunt, commonsense advice about how not to create a Web page. This unique site is much more than a mere hodgepodge of information. It's a full course in HTML Don'ts — complete with lectures, commentary, and dozens of examples.

The premise of Flanders's site is simple. Options for Web page designers, which include everything from HTML tags and animated GIF images to JavaScript, VBScript, and deluxe Web creation suites, have created a Web page buffet table of bacchanalian proportions. And like some people at a buffet, webmasters sometimes load their plates a little too full. The result is a Web page that fits nicely into Vincent Flanders's curriculum.

Webmasters often lose sight of the overall goals of their site. Flanders suggests that before webmasters start designing a site, they determine four important facts: Why their site exists, whom they are trying to reach, whether the visitors will find what *they* need, and why visitors would visit the site a second time. Keeping the visitor in mind at all times is critical to the success of a Web site.

Be considerate. Are you so sure that the visitor will want to see a 90K half-screen rendition of your corporate logo that you'll put it on your opening page — without an option to bypass it? You'd better take a look at Flanders's lesson on avoiding pretentiousness. Does your boss want the company mission statement, customer service pledge, and vision for the future all on the same page? Your boss needs to read "Too Much Tooting," another of Flanders's lessons.

And don't think that Vincent Flanders is scared of anyone. Law firms, art guilds — you name it — all get nailed for their lack of good Web design and abundant use of clichés. One thing is certain: Web Pages That Suck is a terrific place to visit, but I certainly don't want to be featured there.

CHAPTER ELEVEN

CREATING TABLES

IN THIS CHAPTER YOU LEARN THESE KEY SKILLS

11

Not so long ago, Web browsers couldn't work with tables; all they could manage was single columns of text. Combined with the fact that you couldn't use tabs or multiple spaces in Web pages, this presented a real problem to anyone trying to produce an attractive Web-page layout. Options were severely limited.

Then came tables. Only problem was, they were a little awkward to create. You had to combine a variety of HTML tags to describe the outside of the table and each cell within it. It was easy to learn the tags you needed, but sometimes actually typing them correctly to get exactly the table you wanted was a little frustrating.

But FrontPage has gone a step further, of course. No more combining those confusing <table>, <tr>, <td>, and <td> tags, and then using the font format tags to modify the contents of the cells. (Once you've created a few tables, take a look at the HTML source — View → HTML — and you'll see just what a complex mess table-coding can turn into.) Just point, click, drag, and you've got your tables. This chapter will explain exactly how to use the table features.

Creating a Table

Click in your document where you want to place your table. Then use one of these two methods to create the table:

Method 1: Click the Insert Table button, then drag the mouse pointer to select the number of columns and rows you want (see Figure 11-1).

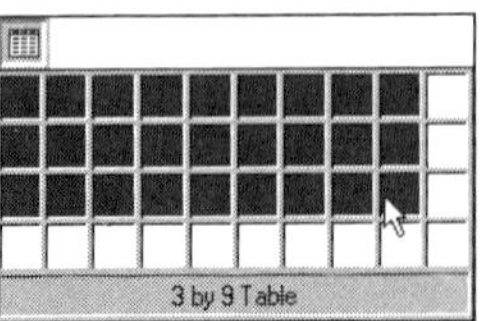

Figure 11-1 Drag the mouse pointer to create your table.

Method 2: Select Table → Insert Table. The Insert Table box opens (Figure 11-2). Select the number of rows and columns, then click OK. (We'll look at the rest of these settings next, under "Setting the Table Properties.")

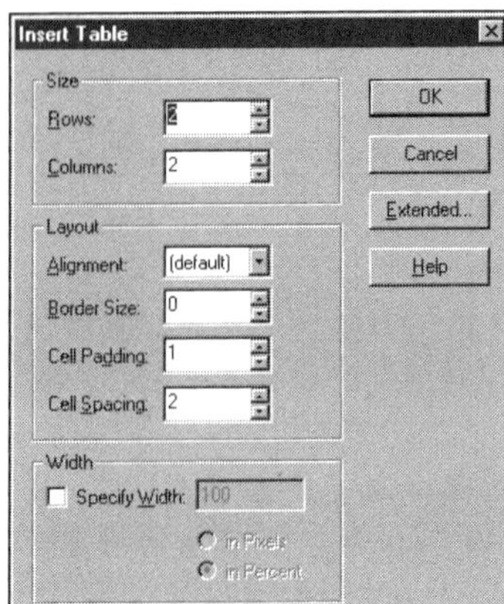

Figure 11-2 You can also create a table here.

Setting the Table Properties

To set your table's properties, right-click inside the table and select Table Properties (or click once and select Table → Table Properties). The Table Properties dialog box opens (Figure 11-3).

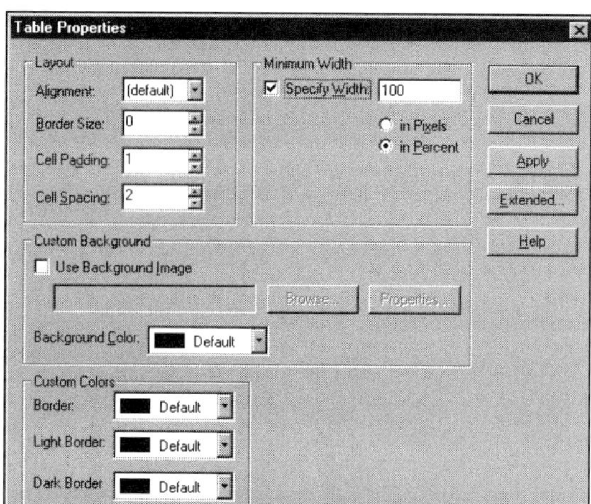

Figure 11-3 The Table Properties dialog box

Here are the settings you can work with:

Alignment This defines how the table is aligned within the page. If you keep the default setting, the table is placed in the document without any attempt to position it — it'll sit at the left side of the window. If you use one of the other settings, though, FrontPage uses the <div> tag to align the table. The <div> tag is a fairly new one that's similar to the normal <p> paragraph tag, except that it doesn't add a blank line after. This may not be intentional, though, as there's an align attribute that can be used within the <table> tag; the way this works right now means that you can't wrap text around tables. (See "Wrapping Text around Tables," later in this chapter.) You can align the table to the right, in the middle, or to the left using these settings.

Border Size Leave this set to 0, and the table will have no visible borders ¶ (you'll see them in the Editor, if you click the Show/Hide toolbar button, but not when viewing the document in a browser) — a great way to line up columns of text. Or you can create a visible table by creating a border. Simply enter a border size to adjust the size of the outside border (it has no effect on the cell border sizes).

Cell Padding This is the distance from the contents of a cell within the table to the edge of the cell (see Figure 11-4).

Cell Spacing This is the space between cells in the table. If you are using borders you can set the cell spacing to 0 to create a table with solid lines between cells. You can use this technique to create a box around text; simply create a single-cell table, with a cell-spacing value of 0 — you'll get an external border but no internal cell border.

Minimum Width This setting defines how far the table must stretch across the browser window. Note that it's the minimum size; if the table is very large, the browser will not squeeze it down to make it fit the window.

Custom Background You can use a background image or background color. As you'll see in a moment (under "Setting Individual Cell Properties"), you can specify background colors for particular cells, too.

Custom Colors Either select a border color to set the color of all the borders, or set the light border color (the left vertical lines and top horizontal lines) and/or the dark border color (the right vertical lines and bottom horizontal lines) individually. You can also set colors for particular cells.

Use the Apply button in this dialog box to experiment with different settings before closing the dialog box.

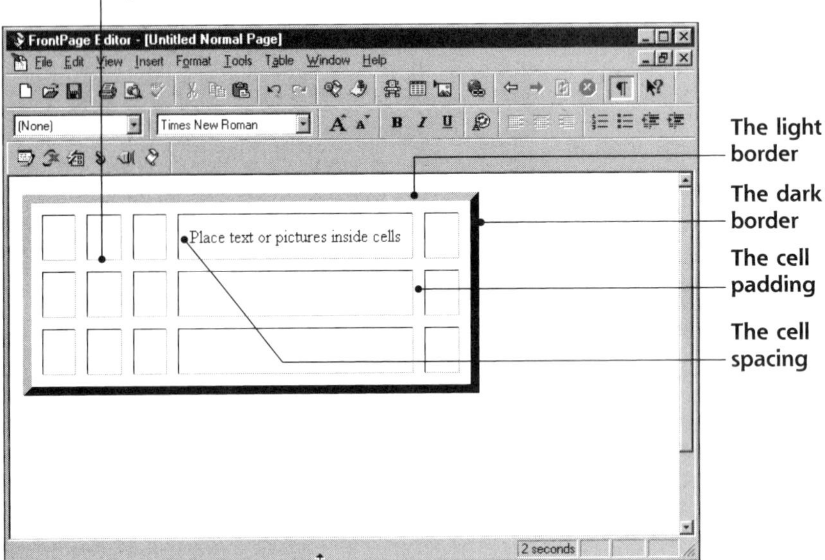

Figure 11-4 The components of a table

Netscape Navigator currently handles colors very differently from Internet Explorer. It won't display border colors, and only displays background colors within cells, not within the cell spacing.

Setting Individual Cell Properties

You can modify specific columns. Right-click inside the table and select **Cell Properties**, or click once and select **Table** → **Cell Properties**. The Cell Properties dialog box opens (Figure 11-5).

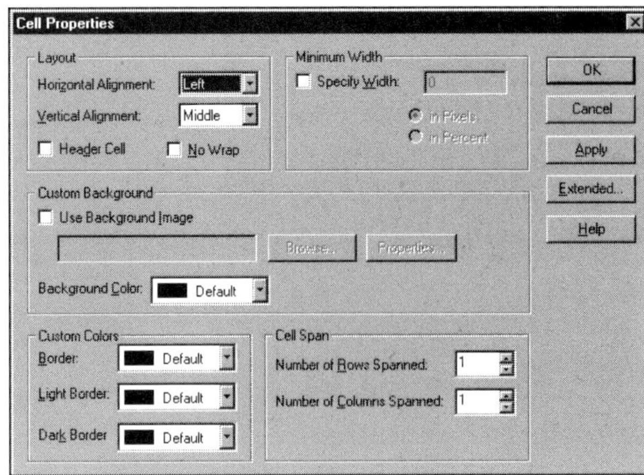

Figure 11-5 The Cell Properties dialog box

These are the cell settings:

Horizontal Alignment By default, the contents of each cell are aligned with the left side of the cell (allowing for the cell padding, of course). You can align them in the center or on the right if you wish.

Vertical Alignment By default the contents are in the vertical middle of the cell; you can shift them to the top or bottom.

Header Cell If you select this, the cell will become a header cell — the text inside the cell will be bold. (These cells are defined using a special HTML tag, the <th> tag.)

No Wrap Text will normally wrap within a cell to allow for long lines. You can check this box to stop the text from wrapping.

Minimum Width You can force a minimum cell-width size with this setting. Select either a size measured in pixels, or the percentage width of the table. Note, however, that although the table may look correct when displayed in a browser, in FrontPage Editor itself it may not show the correct widths.

Custom Background You can override the table's background image or color by setting the background for individual cells.

Custom Colors You can override the table border colors here.

Cell Span You can modify the cell span, merging one cell into several others.

TIP **Set several cells at once by selecting the cells and then opening the Cell Properties dialog box. And you can merge several cells in one direction; select several cells in a row, or an entire row or column (Table → Select Row or Table → Select Column) and then select Table → Merge Cells .**

Be careful when playing with the Cell Span and Minimum Width settings. These settings often provide unpredictable results, so experiment and be sure to preview the results. Be especially careful not to enter span values larger than the number of cells in the row or column. And remember Edit → Undo .

Inserting and Deleting Rows and Columns

If you need to add more cells to your table — complete rows and columns or individual cells — you have a couple of ways to do so. Place the cursor where you want to insert a new row or column, and select Table → Insert Rows or Columns . The dialog box shown in Figure 11-6 will open.

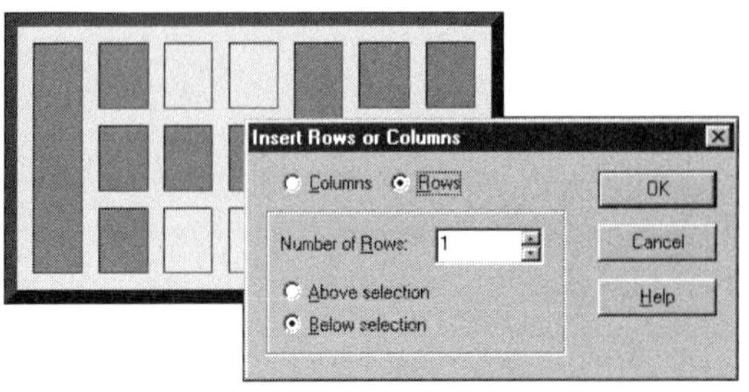

Figure 11-6 Insert a row or column.

Begin by selecting whether you want to insert rows or columns, then select the number you want. Finally, decide whether you want to place the columns to the Left of Selection or Right of Selection, and the row Above Selection or Below Selection. Click OK and the columns or rows are inserted.

The other method is to insert individual cells. Place the cursor into a cell and select Table → Insert Cell . A cell is inserted for you. Where? Goodness knows. That all depends on . . . well, I'm not entirely sure what it depends on. Generally cells are placed to the right of the current cell, shifting existing cells to the right to make room if necessary. But if there are already blank spaces to the right and below the cell, then the new cell might end up on the row *below*. Play with this; it's a mite unpredictable.

Splitting Cells

Another way to add cells is to split existing ones. Click inside the cell you want to split, then select Table → Split Cells. In the dialog box that opens (see Figure 11-7), select whether you want to split the cell into columns or rows, pick how many you want, and then click OK.

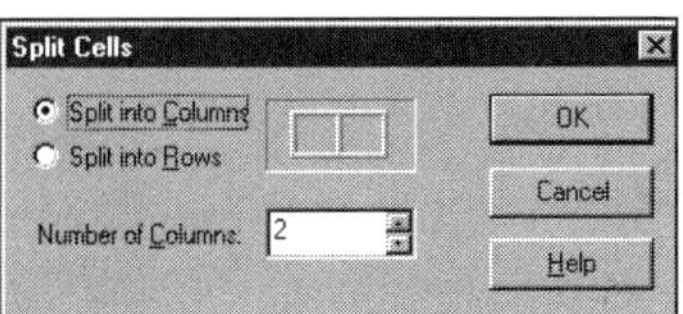

Figure 11-7 You can split cells horizontally or vertically.

This is a neat little feature. Sometimes it even works correctly. All this cell-manipulation stuff is a little shaky, although the main table features work well.

Deleting Cells and Tables

To delete a cell — leaving a blank space in its place — remove all cell contents, click inside the cell, and press Backspace. This can do weird things to tables, so you may have to end up splitting or adding cells. Deleting tends to skip cells that have spanned multiple rows or columns, for instance, and leave spaces in strange places.

Deleting an entire table is sometimes awkward, depending on where it's set in the page. If it's right at the top of the document, and there's nothing else in the document, for instance, getting rid of the thing is tricky; it just doesn't seem to want to die. Still, this method should always work: Click inside the table, then select Table → Select Table, and then press Delete.

Adding a Table Caption

You can add a caption to a table if you wish. This is simply text that remains attached to the table, at the top or bottom of the table. This is not simply ordinary text placed above or below the table; it's actually created using a special HTML tag, the <caption> tag. The manner in which the caption is displayed depends on the browser; in Internet Explorer it's bold text, displayed on the same background color as the table itself. In Netscape Navigator it's not bold, nor is it displayed on the table-background color, and it tends to sit a little higher above the table if placed above it.

TIP **You can use the text-formatting tools — color, bold, italic, size, and so on — to modify the caption.**

Simply click anywhere in the table, then select Table → Caption. FrontPage makes a little space at the top of the table for the caption (don't worry, I'll show you how to move it to the bottom in a moment). Type the caption into this space, and format it if you wish.

To move the caption, click it and select Table → Caption. A dialog box opens that lets you select Top of Table or Bottom of Table. To remove a caption, delete all the text and then, with the cursor in the caption space, press Backspace.

TIP **Now and then, you'll find that you can't insert something immediately before or after a table. For instance, if you put a table right at the top of the document, there's no way to add text before the table later. Here's how to get around this problem: Select View → HTML to see the source, and look for the tag that begins with <table. Type some text — anything — immediately before the tag, then click OK. FrontPage will insert the text into your document on a new line immediately before the table. The table has been shifted down and you can now work on the new line.**

Wrapping Text Around Tables

You can align text around a table if you enter the align=attribute yourself (click the Extended button in the Table Properties dialog box). You can use align="right" or align="left" attributes. (The align="center" attribute doesn't wrap text around the table in current browsers; it simply places it in the middle of the page and pushes the text down below. If you use the alignment settings in the Table Properties dialog box, FrontPage uses the <div> tag to align the table in the center or on the right; this does not wrap text around it.

TIP **There is a way around this problem. See "Tables within Tables," near the end of this chapter.**

Using Tables to Lay Out Pages

HTML, for all the hype, is not the world's most sophisticated page-layout system. For instance, you can't lay out text in columns — not real columns, anyway, in the way you can in a word processor. It's much better than it was just a year or so ago, but it still can't match a desktop publishing program or a sophisticated word processor. After all, those technologies have been developing for a couple of decades.

Because HTML doesn't have all the fancy page-layout tools you may be used to, you have to trick it into letting you put things where you want them. And that's generally done using tables. With tables you can produce varied layouts, mixing graphics and text in lots of different ways. You simply create a table without borders, then place things in the cells. Modify the cells to get everything into the positions you need; adjust alignments within the cells and cell sizes. Split cells, merge cells, delete and add cells. As you can see in Figure 11-8, you can put things all over the place without the user even realizing that he or she is looking at a table.

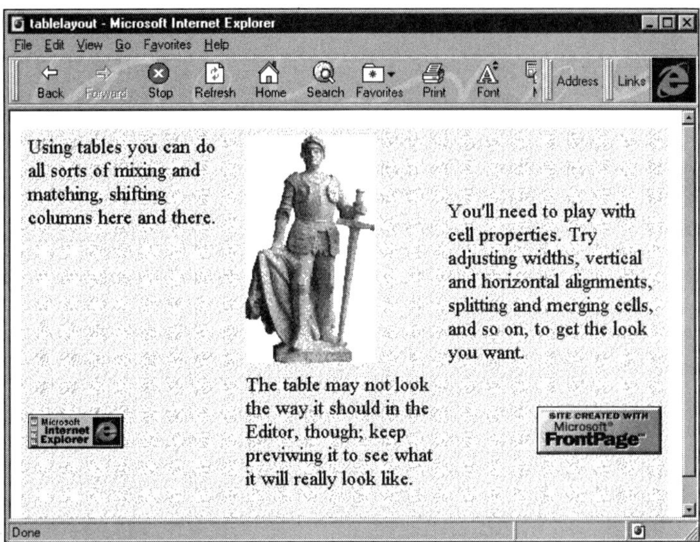

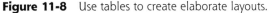

Figure 11-8 Use tables to create elaborate layouts.

As you can see in Figure 11-9, you can even use this method to create a newspaper-type layout. However, remember that Web pages are not paper, so some types of layout that might seem quite appropriate are not. For instance, you really wouldn't want to have very long blocks of two- or three-column text.

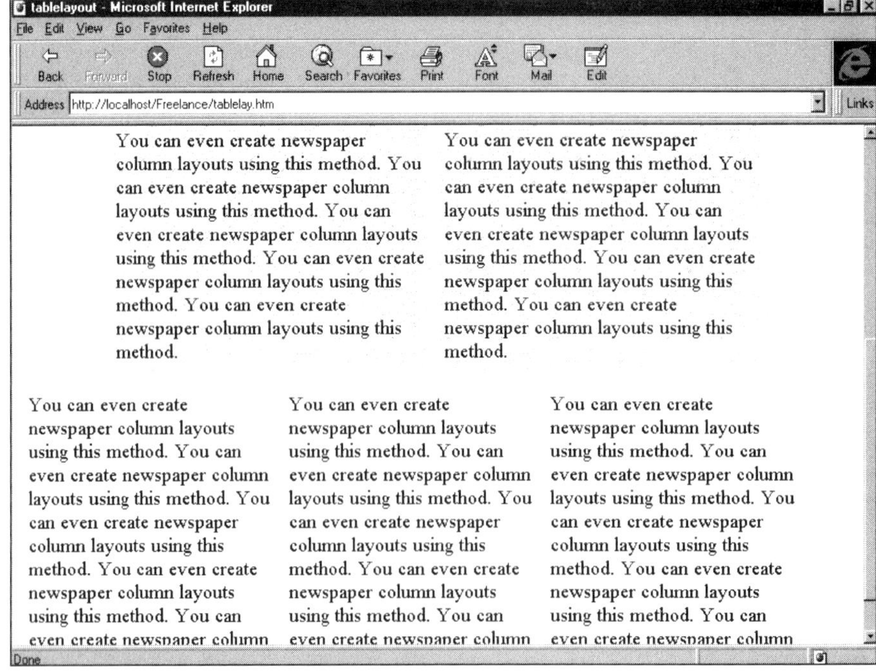

Figure 11-9 Create multiple columns of text if you wish.

BONUS

Tables within Tables

You can build tables within tables if you wish, providing even more flexibility in how you lay out your pages. Simply click inside a cell, then create a new table: use the Insert Table toolbar button, or **Table** → **Insert Table**. Then begin formatting the table in the normal way. Note, by the way, that when you adjust the table width by entering a percentage, you are defining the percentage of space to be taken up within the cell in which you placed the new table.

In Figure 11-10 you can see an example of two tables within tables. The two blocks with the pictures are separate tables, inserted into cells within two other tables.

There's just one problem with this, as you can see in Figure 11-11. FrontPage doesn't always display tables correctly, especially when you start doing odd things like putting tables into tables. Don't worry, though. Preview the document to make sure it looks correct in the browsers — that's all that really counts. And anyway, you may find that when you make some minor adjustment within FrontPage Editor, all of a sudden the tables jump back to their correct positions.

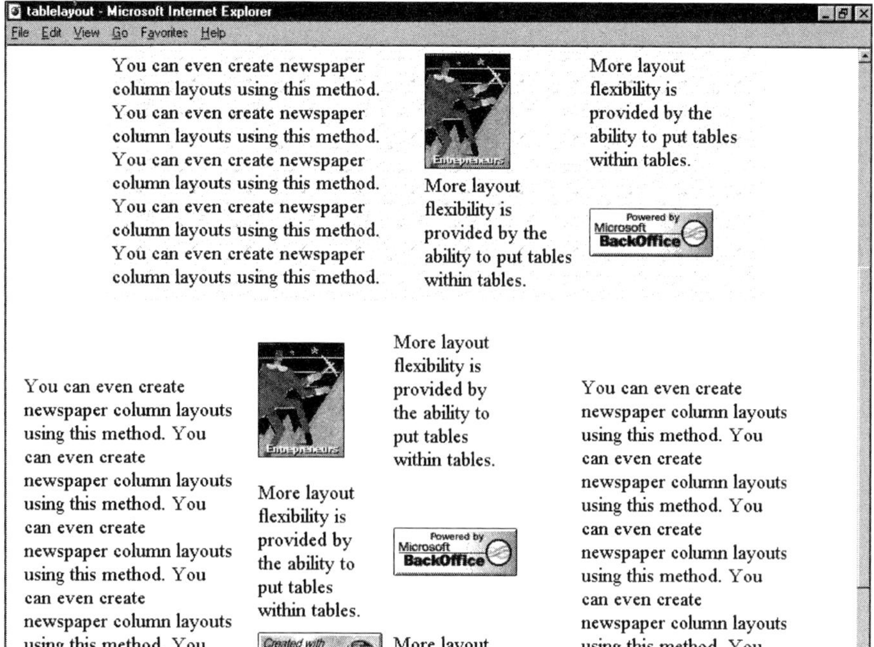

Figure 11-10 Insert tables within tables for even more layout flexibility.

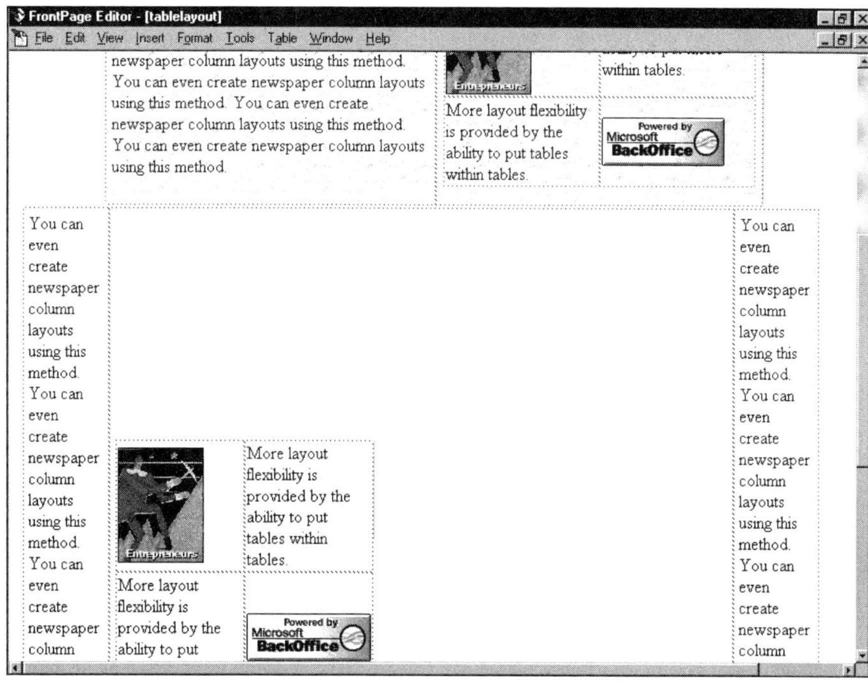

Figure 11-11 This is what the tables-in-tables layout might look like in FrontPage Explorer — not quite correct!

Summary

Tables are not just for tables. HTML tables certainly work in the way that you might use tables in a word processor or desktop publishing program, enabling you to format columns of numbers, for instance. But they're a very important page-layout tool. Take a look at pages you see on the World Wide Web. If you know a little about HTML — but not a lot — you may have looked at some pages and thought, How'd they get it to look like that? Well, very often they've used tables.

Without tables, HTML would greatly limit the manner in which you could display things. You'd be able to wrap text around images, but that's about as fancy as you could get. No multiple columns of text, no spreadsheet-type columns, no mixtures of text and pictures spread around the page in unusual configurations. So play a little with tables. They're really quite easy to work with, and they provide a way to make your pages attractive with minimal effort.

CHAPTER TWELVE

USING FRAMES AND TARGETED WINDOWS

IN THIS CHAPTER YOU LEARN THESE KEY SKILLS

Hypertext has been around for years, and it's actually a fairly well developed medium. The World Wide Web, though, has been in wide use only since the middle of 1994 (and even so, most of today's Web users probably didn't even know what the Web really was back then). Back in 1993 and 1994, hypertext on the Web was in many ways quite crude, a very simple form of hypertext.

The Web was limited in the manner in which it could display data. Click a link and you'd replace what was in the browser with the document referenced by the link. Click another link and you'd replace that document with something else. Compared with other forms of hypertext this was primitive, and in fact it presents real problems to hypertext users. One of the major problems with hypertext is that people tend to get lost, not quite sure where they are or how they got there. And even if they know where they are, they tire of continually having to return along a path they've just followed: go forward, go back, go forward, go back, and so on, can get rather irritating after a while.

The designers of other hypertext systems had developed a variety of methods to alleviate this problem. One method for keeping readers oriented was quite simple. There's a basic principle in hypertext authoring that might be stated as Don't take the reader away if he or she doesn't need to go — or perhaps, Whenever possible bring the information to the reader, not the reader to the information.

Instead of replacing the information the reader is currently viewing with whatever is referenced by the link, why not keep the document and bring the referenced document to the reader as well? This can be done in a variety of ways. Some systems use *pop-ups*, little boxes that appear above the original document — a great way to provide a little piece of information, such as a word's definition, while keeping the reader in the same place. (Pop-ups will start appearing in Web pages in 1997 — Internet Explorer 4.0 will be able to work with them, initially using a system called HTMLHelp. Currently FrontPage 97 does not support this, though.)

Another way to bring information to the user is to use different panes; split the window into two or more sections, keep the first document in one of these panes, and display the referenced documents in the others. And that's what you're going to learn about in this chapter, a feature known in the HTML world as *frames*. Netscape Navigator was the first browser to work with frames, but now Internet Explorer also works with them. You can see an example of a framed page in Figure 12-1.

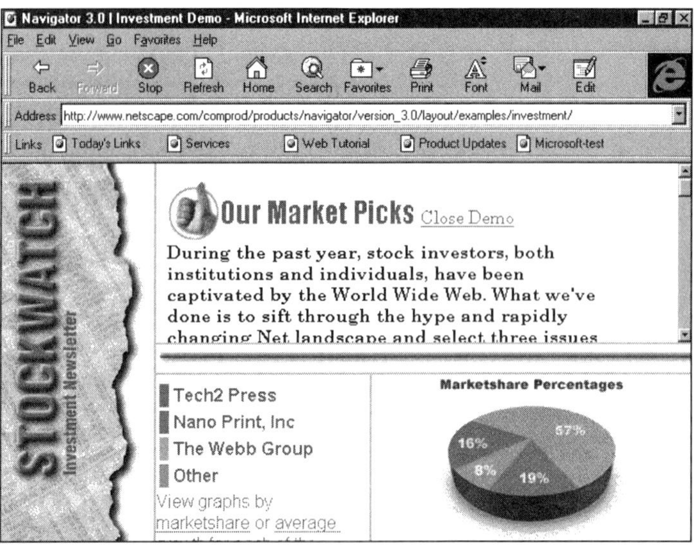

Figure 12-1 A demo page showing frames in action; this page has three frames, one with its own scroll bar.

Before I explain how to use FrontPage to create frames, here's a little more orientation. I need to explain how HTML handles frames. When the user clicks on a link to a set of documents that are displayed in a *frameset* — the structure of two or more individual panes or frames within the browser window — the first thing that happens is that a very simple file is transferred to the browser, a file that is not even displayed to the user (unless the browser doesn't support frames). This document, known as the *frame-definition document*, tells the browser how to set up the frames, where to put the individual frames within the browser window, and what document to load into each frame. So the browser reads this document, then creates the frames in its window, and then transfers the documents to place into each frame.

So if you are creating two frames, you have to create three documents: the frame-definition document and the documents that you want to place inside the frames. Three frames require four documents, five frames require six documents, and so on; you've always got that frame-definition document that the user doesn't see, but which instructs the browser what to do. FrontPage helps you create the frame-definition document by providing a wizard that steps you through the process.

Here's a quick rundown of the procedure you'll follow when working with frames. Depending on whether you use one of the FrontPage templates (see "Using a Frames Template" later in this chapter) or create your own frameset from scratch (see "Create Your Own Frameset").

12

Using a Template

1. Create a file containing a message that will be displayed in non–frames-compatible browsers.
2. Start the Frames Wizard. The wizard creates the frame-definition document. It also creates a document for each of the frames you defined.
3. Modify the documents that the wizard created, placing the information you want to appear in the browser frames in the documents that the wizard created for you.
4. Preview the frameset in a browser, then make any modifications that are required to each page.

Creating Your Own

1. Create a file containing a message that will be displayed in nonframes browsers.
2. Create the files that will be placed inside each frame within the frameset.
3. Start the Frames Wizard. You will tell the wizard how many frames you want, and which documents to place inside each one. The wizard will then create the frame-definition document.
4. Preview the frameset in a browser, then make any modifications that are required to each page.

Creating a Message for Non–Frames-Capable Browsers

When you create your frameset, FrontPage is going to ask you what you want to display in a browser that doesn't support frames — as perhaps 5 to 10 percent of browsers currently don't. Before you use the wizard you should create a document that contains the message you want to have appear, just as you want it to appear.

For instance, let's say you're creating a frame with a table of contents in the left frame, and in the right frame is the information that is referenced by the links in the table of contents. What do you want someone to see if their browser can't use frames? A simple table of contents, probably the same one, in fact. So create and save that page first, then use the wizard. When prompted, you'll tell the wizard to use this page as the one that is displayed when a user without a frames-capable browser comes to your site. The user won't even realize that there's a framed version of the table of contents.

Many web authors place a simple message telling users that their browsers can't use frames, and provide a link to another page. That may be appropriate in some cases, but you don't have to do it that way. You can simply include the page you want them to see in the frame definition document.

Using the Frames Wizard

Creating frames can be a little confusing in HTML, but that's okay, of course; you're not using HTML. FrontPage does all the HTML coding for you. FrontPage provides a special wizard that leads you through the process of creating a frameset. Here's how it works:

1. Select File → New.
2. In the New Page dialog box select Frames Wizard and click OK. The dialog box shown in Figure 12-2 opens.
3. Select Pick a Template if you want to use a ready-made frameset. Or pick Make a Custom Grid to set up all the specifications for the frameset yourself.

We'll look at both of these methods in turn.

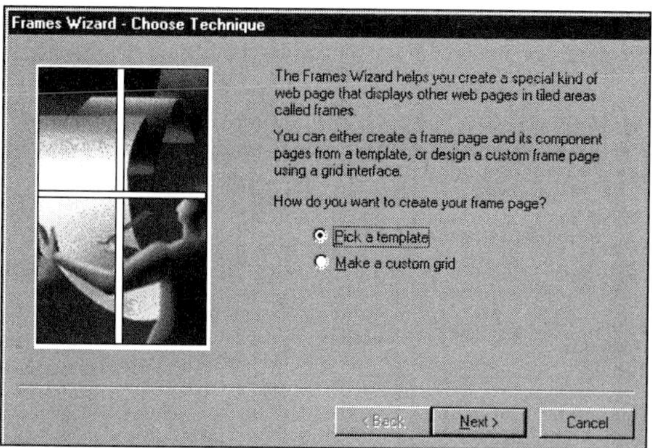

Figure 12-2 You can use a frames template or customize the frameset.

Using a Frames Template

Personally I think it's easier to use the other method for creating frames, because if you use one of the templates you'll have to fiddle around trying to figure out what FrontPage has already done for you — what frame names it used, what it named the files it created to put in each frame, and so on. With the other method you get to define all those things for yourself. Still, we'll begin by quickly looking at the template procedure.

1. Select Pick a Template in the first page of the wizard and click Next. The box shown in Figure 12-3 opens.

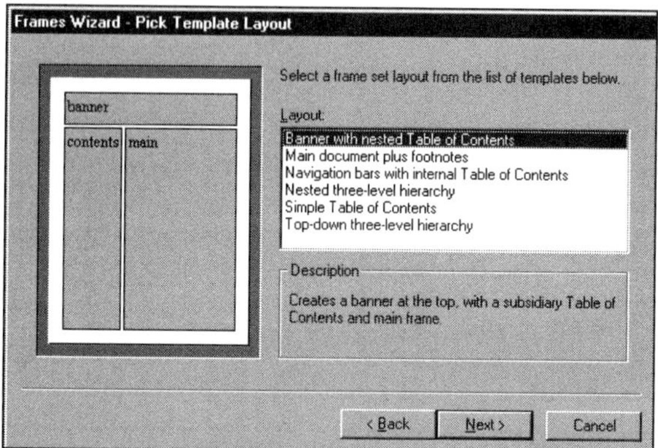

Figure 12-3 Click a template to see what it looks like on the left.

2. Click the entries in the Layout box, and you'll see what each template looks like in the sample on the left. Keep in mind that the more frames you have, the more cluttered the page will be in VGA mode (see "Bonus" near the end of this chapter for more about this).

3. You can modify frame sizes by pointing at a frame border and then, when you see the two-headed arrow, dragging the border.

4. When you've selected the template you want, click Next. The box shown in Figure 12-4 opens.

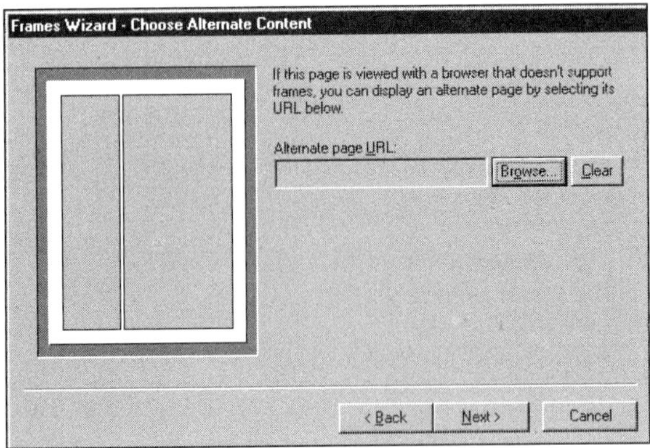

Figure 12-4 Specify which document should be used for nonframes browsers.

5. Click Browse to find the document that the user's browser can display in place of this frameset if his or her browser does not support frames — the document I discussed under "Creating a Message for Non–Frames-Capable Browsers" earlier. If you don't want to bother with an alternative page, simply ignore this option.

Use this feature only if you are working with a FrontPage-enabled server. This uses the Include WebBot to insert the specified document into the frame-definition document. If you are working with a non–FrontPage-enabled server you can edit the frame-definition document. See "Previewing the Frames," later in this chapter, for information on loading the frame-definition document into the Editor.

6. Click Next to see the box in Figure 12-5.

7. Type a title and filename for the file, or simply accept the ones provided by FrontPage, then click Finish. (You'll probably want to pick a more descriptive title, as this is the title that will appear in browser history lists and bookmark lists.)

The wizard now creates your frame definition page, using the name you provided. It also creates two or more additional files, one for each of the frames you've created. See "Viewing Your Files," later in this chapter.

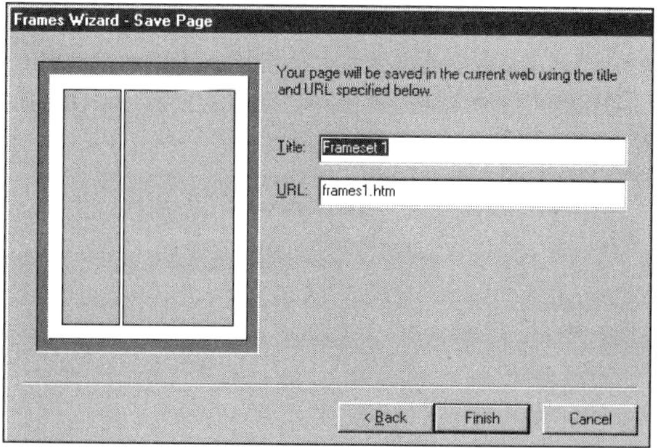

Figure 12-5 Provide a title and filename for this file.

TIP **If you want users to view this page as soon as they enter your Web site, you can delete the index.htm file and name the frame-definition file index.htm instead.**

Create Your Own Frameset

Follow this procedure to customize your own frameset:

1. Select Make a Custom Grid in the first page of the wizard and click Next. The box shown in Figure 12-6 opens.

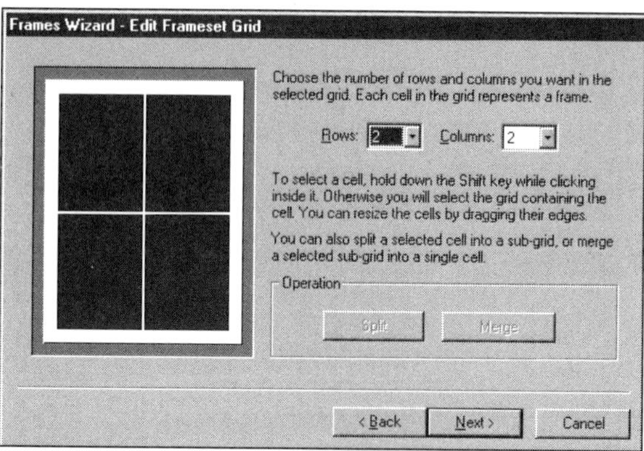

Figure 12-6 Begin by defining your rows and columns.

2. Enter numbers into the Rows and Columns boxes to define how many rows and columns you want. This may not give you exactly what you want, but you'll be able to split and merge cells to get what you want.

3. If you want to split a cell into more cells, press the Shift key and then click the cell. Click Split and the cell is split into more subcells. You can then select the number of rows and columns you want from the little drop-down list boxes.

4. If you make a mistake and want to merge the cells you've just created back into one cell, click the cell containing those smaller cells; no need to hold down Shift (if you do so you'll select one of the subcells). Then click Merge.
5. Size the cells by dragging the borders.
6. Click Next and the dialog box shown in Figure 12-7 opens.

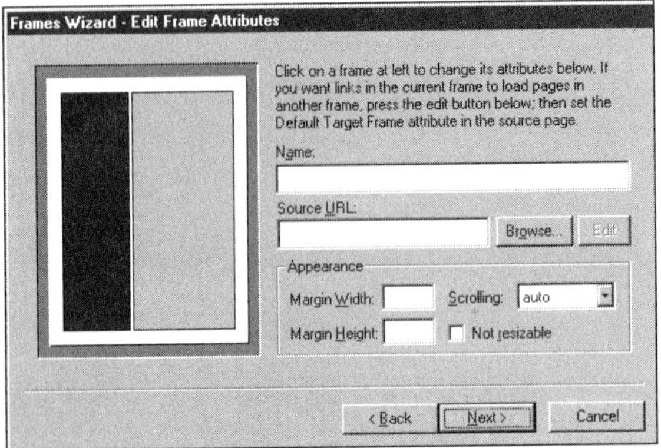

Figure 12-7 Set each frame's properties.

7. When you first see this dialog box all the options are disabled. Click one of the frames and all the options will be enabled.
8. Type a name into the Name text box. This is not the document title — or anything to do with the document itself, really. Rather, it's the name you are giving to the frame. The frame name is used by targets to correctly place documents into the frame, as you'll see under "Creating Links between Frames," later in this chapter. You might use names like left, right, top, bottom, and so on.
9. Click Browse and find the document you want to place into this frame.
10. The Edit button is used to define the target frame, the name of the frame that documents should be loaded into when a link is clicked upon. For instance, if you have a table of contents in the left frame that loads documents into the right frame, you'd want to use the right-frame name as the target frame for the document in the left frame. When you click Edit, the document you are loading into the frame is opened in FrontPage Editor, so you can modify the Page Properties. Did you get all that? Don't worry, we'll come back to it later in this chapter, under "Creating Links between Frames." If you don't understand this right now, ignore it and you can enter the target-frame name later.

11. If you wish, you can enter the frame border thicknesses by entering values in the Margin Width box (the thickness of the vertical borders) and Margin Height box (the thickness of the horizontal borders). The sizes are measured in pixels.

12. If you want to fix the borders in place, click the Not Resizable check box. (I've seen too many framesets in which it was not possible to view all the text, yet the borders were fixed so you couldn't move them — so be careful with this setting.)

13. Select an option from the Scrolling drop-down list box. This defines whether there will be a scroll bar in this frame. Select Auto to let the browser add one if it needs one, Yes to put one in even if it's not required, and No to stop the browser from using one even if it *is* required. (Again, be careful with this last setting. In most cases the No setting is a bad choice.)

14. Repeat for each frame in the frameset, then click Next. The box you saw back in Figure 12-4 appears.

15. As before, you'll select which file contains the message that you plan to use for browsers that can't work with frames. This may actually be a copy of one of the files that you have already inserted into one of the frames (Step 9). For instance, if you have a document named toc.htm, you could place it in a frame, and you could also make a copy of it and use the copy as the document to show the nonframes browsers, so the same table of contents document will be seen by users working with both frames and nonframes browsers. In a nonframes browser the document will appear in window by itself, and when the user clicks on a link the referenced document will load into that window. In a frames browser the document will appear within a frame, and when the user clicks on a link the referenced document will load into the targeted frame. (As you'll see under "Creating Links between Frames," special tags and attributes are used to define which frame is targeted; you won't target a frame in the copy's links, though.)

Use this feature only if you are working with a FrontPage-enabled server. This uses the Include WebBot to insert the specified document into the frame-definition document. If you are working with a non–FrontPage-enabled server you can edit the frame-definition document. See "Previewing the Frames" for information on loading the frame-definition document into the Editor.

16. Click Next.

17. Provide a Document title and filename, then click Finish.

Viewing Your Files

Now that you've created your frameset, what have you actually got? Look at Figure 12-8 and you'll see an example of a simple frameset, shown in FrontPage Explorer. This frameset had two frames.

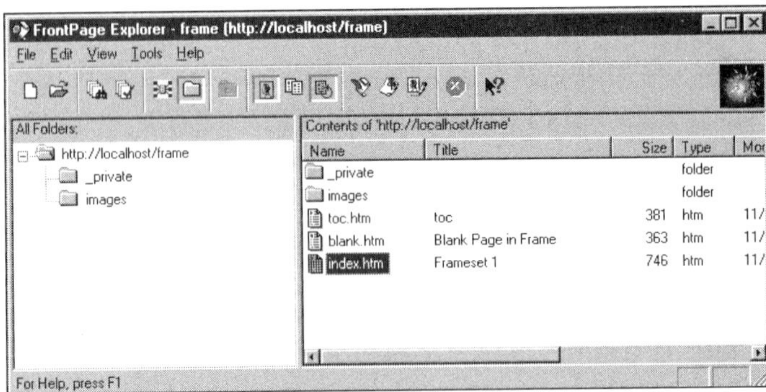

Figure 12-8 A simple frameset in FrontPage Explorer

Here's what we have:

index.htm In Step 17 above (in "Create Your Own Frameset") — or in Step 7 of the "Using a Frames Template" procedure — I gave the frame-definition document the name index.htm. That way, when users first arrive at this site they'll see the frames immediately. The title of this file is Frameset1, because I accepted the title provided by the wizard.

toc.htm Although you can't tell here, I used the file toc.htm as the file to be used in the left frame (my frameset has two vertical frames).

blank.htm This document has the title Blank Page in Frame, a title I gave it when I assigned it to the right frame in the frameset. (Actually, as you'll see in a moment, the document is not blank; it contains a very short message.)

first.htm, second.htm, third.htm, fourth.htm These are pages that are referenced by the table of contents, as you'll see in a moment. When the user clicks on a link in the table of contents in the left pane, one of these pages is loaded into the right pane.

This is from a frameset that I created. If I'd used the template method, then FrontPage would create the files that go in the frames for me (in addition to the frame-definition document) and name them for me too. If you use a template, look for files with titles such as Banner Frame in Frameset 1, or Main Frame in Frameset 1, or something similar. The title will always use the name that you gave to the frameset, so you can easily identify the files.

Previewing the Frames

Time to see what all this looks like . . . how does one do that? Well, first you need to open the frame-definition document in the Editor, but you can't do that in the normal way. If you double-click the frame-definition document, or right-click and select **Open**, the Frames Wizard starts, letting you edit the frame-definition document. So in order to preview the document, do this:

1. In FrontPage Explorer, right-click the frame-definition file. It's probably called Frameset (followed by a number) or whatever you defined as the title for the document.

2. Select **Open With**. The Open with Editor box opens.

3. Select FrontPage Editor and click OK.

4. The file is opened in the Editor. You'll see the message that is displayed to users of nonframes browsers. If you created the frameset using a template, you'll see a comment WebBot, which you can delete if you wish. You can modify the message as well. (If you want to see the instructions that tell a browser how to create a frameset, select **View** → **HTML** and look for the <frameset> tag.

5. Click the Preview in Browser toolbar button. The document is opened in your browser. However, if the browser is capable of displaying frames, then you won't see this document. Rather, the browser reads the document and creates the frameset as defined in the document's instructions, placing the appropriate files inside each frame. You can see an example in Figure 12-9.

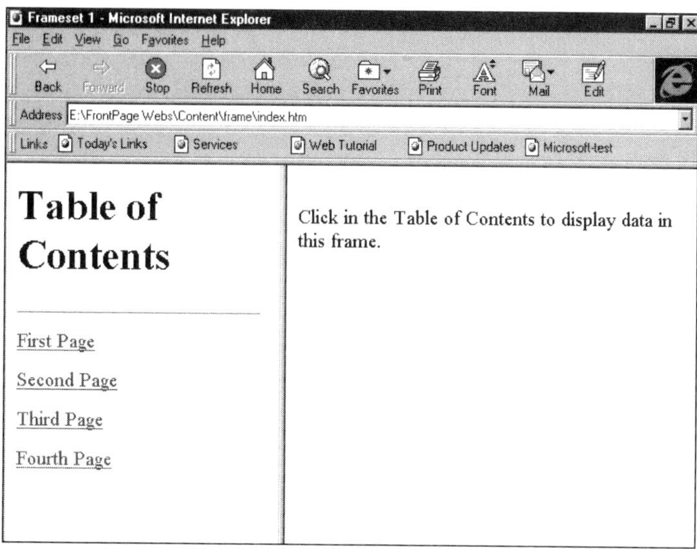

Figure 12-9 Here's what the example frameset looks like.

12

What happens when you click one of the links in the left pane? You can see in Figure 12-10 that another document is loaded into the right pane.

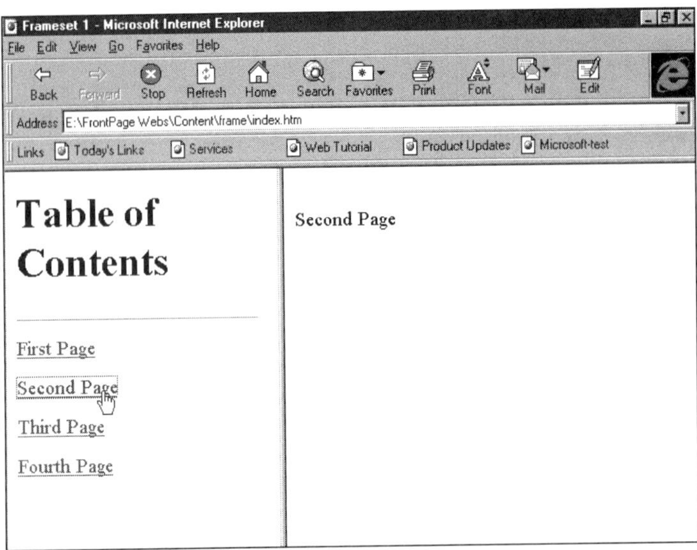

Figure 12-10 Once the links are correctly configured, clicking a link in the left pane loads the right pane.

How did the browser know that it was supposed to put the referenced document in the right pane? If we'd created normal links, the browser wouldn't do that. Instead it would completely reload the window, removing the frameset and displaying only the referenced document. So we have to tell the browser to load the document into a particular frame. I'll explain how to do that next.

Creating Links between Frames

In the above example, you want to load a document into the frame on the right when the user clicks a link on the left. How does one do that? There are three ways.

- Define a default target frame, so the page loads all referenced documents into a particular frame.
- Define target frames for each link, so links can load into different frames.
- Define a default target frame *and* define target frames for just some of the links.

Defining a Default Target Frame

As you saw in Chapter 4, when you set up the Page Properties you can enter a default target frame name. Open the Page Properties dialog box (File → Page Properties) and click the General tab. Then, in the Default Target Frame text box (see Figure 12-11), type the name of the frame you want all the links to load.

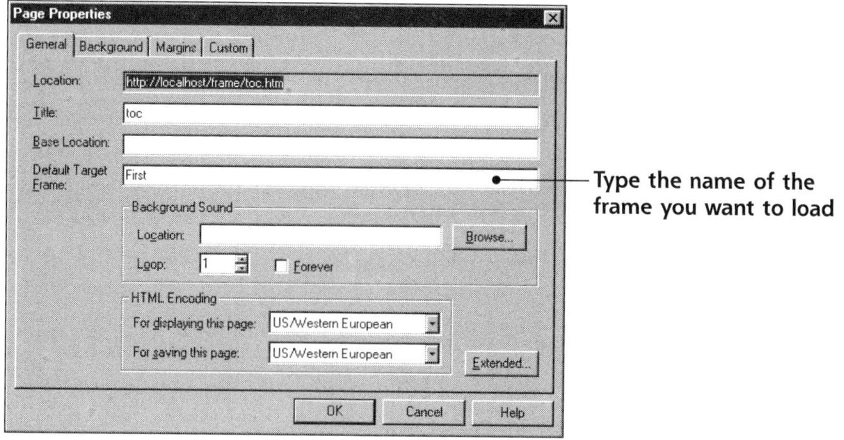

Figure 12-11 Define a default target frame for the document.

Where do you get the name of this frame? If you used a template (see "Using a Frames Template"), the wizard named the frames for you; it showed you the names inside each frame when it displayed the samples in the Frame Wizard–Pick Template Layout dialog box. When you open the documents created by the wizard you'll probably see a note telling you if the default target frame was set.

If you created your own frameset using the custom method (see "Create Your Own Frameset"), you entered the names in the Name text box (see Figure 12-7).

TIP **If you don't remember the names of the frames, double-click the frame-definition document in FrontPage Explorer to load it into the Frames Wizard, then click Next. Then click each frame to see the frame name displayed in the Name text box. (Write the names down!)**

Once you've set the Default Target Frame in the Page Properties box, *all* the links in the document will load documents into that frame . . . unless you define a different frame for a particular link.

Defining a Link's Target Frame

The other way to define which frame is used is to do so for each link. As you saw in Chapter 7, when you create a link you'll see a Target Frame text box (see Figure 12-12), regardless of which pane in the Create Hyperlink dialog box you use. This is where you type the name of the frame you want the referenced document to load into.

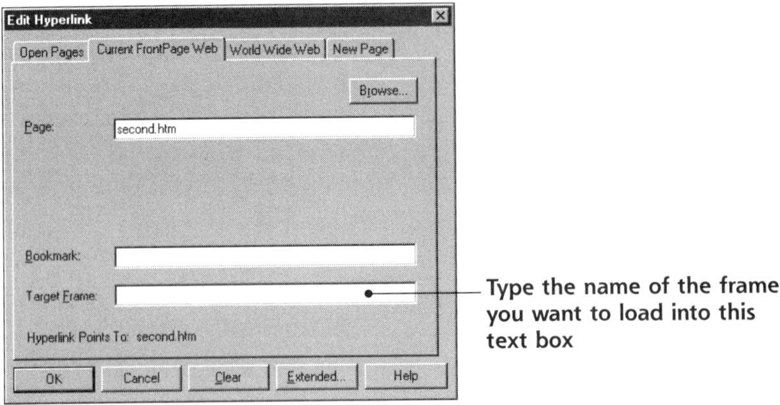

Figure 12-12 Define a target frame for a specific link.

If you specify the name of the target frame for a link, it overrides the Default Target Frame that you've set for the Page Properties, if any.

Defining Both Default and Link Target Frames

If you want all the links in a document to load their referenced documents into the same frame, you can quickly make them do so by setting the default target frame. But if you need some links to do one thing, and some to do another, you'll have to either set all the links individually, or set a default target link and then set some of the links individually.

Perhaps the most common case in which you want to do this is when you have a document — a table of contents, perhaps — that loads most referenced documents into a particular frame, but has one or two links that take you all the way out of the frameset, perhaps back to the Web site's main page.

To do that, you'll set the Default Target Frame in the Page Properties dialog box using the name of the frame into which most documents will load. Then you'll modify the link or links that *don't* load into that frame. Of course, if the links load into a different frame you'll have to use the other frame's name. But how do you make the link remove the frames entirely? Or, perhaps, load the referenced document into the *same* frame — that is, remove the document containing the link and replace it with the document referenced by the link? There are some special frame names you can use to carry out special operations:

_self The document containing the link is removed, and the referenced document is placed into the same frame.

_parent In most cases the browser will remove the frameset entirely and display the referenced document in the browser window by itself. However, note that because HTML lets you create framesets within framesets — a subject I have no intention of touching — if the document is in a subframeset, the subframeset is removed and the referenced document is displayed in the frame that held that subframeset.

_top The frameset is removed, and the referenced document is displayed in the browser by itself. (That's what happens even if the document is in a subframeset.)

_blank This opens a brand new window and loads the document — see "Opening Targeted Windows," later in this chapter.

Editing Your Frameset Documents

Modifying your frameset really comprises three distinct processes:

- You can modify the frame-definition document in the Frames wizard.
- You can modify the nonframes message in the frame-definition document in the Editor.
- You can modify the individual documents that are displayed within the frames in the FrontPage Editor.

12

If you double-click the file in FrontPage Explorer, the file is loaded into the Frames Wizard. You can then follow the process explained under "Create Your Own Frameset," earlier in this chapter, to modify the frameset.

TIP **Use this method to edit any frameset, whether it was originally created using a template or the custom method.**

To modify the message shown to nonframes browsers, right-click the name of the frame-definition document in Explorer and select **Open With**; select FrontPage Editor; click OK. You can now edit the text in this document. (Remember, though, if you specified a document that should be used to provide the message text, you'll edit the text within that document, not within the frame-definition document.)

To modify the files that are displayed into the frames, open them in the Editor and then make your changes. You may want to open all the files contained by the frameset in the Editor at once. Then you can modify and preview the files all at once, in the frames in which they'll appear in the document (see "Previewing the Frames," earlier in this chapter).

Opening Targeted Windows

There's another method used by hypertext authors to help users find their way around without getting lost. Many hypertext systems enable the author to place a document in a new window, so the original document remains in the first window, while the document referenced by the link is placed in the new window.

This feature was added to Web browsers along with frames. In the hypertext world it's often known as *secondary windows*, but in the world of HTML it's more commonly called *targeted windows*.

Making a browser do this is very easy. Simply use the _blank name in the Target Frame box in the Create Hyperlink dialog box (see Figure 12-12). This feature really has nothing to do with frames. You can use it anywhere, in any of your documents, whether or not you've placed these documents in framesets. When the user clicks a link that has one of these _blank target-frame names, a new window opens and the referenced document is loaded into it. If the user is using a nonframes browser (and, therefore, a non–targeted-window browser, as the features are associated), the link acts like a normal link, loading the document into the same window.

Note, however, that there's a significant problem with using targeted windows: If the user isn't paying close attention — if he or she clicks on a link and then turns away from the computer, or even if he or she simply has a very fast computer and happens to blink — the user may not see the new window open. So, away goes the user, following links in the new document, not realizing he or she is working in a new window. Later, the user tries to return and discovers that the history list has disappeared — because the new window started afresh. (Actually with Internet Explorer the history list *doesn't* do this, but with Netscape Navigator, the most popular browser by far right now, it does.) So, again, this is a feature you should use carefully.

BONUS

Should You Use Frames?

Frames, used properly, are a fantastic tool to make your Web site easier to use. Used improperly they are a real nuisance. When frames first appeared they were the cool thing to use. Now people have backed off a little and are using them a little more carefully. The Netscape site, for instance, started using frames immediately. Netscape soon discovered its mistake, and now if you visit the Netscape site you'll find that the page is not framed (`http://www.netscape.com/`), although sometimes the page has a button that lets you display a framed version.

So what's wrong with frames? Well, the first problem was that Netscape Navigator 2, the first browser to support frames, didn't do so very well. Using the browser to display framed documents could crash the browser. Or frame borders might disappear. And the Back command would take you right out of the set of framed documents rather than back to the previous document you viewed within a frame. A system designed to help users navigate hypertext without getting lost sometimes did the opposite!

It's true that Netscape Navigator 3 and Internet Explorer 3 handle frames very well, fixing most if not all of the previous problems. However, Netscape Navigator 2 is still in wide use at the time of writing, so this is still a significant problem, even though Version 3 has been available for a long time. (Many major service providers still distribute Netscape Navigator 2 to their customers.)

Another problem is that a framed document that might look great at a high resolution may look absolutely awful at VGA — and a significant number of users are still working with VGA. Look at ads for computers in the computer magazines and your local newspaper, and you'll see that most are still being sold with 15-inch monitors and many with 14-inch monitors; most of these users are working with VGA resolution, 640 × 480. If you are going to create frames, it's *essential* that you check them out at VGA resolution. You may find the view so cramped, especially if you use three or more frames in a browser at once, that the system is unusable. Take a look at Figure 12-1, for instance. You'll see that some of the text has disappeared below the bottom of the window, and there's no way to view it. This illustration was created at a resolution of 640 × 480, but some text is still hidden even at 800 × 600. Perhaps the author was working at a resolution of 1024 × 768 and didn't bother to check.

Consider also that a still-significant number of users are working with browsers that can't display frames at all — perhaps 10 percent of all users. So you should seriously consider providing both a framed version of your site and a normal, nonframed version.

Some people really do hate frames! If you want to hear why, see Web sites such as The Campaign against Frames, The Crash Site ("using frames and not-too-tricky techniques, I intend to crash your browser!"), Why Frames Suck, and Frames Are Pure Evil. You can find links to these sites at Yahoo's http://www.yahoo.com/Computers_and_Internet/Internet/World_Wide_Web/Browsers/Netscape_Navigator/Enhancement_Humor/Frames page.

Summary

Frames are fun. Frames are easy. Frames can be a nuisance. I've shown you how to create frames, and I've explained why you might not want to. I personally think that frames are really handy, but there are too many Web authors using high-resolution monitors and not considering what their viewers may be working with. This is a problem with many aspects of authoring for the Web, but it's of particular importance with frames, because frames can make a site next to useless for people using low-resolution monitors.

There's a tendency in computing for users to quickly adopt tools that are fun and easy to use, and then to overuse them. Not so long ago, when working with multiple fonts became something that many computer users could do, half the world started turning out documents that looked like ransom notes — half a dozen different typefaces on a page. Now that color printers are getting cheap, we'll probably see all sorts of horrible color combinations on paper (as we already do on the Web). So before you use frames everywhere you can, and in particular before you start using more than two frames in a frameset, think about whether you are using the technique for the user's benefit or for your own. If Netscape Communications has seen the wisdom of using frames sparingly, so should you!

CHAPTER THIRTEEN

GETTING STARTED WITH FORMS

IN THIS CHAPTER YOU LEARN THESE KEY SKILLS

You've seen forms in Web pages. You know, forms into which you can type information about yourself and register, forms that let you search for information at the Web site, forms that allow you to send information to the owner of the Web site, and so on.

But forms really comprise two main parts. There's the physical form itself that you can see and use — the check boxes, text boxes, buttons, and other components. Then there's the program, the script, that carries out the actions when you submit the information that was entered into the form.

Creating the first part, the physical form, is quite easy and always has been. For instance, type this into an HTML document:

```
<form>
<input type="text" size="20">
<input type="submit">
</form>
```

You've just created a text box and a submit button. But what good are these? What can they do for you? Nothing, at least not without the second part of the system, the script. And that's where things get tricky. You can teach anyone to use HTML to create a form in a few minutes, and FrontPage makes it even simpler, of course. But creating a script is not so easy, and it's not easy to learn, either. For instance, you may want a form to be *validated*, that is, checked for incorrect input, so the user doesn't type a number into a name field, or a word into a zip code field, and so on. Then, what happens when they submit the form? Is the information placed into a text file? Placed into a Web page? All these things are carried out using scripting of some kind, and to script you need to understand the script language you are using, and have at least some basic programming skills. Unless, that is, you are using FrontPage.

TIP **You can create forms whether or not you are using a FrontPage-enabled server. However, as you'll see in Chapter 15, some of the page handlers will run only if you are using a FrontPage-enabled server, that is, one with the FrontPage server extensions installed. Forms will not actually do anything unless you have set up a form handler of some kind. So if you are not using a FrontPage-enabled server you will need to use CGI scripts or something similar.**

FrontPage makes creating forms very quick and easy, as you'll see in this chapter. FrontPage gives you two ways to create forms. You can create them from scratch, by placing form components into your Web pages one by one and telling FrontPage what to do with each one. Or you can use a wizard or template to create a particular type of form in just a few seconds or minutes. I'm going to begin by showing you how to use one of the templates to create a form. Then I'll show you how to use the Form Page wizard. In the following chapter you'll learn how to modify the form that is created by the template or wizard, by adding more fields or configuring the ones you've got.

Using Wizards and Templates

You'll probably find that the form you want to create is already available, just waiting for you to run the wizard or pick a template and create it. Here's what's currently available; these are the templates and wizards available in FrontPage Editor's New Page dialog box:

Confirmation Form — Use this in conjunction with another form page; this one displays a message thanking the user for the submission. You can insert a Confirmation Bot (see Chapter 15) to show the user what he or she submitted.

Feedback Form — A form collecting information from the user and saving it in a text file. We'll look at this form in a moment.

Form Page Wizard — A wizard that helps you create a form. You pick the information that you want to collect, format the form, tell FrontPage how you want the submitted data saved, then save the form as a Web page or copy it to an existing page. See "Creating a Form with the Form Page Wizard," later in this chapter.

Guest Book — More correctly called a comments book, really, though it could be modified to also collect names and e-mail addresses. The user types a comment, which is added to the bottom of the Web page using the Include Bot. You can also modify the page to do something different with the information submitted. See Chapter 16.

Product or Event Registration — The user enters registration information, selects from a list of options, chooses an option button, and submits the data. See Chapter 16.

Search Page — A simple text-search form that will search the Web site, along with instructions on how to enter a search query. See Chapter 16.

Survey Form — A form split into four sections. Responses are saved in a text document. See Chapter 16.

User Registration — Creates a self-registration form. The user enters a name and password. This information can be used on subsequent visits to confirm his or her identity. See Chapter 17.

The following wizard is accessed from FrontPage Explorer's New FrontPage Web dialog box:

Discussion Web Wizard — A wizard that quickly creates discussion groups. See Chapter 17.

TIP **Other wizards may become available later. Wizards are executable program files — you'll find them in the \Program Files\Microsoft FrontPage\Pages\ directory, in subdirectories named wizardname.wiz — along with various associated files, so you can easily add new ones by creating a new directory and placing the wizard files inside it.**

13

We'll be looking at these wizards and templates in more detail. In this chapter we'll look at the Feedback Form and the Form Page wizard. See Chapter 16 for details about the others.

Using the Feedback Form

Let's get started by using the Feedback Form template. This is a form in which users can send you suggestions about your Web site. They can pick a category (Complaint, Problem, Suggestion, Praise), enter a comment, and include contact information if they wish.

1. In the FrontPage Editor select File → New.
2. In the New Page box select Feedback Form and click OK. FrontPage creates the document you see in Figure 13-1.

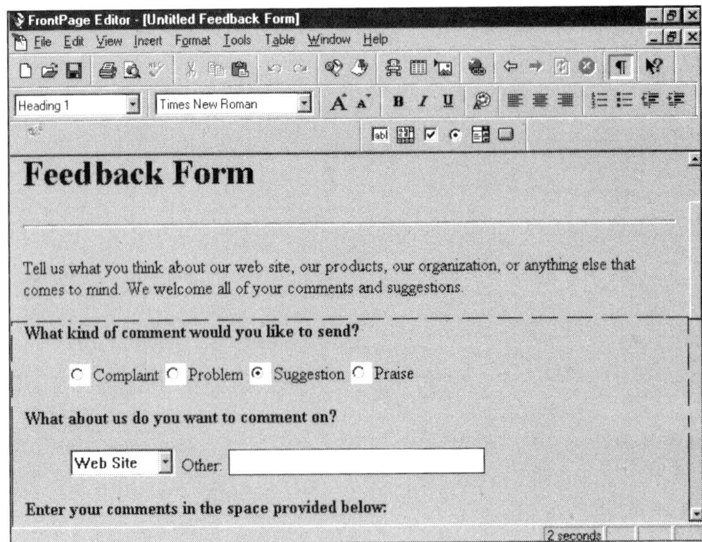

Figure 13-1 The Feedback Form

3. At the very top of the page is a comment (not shown in the illustration); click the comment and press Delete to remove it.
4. Modify the text in this page, if you wish. For instance, you might replace the title, Feedback Form, and modify the text immediately above and below the form.
5. Save the document.
6. Preview the document in a Web browser (see Chapter 5). You can see part of the form in Figure 13-2.

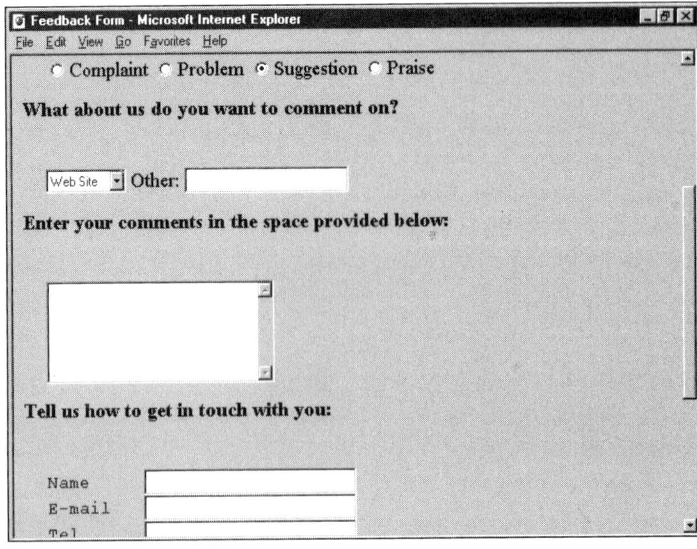

Figure 13-2 Here's what the form looks like in a Web browser.

7. Try the form; enter data into the form, then click the Submit Comments button at the bottom.

8. You'll see a Form Confirmation page, showing the information you've submitted.

9. Switch to FrontPage Explorer and select Tools → Recalculate Hyperlinks.

10. When FrontPage Explorer has finished recalculating, look in the _private\ directory. You should see the feedback.txt file.

11. Double-click the file to open it in Windows Notepad.

That was easy. You've just created a form, and it took you all of 30 seconds. Of course it may not be quite what you want, so you can modify it, as you'll see in Chapter 14.

Viewing the Submitted Data

Open the feedback.txt form in a word processor or text editor, and you'll see something like this:

```
"MessageType"    "Subject"     "SubjectOther"      "Comments"
  "UserName"     "UserEmail"   "UserTel"     "UserFAX"
  "ContactRequested"    "Date" "Time" "Remote Name" "Remote User"
  "HTTP User Agent"
"Complaint"      "Products"     ""      "Your program stinks! It's
  about as much use as a pig on a bicycle!""Peter Kent"
  "pkent@arundel.com"  "303-555-1869"       ""
  "ContactRequested"   "11/25/96"    "11:56:34 AM" "127.0.0.1"
  "Mozilla/2.0 (compatible; MSIE 3.0; Windows 95)"
```

13

This is a bit of a jumble, really. However, it's intended for use by a database program. Import this into your database program and you'll quickly see that you have a series of columns. The first entries in this file are the column headings, starting with MessageType and finishing with HTTP User Agent. The rest of the data are the individual form submissions. So, in this case, the MessageType was Complaint, the Subject was Products, the SubjectOther was left blank, and so on.

The very last column, HTTP User Agent, is not shown in the form itself but is the type of the Web browser used by the person submitting the information. *Mozilla/2.0* refers to Netscape Navigator (Mozilla is its code name), but *compatible; MSIE 3.0;* means that this browser is not actually Navigator 2.0 but is a Navigator 2.0–compatible browser, MS Internet Explorer 3.0. You can also see that it was running on Windows 95.

Modifying the Form

You may want to modify this form, for a variety of reasons. You might want to add new fields, or remove some that are already there. You might want to rename the fields the Form Confirmation page was a little messy, really, containing names like SubjectOther, UserName, UserEmail, UserTel, and UserFAX.

You might also want to set up form validation, to make sure the user enters information correctly. For instance, you may want to accept submissions only from users who enter a phone number. You can validate the form, to make sure that the user has entered a phone number into the phone number field.

To modify a form, right-click a form component and select one of these:

Script Wizard	Opens the Script wizard (see Chapter 9), so you can write a JavaScript or VBScript associated with the form component.
List Properties	FrontPage lines up some form components — such as collections of text boxes or option buttons — using HTML list format. You can use this to modify the type of list format used. See Chapter 6.
Form Properties	Opens the Form Properties dialog box, so you can modify the properties for the entire form. See Chapter 14.
Form Field Validation	Opens a box in which you can set up field validation, to make sure the user enters the right sort of information. See Chapter 14.
Form Field Properties	Opens a Field Properties dialog box so you can modify the field element's name, value, size, and so on. See Chapter 14.

TIP **Double-click a form element to open its Properties dialog box.**

We're not going to see how to modify the form components right now; I'll explain that in Chapter 14.

Creating a Form with the Form Page Wizard

The Form Page wizard helps you build a customized form to your specifications. Here's how to use it:

1. In FrontPage Editor, select File → New, select Form Page Wizard, and click OK. The Form Page Wizard dialog box opens. Click Next to begin and you'll see the dialog box shown in Figure 13-3.

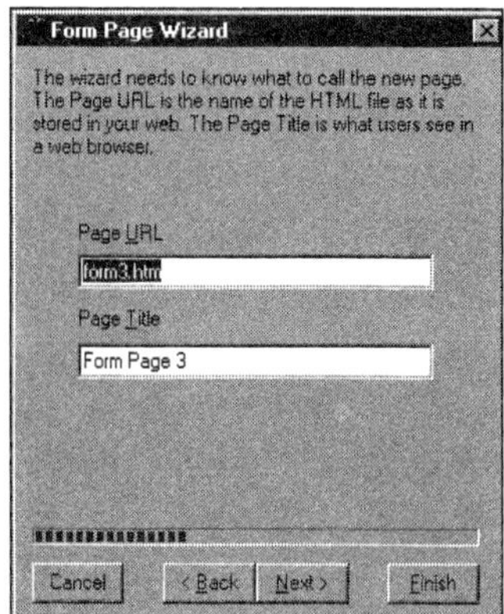

Figure 13-3 The Form Page wizard

2. Type a filename into the Page URL text box, and a page title into the Page Title text box, then click Next to see the dialog box shown in Figure 13-4.

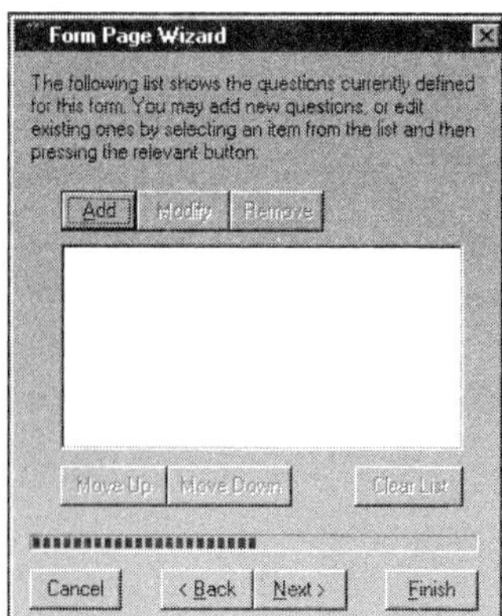

Figure 13-4 Add form elements here.

3. Click Add to add the first form element. You'll see the information shown in Figure 13-5.

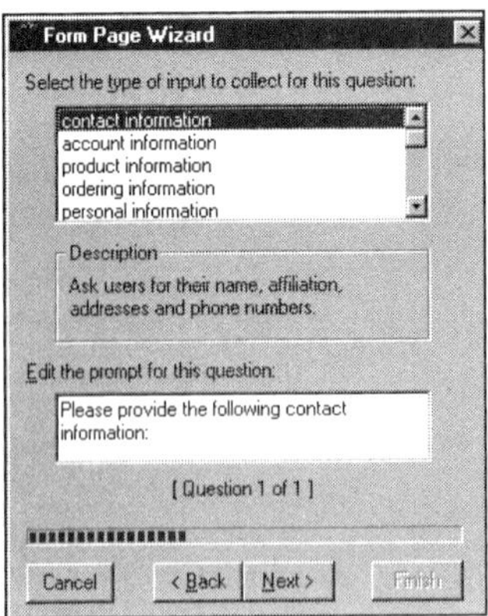

Figure 13-5 Select the type of information you want to collect.

4. The top text box shows you the type of information that you can collect; when you click one of these, look in the lower text box and you'll see the field label that the user is shown in the form. This will give you a better idea of what the field is for. For instance, select Paragraph in the top text box, and the lower box displays *What do you think of...?*

5. When you've selected the first field you want to add to the form (you can only select one, but don't worry — you'll get a chance to add more), click Next and you'll see configuration information for the type of field you are adding. We'll look at these in more detail under "The Form Page Wizard's Fields," in a moment.

6. Make any modifications to the field configuration information, and click Next. You'll find yourself back at the box you saw in Figure 13-4. To add another field click Add.

7. When you've added all the fields you want, click Next in the box shown in Figure 13-4. You'll see the information shown in Figure 13-6.

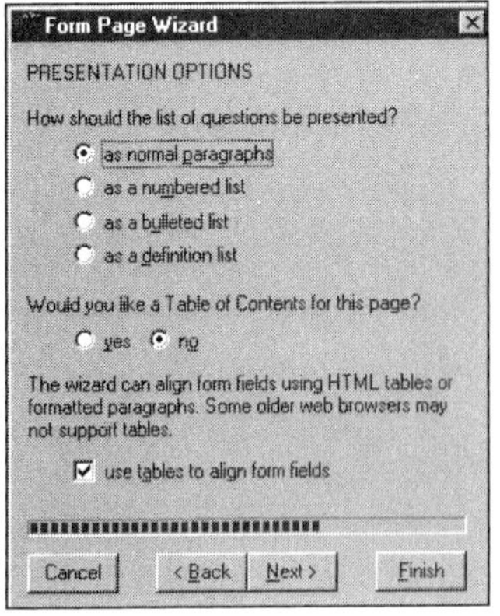

Figure 13-6 Tell FrontPage how this form should be formatted.

8. Select one of the option buttons to define how the fields should be listed: just as normal paragraphs, or as one of the list types.

9. Select whether or not you want a table of contents created for the page. If Yes, then FrontPage creates a series of links near the top of the form, linking down to bookmarks it creates for every group of form elements you added.

10. Leave the Use Tables to Align Form Fields check box checked if you want to let FrontPage use tables to format the form, to line everything up. While it's true that some older browsers can't display tables, the vast majority can, including all versions of Netscape and Internet Explorer; so more than 95 percent of World Wide Web users are working with table-enabled browsers.

11. Click Next to see the information shown in Figure 13-7.

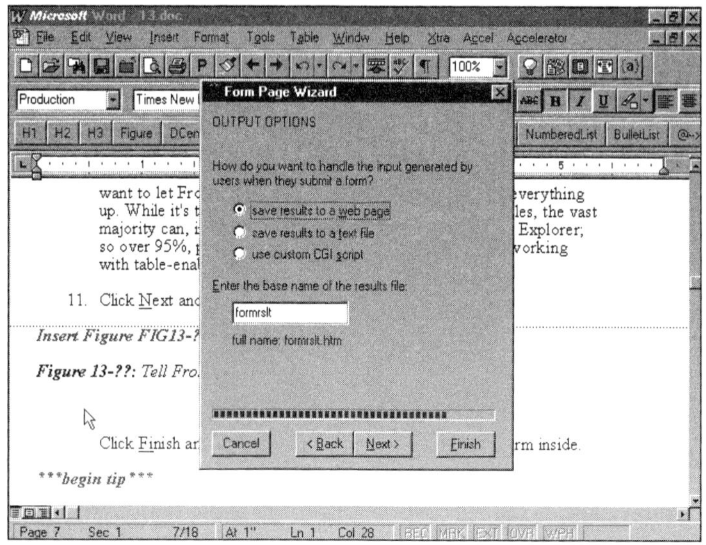

Figure 13-7 Tell FrontPage how to handle the data submitted.

12. Select one of the ways to handle submitted data: Save Results to a Web Page (the data is taken from the form and added to an HTML page), Save Results to a Text File (the data is taken from the form and added to a text file), or Use Custom CGI Script (the data is sent to a Common Gateway Interface script).

13. If you selected one of the first two options, you can type a filename to be used for the .htm or .txt file (or simply accept the name provided).

14. Click Next, then click Finish, and FrontPage creates a Web page with your form inside.

The form may be completely finished, or it may not. For instance, if you chose Use Custom CGI Script in the wizard, you now have to tell FrontPage where to send the data. That's done by clicking the Settings button in the Form Properties dialog box; see Chapter 14.

The Form Page Wizard's Fields

The following tables show the different fields that you can select in the Form Page wizard (see Figure 13-5), with a quick description of each. The selections you see in each box are not necessarily the defaults; I've tried to display most of the elements in the sample illustrations showing the form that is created.

Notice that every form element or group of elements has a text box labeled something like Enter the Base Name for This Group of Variables, or Enter the Name of a Variable to Hold This Answer. Each field needs a name, so that when data is submitted the form handler working with the data (see Chapter 15) is able to identify the data from the field. In cases where you're creating multiple fields at once, you enter a base name, and FrontPage uses that as a prefix: for instance, if the base name is Contact, then the field names are Contact_FullName, Contact_Title, Contact_WorkPhone, and so on. In some cases you are creating a single form field, so you get to enter the full name.

CONTACT INFORMATION

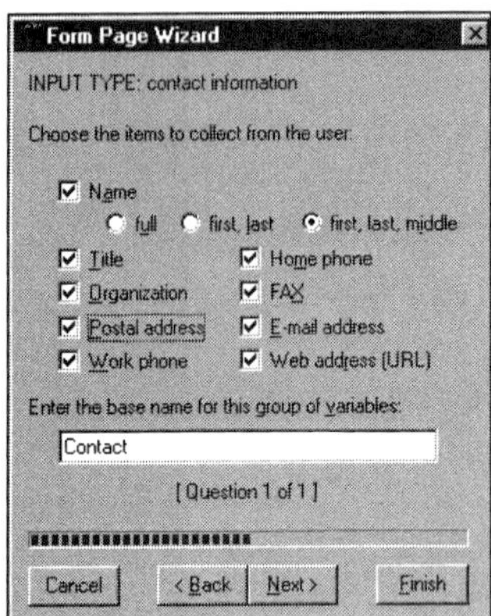

This information is presented as a column of text boxes. If you select Name, you can pick one of the radio buttons, which define how many text boxes you get for the name: one, two, or three.

bigform - Microsoft Internet Explorer

File Edit View Go Favorites Help

Please provide the following contact information:

First name
Last name
Middle initial
Title
Organization
Street address
Address (cont.)
City
State/Province
Zip/Postal code
Country
Work Phone
Home Phone
FAX

ACCOUNT INFORMATION

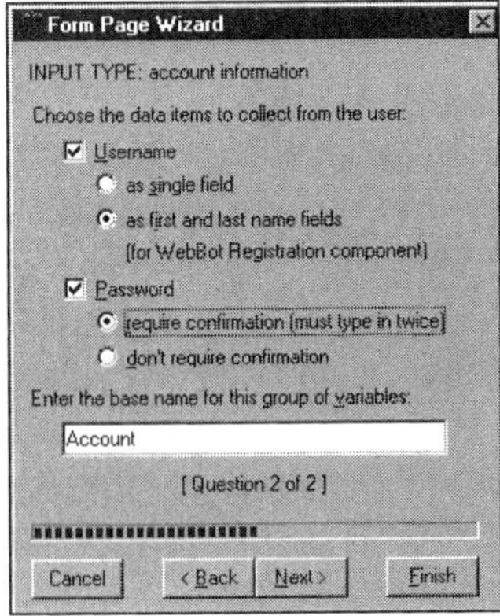

This information is typically used to create a little log-on form, used by the WebBot Registration Component form handler (see Chapter 15 for information about form handlers). The option buttons in both cases let you choose either one field or two fields.

Please provide your account information:

First name
Last name
Password
Confirm password

PRODUCT INFORMATION

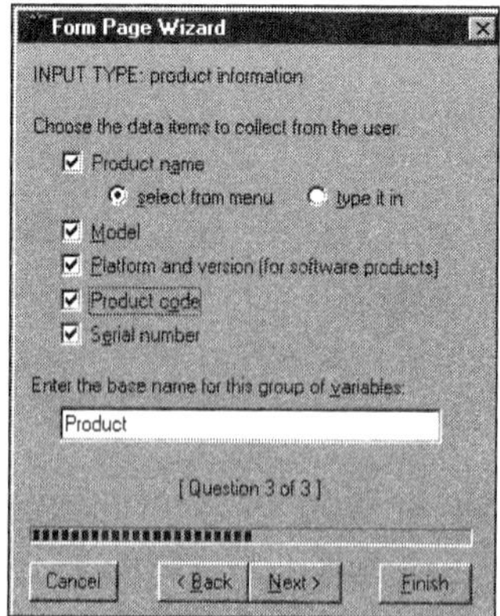

This form is used to gather information about a product the user is working with. All fields are text boxes, unless you select the first option button, Select from a Menu, which actually means Select from a Drop-Down List Box.

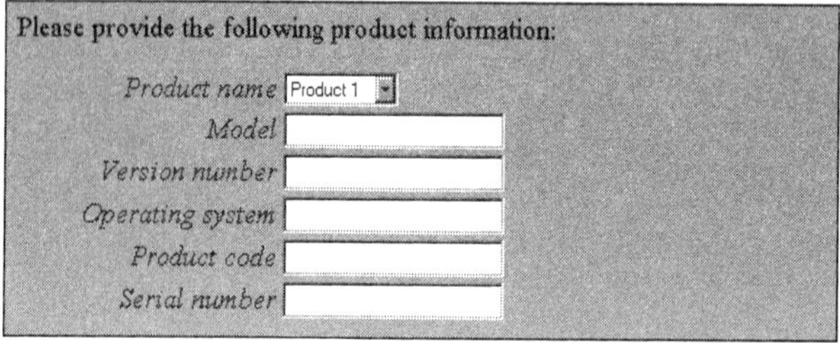

ORDERING INFORMATION

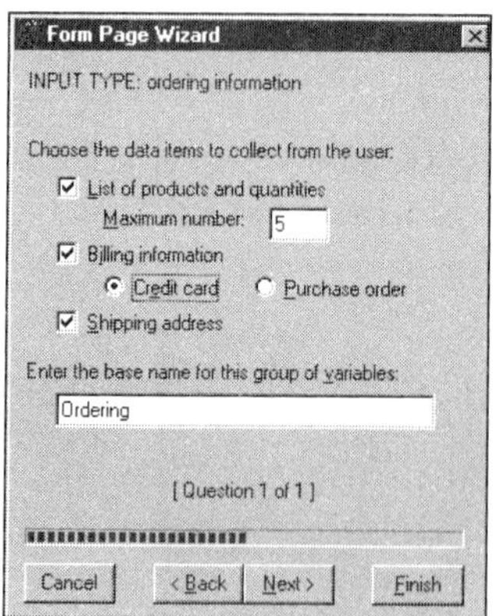

This is a form that takes ordering information: products and quantities, billing and shipping information. All the fields are text boxes, unless you select the Credit Card option button, in which case you'll see a drop-down list box for credit card types.

Form Page 8 - Microsoft Internet Explorer
File Edit View Go Favorites Help
QTY DESCRIPTION
BILLING
Credit card VISA
Cardholder name
Card number
Expiration date
SHIPPING
Street address
Address (cont.)
City

PERSONAL INFORMATION

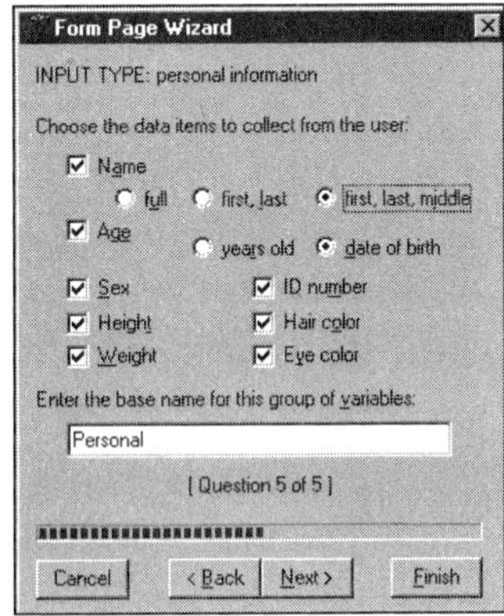

This one collects personal information. Most of the elements are text boxes, with the exception of Sex (option buttons), and Hair Color and Eye Color (drop-down list boxes).

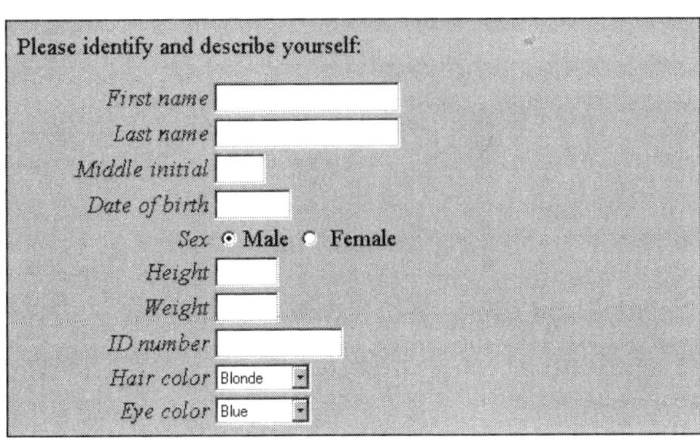

ONE OF SEVERAL OPTIONS

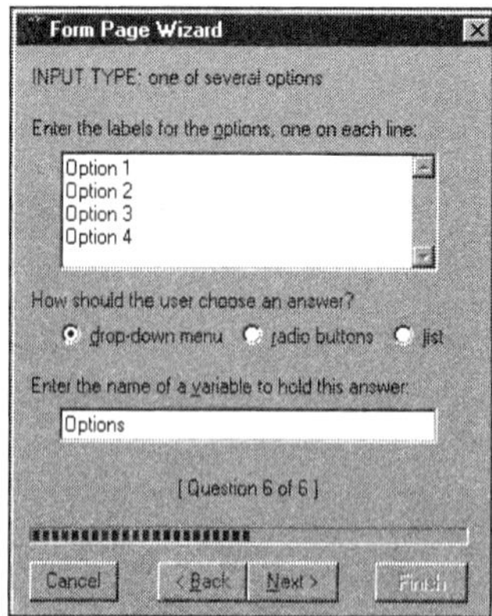

This creates an element that is used to select *only one* option from a group of possible selections. You can choose a drop-down list box, radio buttons, or an open list box. Type the names of the options into the list box; press Enter after typing each one.

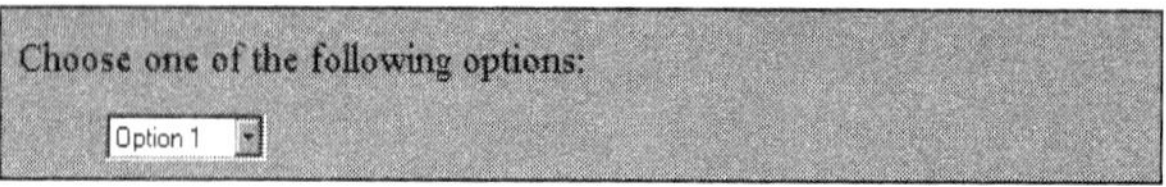

ANY OF SEVERAL OPTIONS

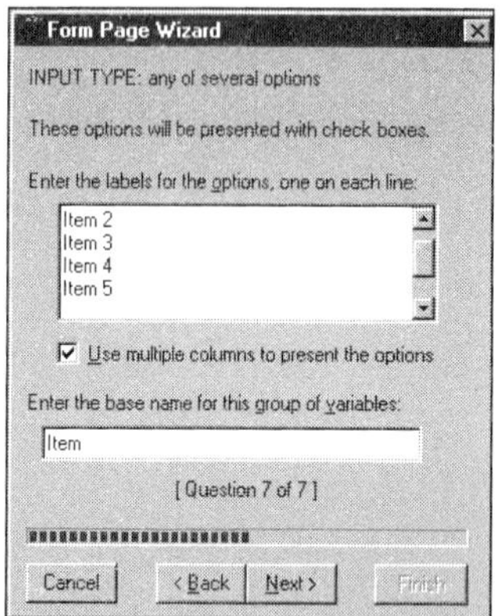

This form is used to select *one or more* options from a group of possible selections, by clicking check boxes. Type the names of the options into the list box; press Enter after typing each one. If you want to allow FrontPage to spread the check boxes across the page, select Use Multiple Columns to Present the Options; otherwise you'll get a single column.

Select any of the following options that apply:

☐ Item 1 ☐ Item 2 ☐ Item 3 ☐ Item 4
☐ Item 5 ☐ Item 6 ☐ Item 7

BOOLEAN

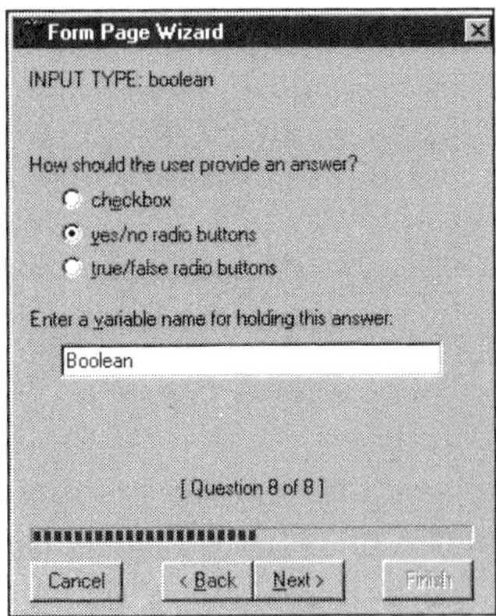

This form lets the user enter a simple *Boolean* yes or no answer. (Boolean logic is a system in which variables are manipulated through the use of various operators: AND, OR, NOT, and so on.) You can select Checkbox (in which case you get a single check box that, when clicked on, submits the value ON; you'll learn about how forms submit information in Chapter 15), Yes and No radio buttons, and True and False radio buttons.

DATE

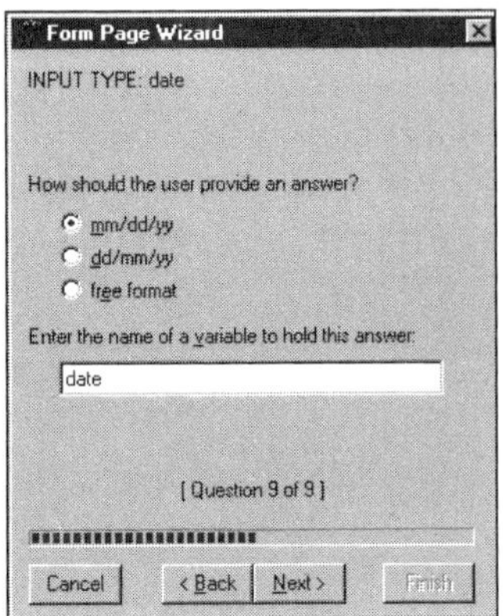

This field enables you to collect a date from the user. The date is entered into a text box; the option buttons merely define what label should appear next to the text box. FrontPage does not validate the date, regardless of which option button you select (see Chapter 14 for information on validation).

TIME

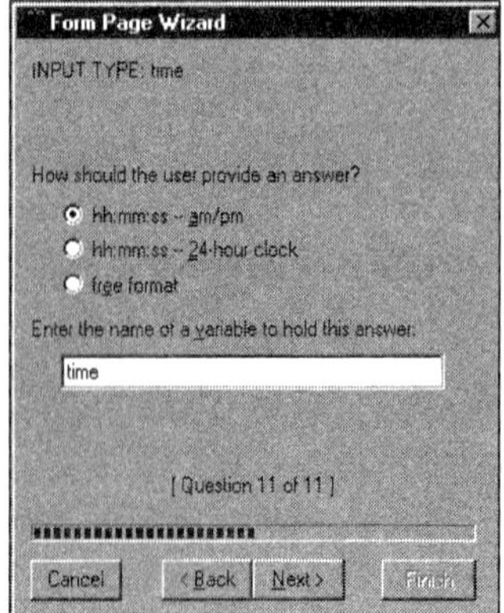

This is just like the Date field, only for time. Again, the option buttons merely define the label that appears next to the text box, and FrontPage does not set up validation criteria.

RANGE

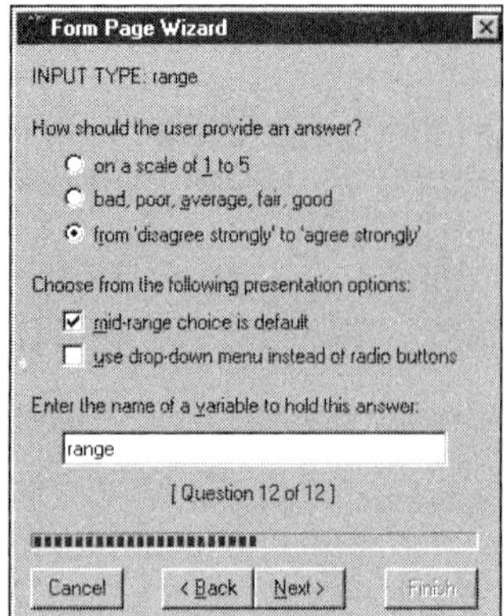

This lets the user select an option, either from radio buttons (the default) or from a drop-down list box (check the Use Drop-Down Menu Instead of Radio Buttons check box). This is functionally the same as the One of Several Options field group, with the difference that FrontPage enters five options for you to choose from, and you can select their names using the radio buttons. Also, check the Mid-Range Choice is Default check box to automatically select the middle option. Otherwise none of the options will be selected, even if you are using radio buttons.

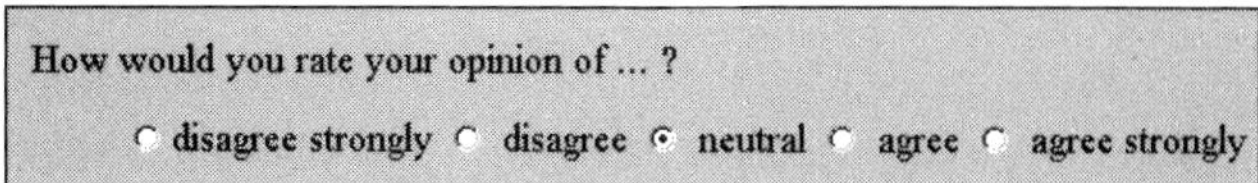

NUMBER

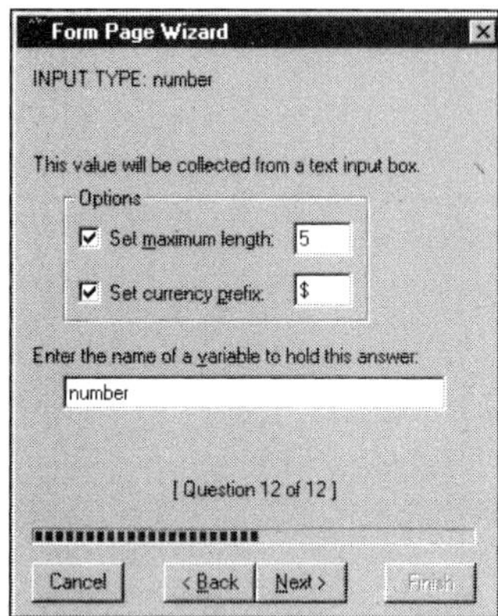

This form element enables you to collect a number or currency value. You can define the maximum length of the box (no, this isn't the maximum value, merely the number of characters that will fit in the box) and provide a currency prefix, too. (To use a different currency prefix you can copy a symbol from the FrontPage Editor; see Chapter 6 for information about using the Symbol dialog box.)

STRING

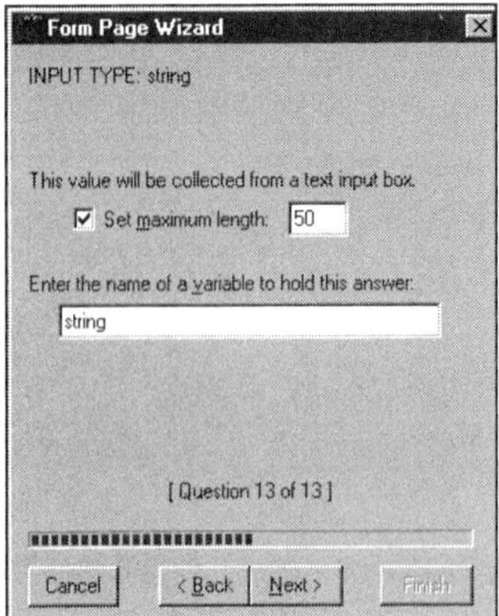

This form element is a text box into which the user may type a short note. If you wish, you can define the maximum number of characters that may be typed into the comment.

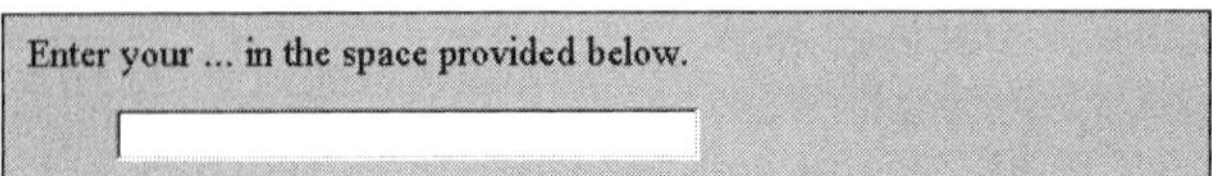

PARAGRAPH

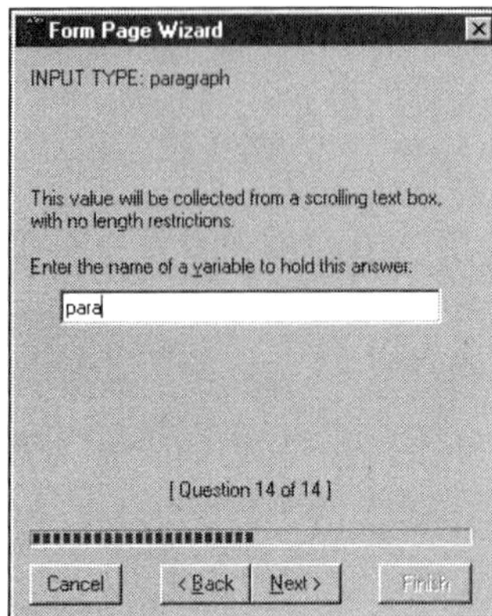

This form element is simply a larger version of the previous element; rather than getting a text box you get a *textarea* — a scrolling, multiline text box — so the user can type a comment as large as he or she wishes. There are no configuration options for this element.

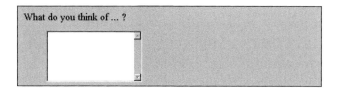

What do you think of ... ?

BONUS

Moving and Formatting Forms

Do you want to place a form directly into a page, rather than create a new page? The templates and wizards all create new pages, but that's OK, because you can quickly move the form to another page.

To copy a form, point at the top left corner of the form. (If you can't see the dotted-line box around the form, so you're not quite sure where the corner is, ¶ click the Show/Hide toolbar button.) Make sure the arrow is pointing up and toward the left, not the right, then double-click and the form is selected. Press Ctrl+C and the form is copied to the Clipboard (or Ctrl+X and it's removed from the page and placed into the Clipboard). Then go to the page where you want to put the form, place the cursor in the insertion position, and press Ctrl+V.

TIP **This also provides a quick way to delete a form. Select the form and then press Delete.**

You can also format forms using all the normal text and paragraph formatting tools, to get the form to look just right. You might also want to consider linking from some of the field labels to pages that explain what these fields are for, to help the user fill out the form. Remember to have a link on the explanatory form taking the user back to the form at the position he or she left the form.

Summary

Getting FrontPage to create forms for you is very quick and easy. It can take literally seconds to create forms using the templates and wizards. In this chapter you've seen how to use a simple form template and how to use the more complicated Form Page wizard. In the next chapter you'll see how to create forms from scratch, by inserting individual form components into your page and configuring them.

But most users probably won't create many forms from scratch. They'll use the templates and wizards and modify them to their needs. That's OK, though. Read about how to create forms from scratch, because then you'll learn how each form component works, so you'll be able to modify them when you need to.

We'll be returning to templates and wizards later, in Chapter 16, when you'll see how to use them to create several common types of forms.

CHAPTER FOURTEEN

CREATING AND MODIFYING FORMS

IN THIS CHAPTER YOU LEARN THESE KEY SKILLS

I've already recommended that you not create a form from scratch if you can help it. So why do we have an entire chapter devoted to creating forms? Because you still need to know how to modify the forms, and the simplest way to explain that is to show you how you add form elements to a form, and how you configure those elements.

In this chapter you'll see how to create a form, but more important, the information will help you to modify forms. Whenever possible, use one of FrontPage's templates or wizards to create your forms, then edit them to suit. For instance, if you want a discussion group at your Web site, you could create it from scratch, but it would probably take several hours of figuring it all out. Or you could spend five minutes or less using the Discussion Web Wizard to create it.

Creating a Form

You begin creating a form by simply placing a form element into your page. You can do that by using the forms toolbar (select **View** → **Forms Toolbar**), or by selecting an option from the **Insert** → **Form Field** menu. When you do this, FrontPage places the element into the page inside a large dotted-line box

¶ (if you can't see the dotted-line box, click the Show/Hide toolbar button). This dotted-line box shows the boundaries of the form. As long as you add more elements within the box they are placed within the form. Enter a form element outside the form, and FrontPage creates a new form.

TIP **You can also type inside a form to add form labels and explanatory text. I'm going to explain how to work with the form elements; use the text-formatting techniques you've already learned to lay out the form and add text.**

Table 14-1 shows you the toolbar buttons, along with a description of the form field that each creates and a picture of that field.

TABLE 14-1 The Forms Toolbar and Form Fields

Button	Field	Description
abl		A text box (HTML type="text") or password box (HTML type="password"). A user can type a single line of text into this.
		A textarea (HTML type="textarea"). A multiline text box. (FrontPage refers to this as a scrolling text box.)
		A check box (HTML type="checkbox"). A user can click this box to make a selection.
		An option or radio button (HTML type="radio"). A user can select one button in a set of buttons.
		A selection list (HTML type="select"). A user can select an entry from the list. The list may be a drop-down list box displaying one entry or a static list displaying several, depending on how it's been set up. (FrontPage refers to this component, ambiguously, as a *drop-down menu*.)
	Submit	A command button (HTML type="reset" or "submit" or "button" — by default it's a submit button). The user clicks a button to carry out an action. (FrontPage refers to this as a *push* button.)

When you click one of these buttons or select the menu option, FrontPage drops the default component into the form. You can then edit it by double-clicking it.

Working with Form Fields

Let's examine each form field in turn. I'll show you how to create it and, more important, how to modify the manner in which it works.

Creating a Text Box

abl To create a text box, select **Insert** → **Form Field** → **One-Line Text Box**, or click the One-Line Text Box button. Double-click the element to open the dialog box in Figure 14-1.

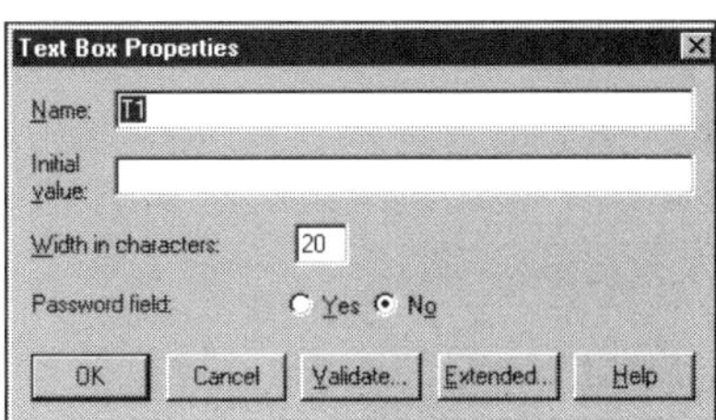

Figure 14-1 The Text Box Properties dialog box

Provide this information:

Name FrontPage has already provided a name for this field. You can, if you wish, rename it to something that you'll more easily remember. This is the name that will appear in, for instance, the text file that is used to store submitted information, so you'll almost certainly want to provide a new name. It may also appear in a confirmation field or procedure-failure field, so you'll almost certainly want to make sure the name makes sense to the user.

Initial Value This is the text, if any, that appears in the text box when the user first views the form. You can leave it blank if you wish, or provide default text.

Width in Characters How wide the box should be, measured in characters.

Password Field If you click the Yes option button, this field will not be a true text field; it will be an <input type="password"> field. This is commonly used in forms in which the user must type a password, such as forms in which he or she registers (see Chapter 15). The user won't see what he or she types into the field; rather, the user will see asterisks.

Validate You can validate the contents of this box, to make sure that the user enters the correct information (or, at least, information that appears to be in the correct format). By default this box is set up so that the form is accepted even if the user enters no information. If you want to set validation information, click Validate and the dialog box shown in Figure 14-2 opens.

14

VALIDATING YOUR DATA

You can automatically validate form entry, to make sure that the user has entered data that is appropriate. FrontPage can validate data in two ways: by creating a JavaScript or by creating a VBScript. (JavaScript is used in most browsers, VBScript currently in few.)

That doesn't mean that the validation procedure will work even if you place your Web pages at a non–FrontPage-enabled Web server, though. Yes, JavaScript and VBScript are scripting languages that are built into browsers. But FrontPage creates those scripts using the FrontPage server extensions (it uses a special GeneratedScript WebBot), so unless the page is at a FrontPage server, the scripts won't be created.

Which method, then, should you use? You should probably use JavaScript. Don't use VBScript unless you are sure that all your site users are working with VBScript browsers — something that is likely only on a corporate network using Internet Explorer. Most browsers currently do not use VBScript.

TIP **To define which sort of script is used to validate data, select Tools → Web Settings in FrontPage Explorer, click the Advanced tab, then select from the Validation Scripts Language drop-down list box. Select JavaScript, VBScript, or <None> (meaning FrontPage server extensions).**

Click the Validate button in the Text Box Properties dialog box. As you can see in Figure 14-2, when you first open the Text Box Validation dialog box the Data Type is set to No Constraints. That means the user can type anything — the form is not validated. Most of this dialog box is therefore disabled until you select an option from the Data Type drop-down list box. And once you've done this, inappropriate parts of the box remain disabled.

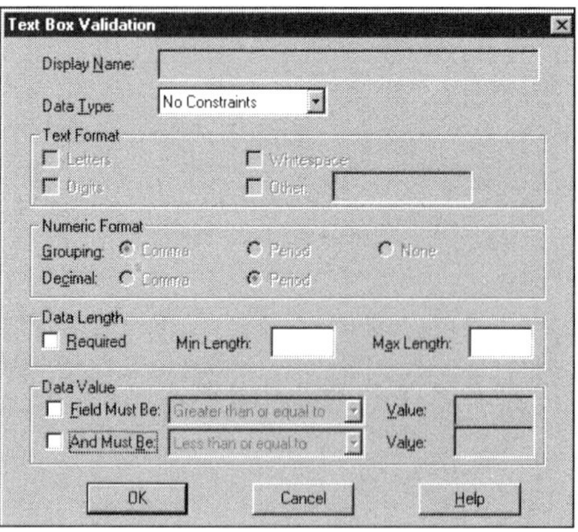

Figure 14-2 The Text Box Validation dialog box

Here are your options:

Display Name The name that will appear in the error-message box when referring to this field. For instance, you might have a field called FName, but it would make more sense to call it First Name in the error message. If you don't enter a name, FrontPage will use the field name instead.

Data Type Select No Constraints (the user can type anything); Text (the user can type any letters, numbers, or characters, depending on the settings in the Text Format area); Integer (the user can type whole numbers, but no text or decimal places — except for a comma or period used for grouping digits, as explained under "Grouping" below); or Number (the user can type a number including a decimal place, but no text).

Text Format This is where you define the text format, if you select Text in the Data Type.

Letters Check this if you want to allow the user to type letters.

Digits Check this if you want to allow the user to type numbers.

Whitespace Check this if you want to allow the user to include spaces and tabs.

Other Check this if you want to allow the user to type other characters. You must then type the characters (such as commas, the @ symbol, and so on) into the text box.

Numeric Format This is where you define the integer or number format, if you selected Integer or Number in the Data Type section.

Grouping The character the user may enter to divide thousands, as in 55,100. In North America the character is the comma, but in some areas of the world the period is used.

Decimal The character used to mark the number's decimal place; in North America the character is the period, but in some areas of the world the comma is used.

14

Data Length You can check to see how many characters have been entered into the field. If you expect a number that is at least 100, then you can specify a minimum length of 3, for instance. If you want to specify a minimum but not a maximum, or vice versa, simply leave one box empty and specify the other length.

Required The way this check box works is a little ambiguous. If the Required check box is cleared, then the user doesn't have to enter anything into this field; if he or she does enter something, though, it must be within the minimum and maximum values, if any. If the Required check box is checked, the user *must* enter something — unless the Min Length box is empty.

TIP **To make sure that the user enters something, you must check the Required check box *and* enter a value into the Min Length box.**

Data Value These settings make the validation procedure compare what the user has typed with something that you specify. You can select two matches, so you can make the data match two different criteria. The criteria are Less Than, Greater Than, Less Than or Equal To, Greater Than or Equal To, Equal To, and Not Equal To.

By the way, the data values can work with both numbers and text. With numbers it's obvious how these work, of course; for instance, if the field is an age field, and the user must be at least age eighteen, you could enter the number 18 in the Field Must Be Value box, and select Greater Than or Equal To. If the user enters 15, for instance, he or she gets an error message.

If the field is a text field, or has no constraints specified, the validation process compares the value's alphabetical order. A is less than B, B is less than C, and so on. (Also, note that a is not the same as A; b is not the same as B.)

Creating a Textarea

To create what is commonly known as a textarea, or what FrontPage calls a scrolling text box, select Insert → Form Field → Scrolling Text Box, or click the One-Line Text Box button. Double-click the element to open the dialog box in Figure 14-3.

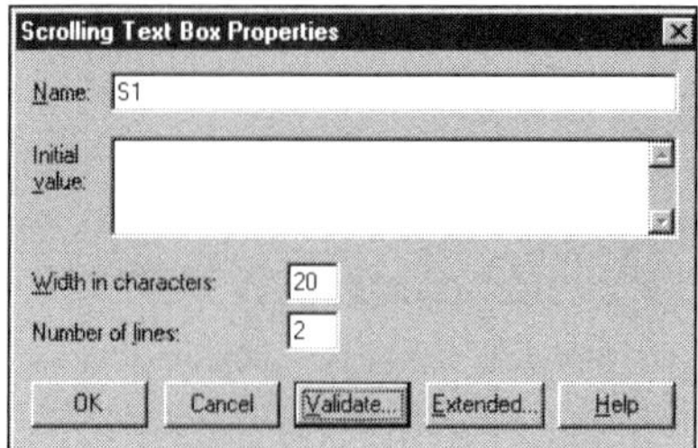

Figure 14-3 The Scrolling Text Box Properties dialog box, where you modify a textarea

These are your options:

Name Type the name of the element.

Initial Value This is the text that will appear in the textarea when the user first views the form.

Width in Characters The width of the textarea.

Number of Lines The number of lines visible in the textarea. The box will have scroll bars, so if all the text is not visible the user can scroll down to read more. As the user types, the box will scroll down to make room for more.

Validate Click here for validation information. It's the same as for the text box, so see "Validating Your Data," earlier in this chapter. Use this only if working with a FrontPage-enabled server.

Creating a Check Box

To create a check box, select **Insert** → **Form Field** → **Check Box** or click the One-Line Text Box button. Double-click the element to open the dialog box shown in Figure 14-4.

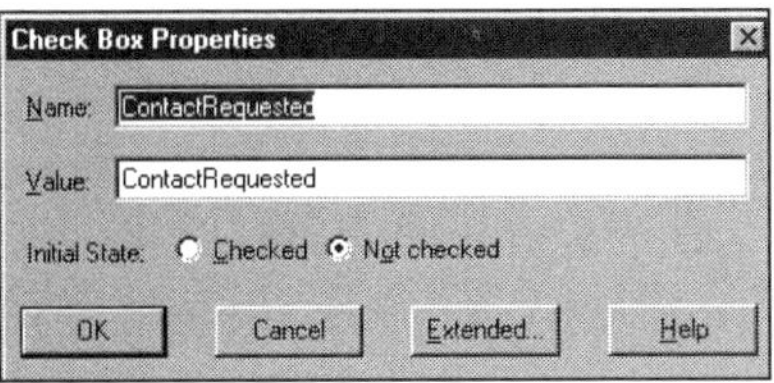

Figure 14-4 The Check Box Properties dialog box

These are the options:

Name Provide a name for the element.

Value This is the text that is submitted if the check box is checked when the user clicks the form's Submit button. For instance, in the Feedback Form we saw earlier, there's a check box at the bottom of the form that is labeled Please Contact Me as Soon as Possible Regarding This Matter. The check box's value is ContactRequested. In other words, if the user checks the box, the text ContractRequested is submitted and placed into the feedback.txt file. If the check box is not checked, no text is submitted.

Initial State You can define whether the check box is checked or not when the user first sees the form.

Creating an Option (Radio) Button

To create an option, or radio, button, select **Insert** → **Form Field** → **Radio Text Box**, or click the One-Line Text Box button. (*Option button* is the original Windows term. *Radio button* comes from the Macintosh world. On the Web the term is usually option button.)

Unlike check boxes, option buttons work only in sets. A single option button is always selected, and only one button in a set can be selected. So if, say, you have five buttons and the first is selected, when you click the fifth, that one is now selected and the first button is not. That's why option buttons are also known as radio buttons — they're like the old-style mechanical memory buttons used in car radios. When you press one button in, another pops out.

When you place an option button on a form, you've just begun a set. Place the next, and the next, and so on, and they're all part of the same set. In fact FrontPage, unless told otherwise, will assume that all option buttons in a form are part of the same set. In order to start a new set you must place the first button of the new set, double-click the button, and then type a new Group Name and click OK. From then on the buttons you create will be part of this new set.

Double-clicking the element opens the dialog box shown in Figure 14-5.

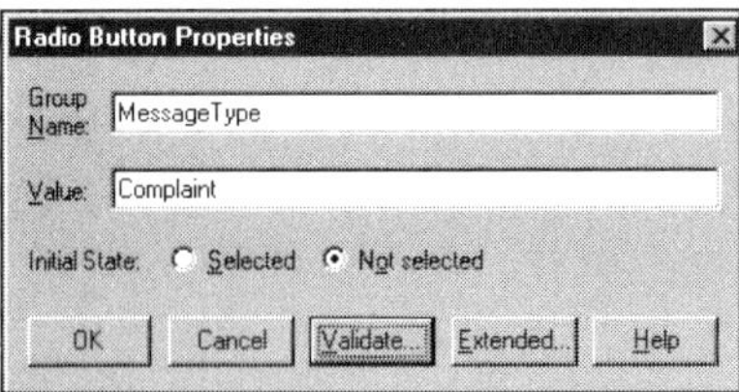

Figure 14-5 The Radio Button Properties dialog box

These are the options:

Group Name This is the name of the group of buttons of which this one is a member. To move a button from one group to another, or to start a new group, simply type a new name.

Value This is the text that is submitted if the option button is selected when the user clicks the form's Submit button. For instance, in the Feedback Form we saw earlier, there are four option buttons. Each has a different value: Complaint, Problem, Suggestion, and Praise. It's this text that is sent to the feedback.txt file, depending on which button is selected.

Initial State Click Selected to make this the selected button in the group; doing so removes the selection from the currently selected option button. Notice that you can also click Not Selected to make a button not selected. That's unusual, of course, as option button sets in programs normally have a button already selected, but HTML enables you to create sets with nonselected buttons.

Validate Click here to validate the option button set (you are defining validation for the entire set, not just the single option button you are configuring). You'll be able to select the Data Required check box. If this is checked, one of the option buttons must be selected before the user submits the data (remember, you can create option button sets with nonselected buttons, so this is a way to force your users to make a choice). You'll also be able to enter the Display Name, the name that the error message will contain when referring to this option button set.

Creating a Selection List

To create a selection list box, select Insert → Form Field → Drop Down Menu, or click the One-Line Text Box button. (Drop-Down Menu is an incorrect and ambiguous term — it may not drop down, and it's not a menu — so I'm going to call it a selection list.) Double-click the element to open the dialog box shown in Figure 14-6.

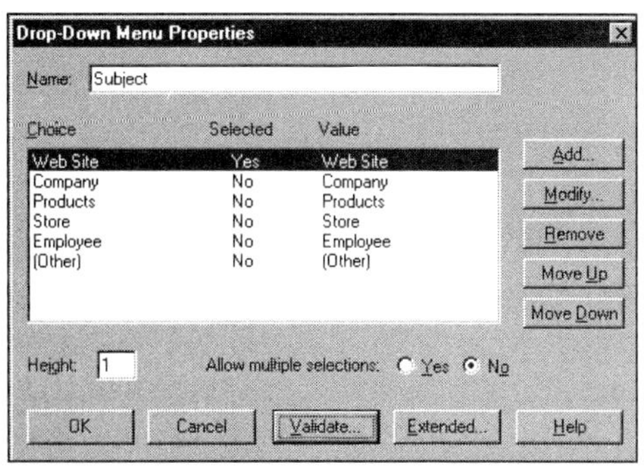

Figure 14-6 Configure selection lists here.

These are your options:

Name Provide a name for the element.

Choice This column shows the list of choices from which the user can select. Figure 14-6 shows the choices in the Feedback Form's drop-down list box: Web Site, Company, Products, and so on.

Selected This column shows if the entry is highlighted in the list. However, see the "Allow Multiple Selections" option below.

Value This is the text that is submitted if the entry is selected when the user submits the data.

Height This defines the size of the box. If you enter 1, then a drop-down list box is created — a box that shows a single entry, but which, when clicked upon, opens up and shows more entries. If you enter 2 or higher, the box is a multiple-line box with a scroll bar.

Allow Multiple Selections If Yes is selected, the user can select more than one entry in the list. If No is selected, when the user clicks an entry the currently selected entry is unselected. If you've set more than one item in the list to Yes under the Selected column, though, and if Allow Multiple Selections is set to No, then the last item in the list set to Yes is the one that will be selected.

Validate Click here to validate the selection list.

ADDING ITEMS TO THE LIST

To add an entry to the list, click Add. You'll see the dialog box shown in Figure 14-7. Type the entry text that you want to see in the list into the Choice box. You'll see that as you type, the second text box is filled in for you. In other words, the text that will be submitted with the form if this entry is selected in the list box is the same as the text you type into the Choice box. If you prefer, you can enter your own Value text; click Specify Value and then enter the text.

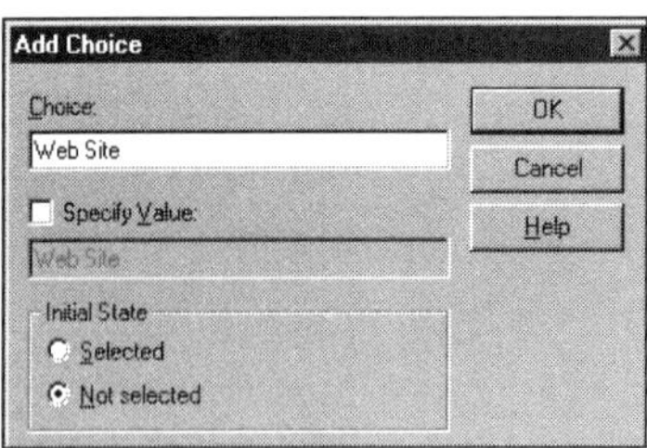

Figure 14-7 Enter a new selection-list entry.

Click the Selected or Not Selected option button, then click OK. If you want to edit any entries in the list you can just double-click them, or click once and then click Modify. Notice also that the entries can be moved up and down in the selection list using the Move Up and Move Down buttons in the Drop-Down Menu Properties dialog box, or removed from the list by clicking Remove.

VALIDATING THE LIST

If you wish you may validate the list. Click Validate in the Drop-Down Menu Properties dialog box. The dialog box shown in Figure 14-8 opens.

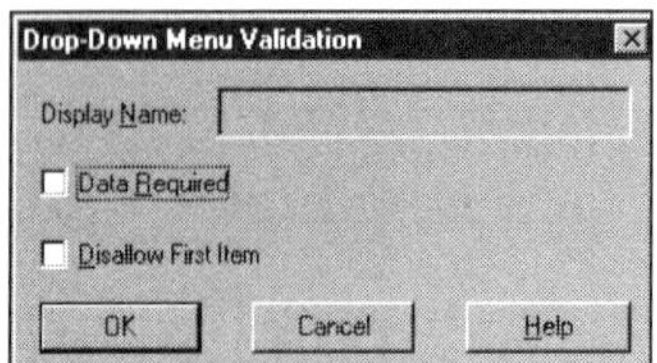

Figure 14-8 The Drop-Down Menu Validation box

These are your options:

Display Name If you check one of the check boxes, you turn on validation. This text box is then enabled so you can enter the name you want used for the field when displayed in the error message.

Data Required Checking this means that the user must make a selection in this box.

Disallow First Item Check this item to not accept the first entry in the box. You can then use the first entry as a description — Pick a Location From This Box, for instance — and FrontPage will ignore it, realizing that it's not an acceptable choice.

Creating a Command Button

abl To create a command button, select Insert → Form Field → Push Button or click the One-Line Text Box button. Double-click the element to open the dialog box shown in Figure 14-9.

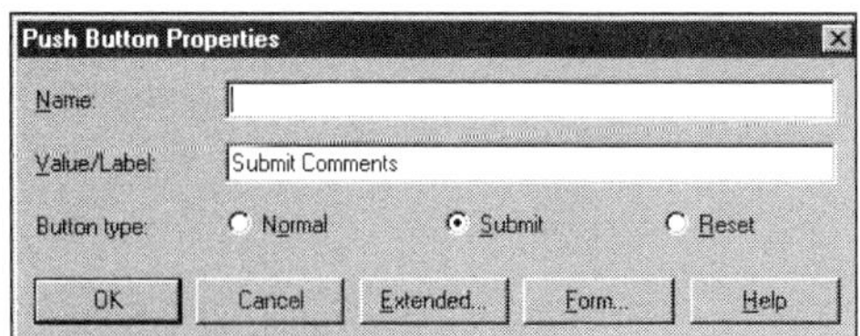

Figure 14-9 The Push Button Properties dialog box

These are the options:

Name An optional button name. It's not always required, but it may be if you have more than one button and need to determine which button was clicked.

Value/Label Pair This is the buttons value, the name that appears on the button. If you select the Normal option button at the bottom of the dialog box, the button has no label unless you enter one; select Submit and the button's label is Submit, select Reset and the button's label is Reset. You can assign whatever label you want (Submit the Form, Submit the Data, Send the Data, Clear the Form, or whatever) by typing text into this text box.

Normal This creates a normal button, the <input type="button">.

Submit This creates a submit button, the <input type="submit">. When the user clicks this button the data is submitted to the *form handler*, the system you will define to handle form submissions. We'll be looking at form handlers in Chapter 15.

Reset This creates a reset button, the <input type="reset">. When the user clicks this button the form is reset back to its default values, in effect clearing the form.

Form Click this button to set the Form Properties. See "Making the Form Work," later in this chapter.

Creating Image Submit Buttons

You can insert an image into your form and use it as a submit button. Place the cursor where you want the image, then select **Insert** → **Form Field** → **Image**, select the image you want to use, and click OK. This image will act just like a submit button. For instance, if you modify the Feedback Form, you can add an image to the form, (or replace the submit button with the image), and when a user clicks the image the form contents are submitted in the normal way.

You can then double-click the image to open the Image Form Field Properties dialog box (Figure 14-10). All this box lets you do is edit the image (click Image Properties) in the normal way — see Chapter 8 — and modify the image name.

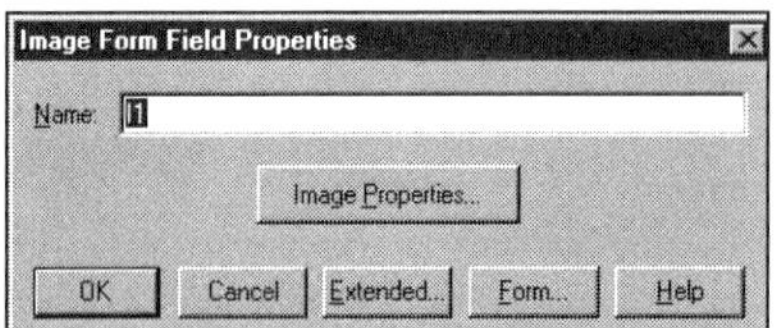

Figure 14-10 The Image Form Field Properties dialog box

Creating Hidden Fields

There's another type of form component: the hidden element (<input type="hidden">). You'll use the Form Properties dialog box to create these elements, which are used to pass background information — info the user doesn't need to see — to CGI scripts. See "Making the Form Work," next.

Making the Form Work

Once you have your form components in place, you can tell FrontPage how you want the form to work. This is done in the Form Properties dialog box (see Figure 14-11), which can be opened in two ways:

* Right-click anywhere inside the form and select **Form Properties**.
* In the Push Button Properties and Image Form Field Properties dialog boxes, click Form. (Currently only the Push Button Properties and Image Form Field Properties dialog boxes have this button.)

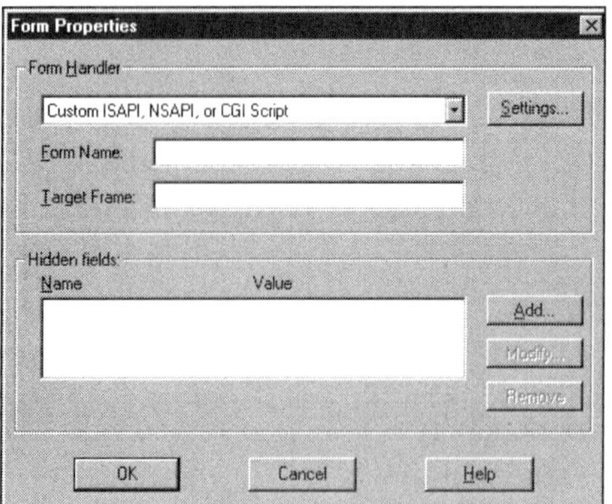

Figure 14-11 The Form Properties dialog box

These are the options in this dialog box:

Form Handler Select the form handler you want to have process the form. You'll learn more about form handlers in Chapter 15.

Settings After selecting a form handler, you can click Settings to configure that form handler; see Chapter 15.

Form Name You can provide the form with a name; this may be necessary when referring to the form from a script.

Target Frame This is the frame, if any, in which you want to display the results from the script that handled the submission from this form.

Hidden Fields If you have hidden fields in this form, which may be required by some scripts, they'll be listed here; you'll see the Name of the field and the Value that it holds. A hidden field (<input type="hidden">) is a field that holds information that is not seen by the user.

Add Click Add to add a new hidden field to the list.

When the user clicks the Submit button, the data is sent to the form handler. By selecting a form handler you are telling FrontPage what you want done with the data that the user enters into the form, or the options that the user selects from the form.

So you have now created a form that works, in that it sends information to the form handler. But what does the form handler do with that information, and is the form handler set up correctly? For that information you'll have to turn to the next chapter.

BONUS

A Couple of Text Box Validation Examples

Here are a couple of validation examples using the Text Box Validation dialog box (Figure 14-2). Let's say you create a text box into which the user must type an e-mail address. Set up the Text Box Validation dialog box like this:

Display Name Enter the field name; E-mail Address, for instance.

Data Type Select Text.

Letters Checked.

Digits Checked.

Whitespace Cleared. E-mail addresses can't contain spaces.

Other Cleared. There are a number of different characters that can be placed in e-mail addresses, so it's safer to leave this cleared.

Data Length Required Checked.

Min Length 7. The minimum size e-mail address is seven characters.

Max Length Leave clear.

Data Value Leave these check boxes cleared.

Here's what you could do for a phone-number field:

Display Name Enter the field name; Phone Number with Area Code, for instance.

Data Type Select Text. Yes, it's a number, but you have to allow for dividers such as - and ().

Letters Cleared.

Digits Checked.

Whitespace Cleared, perhaps. Some people may enter blank spaces to divide their numbers.

Other Checked. Then type **. ( )** - into the box. While the dash and parentheses are commonly used to divide numbers in North America, the period is used in many other areas.

Data Length Required Cleared, perhaps. It's difficult to know exactly how many characters will be typed, because phone numbers vary in length among countries, and you don't know for sure what dividing characters, if any, the user will enter. You could enter a low value of, say, 7, though (if not including area code), and 10 (if including it), and a high value of enough digits for a user to enter all necessary dividing characters, plus phone number, area code, and country code, if you can figure that out!

Data Value Leave these check boxes cleared.

This validation system is not perfect. But even if it's only close, as with the telephone number validation above, it will at least stop people accidentally typing a name, for instance, into a phone number field.

Summary

In this chapter I showed you how to create a form. I even showed you how to set up a few form-configuration options. You now have most of the information you need in order to modify one of the forms created by a FrontPage wizard or template.

However, there's an important piece we haven't yet covered. Once the data is sent to the form handler, what happens next? That depends on which handler you've chosen. The WebBot Save Results form handler, for instance, is very simple. The data entered into the form is taken and saved into a text file, though we haven't yet told the form handler which text file and where.

So if you've created a form from scratch, you haven't quite finished. And even if you want to merely modify a form, you should really understand how form handlers work in order to do so. We'll cover form handlers in Chapter 15.

CHAPTER FIFTEEN

WORKING WITH FORM HANDLERS

IN THIS CHAPTER YOU LEARN THESE KEY SKILLS

An HTML form by itself is nothing much. It lets the user enter information and make selections from check boxes, option buttons, and selection lists. But what good is all that? Something has to be done with the user's entries and selections. When the user clicks the Submit button (see "Creating a Command Button" in Chapter 14), or an Image Submit button (see "Creating Image Submit Buttons" in Chapter 14), the browser sends the information to the selected form handler. The handler then carries out certain procedures; it may save the information in a text file or a Web page, or use it to search for information, or run a program of some kind.

In the previous couple of chapters you've seen how to create forms, from adding the first field and configuring it, to selecting the form handler that will work with the data submitted by the form. Now it's time to consider what those handlers are and how to get them to work properly.

Setting Up Your Form Handler

The *form handler* is the script or program that does something with the information that is submitted from your form. As you saw in Chapter 14, you select the form handler in the Form Properties dialog box (right-click in the form and select Form Properties). These are the form handlers you can work with:

Custom ISAPI, NSAPI, or CGI Script These are scripts that run on the Web server and have nothing to do with FrontPage — FrontPage submits the information to the scripts, but from then on it's all out of FrontPage's hands.

WebBot Discussion Component This is part of the FrontPage server extensions and is used in a Web-page discussion system; the handler takes the information from the form, adds it to a Web page, and includes the data in a table of contents and an index.

WebBot Registration Component This handler is part of the FrontPage server extensions and is used in a registration system, taking the information from the form and adding it to an authentication database, so the user can log in to the Web site later.

WebBot Save Results Component This handler is part of the FrontPage server extensions and is used to take information from a form and save it in some form at the Web server.

Internet Database Connector This is a script that runs on the Microsoft Internet Information Server and allows users to send queries to databases (see Chapter 9). We won't be looking at this handler.

Note that several of these form handlers are built in to the FrontPage server extensions — no FrontPage-enabled server, no form handler! See Chapter 1.

Saving Form Entries — the Save Results Handler

This is, perhaps, the simplest form handler to understand and use, so that's where we'll start. This handler is used to collect information from the form and then place it in a file of some sort — a text file you can read later, a text file formatted so the text can be imported into a database, a Web page so the information can be viewed by other people (for a comments page, for instance), and so on.

Select WebBot Save Results Component in the Form Properties dialog box, then click Settings. The dialog box shown in Figure 15-1 will open.

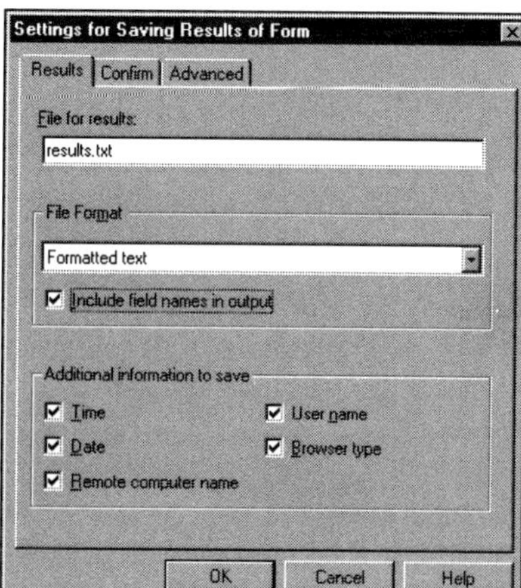

Figure 15-1 Use this box to set up the WebBot Save Results handler.

Here are the options you can work with in the Results pane:

File for Results Type the name of the file in which the information from the form should be saved. You may also want to include a directory name. For instance, if you enter _private/filename.txt the file is saved in the _private directory, so it can't be seen by Web users. (Remember, use a forward slash, not a backslash!) Include a file extension; FrontPage won't add one for you.

File Format Select the type of file you want created.

HTML: A Web page with the submitted information displayed, showing the field name first and then the submitted data.

HTML Definition List: A Web page with the data in a definition list.

HTML Bullet List: A Web page with the data in a bullet list.

Formatted Text within HTML: A Web page with the data inserted between <pre> and </pre> tags, so that it appears in monospaced font and with all spaces and blank lines shown.

Formatted Text: A text file with spaces used to line the submitted data up in a column to the right of the field names, and a line of asterisks above the entry separating it from previous entries.

Text Database Using Comma as a Separator: A text file with the entries placed one after another, with a comma between, so it can be imported into a database.

Text Database Using Tab as a Separator: As before, but using tab characters to separate items.

Text Database Using Space as a Separator: As before, but using spaces to separate items.

Include Field Names in Output Clear this check box and the field names are not submitted with the user's entries.

Additional Information to Save You can tell the browser to send additional information to the handler, too: the Time, Date, Remote Computer Name (the computer's network name or IP address), User Name (if the user logged in to a Web site that requires registration), and Browser Type.

TIP **The Text Database Using Comma as a Separator option is appropriate only if you have created a form in which the user is unable to enter spaces.**

This is really quite straightforward — it simply defines how the submitted data is saved. Is it saved in an HTML file, for instance? If so, you could provide a link to that HTML file so that your Web site users can read the submission, as in a comment or guest book. Each time information is submitted using that form, the information is added to the bottom of the page.

Is the data submitted to a text file? You could pick one of the database text file options, so that you can import the data directly into a database periodically. Again, each time someone submits data, it's added to the bottom of the file. Import the file, then delete it so that all the new data is added to a new file.

TIP **By default the form handler will save the values of all fields, even the Submit and Reset buttons, which really isn't much use to you. However, you can define which fields are saved in the Advanced pane, which we'll look at under "Saving Data Twice," later in this chapter.**

Adding a Confirmation Page

The form handler will automatically create a confirmation page, but it's a little ugly. It will use all the field names, which may appear like gibberish to the user. And it will show all the submitted data, including values from command buttons that are irrelevant to the user. So it's a good idea to tell the handler to use a confirmation page.

First you need to actually create the confirmation page, so we'll look at that process first. You can use the Confirmation Form template or create a page from scratch. We'll look at the template, and once you've seen that you'll easily figure out how to create one from scratch.

1. Select File → New, and in the New Page dialog box select Confirmation Form and click OK. The form you see in Figure 15-2 is created.

2. Click the purple text at the top of the page and press Delete to remove the comment.

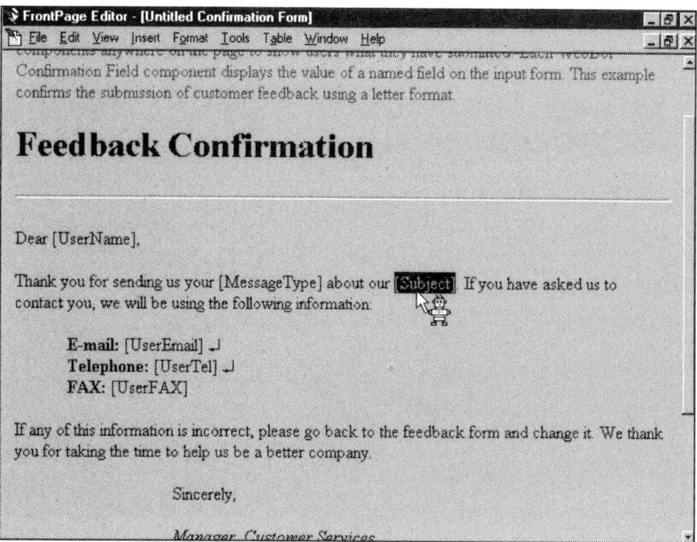

Figure 15-2 The Confirmation Form page

3. The text shown in the [ ] brackets was placed there using the Confirmation Field WebBot. Point at one and you'll see the Robot mouse pointer. Double-click one of these text blocks to open the dialog box in Figure 15-3.

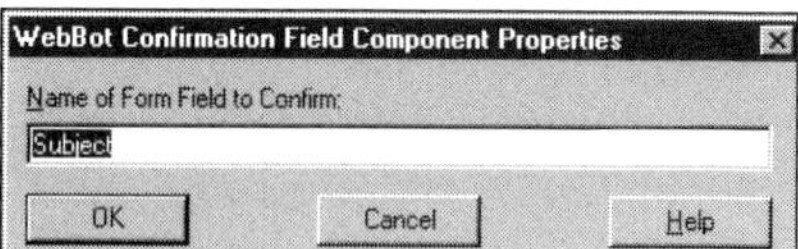

Figure 15-3 Tell the WebBot which field will provide the data to this block of text.

4. Double-click each of the WebBot text blocks in turn, and enter the name of the field, in the form in which the user will enter data, that you wish to use to provide data. For instance, if your form has a field called Email in which users type their e-mail address, you'd double-click [UserEmail], type **Email**, and click OK.

5. Remove any of the blocks that are not appropriate, along with any introductory text. For instance, you may want to remove "Dear [UserName]," — the form handler will try to place the user's name here, but if you are not collecting that data, or if the form is not at a Web site at which the user must register and log on (see "Registering Users — the Registration Handler," later in this chapter) then this line is not needed.

6. Add any new entries you need. For instance, if the user submits a company name, and the company-name field is called Cname, you could add this:

Company Name: [Cname]

You wouldn't type the [Cname] bit directly, of course — you'd use the Confirmation Field WebBot. Select Insert → WebBot Component, click Confirmation Field, click OK, type **Cname**, and then click OK.

7. When you've completed the form, save and close it.

Once you've created your confirmation page, you should return to the original form and open the Form Properties dialog box, click the Settings button, then click the Confirm tab. You'll see the pane shown in Figure 15-4.

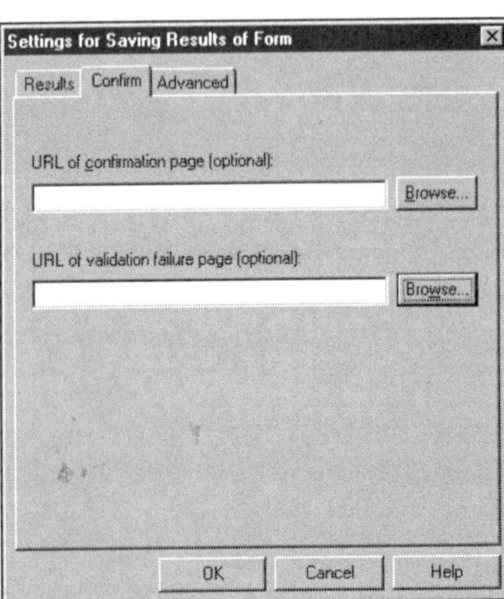

Figure 15-4 Define a confirmation page.

You'll place the name of the confirmation-page file into the first text box (along with the directory name if necessary); use the Browse button to find it.

Using a Validation-Failure Page

You'll notice in Figure 15-4 that you can also define a validation-failure page. (This text box is disabled unless you've defined a validation process for one or more form field.) That's a page that appears if the user has not entered information into the form correctly, and if you have made FrontPage use the FrontPage server extensions to validate data (see Chapter 14). If you are using VBScript or JavaScript to validate data, the browser will display a message box explaining which field was filled in incorrectly.

If you are using the FrontPage server extensions to validate the form, and if you leave this field blank, the server extensions will create a page for you — and I recommend that you allow it to do so. You can see what this page looks like in Figure 15-5, and I think this works well. It shows the error and has a link back to the form. There's no way for you to create a good validation-failure page, so use the default.

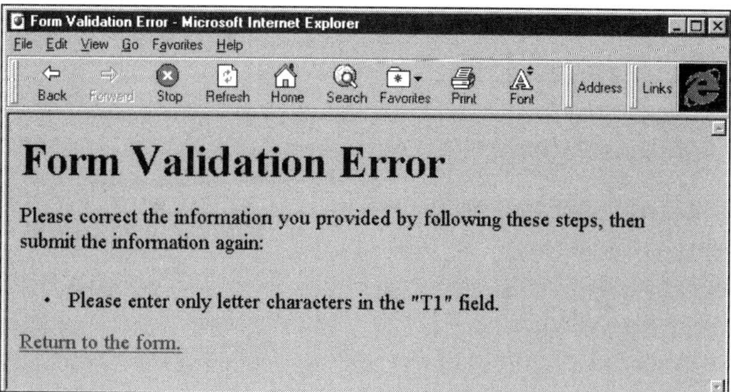

Figure 15-5 A Form Validation Error page

Saving Data Twice

You can save submitted data twice if you wish, by entering data into the Advanced pane (click the Advanced tab to see the information shown in Figure 15-6). Why would you want to do this? Well, maybe you want to store information shown in a text file so you can import it into a database, and you also want to display it in a Web page, for instance. Or perhaps you want to store just part of the data; the Advanced tab lets you define which fields are stored and in which order.

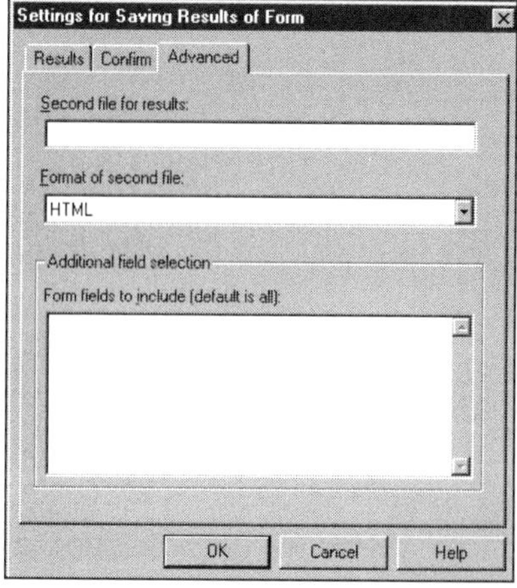

Figure 15-6 Define a second data-storage file.

As you did in the Results tab, enter a filename into the text box and select the format in which the data should be stored in the drop-down list box.

If you want to define which fields are stored, or in which order, type the field names into the large text box, separating them with commas. Note that this box affects the file you define in this pane *and the one you define in the Results pane*. If you leave this large box empty all the fields are stored in the file, in the order in which they appear in the form.

Registering Users — the Registration Handler

SERVER EXTENSIONS

The WebBot Registration handler can do two things. You can use it to enable people to register to use your Web site or a portion of the Web site. And you can also use it to save form entries, in the same way that the Save Results handler does. (You must be using a FrontPage-enabled Web server in order to use the WebBot Registration handler.) Here's how it works.

You have to create a registration form that's saved in the root web and that allows people to register to gain access to one of the subwebs that you've created inside the root web. Later, when the user uses a link to get to that web or enters the URL for that web, he or she will see the dialog box shown in Figure 15-7. The user will type his or her username and password and then will be allowed to view the pages in that web. (The user will be given three chances to get the correct username and password, and if the correct information hasn't been entered, the Web server will display an error message.)

What's the point of getting users to register to get into your site? It's not security, after all; it doesn't stop people getting in — it just makes them register first. Well, it's a way to get information from them. You could include in the registration form an e-mail address field, for instance, and set up validation so they can't get in without entering something into the e-mail form. If they want to view your site, they have to provide the information! True, some people will enter fake information, but most won't. It also means that the person's username can be grabbed each time he or she fills in a form subsequently. Remember the User Name check box when we looked at how to set up the Save Results handler? That works only in a registration site, in which the user has to log on. And some Web authors believe it helps provide a sense of community. Users register, and each time they return they have to enter an account name and password, and so they may feel a little different about this site, almost as if they've joined a club — which, in a sense, they have.

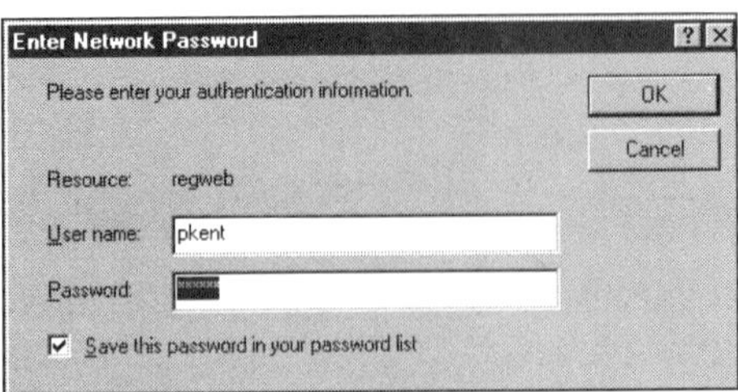

Figure 15-7 Before the user can view the Web site he or she will have to log in.

Before you use this handler, you should set permissions for the web, in FrontPage Explorer, so that only registered users can view the web. You'll see how to do that in Chapter 17.

You'll also want to create a form with at least one text box for a name, and at least one — preferably two — text boxes configured to be password boxes (see Chapter 14).

TIP **The quickest and easiest way to set up a registration form is by selecting the User Registration template in the New Page dialog box.**

Select WebBot Registration Component in the Form Properties dialog box, then click Settings. The dialog box shown in Figure 15-8 will open.

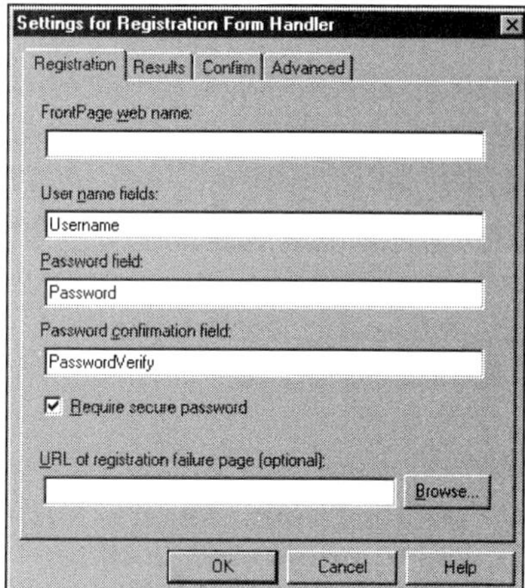

Figure 15-8 Use this box to set up the WebBot Registration handler.

As you can see, this handler has four panes. The last three, Results, Confirm, and Advanced, work in the same way as for the WebBot Save Results handler, so see the information earlier in this chapter to learn how to use them. The other pane, Registration, is shown in the illustration, and this is where you set up the registration criteria, as follows:

FrontPage Web Name Provide the name of the web to which you want to provide access.

User Name Fields Type the name of the field into which the user will type his or her log-on or account name. You may have a single box into which the user can type a log-on or account name. Or the handler can take the entries from two or more boxes (First Name and Last Name, for instance) and string them together to form a log-on or account name, joining each of the user's entries with an underscore: Peter_Kent, for instance. If you have more than one field providing the name, type all the field names separated by commas.

TIP **Make sure that none of the name fields have spaces within the names — use UserName rather than User Name, for instance — or the handler won't work correctly.**

Password Field Type the name of the field into which the user will type the password.

Password Confirmation Field It's a good idea to have two password fields, to make sure the user typed what he or she thinks he did; if the entries in both text boxes don't match, the process fails. Enter the name of the confirmation field here.

Require Secure Password If you check this box the handler will not allow the user to enter a password less than six characters long, or one that contains part of the user name.

URL of Registration Failure Page You can define a message to be displayed if the registration procedure fails, although you should probably let the FrontPage server extensions handle this for you. They'll explain the reason that the procedure failed: passwords not matching, password too short, the user picked a name someone else is already using, and so on.

When you close the dialog boxes you'll see a message reminding you to save the registration form in the root web; do not save it in the web for which you are setting up registration. If necessary go to FrontPage Explorer, close the current web, open the root web, then return to the FrontPage Editor and save the registration-form page.

Make sure you have the registration form where people can get to it. For instance, you might have a link from your main page in the root web to the page containing this form. The user can then register and immediately go to the web for which he or she registered. And if you want a link to this web from *another* web, one that isn't the root web? Then you'll have to link from that other web to the registration form in the root web first.

TIP **To make a Web site completely private, accessible only to users for whom you have created an account, see the information about permissions in Chapter 17.**

Creating Discussion Groups — the Discussion Handler

The WebBot Discussion handler is used to create discussion groups, a system in which people can leave messages that others can view and respond to. You could use this to set up a true discussion group, like an Internet newsgroup. You could also use it to allow people to place classified ads, or to provide technical support to users (the user can leave a message and someone in your company can answer it).

If you want to set up a discussion group, I'd advise that you use the Discussion Web Wizard in FrontPage Explorer and then modify it, as it's quite complicated to set up the collection of pages you'll need. This wizard will create all the forms for you and set up the handler for you, too. (Check Add to the Current Web in the New FrontPage Web dialog box to place the discussion group in the current web.) I'm going to use the settings that are created by that wizard. For more information about this wizard see Chapter 16.

Open the discussion group's submission form (if you used the wizard, it's the file with the title Groupname Submission Form) in FrontPage Editor. Open the Form Properties dialog box for this form; you'll see WebBot Discussion Component in the drop-down list box. Click Settings. The dialog box shown in Figure 15-9 will open.

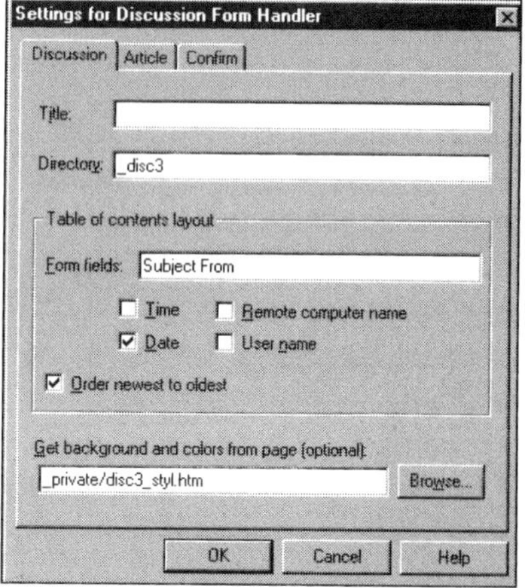

Figure 15-9 Use this box to set up the WebBot Discussion handler.

These are the settings in the Discussion pane:

Title This is a title that will appear near the top of a page in which a message is displayed (below the message subject). It seems superfluous to me, so I'd leave it blank, but it may be useful in some cases, I guess.

Directory This is the directory in which the messages posted by users are saved.

TIP **Each message to the discussion group is placed in a separate file and saved in the directory specified here. You can't see these files unless you select Show Documents in Hidden Directories in the Advanced pane of the Web Settings dialog box.**

Table of Contents Layout This is where you set up how the list of messages looks. Users will be able to read this list to see what messages have been posted to the group.

Form Fields Name the fields you want to place in the message listing. The first field you enter will be the one that has a link placed on it so the user can read the message. That field is also the one that will appear as the message title in the page that displays the message, so in most cases you'll want the first one to be the message subject. Separate the fields with spaces or commas.

TIP **Make sure the names of the fields in your form do not have spaces in them, or the handler won't be able to create the table of contents correctly.**

Time Check this to include, in the table of contents, the time that the message was posted.

Date Check this to include the date the message was posted.

Remote Computer Name Check this to include the name of the computer from which the message was posted. This is generally not very useful on the Internet, but might be handy on a corporate intranet.

User Name If this discussion group is in a private web site, or one that the user has to register with to use, you can check this to include the user's name.

Order Newest to Oldest Check this to sort the list of messages with the newest messages at the top.

Get Background and Colors from Page You can set up a page template, as discussed in Chapter 4, to define the background color and pattern, and the text colors, for all the pages in the discussion group. If you do so, name the template file here.

Setting Up Articles

Click the Article tab to see the settings shown in Figure 15-10. Article here means message. The term *article* is commonly used on the Internet to refer to a message in a discussion group. So this pane is used to set up the pages in which the messages are displayed.

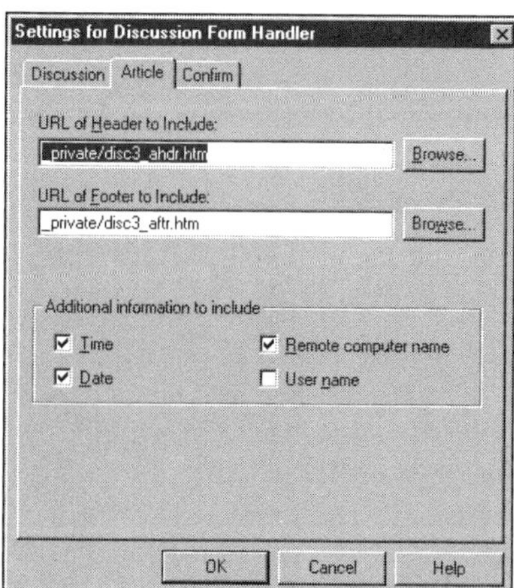

Figure 15-10 Set up the article (message) pages here.

These are the settings:

URL of Header to Include This is the file that the handler places at the top of a message page, using the Include WebBot (see Chapter 10). If you are using the wizard, this file contains links to the home page, and to search the discussion group, post a message, reply to a message, and so on.

URL of Footer to Include You can also include a footer using the Include WebBot.

Additional Information to Include Use these check boxes to define what additional information will be displayed at the top of the message page, below the included header but before the actual message.

CONFIRMATION AND VALIDATION PAGES

To set up the confirmation and validation pages, click Confirm (see Figure 15-11).

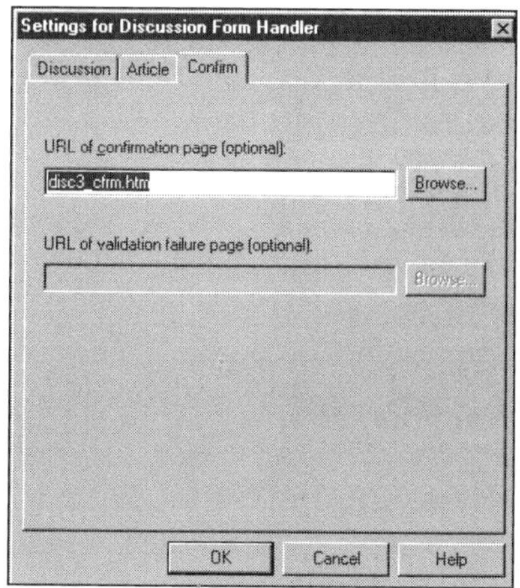

Figure 15-11 Define the confirmation and validation pages here.

A confirmation page should tell the user that the message has been posted, and have links to the main discussion group page (and a note telling the user to reload the main page to see the new list of messages), the home page, the message-post page, and search page, and so on.

As for the validation-failure page, this works in the same way as before; the text box is disabled if you have not set up any form fields for validation; and in any case, you'll probably want to let the handler handle validation-failure pages for you. See "Using a Validation-Failure Page," earlier in this chapter.

TIP **The Discussion wizard uses several special WebBots that are not directly available to you from the Insert WebBot Component dialog box (though you can type them directly into the HTML source): the REPLY, NEXT, PREV, and UP WebBots. Another reason to use the wizard to set up your discussion group.**

Using Scripts — the Script Handler

The Custom ISAPI, NSAPI, or CGI Script handler is used to send information from the form to a non–FrontPage script — a CGI (Common Gateway Interface), ISAPI (Internet Server Application Programming Interface), or NSAPI (Netscape Server Application Programming Interface) script. The script can carry out some kind of process, such as carrying out a search and returning information, or placing the information in an e-mail message and sending it somewhere. You may want to use such scripts to carry out functions that FrontPage's server extensions are not set up to do.

You do not need to be using a FrontPage-enabled server in order to use this script handler. You can still use the script handler if you are using a FrontPage-enabled server, though.

FrontPage can't help you create these scripts; all it can do is send the information to the scripts. It's up to you to create or find the scripts themselves and configure the form correctly. Many web-hosting companies provide libraries of scripts that you can use.

Select Custom ISAPI, NSAPI, or CGI Script in the Form Properties dialog box, then click Settings. The dialog box shown in Figure 15-12 will open.

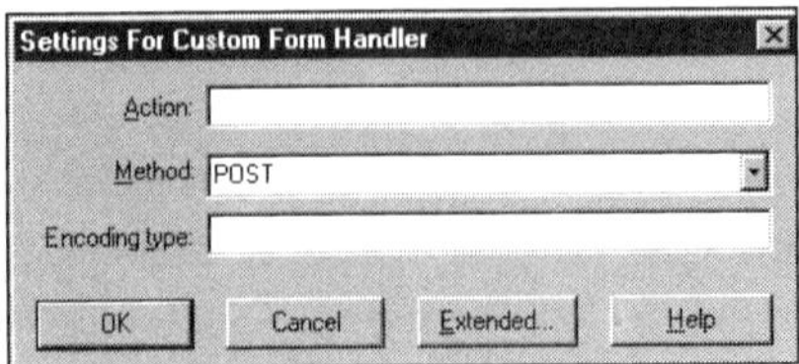

Figure 15-12 Use this box to set up a handler to work with non–FrontPage scripts.

Here's the information you must enter:

Action Enter the URL of the script to which you want to send the information submitted from the form. If you are not sure of this, check with the server administrator.

Method Select the submission method. There are two methods, GET and POST. With GET, the information from the form — the field names and their values — are tacked onto the end of the script's URL and sent to the server. The server then places the data into an environment variable (a special data-storage variable) called QUERY_STRING and then sends it to the script. With POST, the data is sent in a stream of data, through the server to the script. The POST method is the preferred method, because it can handle much more data, so use POST unless your server administrator tells you that you must use GET.

Encoding Type You probably won't need to enter anything here. This defines the manner in which the data is transferred across the World Wide Web or corporate intranet — the MIME (Multipurpose Internet Mail Extensions) content type, to be exact. But the default MIME type (x-www-form-encoded) is almost always acceptable, so just leave this blank.

When you are creating a form that will be used by a script, you may need to create some hidden fields; you do this in the Form Properties dialog box, as you saw in Chapter 14. You can see an example of this later in this chapter, under "A Real-Life Script Example."

BONUS

A Real-Life Script Example

Here's an example of a form that submits data to a CGI script. My Web-hosting company has a script that it provides that takes data from the form and places it in an e-mail message, which it then sends to the e-mail address you specify. (This is the FormMail script, available from Matt's Script Archives at `http://www.worldwidemart.com/scripts/`.)

Your server's system administrator should be able to tell you where to find CGI scripts that run on the Web server. (You must use scripts written for the Web server's operating system.) Or go to Yahoo (`http://www.yahoo.com`) and search for cgi; you'll find links to all sorts of CGI resources.

Here are the details.

Script name formmail.cgi

Location `http://www.digiserve.com/cgi-bin/`

Hidden fields Three hidden fields are necessary: recipient (the e-mail address to which the message is sent), redirect (the address of a Web page that is displayed after the form information has been submitted), and subject (a word or two that describes the content of the message that is placed in the subject line of the e-mail message).

Name field One of the fields has to be called realname; the data from that field is placed into parentheses at the top of the e-mail message, as you'll see in a moment.

It took me about five minutes to set all this up. Here's how I did it.

1. I created the form with the fields that the user would enter information into and selection options, the information that will be placed into an e-mail message. The field in which the user will type his or her name I called realname.
2. I opened the Form Properties dialog box (see Figure 15-13).
3. I used the Add button to add the three hidden fields.

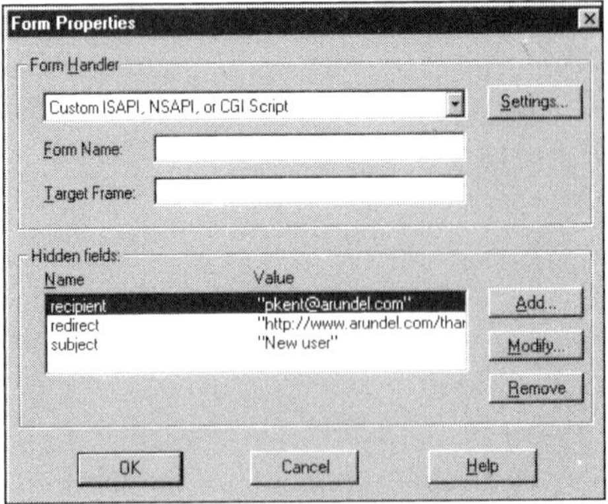

Figure 15-13 I selected the Custom ISAPI, NSAPI, or CGI Script option and then created the hidden fields.

4. I clicked Settings and entered the URL to the script in the Action box, and selected the POST Method (Figure 15-14).

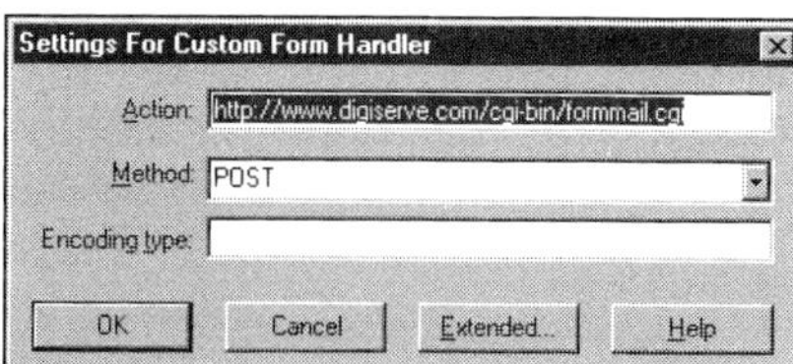

Figure 15-14 Here's how the Settings for Custom Form Handler box is set up.

5. I closed these dialog boxes, then created the page that is referred to by the redirect hidden field, the page that the user sees after submitting the data.

That's it; it's really quite easy. (The difficult part is writing the script, or finding a script and figuring out from the documentation how to set it up.) Now, when the user submits information I'm sent an e-mail message that looks like the following:

```
Below is the result of your feedback form. It was submitted by
  (John Smith) on Wednesday, April 30, 1997 at 12:10:08
_______________________________________________

Field 1: Field Value
Field 2: Field Value
Field 3: Field Value
Field 4: Field Value
_______________________________________________
```

TIP **What exactly are these hidden fields? They're just like the other input fields, except that the browser won't display them. They're simply used to hold information that the script needs. For instance, here's one of the hidden fields from the above script:**

```
<input type="hidden" name="recipient" value="pkent@arundel.com">.
```

Summary

There are a number of theories about how to make your Web site popular. As you've probably figured out, I'm not a proponent of the "Make it cool and they will come" theory. Lots of video, java, animations, and the like slow things down and can actually keep people away from your site.

Another, more plausible theory is that you need to create a sense of community at your site. The nice thing about this theory is that you can add community a lot more easily — and a lot cheaper — than adding cool. The form handlers that you've seen here, in particular the Discussion handler, can help you do that. Forms provide interaction, a way for your site's users to get involved with your site — to talk to one another, to give you suggestions, to answer your questions, to order things, and so on. Spend an hour or two learning these tools, then put them to work.

CHAPTER SIXTEEN

USEFUL FORMS YOU CAN CREATE

IN THIS CHAPTER YOU LEARN THESE KEY SKILLS

Now that you've learned how to create forms, let's see why you may not need to. We're going to look at the forms that FrontPage can create for you. Create them and then modify them to your specifications. These are the wizards and templates provided:

- **Confirmation Form** — We covered this in Chapter 15.
- **Feedback Form** — We did this one in Chapter 13.
- **Form Page Wizard** — We also did this one in Chapter 13.
- **Guest Book**
- **Product or Event Registration**
- **Search Page**
- **Survey Form**
- **User Registration** — We covered this in Chapter 15.
- **Discussion Web Wizard** — We looked at the discussion handler used by the wizard in detail in Chapter 15, but we'll look at the wizard itself in this chapter.

All but the last of these is opened from FrontPage Editor's New Page dialog box. The last is opened from FrontPage Explorer's New FrontPage Web dialog box.

SERVER EXTENSIONS

By the way, all the forms we're going to look at in this chapter are set up to work with the FrontPage server extensions. Some of these forms could be modified to work with a CGI script, but some of them cannot — they work only with the FrontPage server extensions. The Search Page and Discussion Group work only at a FrontPage-enabled server; they cannot be modified to work with a script.

Creating a Guest Book

To create a guest book or simple feedback form, select Guest Book in the New Page dialog box. FrontPage creates the form displayed in Figure 16-1.

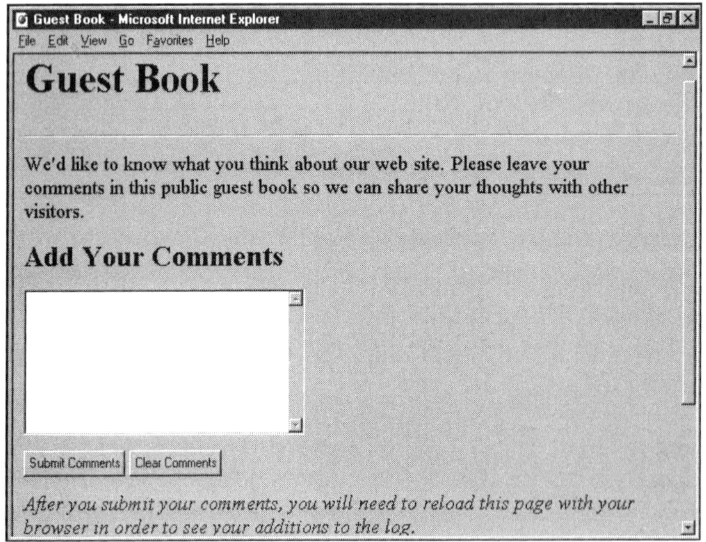

Figure 16-1 The Guest Book

This form has an Include WebBot (see Chapter 10) at the bottom of the page. The comments submitted by a user are placed into an .htm file, which is then included using this WebBot underneath the form, so the user can view the comments of others. You might want to modify this so that the comments are shown on a different page (remove the Include WebBot and use a link to the other page) or appear above the form (move the Include WebBot).

Registering for a Product or Event

To create a form with which users can register for a product or event, select Product or Event Registration from the New Page dialog box. You'll see the form in Figure 16-2.

Registration Form - Microsoft Internet Explorer
File Edit View Go Favorites Help

Registration Form

[The instructions for registration go here.]

User Information

First Name:
Last Name:
Title:
Company:
Street Address:
City:
State:
Zip Code:
Telephone:
FAX:

Figure 16-2 The Product or Event Registration form

You'll need to modify the text, the registration instructions, and titles, of course. You'll probably also need to add and remove some fields. And lower down in the form you'll find a drop-down list box and some check boxes that should either be removed or set up with appropriate names and values.

This form saves the data that's submitted into an .htm file. You'll probably want to modify that, to save it into a text file that can be imported into a database.

Building a Search Page

This is a very handy form that enables your users to search your Web site for the information they need. Select Search Page from the New Page dialog box and FrontPage will create the form shown in Figure 16-3.

This search form will not work unless you are using a FrontPage-enabled server.

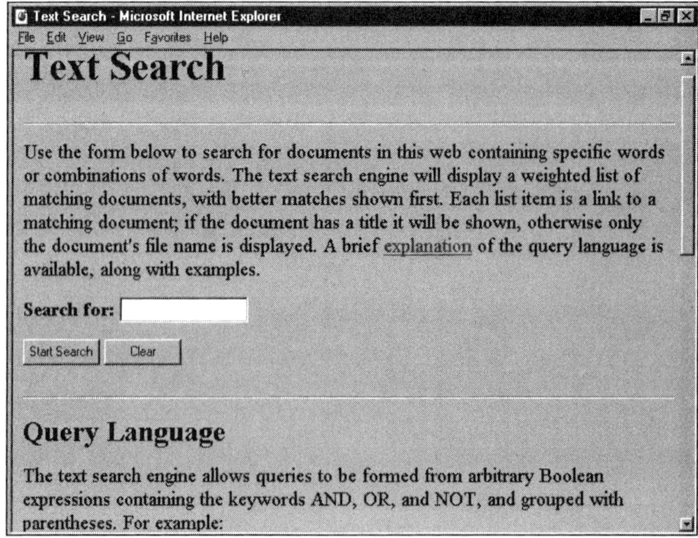

Figure 16-3 The search page

This page doesn't require much customization at all. You'll find that the form is not a true form at all — it's a WebBot. Double-click it and you'll see the dialog box shown in Figure 16-4.

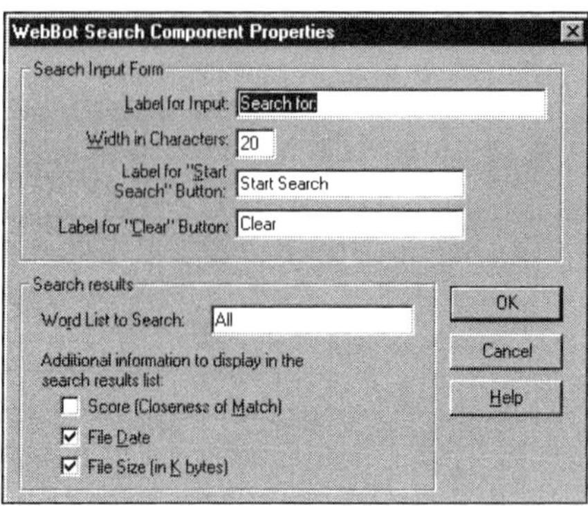

Figure 16-4 You can modify the manner in which the search page works.

These are the settings you can modify:

Label for Input You can modify the title shown to the left of the text box.

Width in Characters This is the width of the text box, measured in characters.

Label for "Start Search" Button You can change the label on the Start Search button.

Label for "Clear" Button You can change the label on the Clear button.

Word List to Search This can either show All (meaning "search the text of all the pages in the entire web"), or it can be the name of a particular directory, in which case only that directory is searched. So you can set up a search form to search just the discussion group, for instance (enter the name of the directory holding the messages — see "What's It Called?" later in this chapter), or to search a particular portion of the web.

Score (Closeness of Match) When the user searches for text, the results are shown in a table. The table contains a column showing the links to matching pages. If you check this box it will also have a column showing a number representing the quality of the match: the higher the number, the better the match.

File Date If this box is checked, the table also contains a column showing the pages' modified dates.

File Size (in Kbytes) If this is checked, the table also has a column showing the pages' file sizes.

Creating a Survey Form

A survey form is really the same thing as a feedback form. This form is much larger than the Feedback Form you saw in Chapter 13, though. It's split into three parts and contains more-varied questions. Select Survey Form in the New Page dialog box and FrontPage creates the form shown in Figure 16-5.

This one needs extensive modifications. Not only will you have to modify the explanatory text and headings, but unless you're carrying out a survey about television use you'll have to modify all the fields, too. You may find it easier to start from scratch and use the Form Page wizard (see Chapter 13).

The Survey form is set up to save the submitted information in a text file formatted so that it can be imported into a database — a file with tabs used as separators.

Creating a Discussion Group

In Chapter 15 you saw how the Discussion handler, which takes data from a form and places it into a discussion group, can be configured, so I won't go into detail about that again. I will, however, lead you through the Discussion Web wizard and give you a few pointers.

This discussion group will not work unless you are using a FrontPage-enabled server.

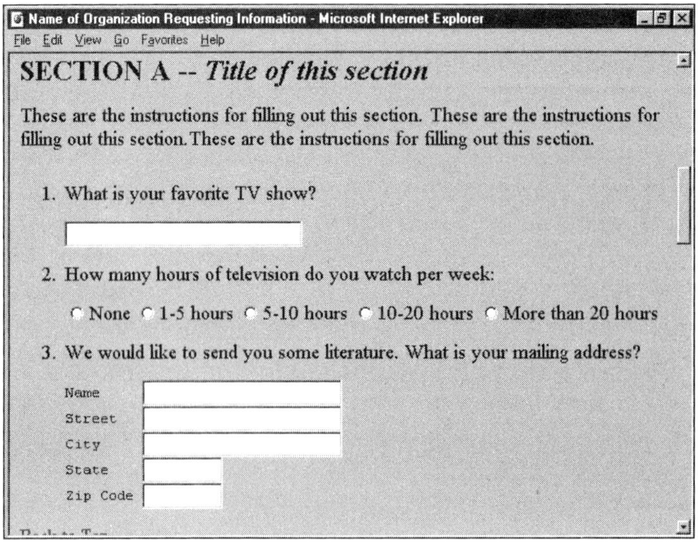

Name of Organization Requesting Information - Microsoft Internet Explorer

File Edit View Go Favorites Help

SECTION A -- *Title of this section*

These are the instructions for filling out this section. These are the instructions for filling out this section. These are the instructions for filling out this section.

1. What is your favorite TV show?

2. How many hours of television do you watch per week:

   None 1-5 hours 5-10 hours 10-20 hours More than 20 hours

3. We would like to send you some literature. What is your mailing address?

   Name

   Street

   City

   State

   Zip Code

Figure 16-5 The Survey Form

You start this wizard from FrontPage Explorer. Select Discussion Web Wizard from the New FrontPage Web dialog box. If you want to include the discussion group in the current web, rather than create a brand new web, check the Add to the Current Web check box.

Let's look at each of the wizard's dialog boxes one by one.

What Features Do You Want?

When you see the first box, click Next to see the information shown in Figure 16-6. This lets you select which features you want in the discussion group.

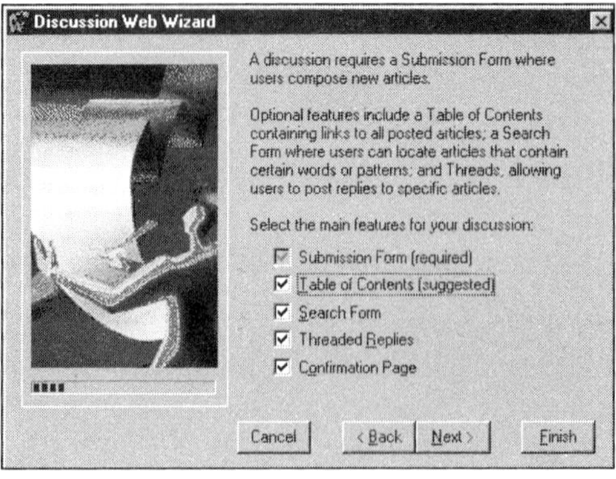

Figure 16-6 Tell the wizard what features you want to include in your discussion group.

These are the features:

Submission Form You must have a submission form (how else would people send messages to the group, after all?), so you can't clear this check box.

Table of Contents This is a list of the messages in the group. The user can view the list of subjects, then click a message to read the message.

Search Form If this is checked, the wizard creates a search page so users can search all the messages at once for a particular word or phrase.

Threaded Replies If this is checked, the wizard sets up a threaded-reply system. That is, users can reply to messages posted earlier. In the table of contents — the message list — replies are shown indented below the original message. If you clear this box, users will be able to post messages to the group but not reply directly to an earlier message.

Confirmation Page When the user submits a message to the group, a confirmation page is displayed, regardless of whether you check this check box or not. However, if the check box is cleared, the user sees a simple confirmation page that the discussion handler creates automatically. If the box is checked, the wizard creates a page and stores it in the web. The handler then uses that page, inserting information about the message into it. So if you check this box you'll be able to edit the confirmation page and add any explanatory text you want. This is the best choice, as the default page that the wizard creates for you has a useful note about refreshing the table of contents page, which isn't displayed in the automatic confirmation page.

The information that the wizard requests from you depends on your choices here, so if you clear some of these check boxes you may not see all the wizard dialog boxes that I'm going to show you.

What's It Called?

When you click Next the information shown in Figure 16-7 appears.

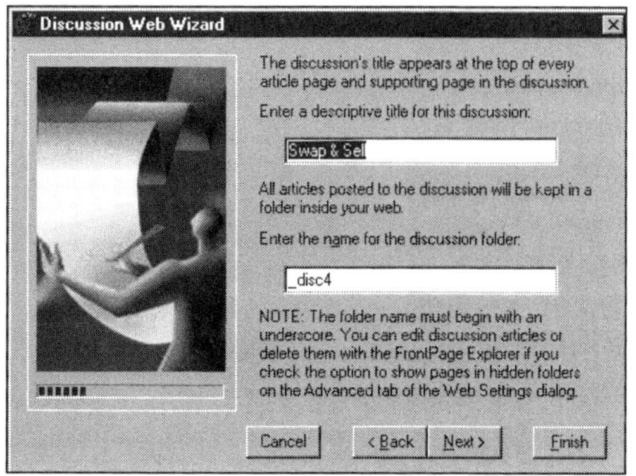

Figure 16-7 Provide a name and directory.

In the top text box enter the name you want to give the discussion group. This name will appear as a title in the group's pages. In the second text box you can provide a name for the directory in which the message files will be stored, or keep the name provided for you. The name must begin with an underscore.

Input Fields

Click Next and you'll see the box in Figure 16-8.

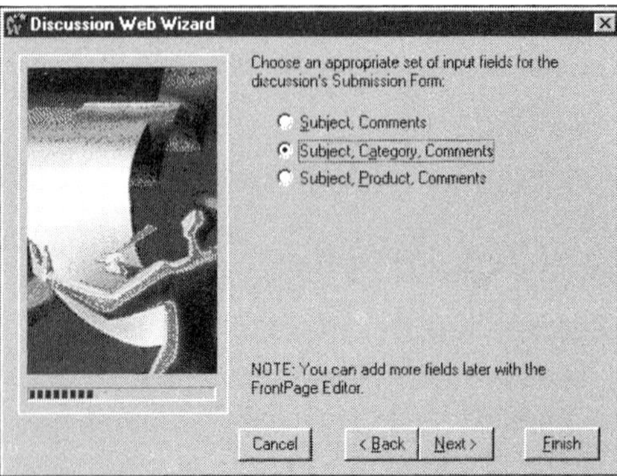

Figure 16-8 Pick your input fields.

When someone wants to post a message to the group or reply to a message, he or she enters information into a form. This box is where you tell the wizard which fields you want in the form. You must have a Subject field (a text box) and a Comments field (a textarea in which the user types his or her message). You can also have a Category or Product field. These are simply drop-down list boxes from which the user can select a category or product title. For instance, if you are creating a technical support forum and you have several products, a user could select the product name from the list box. The name will then appear near the top of the message, under the message subject.

Who Can Join?

Click Next to see the box in Figure 16-9.

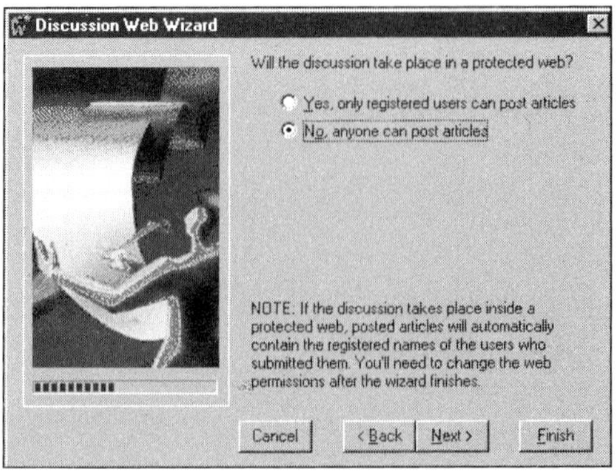

Figure 16-9 Select whether this is a protected web or not.

In this box you'll state whether this discussion group will be *protected:* one in which users must register before entering.

Yes, Only Registered Users Can Post Articles Select this and the wizard creates a registration page for you. (See "The Registration Form," later in this chapter.)

No, Anyone Can Post Articles Select this and the wizard doesn't create a registration form for you. You can still make this a site that requires registration by setting up registration yourself (see Chapter 15).

Up or Down?

Click Next and the box shown in Figure 16-10 appears.

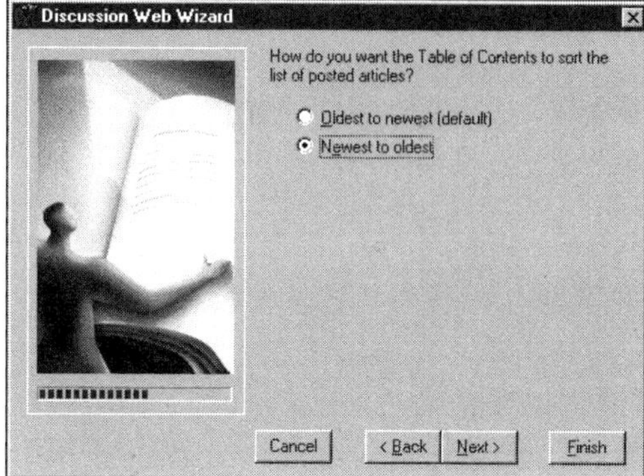

Figure 16-10 Which way do you want to sort messages?

This defines which way the messages will be listed in the message list — the table of contents, or TOC. You can sort them with the oldest at the top or the newest at the top.

Make It the Home Page?

Click Next and you'll see the information shown in Figure 16-11.

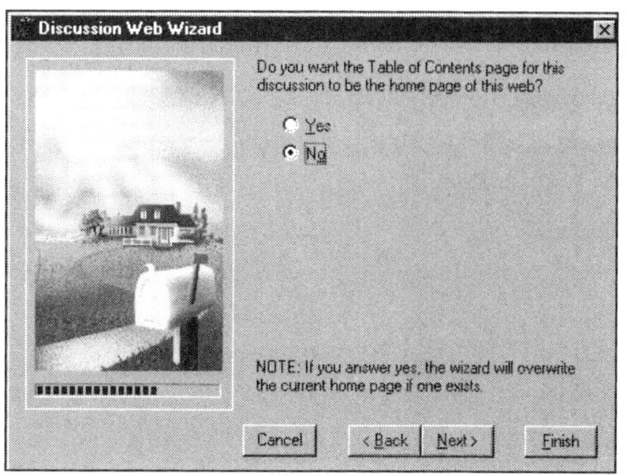

Figure 16-11 Make it a home page?

Be careful with this. If you click Yes, the web's index.htm file is replaced with a new one: the discussion group's main page or, if you are using frames, the frame-definition file. Click No and the index.htm page remains untouched; you may want to create a link from that page, or another part of your web, to the TOC or Frameset For page (see "Finishing It All Off," later in this chapter).

Setting Up the Search Page

If you told the wizard you wanted to include a search page, when you click Next you'll see the information in Figure 16-12.

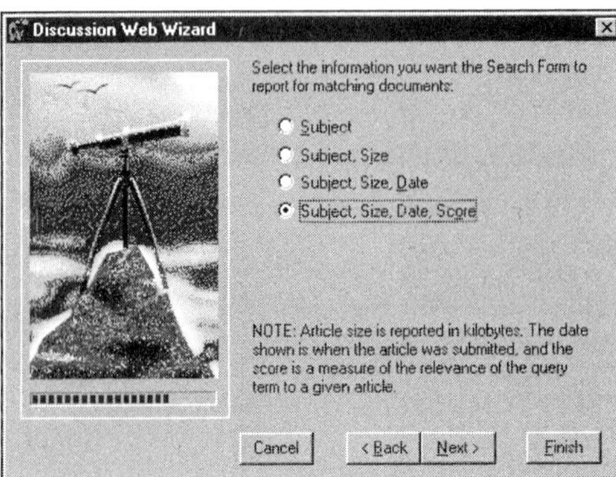

Figure 16-12 Setting up the search page

We learned about the search form earlier in this chapter (see "Building a Search Page"). This wizard's page simply allows you to define which columns appear in the results table when the user does a search. You can modify the search form further later on, by opening it in the Editor and double-clicking the form.

Create a Template

The wizard uses a template to define the background pattern, background color, and text colors used in all the pages it creates. So when you click Next you'll see the information shown in Figure 16-13.

We discussed these templates — and the different settings you see here — in Chapter 4.

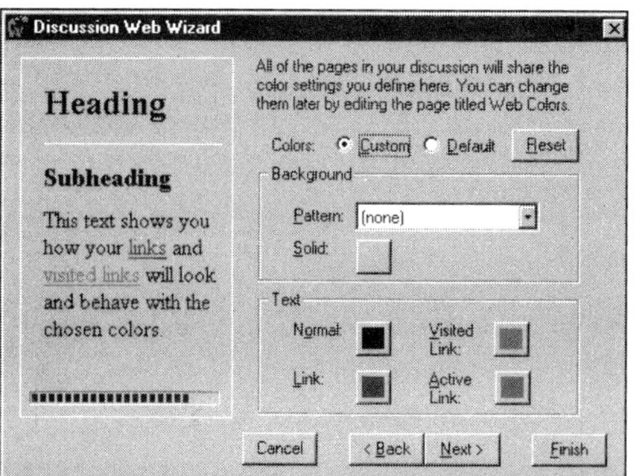

Figure 16-13 You can modify the page template here.

Do You Want Frames?

Click Next and you'll see the box where you can select the type of frames you want to use, if any — see Figure 16-14. (The wizard will create a page with the title Frameset For; by double-clicking this file in FrontPage Explorer later you can open the Frames wizard and modify frame settings.)

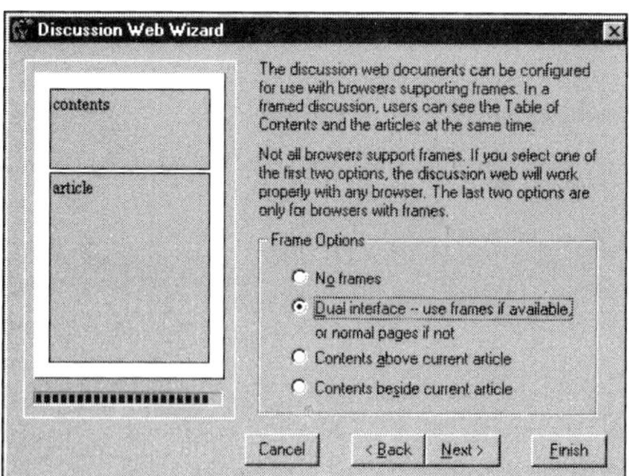

Figure 16-14 Set up your frames.

Discussion groups are a good example of when using frames is a good idea: users will see the list of messages in one frame, and the actual message they've chosen to read in another. They can click different messages in the list to view those messages.

No Frames If you select this, the system won't use frames at all.

Dual Interface This is, I believe, the best choice (it's also the default). Select this and the system will use frames if the browser can work with them, no frames if it can't. There'll be two frames, the list of messages at the top and the messages below.

Contents above Current Article Not such a good idea for two reasons. Users who don't have a frames-capable browser won't be able to use the discussion group. And this choice actually creates three frames: a banner at the top, the list of messages below, and the message below that, adding up to a lot of clutter on systems using a low video resolution. Click this option button and you'll see what the setup looks like in the sample picture.

Contents beside Current Article Another bad idea, for the same reasons explained above.

Remember This Information

Click Next and the wizard will show you the titles it's given to two important files (see Figure 16-15).

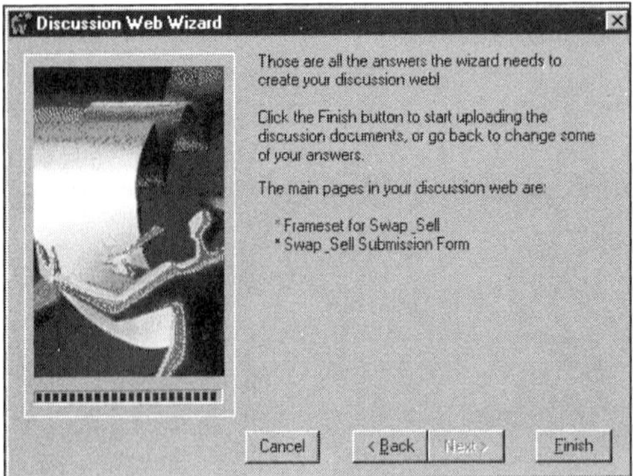

Figure 16-15 Write down these file titles.

These titles are based on the name you gave to the discussion group. In this example the group is called Swap & Sell, so you'll see two of these file titles (the & has been replaced with _, because FrontPage doesn't like & in titles):

Frameset for Swap _ Sell This one appears if you've chosen to use one of the three frame systems.

Swap _ Sell TOC This one appears if you've chosen not to use frames.

Swap _ Sell Submission Form This one always appears. This is the page containing the submission form used to send messages to the discussion group.

Which page will you link to? To the Frameset for Swap _ Sell page or the TOC page. Link from your web's main page or from wherever else you want users to be able to access the discussion group.

The Registration Form

Click Finish and the wizard completes its work, creating all the pages you need. It may then open a page titled Web Self-Registration Form in FrontPage Editor — it does this if you told the wizard that the discussion group will run in a web to which users must register.

You should modify this form — remove the comment and change the explanatory text if you wish. Then go to FrontPage Explorer and open the root web. Return to FrontPage Editor and save the document into the root web. Remember, registration forms must be saved in the root (see Chapter 15).

You should also remember to create links from your web to the registration form. So you may want two links for the discussion group, one that takes users directly to the group — for users who have already registered — and one that takes them to the registration form (you'll have to link out of the web to the form in the root web). When the user registers, he or she sees a confirmation page with a link to the discussion group. Remember also to modify the permissions settings for the web. See Chapter 17.

Finishing It All Off

In Figure 16-16 you can see, in FrontPage Explorer, the files and directories that the wizard created for you. (You may not have all these files, depending on the options you selected in the wizard.)

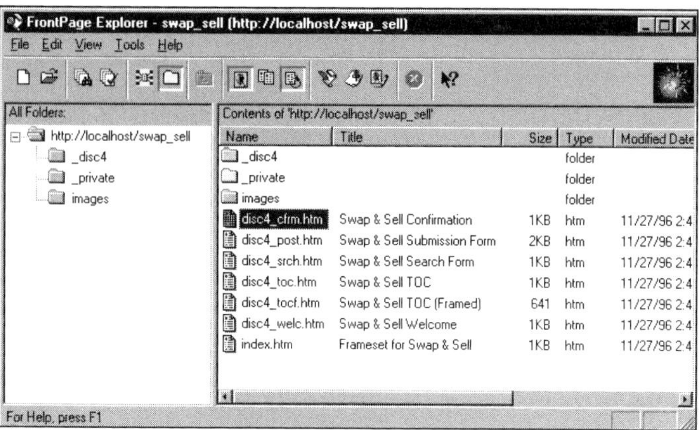

Figure 16-16 The web that's just been created

The chart on the next page shows different types of files and directories, and explains the purpose of each one.

File title or directory name	Purpose
Confirmation	The document displayed after the user submits a message. That's a wizard option, so you won't see this file if you told the wizard you didn't want a confirmation page.
Submission Form	The page holding the form in which the user enters the message.
Search Form	The page holding the form used to search for messages.
TOC	The list of messages used for non-frames browsers.
TOC (framed)	The list of messages used for frames-capable browsers.
Welcome	The page displayed in the main frame (below or to the right of the TOC).
Frameset For	The frame-definition document (see Chapter 12 for information about frames).
Web Self-Registration Form	If you told the wizard that users must register to use the discussion group you'll get this registration form. This page must be saved in the root web, so you won't see it in FrontPage Explorer along with the other files unless you're adding the discussion group system to the root web.
_disc4	This directory is where the Discussion handler will place the messages.
_private	This directory contains the style-sheet document used to set up the pages' background and text, as well as header and footer documents included in some of the pages using the Include WebBot.

What's left for you to do? Here are a few things to consider:

- Open each page one by one and remove the Comment WebBots.
- Read *everything* and replace any text you wish.
- If you selected the Category or Product input fields, edit to add appropriate entries to the drop-down list box.

* Check all the links and modify or remove.
* Add any new links you feel you need.
* Remember to open and modify, if necessary, the include files stored in the _private directory.
* Note that the Included Header and Included Article Header files (these are the file titles; look in the Title column in FrontPage Explorer) will have a link to Home (to the index.htm file) if you set up the web such that the discussion group's main page is not the index.htm file. You may want to modify this link if you are not linking to the discussion group from your web site's main page.
* Create a link from somewhere else in your web or from another web to either the Frameset For page (if you're using frames) or the TOC page (if you're not).
* Test the discussion group by previewing the page from where it is linked and then clicking the link to the group. If you are using frames, remember that in order to preview framed documents you must right-click the frame-definition document, select **Open With**, select FrontPage Explorer and click OK, and then use the Print Preview toolbar button to place the document in the browser (see Chapter 5).
* You won't be able to see the message files in FrontPage Explorer unless you select **Tools** → **Web Settings**, click the Advanced tab, and check the Show Documents in Hidden Directories check box (which is really a Show Hidden Documents check box, as the directory itself is not hidden).
* You can edit message files by double-clicking them in FrontPage Explorer to place them in the Editor.

The discussion group can soon get big. You can simply delete old message files or remove them from the web, and the table of contents will automatically be updated.

BONUS

Finding CGI Scripts

FrontPage has some great form tools, but there are plenty of things that it *can't* do. You may still want to use CGI scripts. You don't have to learn how to program these, though, just how to modify them. The Internet has lots of sites that provide public-domain, freeware, shareware, and commercial CGI scripts. You can download and use the ones you need. Remember, however, that CGI scripts run only in the operating system for which they are designed, so you must pick the ones that are appropriate for the operating system being used by your Web server.

Here are some places you can check for CGI scripts:

wtools (helpful tools for administering a Web site): `http://wwwece.engr.ucf.edu/~mav/Projects/wtools/`

Matt's Script Archives (lots of useful stuff): `http://www.worldwidemart.com/scripts/`

Scripts around the World (examples of CGI scripts in action): `http://www.worldwidemart.com/scripts/examples/`

Selena Sol's Public Domain Script Archive: `http://www.eff.org/~erict/Scripts/`

The Yahoo! CGI Page (links to many useful sites): `http://www.yahoo.com/Computers_and_Internet/Internet/World_Wide_Web/CGI___Common_Gateway_Interface/`

Summary

We've covered all the forms we're going to cover. You've seen how to create them from scratch, how to modify them, and, in this chapter, how to use the templates and wizards to create several for you. These are very useful, particularly in the case of the discussion group, which would be very complicated to set up for yourself.

When I first used FrontPage I'd been looking around for a way to add a discussion group to a Web site. I figured it would take me a while to find a program to do it, and probably a number of hours to set it all up. And I might have to pay a fee to use it, too. One of the first things I did with FrontPage was to create a discussion group, and I was amazed that I could set it up in less than five minutes. And it ran the first time, too! With a tool as easy to use as this, we're going to be seeing many more discussion groups on the Web. As FrontPage grows in popularity, finding a discussion group at a Web site will soon become about as unusual as finding snow at a ski resort.

CHAPTER SEVENTEEN

MANAGING YOUR WEB SITE

IN THIS CHAPTER YOU LEARN THESE KEY SKILLS

Well, we've come to the end. You've seen how to manage webs, how to create Web pages, and how to work with text, multimedia, hyperlinks, and forms. Your Web site has been created.

In this chapter we're going to sort out a few loose ends. I'll show you how to move your web from your computer to another one. You'll need to do that if the Web site is being published on another computer; that is, if its final location, the one at which people will be able to access it, is on another Web server, somewhere else on the World Wide Web or intranet. I'll also explain how to set up permissions, for both authors and users. You can define who is allowed to modify your webs and which users may access the site. And we'll look at To Do List, a little utility that you can use to keep a list of tasks you need to carry out.

Copying Your Web

You've spent a few days — or weeks, perhaps — creating a web. Finally it's ready for public view. Now you want to move it to another location. There are three ways to do that:

* Use the Publish FrontPage Web command to copy your web to a FrontPage-enabled Web server.
* Use the Web Publishing Wizard to copy a web to a non–FrontPage-enabled Web server.
* Use an FTP program — WS_FTP, CuteFTP, Norton File Manager, or any other FTP program — to transfer files to a non–FrontPage-enabled Web server.

Transferring to a FrontPage Server

Here's how to transfer your web to a FrontPage-enabled server.

1. In FrontPage Explorer, open the web that you want to copy.
2. Select **File** → **Publish FrontPage Web**. The dialog box shown in Figure 17-1 opens.

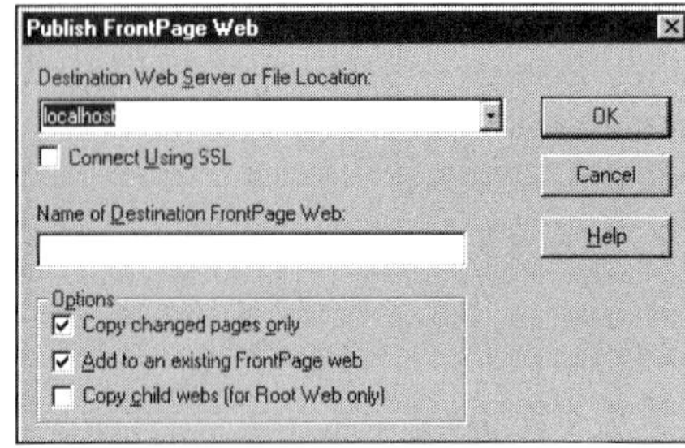

Figure 17-1 The Publish FrontPage Web dialog box

3. In the Destination Web Server or File Location, select (or enter) the name of the server you're copying the file to. If you're not sure what to enter, ask the server's administrator.

TIP **You can use this system to create a copy of your web on your hard disk. Simply type a path to a directory on your own hard disk in the Destination Web Server or File Location box. FrontPage will copy the web to that directory. If the directory doesn't exist it will ask if it should create it.**

4. Enter a name into the Name of Destination FrontPage Web. This is the name of an existing web at the specified server (if you are modifying that web) or a new name (if you are creating a new web at that server). Or leave it blank (or type **<Root>**) to publish to your root web.
5. You'll probably want to leave the Copy Changed Pages Only check box selected. If you are creating a new web this has no effect, but if you are modifying one it speeds up the process by transferring only pages that have changed.

6. If the Add to an Existing FrontPage Web check box is checked, FrontPage looks for the web you named in the Name of Destination FrontPage Web and transfers the files there (or, if the text box is blank, transfers it to the root web). If this check box is cleared, FrontPage creates a new web within the root web and calls it whatever you typed into the Name of Destination FrontPage Web. Remember, if you're creating a new web, you may have to inform the server administrator and wait until the server has been reset before you can use this web.
7. If you opened the root web, you can select Copy Child Webs (For Root Web Only). If you do this, FrontPage will copy the root web *and* all the subwebs stored in the root web.
8. Click OK and the process begins.

TIP **Create an empty web of the same name at the other location early on, and inform the system administrator. You'll remember from Chapter 1 that some Web servers must be restarted before you can use a web, so creating one early, then moving your finished web to that web (rather than creating a new web), will save time, as you'll be able to use the web right away.**

Using the Web Publishing Wizard at Non–FrontPage Servers

If you are copying your web to a server that does not have the FrontPage server extensions, you should use the Web Publishing wizard. You can use it two different ways; I'll explain both, but the second is probably the preferable method in most cases.

TIP **Have you installed the wizard? It's an optional component in the FrontPage Bonus Pack.**

Here's how to use it:

1. Select File → Publish FrontPage Web. You'll see the dialog box shown in Figure 17-1.
2. Enter the hostname of the server in the Destination Web Server or File Location box.
3. Select the Copy Changed Pages Only check box if you want to transfer only the pages that have changed since the last time you updated the Web site.

4. If you are transferring the root web you can select Copy Child Webs (For Root Web Only) to transfer files from subwebs, too, webs stored within the root web. But note that these files will be placed in the same directories as the root web. FrontPage will not create new directories for the subwebs.
5. The Name of Destination FrontPage Web text box and the Add to an Existing FrontPage Web check box have no effect; the wizard ignores them.
6. Click OK. The Web Publishing Wizard begins running — see Figure 17-2.

Figure 17-2 Enter your user name and password.

7. Enter the user or account name and the password you use to access the Web server, and click OK.

TIP **You may have been given an FTP address to use to upload your Web pages, but that's not what this is. You must enter the actual URL of the directory into which you are going to place the files.**

8. FrontPage begins transferring the web.

The Preferred Method

The above method transfers the entire web, including subdirectories that you don't need. Furthermore, this process doesn't always work (some users report that the wizard doesn't always start). If you launch the wizard directly, though, by selecting from the Windows taskbar Start → Programming → Accessories → Internet Tools → Web Publishering Wizard, or by double-clicking wpwiz.exe in the \Program Files\Web Publish\ directory, you'll have more control over the manner in which the wizard operates. When you see the first wizard box, click Next and then follow this procedure (see Figure 17-3):

1. Use the first Browse button to find the directory containing the files you want to transfer.

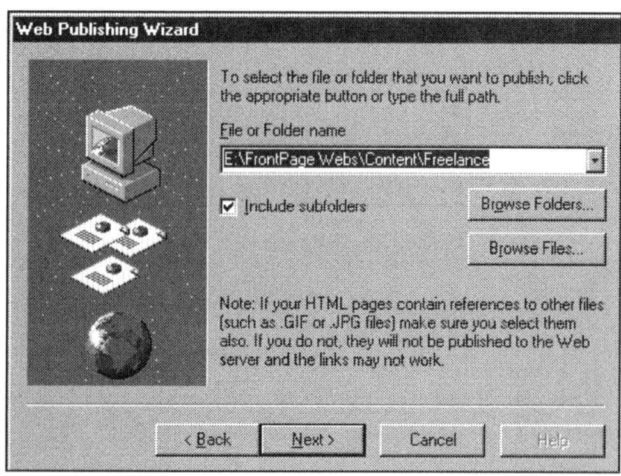

Figure 17-3 The Web Publishing wizard lets you select the directory.

2. Check Include Subfolders if you want to transfer subdirectories within the selected directory — you probably shouldn't, though. The wizard will include the directories containing files that will be used by the FrontPage server extensions, which you won't need transferred. If you are transferring the contents of the root web it'll even transfer webs created within the root web! So it may be better to transfer each directory separately — in which case you should clear this check box.

3. If you prefer to transfer a particular file, use the second Browse button. Note that the information shown in this wizard box is ambiguous, telling you to select the .gif and .jpg files in your web. Ignore this. You can either select an entire directory — in which case all files are transferred — or a single file.

4. Click Next and the box shown in Figure 17-4 appears.

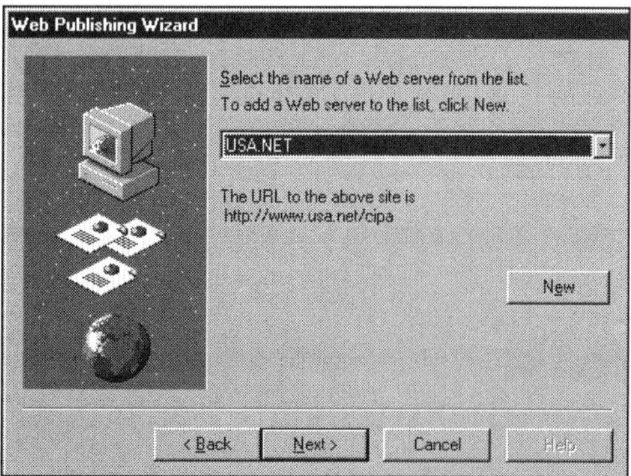

Figure 17-4 Pick a previous connection, or click New.

5. Select the Web site to which you plan to transfer this information from the drop-down list box. If this is the first time you've used the wizard, click New and you'll see the box shown in Figure 17-5.

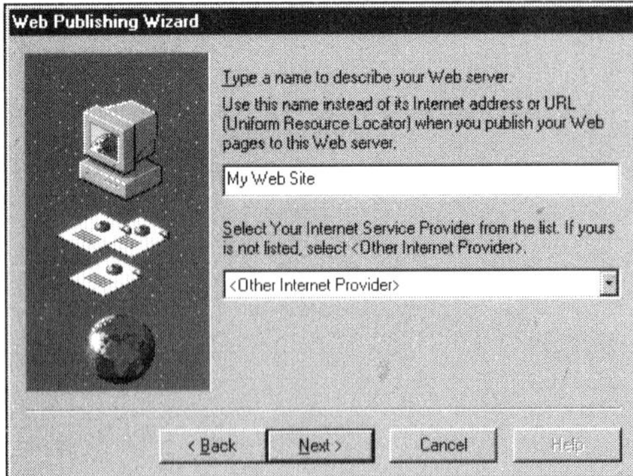

Figure 17-5 Set up a new connection.

6. Type a name for this Web site. This name will appear in the drop-down list box you saw in Figure 17-4 the next time you use the wizard.

7. Open the Select Your Internet Service Provider drop-down list box and see if your service provider is listed. If so, select it. If not, select <Other Internet Provider>. When you click Next, the information you see (Figure 17-6) will depend on your choice here. I'm going to use the <Other Internet Provide> as the example.

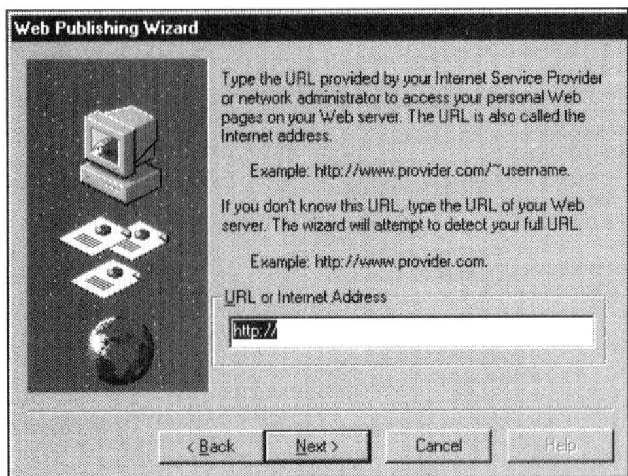

Figure 17-6 Tell the wizard where your Web site is.

8. Type the full URL of the directory in which you have to store your Web pages. Note that this is not the FTP directory that the server's system administrator may have given you; it's the actual Web URL. Talk with the administrator if you're not sure what to enter here.

9. Click Next and you'll see the information shown in Figure 17-7.

Figure 17-7 Pick the type of connection you plan to use.

10. Select the first option if you are working on a network and the Web server to which you are sending the pages is also on the network, or if you are on the network with a connection to the Internet. You'll also have to select this option if you are not on a network but are using a dialing system other than Windows 95's Dial-Up Networking.

Select the second option if you are using Dial-Up Networking to connect to the Internet, and select the Dial-Up Networking connection you use from the drop-down list box. (If that connection is not running when the wizard tries to transfer the files, the wizard opens the specified connection's Connect dialog box . . . which is a bit of a nuisance if you have another connection already running. If you use several Dial-Up Networking accounts, you may want to select the Use Local Area Network option instead. When the wizard tries to connect to the Web server you'll see an error message. You'll then be able to select FTP, click Next, and continue.)

11. Click Next in this box. If you are using Dial-Up Networking, enter a user name and password, click Next, and the transfer begins.

If you chose the Use Local Area Network option, you'll have to click another Next button, and the wizard then tries to connect to the Web server. If it's unable to do so you'll see an error message. Click OK and you'll see a box in which you can select the type of transfer you want to use: FTP or Windows File Transfer. Talk with your system administrator about which to use and how to set it up.

Remember to make sure that your main or home page is using the name that your server's administrator has set up as the default: index.html, default.htm, default.html, and so on. As I mentioned in Chapter 2, you should have been using the correct name all along, so that links to the main page are named correctly. If you forgot, modify the name in Explorer and the links will all be adjusted correctly. Then transfer the pages again.

Using an FTP Program

The Web Publishing wizard can be a little awkward sometimes. You may find it simpler to use the FTP program you are familiar with. Simply copy the files from your web to the server in the normal way (no, I'm not going to explain how to use FTP programs here!).

You don't have to copy all the files in the web, though. FrontPage webs contain a number of files that are used to administer the web, and which are completely useless unless the server extensions are present. Still, you should know which files you need to transfer: the .htm and .html files you've created, along with any image and multimedia files that go with them.

Authors and Users — Setting Permissions

FrontPage enables you to control who can modify and access your Web site. There are basically three things you can do with permission settings:

- Define who can modify your Web pages. Very useful for situations in which two or more people want to work on the same web, or in which a single administrator controls the root web and gives subwebs to authors.
- Make the site private, allowing only certain users the right to view the site (company employees or club members, for instance).
- Make the site a registration site, one that anyone can view, as long as they register first (note that this is not a real security measure, although making people register has certain benefits — see Chapter 15).

Here's how to set permissions:

1. In FrontPage Explorer select Tools → Permissions. The dialog box shown in Figure 17-8 opens. (If you are setting permissions for the root web, the box won't have the Settings pane; skip to Step 5.)

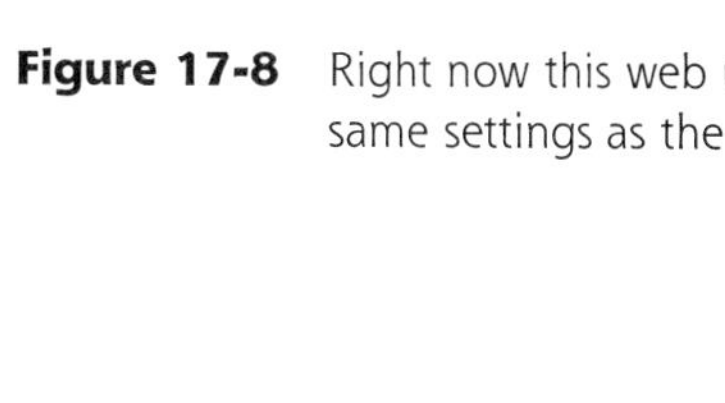

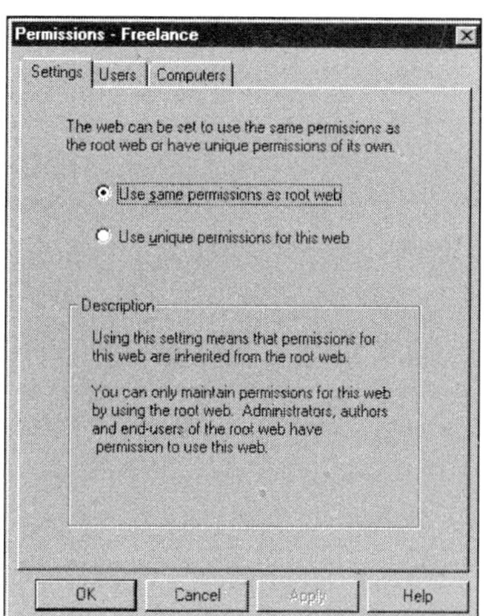

Figure 17-8 Right now this web uses the same settings as the root.

2. If Use Same Settings as Root Web is selected, this web is controlled by the root; people given permission to modify root-web pages can do so in this web, and users with access to the root web can also access this one. To modify those settings you need to open the root web and then open the Permissions dialog box.
3. If you want to modify this web, providing different permissions from those set for the root web, click Use Unique Permissions for This Web and then click the Apply button.
4. Click the Users tab and you'll see the information shown in Figure 17-9.

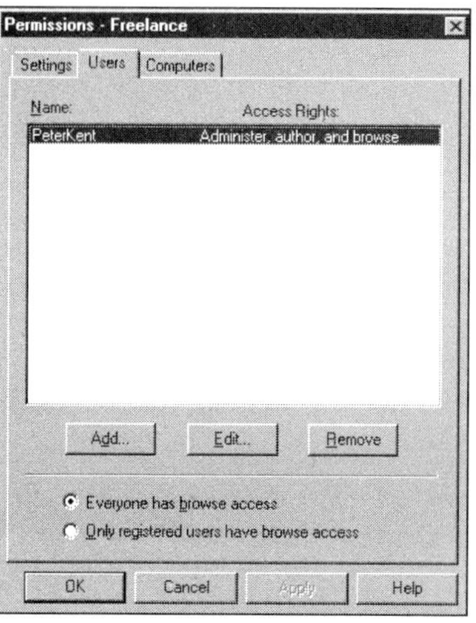

Figure 17-9 You can add administrators, authors, and users.

5. Notice the option buttons at the bottom of the dialog box. If Everyone Has Browse Access is selected, there's no need to set up accounts so users can view your Web site. Anyone with access to the network on which your web is published will be able to see the pages. If you want to restrict access to only people for whom you've specifically provided permission, click Only Registered Users Have Browse Access.

TIP **This is a little ambiguous, because as you saw in Chapter 16 you can force users to register to get onto your Web site. This option button can be used in two ways — once the site has been set up as one that requires registration, there are two ways for a user to gain access. Either you can set up an account for the user and give the user the password you have provided for that user (you'll see how to do that next). Or you can create a registration page (see Chapters 15 and 16), so users can register themselves to gain access to the site. The first method provides security (only people you approve will gain access), the second does not (anyone who registers can get into the site). If it's security you're after, check the Only Registered Users Have Browse access option button, but do not create a registration page for the web.**

6. To create a new administrator, author, or user account, click Add and the Add Users box opens (Figure 17-10).

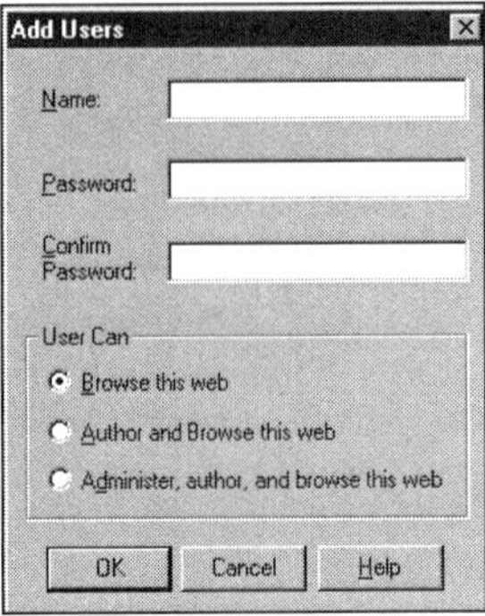

Figure 17-10 You can create a new administrator, author, or user account.

7. Enter an account name, and then type a password in both password boxes.

8. Select the type of access:

   Browse this web — The account owner will be able to view pages at the Web site, but nothing more. Of course, if the Everyone Has Browse Access option button was selected earlier, this sort of account is meaningless; users don't need an account to view the Web site anyway.

Author and Browse This Web — The account owner will also be able to author at the Web site; that is, to create and modify Web pages.

Administer, Author, and Browse This Web — The account owner will also be able to administer the Web site — that is, to add and modify web accounts.

9. Click OK and the new account is created.

10. You may, if you wish, restrict Web use according to the IP number of the computer accessing the web. This is not very useful if all the authors and administrators are working on Dial-Up Networking connections, because in most cases their IP (Internet Protocol) addresses are not fixed (they're assigned when they log on). This may be useful in a corporate setting, though, if you know the IP addresses of the computers on the network. To modify these computer permissions, click the Computer tab and you'll see the information in shown Figure 10-11.

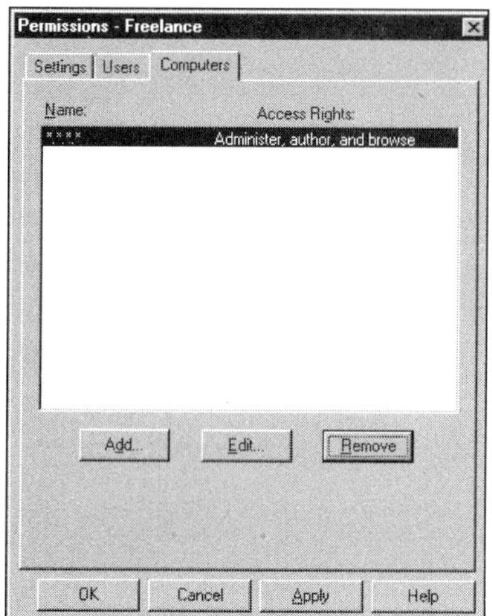

Figure 17-11 Define which computers may use the web.

11. This box shows you which computers may be used to access the web. You could, for instance, limit which corporate users may view the Web site. You could create a Browse account for, say, 182.174.*.*, which would mean that any computer with an IP number that didn't start with 182.174. would not be able to view the Web site.

TIP **For a detailed explanation of this feature, see this Microsoft Knowledge Base page:** `http://www.microsoft.com/kb/articles/q156/9/81.htm`

12. When you've set up your permissions, click OK and they're saved to the web's configuration files.

TIP **What is your computer's IP address? I'll show you how to find out later in this chapter; see "Testing Your Connection."**

Changing Your Own Password

You can change your own password — whether you have administrator or simply author privileges — using the Tools → Change Password command. You type your current password once (to prove you have the right to change a password), and then enter your new password twice. When you type your passwords you'll see asterisks, not what you type, so that someone looking over your shoulder can't steal the password.

TIP **The administrator cannot modify account passwords, except his or her own, so if an author or another administrator loses his or her password the administrator will have to re-create the account.**

A Handy Reminder — To Do List

To Do List is a very simple utility that you can use to keep track of things that you need to do to your web. It holds reminders placed there from various locations throughout FrontPage.

Select Tools → Show To Do List in FrontPage Explorer or the Editor, or click the To Do button, and the window you see in Figure 17-12 opens.

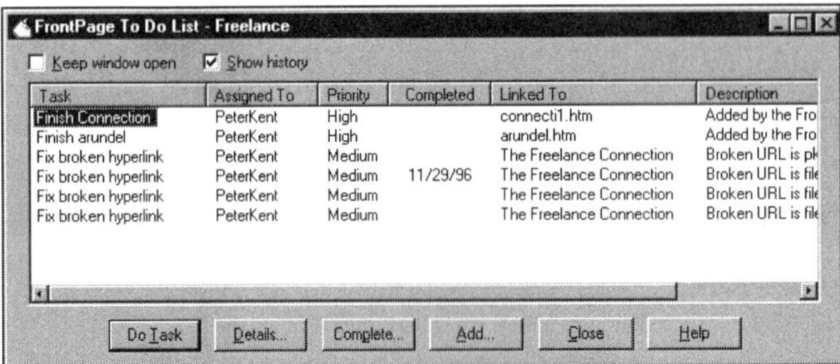

Figure 17-12 To Do List

You can add an item to the list by clicking Add, then entering a task name and a description of the task. You can select a priority, too, and even assign the task to a particular person. You can also add tasks from various other places within FrontPage. When you use the spell checker, find, and search-and-replace features, for instance, or when you search for broken hyperlinks (see Chapter 7), you can click a button to automatically add a task to To Do List. Also, you can select Edit → Add To Do Task in both FrontPage Editor and Explorer, and a box lets you enter information; the task is automatically linked to the open page (in the Editor) or the selected file (in the Explorer).

As you can see, To Do List simply shows a bit of information about the task: the task name, who it's assigned to, the priority, and so on. Here's what all the controls do:

Do Task Select an item and click Do Task. FrontPage opens the referenced document in FrontPage Editor and highlights the portion that needs work: the link that was broken, the misspelled word, or whatever the task was related to.

Details Select an entry and click Details to see a dialog box with the same information that's in the main list, but with two more items: the account names of the people who created the task and, perhaps, who modified the task (though this modified entry doesn't work correctly).

Complete Select an entry and click Complete to see a dialog box in which you can mark the task as completed, or delete it from To Do List entirely.

Add Click here to add a task to the list.

Keep Window Open Click here to keep the window open. If you don't, the window closes when you click Do Task.

Show History Select this check box and you'll see another column, Completed; if any tasks have been completed, but not removed from To Do List, they'll now appear in the list and the Completed column will show the date that they were marked as completed.

And that's that. To Do List is really quite a simple utility, but quite helpful if you actually put it to use.

General Configuration

There are a number of general configuration settings you need to know about, some of which you've seen before, so we'll quickly run through these settings in the Web Settings and Options dialog boxes.

Working with Web Settings

Select Tools → Web Setting in FrontPage Explorer to see the dialog box shown in Figure 17-13.

These are the settings:

Web Name This is actually the name of the directory in which the web is stored.

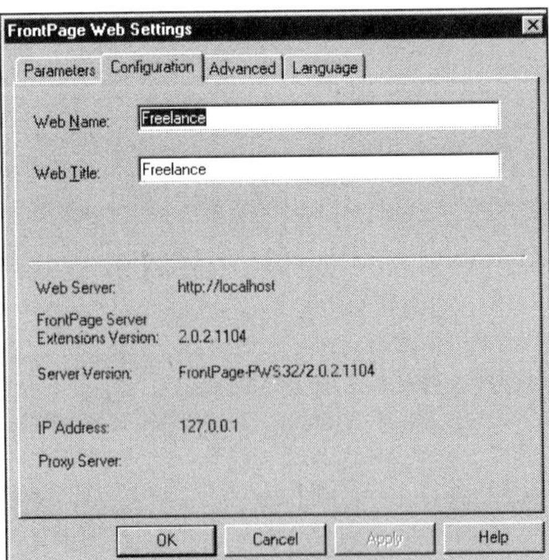

Figure 17-13 The Web Settings Configuration pane

Web Title This is initially the same as the directory name. But you can rename one and not the other, if you wish. The title is the name of the web as shown in the Explorer title bar and the Open FrontPage Web dialog box. (But the web name will be shown in parentheses after the title, if it's different.)

The other data shows general information about your FrontPage and server setup.

Click the Advanced tab to see the pane shown in Figure 17-14.

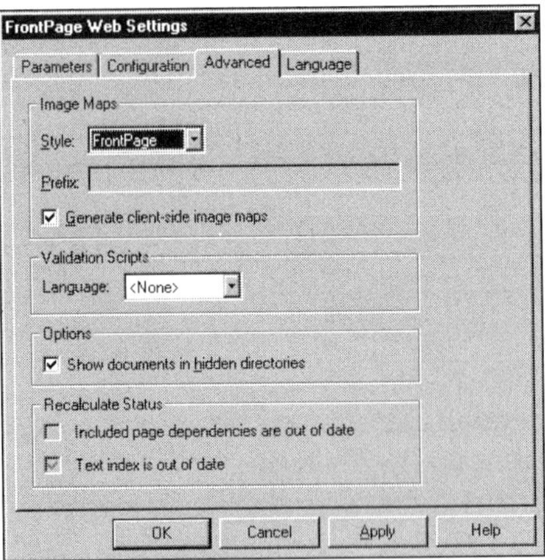

Figure 17-14 The Advanced pane

These are the advanced settings:

Image Maps The information in this area of the box was explained in Chapter 8. It's used to define the type of image maps created by FrontPage.

Validation Scripts This setting is explained in Chapter 14. It defines the type of script used to validate form input.

Show Documents in Hidden Directories This would make more sense if it were labeled Show Hidden Files. Some files are hidden in some of the subdirectories created within your web. Checking this box makes sure that you can see them. It *doesn't* make all the hidden directories in the web visible.

Recalculate Status These check boxes are set by the program itself; you can't modify the settings. They show potential problems, as well as whether you should use the Tools → Recalculate Hyperlinks command. Included Page Dependencies Are Out of Date means that you've included images or files, using the Scheduled Image or Scheduled Include WebBot, and the expiration dates have passed; Text Index Is Out of Date means that you have a Search page in your web (see Chapter 16), but you've added or modified text, so the search index should be updated.

Click the Languages tab to see the pane shown in Figure 17-15.

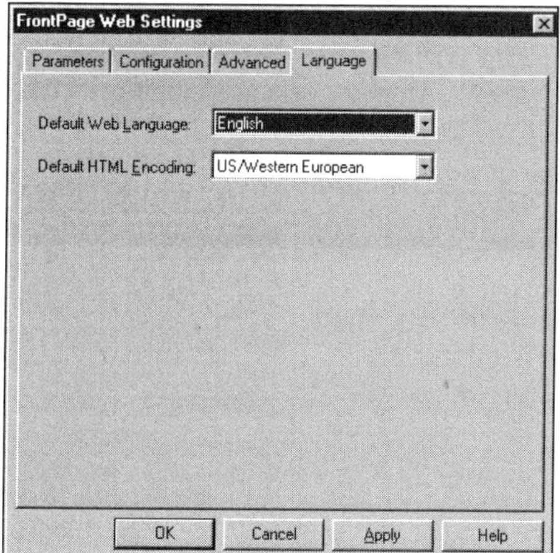

Figure 17-15 The Languages pane

The first setting, Default Web Language, defines which language should be used when error messages are sent to the Web browser. This may not work! It depends on how the server is set up.

The second setting, Default HTML Encoding, defines which character set should be used as the default when Web pages are saved by the Editor. Note that this setting can be overridden in the Page Properties dialog box.

Click the Parameters tab to see the pane shown in Figure 17-16.

In Chapter 10 you learned about the Substitution WebBot. This bot is used to place data that is stored elsewhere into a Web page. If you need to change the data, you can change it in one place and wherever it appears in the web it's changed.

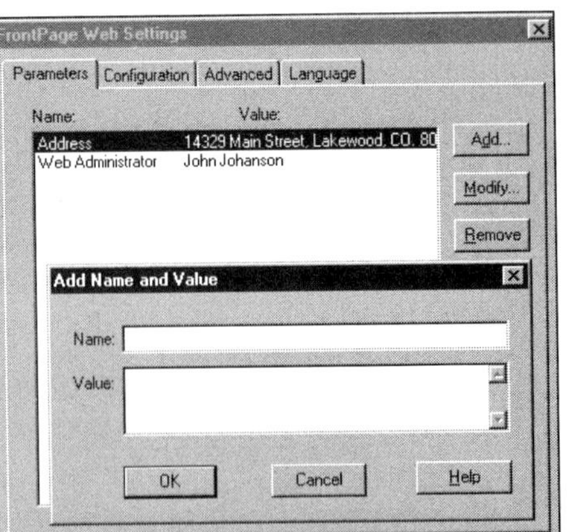

Figure 17-16 The Parameters pane

The Parameters tab is where you enter the data you want to save, such as addresses, phone numbers, personnel names, and so on. For instance, you might put the name of the person administering the Web site in some pages. If you use the Substitution bot that name can be changed throughout the web very quickly if the person quits or is fired!

The Web Options

Almost finished. We have a few more settings in the Options dialog box. Select **Tools** → **Options** and you'll see the information shown in Figure 17-17.

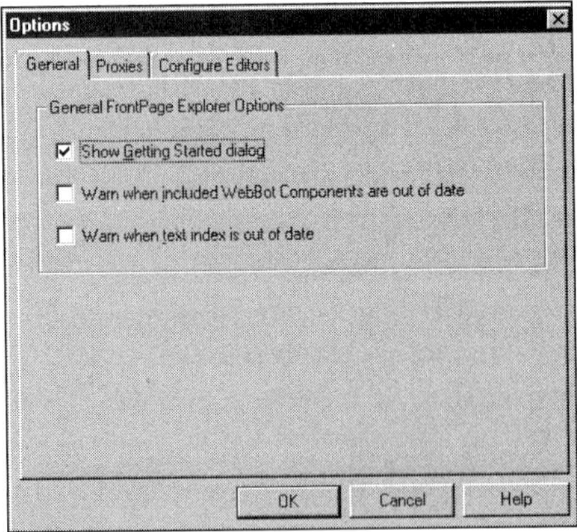

Figure 17-17 The Options dialog box

These are the settings:

Show Getting Started Dialog If this is checked, the Getting Started with Microsoft FrontPage dialog box (see Chapter 2) opens whenever you open FrontPage or whenever you close a web.

Warn When Included WebBot Components Are Out of Date If files or images included in other files, using the Scheduled Image or Scheduled Include WebBot (see Chapter 10), have passed their expired date, when you open the web you'll see a message. (However, this feature does not seem to work.)

Warn When Text Index Is Out of Date If a Search page's text index (see Chapter 16) is out of date, you'll see a message when you open the web asking you if you want to recalculate hyperlinks.

Click the Proxies tab to see the pane shown in Figure 17-19.

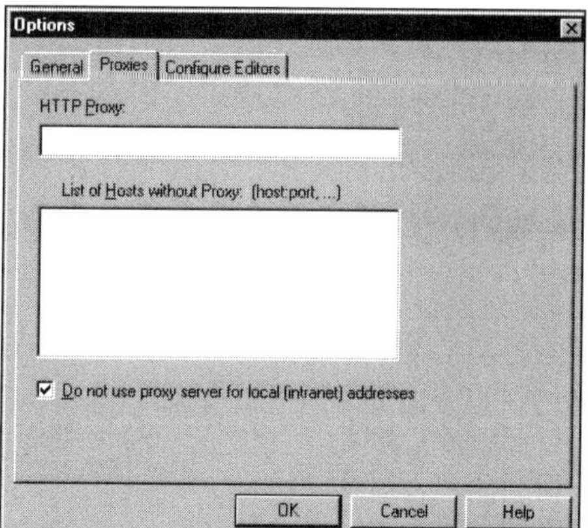

Figure 17-18 The Proxies pane

Networks often use *proxy servers,* special systems that allow access to the Internet but also act as *firewalls,* protecting the network from intruders. If your network uses a proxy server, you provide information to FrontPage so it can find its way out of the network and onto the Internet when it needs to. (If all of your work is within the network, and you don't need access to pages outside the network, then you don't need to configure the proxy server.)

You should ask your network system administrator what to enter into these boxes; you'll need the name and port number of the proxy server for the top box, and the names and port numbers of servers that you use that are *within* the network in the large list box. (Just type them in and separate with a comma.)

Click the Configure Editors tab to see the pane shown in Figure 17-19.

Use this dialog box to tell FrontPage where the editors are that you will be using. For instance, if you've installed a program you use for editing animated GIF files, or JPEG files, for instance, you can enter it here. Then you can open a file by right-clicking the file in Explorer and selecting **Open With**, or by double-clicking it.

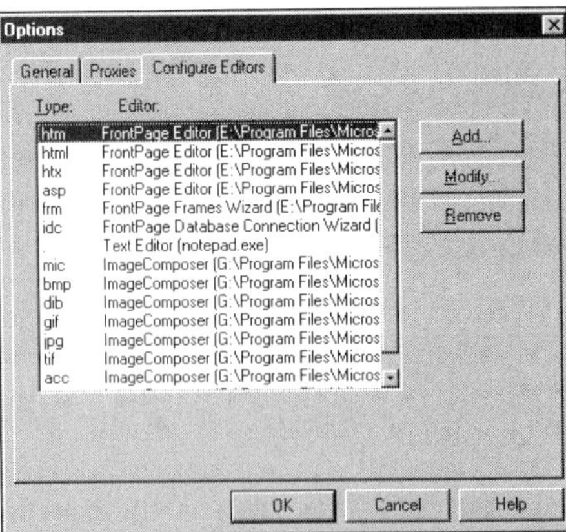

Figure 17-19 The Configure Editors pane

The box is a little awkward, though, because when you add editors you have to enter a file extension, so that FrontPage knows which editor to open when you double-click a file in FrontPage Explorer. If you want to add more than one editor for a particular file type (for instance, another HTML editor so you can edit .htm and .html files with that occasionally), you'll have to trick FrontPage; simply enter a fake extension, such as .ht1. You won't be able to use the editor by double-clicking a file, but you will be able to right-click and select **Open With**.

Testing Your Connection

Hidden away in the About box is a handy little test tool. Select **Help** → **About Microsoft FrontPage Explorer** and then click the Network Test button in the dialog box that opens. When the FrontPage TCP/IP Test box opens, click Start Test (see Figure 17-20). (If your Windows 95 Dial-Up Networking system is set up to open a particular connection, and if you're not currently logged on, you'll see the Connect dialog box; you can simply click Cancel to remove it for now.)

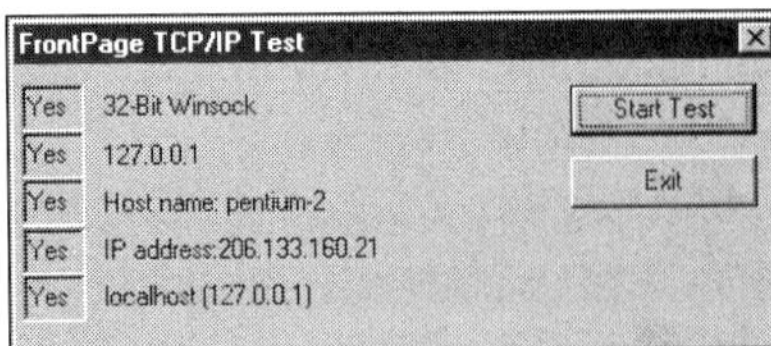

Figure 17-20 The FrontPage TCP/IP Test program

What is all this information? The program tests to see if certain things are present or how certain things are configured, and when that item is OK the test program shows Yes in the little box. Here's what the program found when I did the test:

32-Bit Winsock This shows that my computer has a 32-bit winsock installed. A *winsock* is like an Internet driver, letting Windows programs communicate across a TCP/IP network.

127.0.0.1 This shows that the 127.0.0.1 IP address is present. Most computers will be set up to use that IP address as the local address, the address that is used by the FrontPage Personal Web Server.

Hostname: pentium-2 The test looks for the computer's hostname. It found, in this case, that my Windows 95 Network settings were using pentium-2 as the computer name.

IP Address: 206.133.160.21 This is the IP address my computer is currently using. This number is the number I was assigned when I logged on to my Internet service provider using Dial-Up Networking. The number will be different next time because a number is assigned each time I log on, depending on what numbers are available. If I weren't logged on to my service provider, this would show the address as 127.0.0.1.

localhost (127.0.0.1) This is the IP address of my local host. It will generally be 127.0.0.1.

BONUS

Working with the Server

We haven't dealt much with the server in this book, as it's a complicated subject that requires far more space than we have available. Setting up a web server can be a complicated process, not one to be undertaken unless you're sure you really need to . . . and only then if you're willing to dedicate the time to learning how to do it.

Before we finish, though, I do want to show you the FrontPage Server Administrator. This is hidden away from sight (unless you installed FrontPage 97 over FrontPage 1.1, in which case you'll find this in the Start menu as before) in the \Program Files\Microsoft FrontPage\bin\ directory. Double-click the file named fpsrvwin.exe. You can see the FrontPage Server Administrator in Figure 17-21.

TIP **Notice that you can also open the FrontPage Editor (fpeditor.exe) from the same directory. You can then use the editor to work on files outside your webs, without needing to open FrontPage Explorer first.**

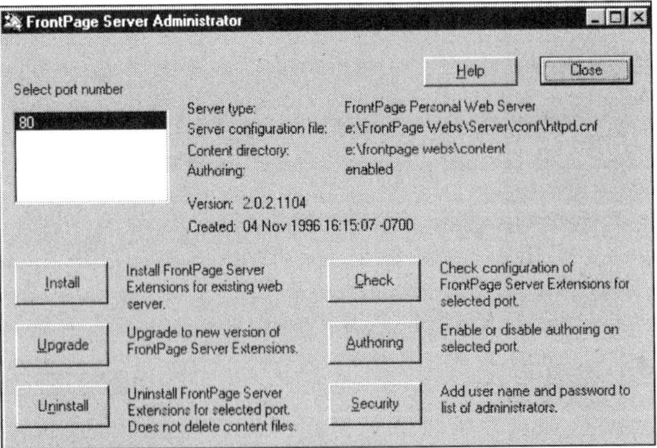

Figure 17-21 The FrontPage Server Administrator.

Note that most users will probably never need to use this program. If you installed FrontPage and used the FrontPage Personal Web Server, everything should already be set up just the way you need it. You may want to use the Security button, though.

This little program can be used to carry out these tasks:

Install Use this to install the server extensions for a server that you've already installed on your system. You have to specify what type of server you are using and the server configuration information.

Upgrade This upgrades a server to the latest FrontPage server extensions.

Uninstall This removes the server extensions from the server.

Check This checks to see if the server extensions have been properly installed on the server.

Authoring This lets you disable authoring (you won't be able to open webs in FrontPage Explorer on the specified server) or to specify that authors can work only if they are doing so with a Secure Sockets Layer connection to the server.

Security Use this to create new Administrator accounts.

Summary

That's it. We've come to the end of the book. If you've gone through this book chapter by chapter, you now know everything you need to know about creating and administering Web sites using Microsoft FrontPage.

No longer is Web publishing a complicated discipline that requires many hours studying books that weigh more than your laptop. Now you can publish on the Web or on an intranet almost as easily as you create memos and letters in your word processor. So go forth and multiply your Web pages. With FrontPage you can create them so quickly and with such ease that you can be as prolific as you wish.

DISCOVERY CENTER

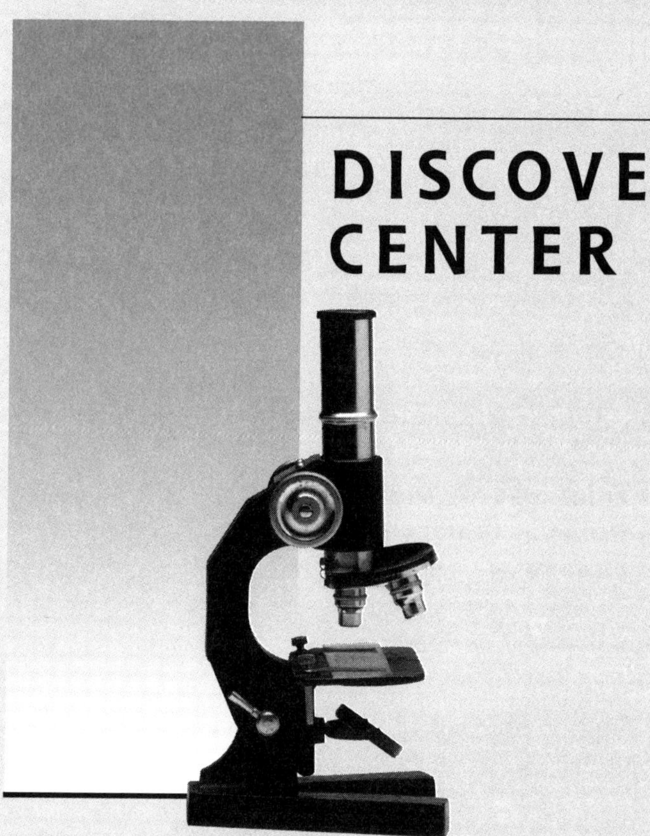

In this section, you'll discover many of the important steps for how to accomplish tasks in FrontPage 97. The Discovery Center serves as a handy reference to the most important tasks in the chapters. These quick summaries include page references referring you back to the chapters if you need more information.

CHAPTER 1

IMPORTANT!

Don't install FrontPage until you've read this chapter. Then you'll be able to decide which Web server you want to install (you must have one installed to use FrontPage): the FrontPage Personal Web Server (the best choice unless you plan to publish your Web pages on your own computer), the Microsoft Personal Web Server, or some other Web server.

FrontPage Is a Collection of Tools (page 10)

* **FrontPage Explorer** — An overview of your Web site and an assortment of web-management tools.
* **FrontPage Editor** — The Web page editor, far more powerful than most. Create tables, frames, and forms.
* **Templates and Wizards** — To help you create Web pages or entire Web sites in a hurry.
* **Image Library** — A library of graphics — backgrounds, headers, bullets, and so on.
* **FrontPage ToDo List** — A simple reminder tool.
* **FrontPage TCP/IP Test** — A program that checks your TCP/IP connection and provides useful information.
* **FrontPage Personal Web Server** — A very simple Web server.
* **FrontPage Server Extensions** — Special utilities that work alongside the Web server to provide services to your Web pages.
* **Server Administrator** — A simple program for managing FrontPage settings on the server. You may be using the FrontPage Personal Web Server or another, more powerful server, but in either case the Server Administrator is used to manage the FrontPage Server Extensions and to set permissions for the Web site; that is, to allow you to decide who may modify or read documents at that Web site.
* **Microsoft Image Composer** — A program that helps you create and edit images, and comes with a collection of clip art and photos, too.
* **Microsoft Personal Web Server** — A more advanced Web server than the FrontPage Personal Web Server.
* **Internet Explorer** — Microsoft's Web browser.
* **WebPost** — A utility that helps you transfer your Web pages from your hard disk to a non-FrontPage Web server on another system.

The Ways You Can Use FrontPage (page 12)

- Create a Web site on your own computer, then transfer it to a computer that has a FrontPage-compatible Web server.
- Create a Web site on your own computer, then transfer it to a computer that has a *non*–FrontPage-compatible Web server.
- Work remotely, with your computer connected to another computer across the World Wide Web or corporate intranet, making changes directly to the Web site.
- Install a Web server on your own computer and create the Web site on that computer, so other users can connect to your computer to view your work.

CHAPTER 2

To Open FrontPage (page 23)

Select **Start** → **Programs** → **Microsoft FrontPage**.

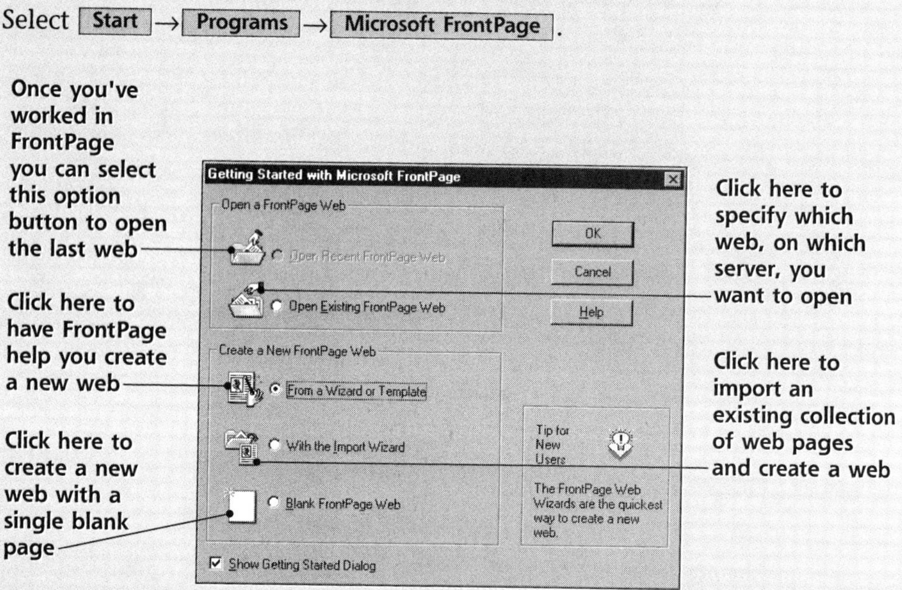

Once you've worked in FrontPage you can select this option button to open the last web
Click here to have FrontPage help you create a new web
Click here to create a new web with a single blank page
Click here to specify which web, on which server, you want to open
Click here to import an existing collection of web pages and create a web
Getting Started with Microsoft FrontPage
Open a FrontPage Web
Open Recent FrontPage Web
Open Existing FrontPage Web
OK
Cancel
Help
Create a New FrontPage Web
From a Wizard or Template
With the Import Wizard
Blank FrontPage Web
Tip for New Users
The FrontPage Web Wizards are the quickest way to create a new web.
Show Getting Started Dialog

The FrontPage Explorer Folder View (page 29)

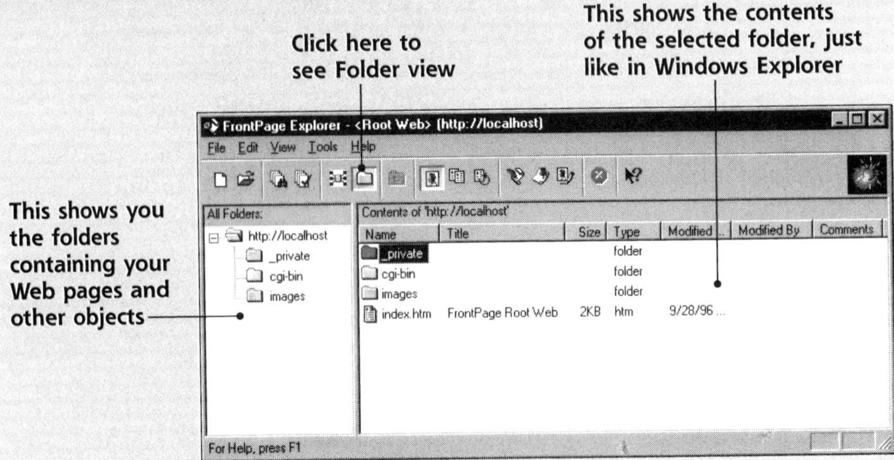

The FrontPage Explorer Hyperlink View (page 30)

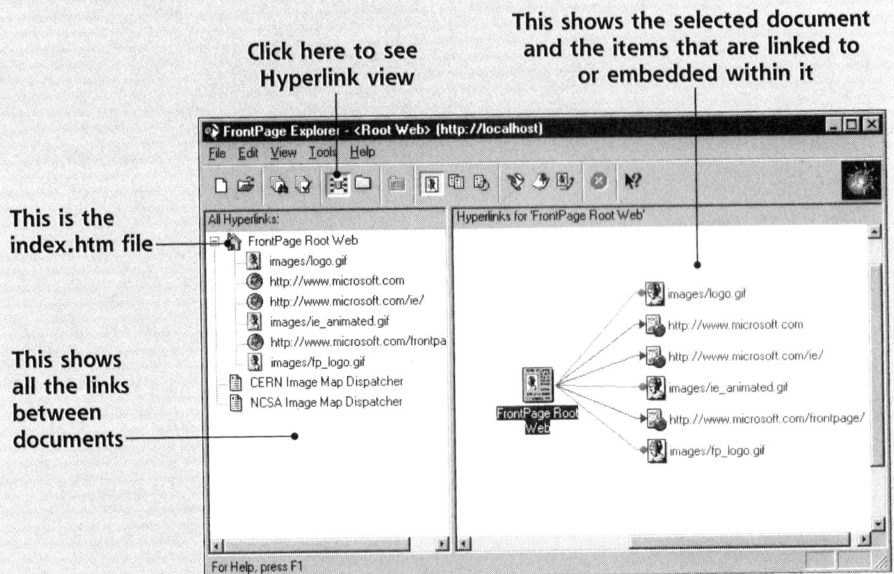

CHAPTER 3

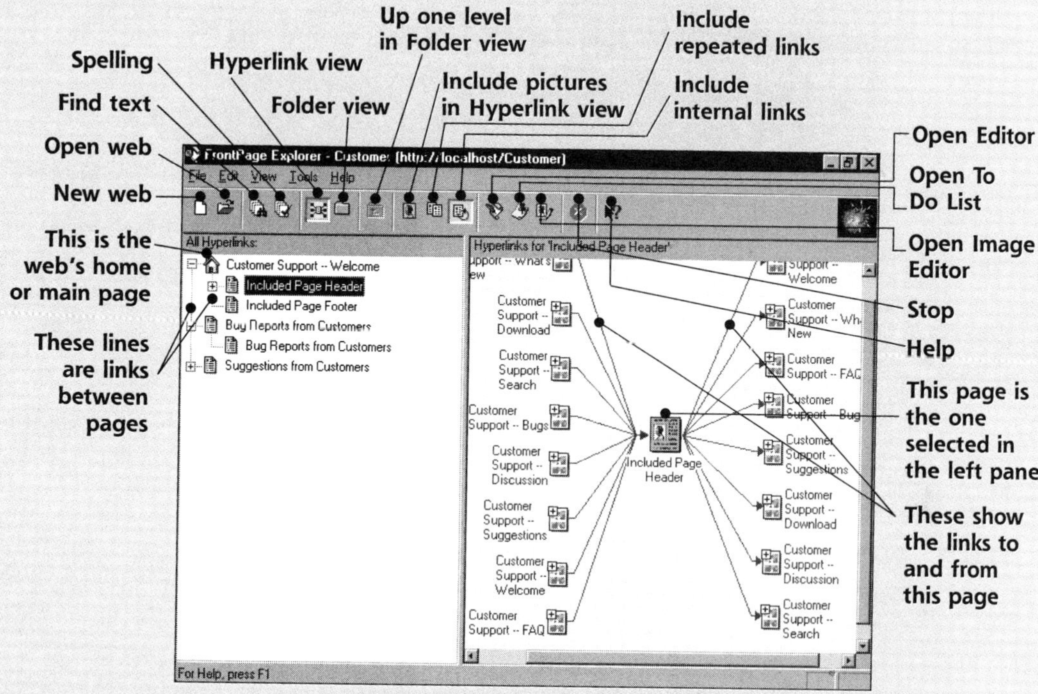

Explorer Icons (page 40)

The home page/main page (the index.htm file).

Click here to expand a portion of the tree.

Click here to collapse a portion of the tree.

A page or program in your web.

A broken link.

A link from one of your pages to something out on the Internet or intranet.

An image.

A mailto: link.

A Web page that contains some kind of web bot error.

The item you clicked in the left pane.

A document within your web that links to, or is linked from, the selected one.

This document has links of its own. Click the + to see what's linked to or from that page.

After clicking the + sign, the icon changes to one with a – sign. Click the – to collapse that part of the view.

An item outside your web, on the World Wide Web or intranet.

The little arrow at the end of this line means the line represents a link.

The little blob at the end of this line means that the object is embedded in the page.

To Work with Webs (page 46)

To copy a web Select File → Publish FrontPage Web. Enter the name of the host where you want to place the copy, and the name of the new web, then clear all the check boxes in the dialog box and click OK.

To merge webs Select File → Publish FrontPage Web again. Check the Add to an Existing FrontPage Web check box, enter the name of an existing web, and click OK.

To rename a web Choose Tools → Web Settings. Click the Configuration tab, then type a new name into the Web Name box. When you click Apply or OK, FrontPage renames the web.

To close the web Select File → Close FrontPage Web or File → Exit. Or simply open another web, and the current web closes automatically.

To open a web Select File → New → FrontPage Web or File → Open FrontPage Web, or select a recently used web from the bottom of the File menu.

To delete a web Open the web, then select File → Delete FrontPage Web.

To import pages Select File → Import, click Add File or Add Folder and find the files or directories you want, then click OK.

CHAPTER 4

To Open a Web Page from FrontPage Explorer (page 51)

* Click the toolbar button.
* Select Tools → Show FrontPage Editor.
* Double-click a file in the right pane.

- Right-click a file and select **Open**.
- Click a file and select **Edit**→**Open**.
- Click a file and press Ctrl+O.
- Drag a file from the Explorer onto the Editor.
- Right-click a file and select **Open With**.
- Click a file and select **Edit**→**Open With**.

To Open a File from within the Editor — a Page from Your Web (page 54)

1. Select **File**→**Open**, or click the Open icon.
2. Double-click a file to select it. That file will be opened in the Editor.

To Open a File within the Editor— a Page from Your Hard Disk or LAN (page 55)

1. Select **File**→**Open**, or click the Open icon.
2. Click the Other Location tab.
3. Click Browse and find the file you want to open.
4. Double-click the file to place it into the Open File dialog box.
5. Click OK and the file is opened in the Editor.

To Open a File within the Editor — a Page from the World Wide Web or Intranet (page 56)

1. Select **File**→**Open**, or click the Open icon.
2. Click the Other Location tab.
3. Click the From Location option button.
4. Type the URL of the page you want to borrow.
5. Click OK.

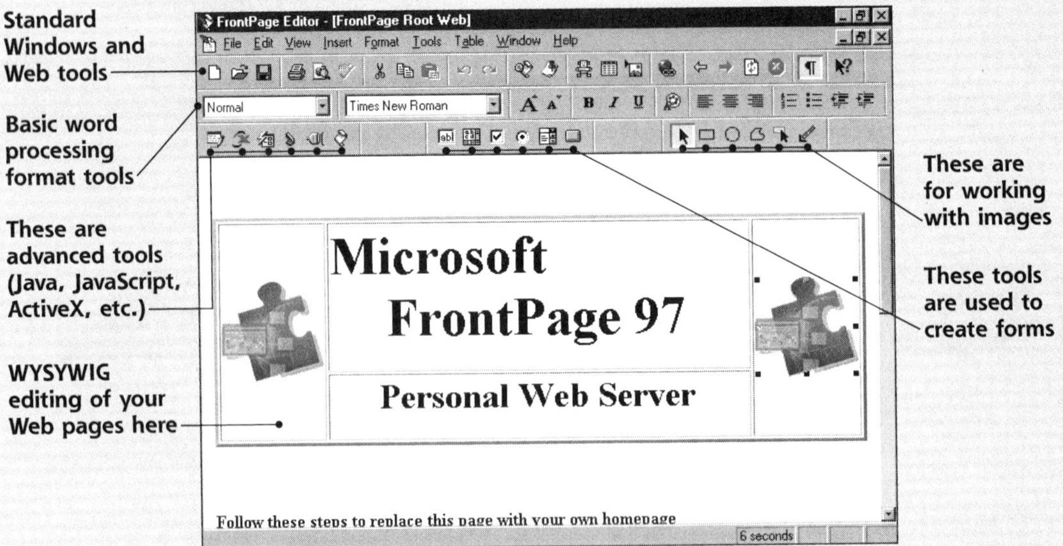
Standard Windows and Web tools
Basic word processing format tools
These are advanced tools (Java, JavaScript, ActiveX, etc.)
WYSYWIG editing of your Web pages here
These are for working with images
These tools are used to create forms
FrontPage Editor - [FrontPage Root Web]
File Edit View Insert Format Tools Table Window Help
Normal
Times New Roman
Microsoft
FrontPage 97
Personal Web Server
Follow these steps to replace this page with your own homepage
6 seconds

CHAPTER 5

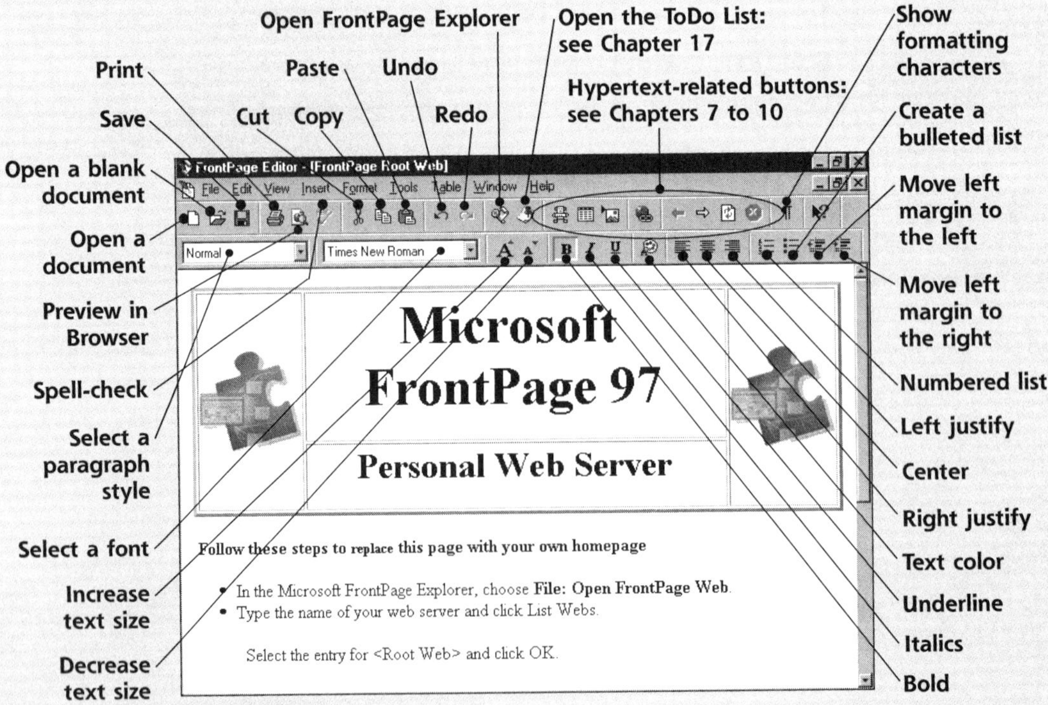
Open FrontPage Explorer
Open the ToDo List: see Chapter 17
Show formatting characters
Print
Paste
Undo
Hypertext-related buttons: see Chapters 7 to 10
Save
Cut
Copy
Redo
Create a bulleted list
Open a blank document
Move left margin to the left
Open a document
Preview in Browser
Move left margin to the right
Spell-check
Numbered list
Left justify
Select a paragraph style
Center
Right justify
Select a font
Text color
Increase text size
Underline
Italics
Decrease text size
Bold
FrontPage Editor - [FrontPage Root Web]
File Edit View Insert Format Tools Table Window Help
Normal
Times New Roman
Microsoft
FrontPage 97
Personal Web Server
Follow these steps to replace this page with your own homepage
In the Microsoft FrontPage Explorer, choose File: Open FrontPage Web.
Type the name of your web server and click List Webs.
Select the entry for <Root Web> and click OK.

To Export a File (page 74)

1. Select File → Save As.
2. Click As File.
3. Find the directory into which you want to save the file.
4. Type a name into the File Name text box.
5. Click OK.

To Save a File as a Template (page 74)

1. Select File → Save As.
2. Click As Template.
3. Type a template title and filename.
4. Type a description if you wish.
5. Click OK.

To View the HTML Source File (page 75)

Select View → HTML.

Purple text = HTML tags

Blue text = the attribute names within tags

Green text = the attribute values

Black text = the text that is visible to someone reading the Web page

To Preview Your Work in a Browser (page 78)

1. Select File → Preview in Browser.
2. Click the browser you want to view.
3. Click the Window size you want to check.
4. Click Preview.

Clicking the button opens the document in the last browser selected in the Preview in Browser dialog box.

CHAPTER 6

To Insert Text from a File (page 82)

Select Insert → File. You can insert .asp, .doc, .htm, .html, .htt, .htx, .mcw, .rtf, .txt, .wpd, .wps, .wri, .xls, and .xlw files.

To Start a New Paragraph (page 82)

Press Enter.

To Insert a Line Break (page 82)

Press Shift Enter.

To Insert a Horizontal Line (page 84)

1. Select Insert → Horizontal Line.
2. Double-click the line, or right-click and select Horizontal Line Properties. A dialog box opens.
3. Select the line width and height.
4. Select the line alignment: Right, Center, or Left.
5. Select a color.
6. If you want a solid line, click the Solid Line (No Shading) check box.
7. Click OK.

To Create Horizontal Lines from Images (page 85)

1. Select Insert → Image.
2. Click the Clip Art tab.
3. Select Lines from the Category drop-down list box.
4. Pick your line and click OK.
5. Right-click the line and select Image Properties to modify the line.

To Insert Special Characters (page 86)

1. Select Insert → Symbol.

2. Click the symbol you want, then click Insert.
3. Click Close.

To Add Comments (page 86)

1. Select Insert → Comment.
2. Type your comment.
3. Click OK.

Comments are visible to you, but not the reader.

To Find Text Anywhere in Your Web (page 88)

In FrontPage Explorer select Tools → Find.

To Find and Replace Anywhere in Your Web (page 89)

In FrontPage Explorer select Tools → Replace.

To Spell-Check the Entire Web (page 89)

In FrontPage Explorer select Tools → Spelling.

To Find, Replace, or Spell-Check in a Single Document (page 88)

In FrontPage Editor select Edit → Find, Edit → Replace, and Tools → Spelling.

CHAPTER 7

To Place a Link to a Document in Your Web Page (page 96)

1. Select the text on which you want to place the link.
2. Click the toolbar button. The Create Hyperlink box show the Open Pages pane (if other documents are open in the Editor) or the Current FrontPage Web pane.

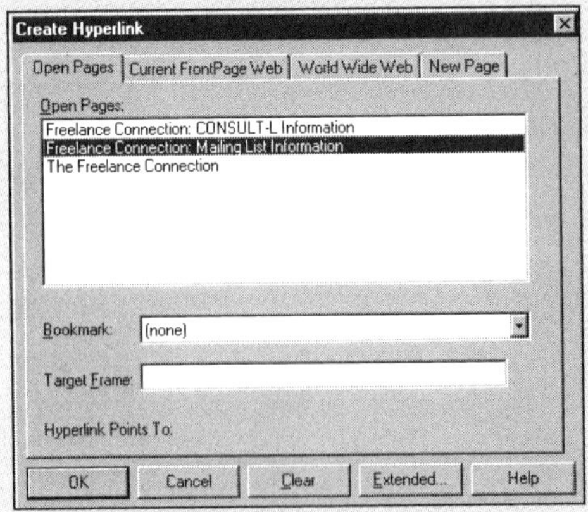

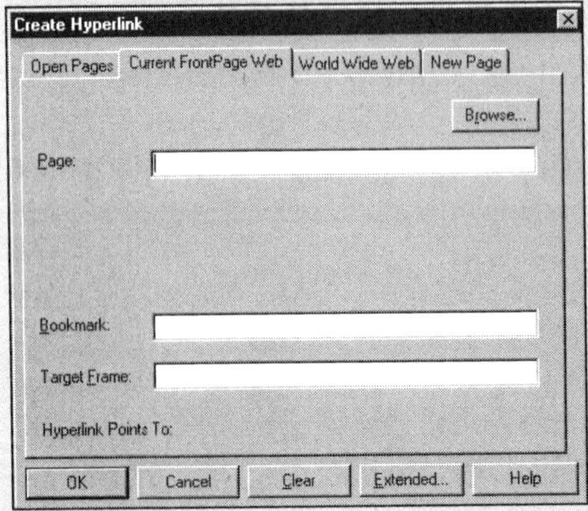

3. To link to an open page, click the page in the Open Pages pane.
4. To link to an unopened page in the current web, click Browse in the Current FrontPage Web pane, and select the file you want to link to.
5. Click OK, and you've created your link.

To Create a Link to a New Page (page 98)

1. Select the text on which you want to place the link.
2. Click the toolbar button.
3. Click the New Page tab.
4. Enter a Page Title box.
5. Enter a filename.
6. If you want to open the page you are about to create in the Editor right away, leave Edit New Page Immediately selected.

7. If you don't want to create the page right now, but want to be reminded to create it later, select Add New Page to To Do List.
8. Click OK and the New Page dialog box opens.
9. Select a page template or wizard, and click OK.

To Create a Link to the Outside World (page 99)

1. Select the text on which you want to place the link.
2. Click the toolbar button.
3. Click the World Wide Web tab.
4. Type a URL. Or click Browse, find the page in your Web browser, then press Alt+Tab to switch back to the Create Hyperlink dialog box. The URL will be entered automatically.
5. Click OK.

Creating Internal Links (page 101)

To create a link to another part of the current document, first create a bookmark, then link to the bookmark.

To Create a Bookmark (page 101)

1. Highlight the text where you want the bookmark.
2. Select Edit → Bookmark.
3. Click OK.

Linking to the Bookmark (page 102)

* When using the Open Pages pane of the Create Hyperlink dialog box, select the bookmark from the Bookmark drop-down list box.
* When using the Current FrontPage Web pane of the Create Hyperlink dialog box, type the bookmark into the Bookmark drop-down list box.

To Move Through Links (page 103)

Hold the Ctrl key and click a link. To move back, use the toolbar's button.

To Find Broken Links in the Current Web (page 105)

In FrontPage Explorer select **Tools** → **Verify Hyperlinks**.

To Find Broken Links to the Outside World (page 106)

1. In FrontPage Explorer select **Tools** → **Verify Hyperlinks**.
2. Click Verify.

CHAPTER 8

Placing an Image into the Document from the FrontPage Web (page 110)

1. Place the cursor where you want your image.
2. Click the toolbar button. The Image dialog box opens.
3. Click the Current FrontPage Web tab.

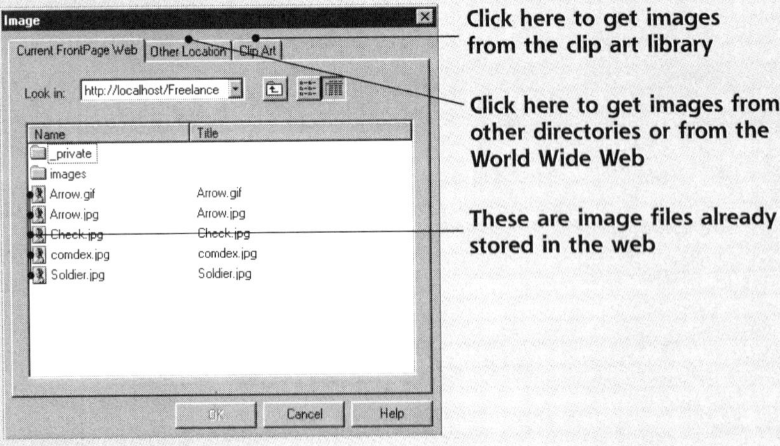

4. Click the image you want to use in the large list box.
5. Click OK.

Inserting Images from the Clip Art Library (page 110)

1. Click the Clip Art tab in the Image dialog box.
2. Select a category from the Category box.

3. Click the image you want to use.
4. Click OK to place it into your document.

Using Images Stored Elsewhere on Your Hard Disk (page 111)

1. Click the Other Location tab.
2. Use the Browse button to find the image you want.
3. Click the OK button.

Using Images from the World Wide Web or Intranet (page 112)

1. Click the Other Location tab again.
2. Type the URL of the image into the From Location text box.
3. Click OK.

To Modify an Image (page 114)

Right-click the image and select **Image Properties**.

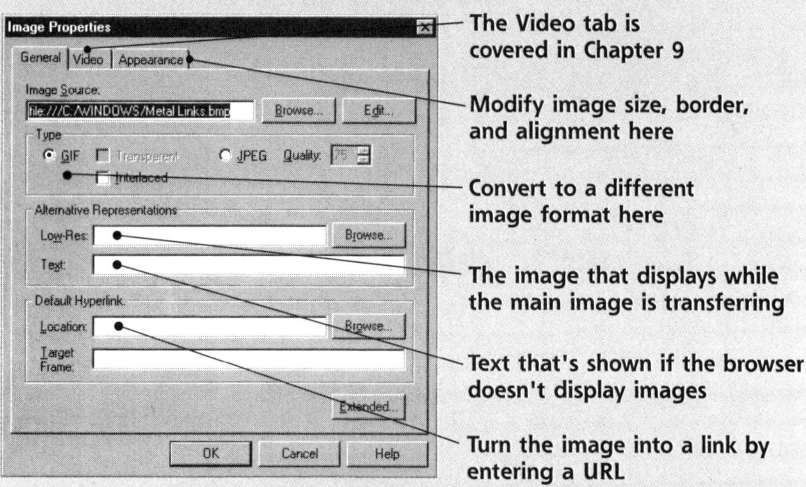

To Create an Imagemap (page 121)

1. Click the image.
2. Click one of the three drawing buttons on the toolbar: insert ▭ (to draw a rectangle or square), ● (to draw a circle), or ⌂ (to draw an irregular shape).

3. With the mouse, draw a shape on the image.
4. When you finish drawing, the Create Hyperlink box opens.
5. Enter the hyperlink information and then close the box.
6. Create the next hot spot by drawing another shape.

CHAPTER 9

To Insert a Marquee (Scrolling Text) (page 126)

1. Type the text you want to appear in the marquee into the document.
2. If you wish you may place a link on the text and format it in the normal way.
3. Highlight the text and select Insert → Marquee.

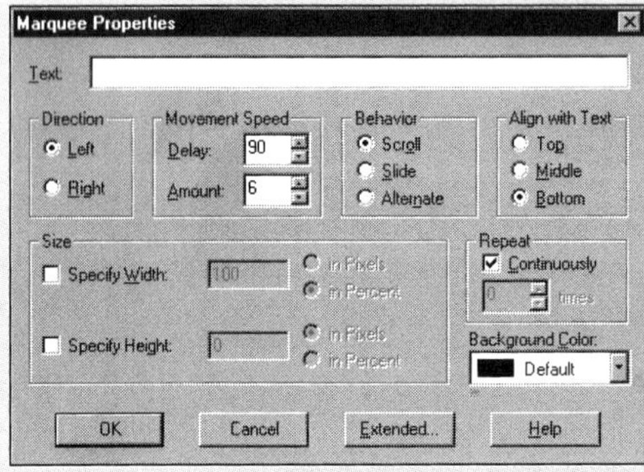

4. Select the direction of movement: Left (meaning from the right to the left), or Right (from the left to the right).
5. Set the movement "speed" using the Delay and Amount settings.
6. Set the Behavior. Scroll makes the text scroll onto the marquee at one end and off at the other; Slide makes it scroll but stop when it gets to the end; Alternate scrolls back and forth.
7. Select the alignment.
8. Specify the size of the marquee.
9. To limit the number of times the marquee moves, clear Continuously and type a number into the Times box.
10. Pick a background color.
11. Click OK and the marquee is created.

To Insert a Video (page 128)

1. Select Insert → Video and pick the .avi video file you want to use.
2. Click OK.
3. Right-click the video box and select Image Properties.
4. Set the video properties and click OK.

Note: This feature is currently only supported by Internet Explorer, so most browser users on the World Wide Web will not be able to view these videos.

Adding a Background Sound (page 129)

1. Select Insert → Background Sound.
2. Pick the sound and click OK.

Modify the sound properties in the Page Properties dialog box. Only Internet Explorer plays these background sounds.

Using Other File Formats (page 129)

You can easily use other file formats by creating hyperlinks to them, making them external files.

To Embed Another File Type (page 130)

1. Select Insert → Other Components → Plug-Ins. The Plug-in Properties dialog box opens.

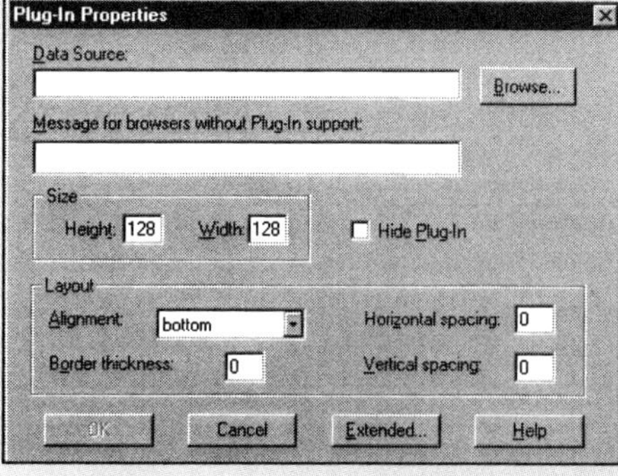

Figure 9-3 The Plug-in Properties dialog box.

2. Click Browse to find the file you want to use, then return to the Plug-in Properties dialog box.

3. Type a message that will be displayed to users working with browsers that don't use the <embed> tag.
4. Modify the size if you wish.
5. Click Hide Plug-in if you want the plug-in to be invisible; if it's playing a sound, for instance.
6. Specify the alignment.
7. Specify the border, if any, and spacing.
8. Click OK.

Linking to Databases (page 132)

If you understand ODBC databases you can use the Database Connection Wizard to link your Web pages to a database. This is complicated stuff though, not for the novice.

To Insert a Java Applet (page 133)

1. Import the .class file into your web, and any associated files.
2. Place the cursor where you want the applet in FrontPage Editor and select Insert → Other Components → Java Applet.
3. Enter the required information to run the Java applet (available from the Java applet's documentation or from the programmer).
4. Click OK.

Using JavaScript and VBScript (page 134)

If you know the JavaScript or VBScript programming languages, you can insert scripts into your pages: select Insert → Script.

Inserting ActiveX Components (page 136)

Another procedure for the expert, not the novice: you can insert ActiveX components into pages. Select Insert → Other Components → ActiveA Control.

CHAPTER 10

WebBots Carry Out Certain Tasks (page 139)

Click the toolbar button, or select Insert → WebBot Component.

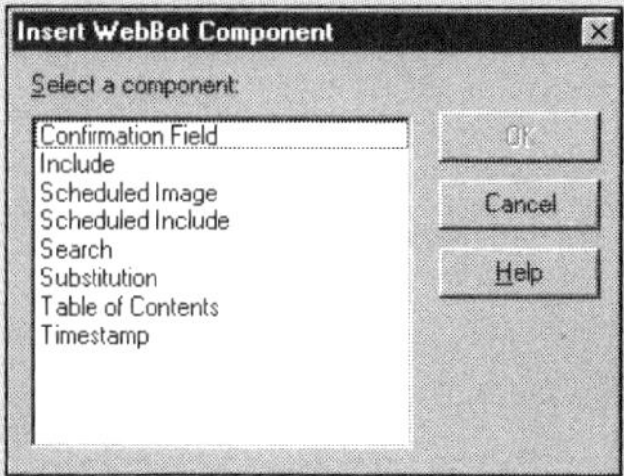

* Include — Insert one HTML document into another.
* Scheduled Include — Insert one document into another at a specified time.
* Timestamp — Insert information showing when the document was last saved.
* Substitution — Insert the author name, document description, and document URL.
* Table of Contents — Create a table of contents of your entire web.
* The other WebBots are described elsewhere in this book.

To Insert One Web Page Into Another (page 140)

1. Select Insert → WebBot Component.
2. Click Include in the list of WebBots, then click OK.

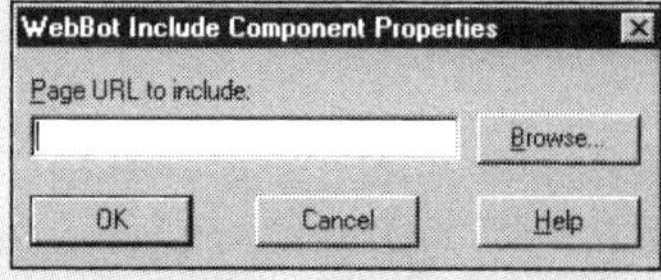

3. Click Browse and find the file you want to include.
4. Click OK.

To Insert a Page at a Specified Time (page 141)

This is exactly the same procedure as inserting an image (Chapter 8); select the Scheduled Include WebBot.

Inserting a Timestamp (page 142)

1. Select Insert → WebBot Component.
2. Click Timestamp in the list of WebBots, then click OK.
3. Select the type of timestamp.
4. Click OK.

Inserting Document Information (page 142)

1. Select Insert → WebBot Component.
2. Click Substitution in the list of WebBots, then click OK.
3. Select the type of information from the drop-down list box (Author, Modified By, Description, Page URL).

Note: The Description is the comments in the Properties dialog box viewed in FrontPage Explorer.

To Create a Table of Contents (page 144)

1. Select Insert → WebBot Component.
2. Click Table of Contents in the list of WebBots, then click OK.

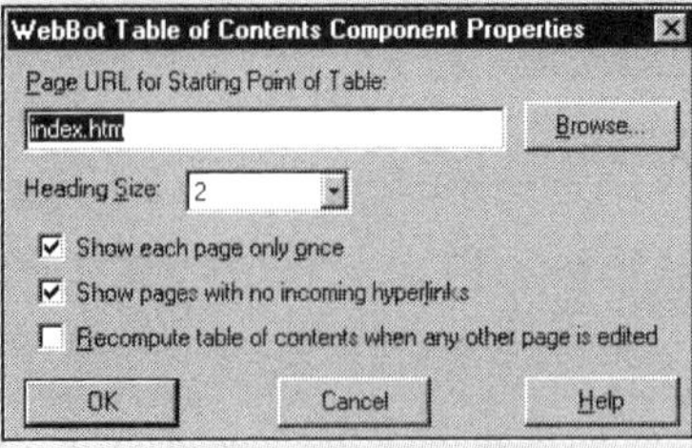

3. Select your table of contents settings.
4. Click OK. A generic table of contents is created; you can see the actual table of contents by previewing the file.

The Four Ways to Modify Your Pages' HTML (page 145)

- Use the HTML Markup WebBot: select Insert → HTML Markup or click the toolbar button.
- Click an Extended button in a dialog box (this is present in many dialog

boxes).

* Select View → HTML, make changes directly to the HTML, then click OK.
* Edit the document in another HTML editor. For instance, right-click a file in FrontPage Explorer, select Open With, then select an editor (such as notepad.exe).

CHAPTER 11

To Create a Table (page 154)

1. Click the toolbar button.
2. Drag the mouse pointer to select the number of columns and rows you want.

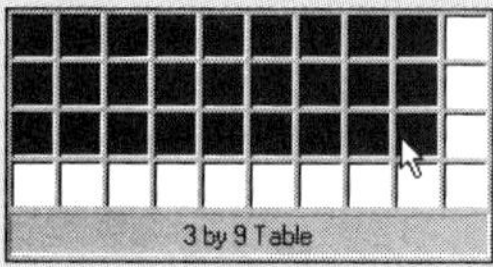

To Set Up the Table the Way You Want It (page 154)

Click the table and select Table → Table Properties.

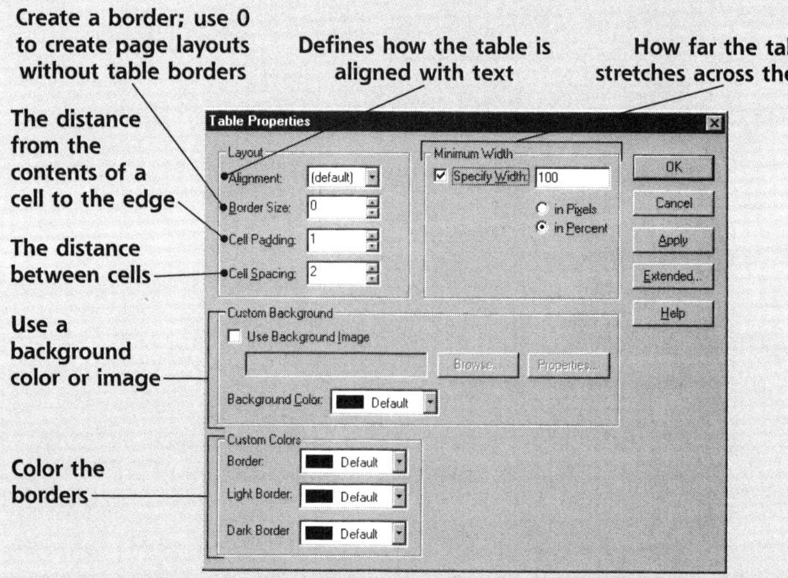

To Modify Individual Cells (page 157)

Click inside the table and select Table → Cell Properties.

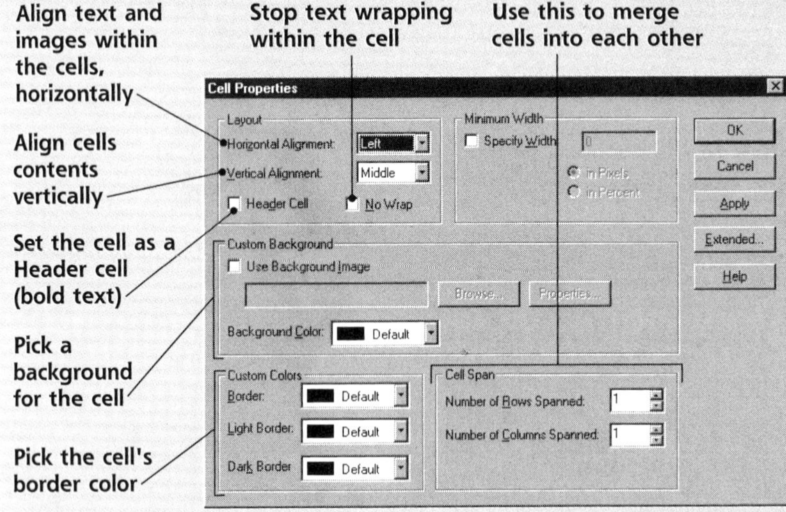

To Select and Modify Several Cells (page 158)

Select Table → Select Row or Table → Select Column, or drag the mouse pointer drag across several cells. Then select Table → Cell Properties.

To Merge Cells (page 158)

Select a row or column and then select Table → Merge Cells.

To Add a Caption (page 159)

1. Click anywhere in the table.
2. Select Table → Caption. FrontPage makes a little space at the top of the table for the caption.
3. Type the caption into this space.
4. If you want to move the caption to the bottom, click in it and select Table → Caption Properties. Then select Top of Table and click OK.

To Create Sophisticated Page Layouts (page 160)

Create a table with no borders (leave the Border setting set at 0.) Use the table to place images and text exactly where you want them on the page. The reader won't be able to see that a table has been used.

To See the Borders in FrontPage (page 155)

Click the ¶ toolbar button.

CHAPTER 12

Two Ways to Create Frames (page 167)

- Start the Frames Wizard and then select Pick a Template.
- Start the Frames Wizard and then select Make a Custom Grid.

Three Terms You Must Know (page 166)

A *frameset* is a group of *frames* in a browser window.

Frames are simply boxes or panes into which you place HTML documents.

The *frame-definition document* is a Web page that tells the browser where to place frames, and what document to place into each frame. It may also contain a message for users of non-frames-capable browsers.

Before You Begin (page 167)

Before you begin creating a frame using the Make a Custom Grid method, create these files:

- A file that is shown to the user of a browser that can't display frames.
- The documents you plan to place into each frame.

Before you begin using the wizard to select a frame template, create the first of these documents.

To Start the Frames Wizard (page 168)

1. Open FrontPage Editor.
2. Select File→New.
3. In the New Page dialog box select Frames Wizard and click OK.

To Edit a Frameset (page 172)

1. In FrontPage Explorer find the frame-definition document (it probably has the title Frameset followed by a number).
2. Double-click the file and the Frames Wizard opens.

To Edit the Message for Nonframes Browsers in the Frame-Definition Document (page 175)

1. In FrontPage Explorer find the frame-definition document (it probably has the title Frameset followed by a number).
2. Right-click the document name and select **Open With**.
3. Select FrontPage Editor.
4. Click OK. The document is loaded into the Editor and you can now see the message.

To Load Documents Linked in One Frame into Another Frame (page 177)

Here's what to do if you want all the documents referenced by the links in a frame to be loaded into another frame (for instance, when you have a Table of Contents in one frame).

1. In the document containing the links, select **File** → **Page Properties**.
2. Click the General tab.
3. In the Default Target Frame text box, type the name of the frame you want all the links to load.

To Target a Frame from One Link (page 177)

When you create a link, enter the name of the frame into the Target Frame text box.

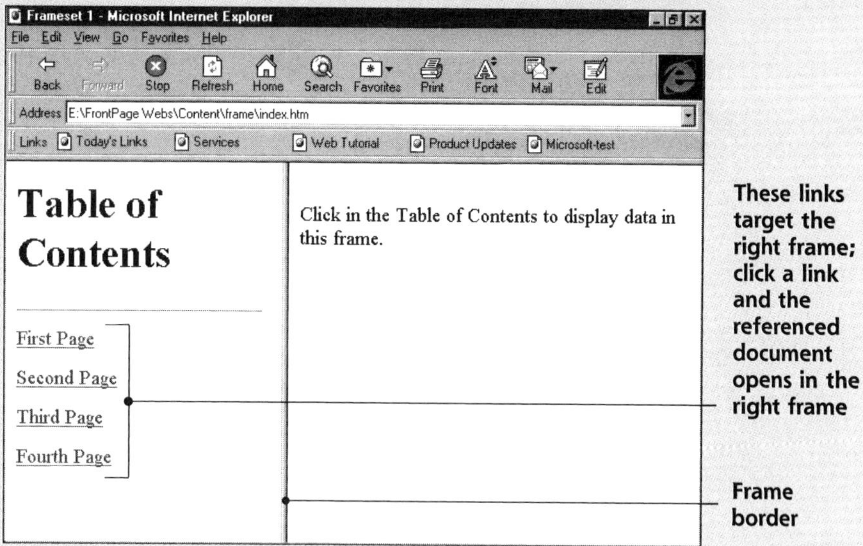

Magic Target Frame Names (page 178)

_self Place the referenced document into the current frame.

_parent Remove all frames and display the document.

_top In most cases (but not all), the same as _parent.

_blank Open a new window and load the document.

CHAPTER 13

To Create a Feedback Form (page 185)

1. In FrontPage Editor select File→New.
2. Select Feedback Form and click OK.
3. Modify the text, if you wish.
4. Save the document.

This document saves the information submitted by the user in a file called feedback.txt, stored in the _private directory.

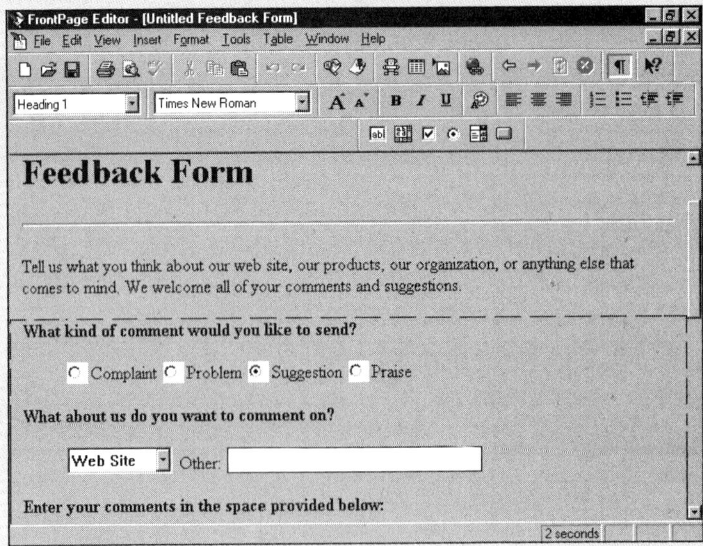

To Modify a Form (page 188)

Right-click the form and select:

- **Script Wizard** Add JavaScript or VBScript to the form component.
- **List Properties** Modify the manner in which the components are formatted within the form.
- **Form Properties** Modify the properties for the entire form.
- **Form Field Validation** Set up field validation, to make sure the user enters the right sort of information.
- **Form Field Properties** Modify the field element's name, value, size, and so on.

To Start the Form Page Wizard (page 188)

1. In FrontPage Editor, select **File** → **New**.
2. Select Form Page Wizard.
3. Click OK.

The Different Form Wizard Fields (page 192)

The Form Page wizard helps you quickly add the following types of form elements:

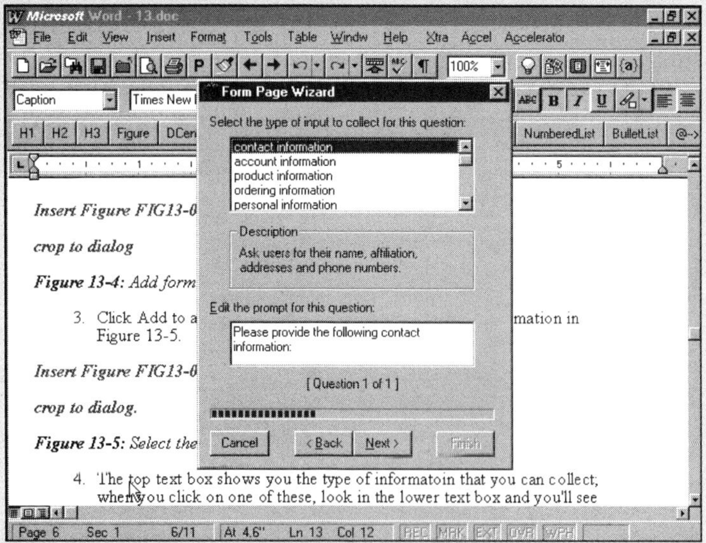

* Contact Information — Getting information about a person.
* Account Information — Users can register with this.
* Product Information — Gather information about a product the person is using.
* Ordering Information — A simple order form.
* Personal Information — Details about the user.
* One of Several Options — The user selects an option from a group of choices.
* Any of Several Options — The user selects one or more options from a group of choices.
* Boolean — The user selects Yes or No, True or False.
* Date — The user enters a date.
* Time — The user enters a time.
* Range — The user selects a single option within a range.
* Number — The user enters a number or currency value.
* String — The user types a short note.
* Paragraph — The user types more text.

CHAPTER 14

To Validate User Entry (page 214)

Different fields have different validation options. Here's what you can do for text boxes.

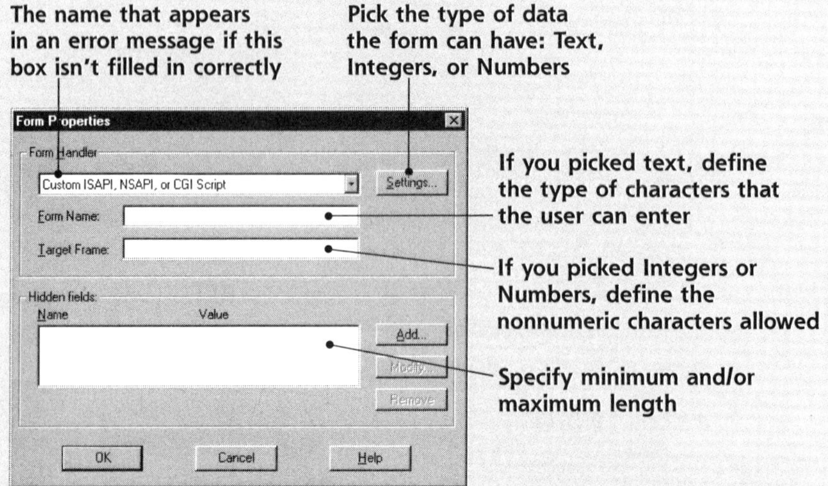
The name that appears in an error message if this box isn't filled in correctly
Pick the type of data the form can have: Text, Integers, or Numbers
If you picked text, define the type of characters that the user can enter
If you picked Integers or Numbers, define the nonnumeric characters allowed
Specify minimum and/or maximum length
Form Properties
Form Handler
Custom ISAPI, NSAPI, or CGI Script
Settings...
Form Name:
Target Frame:
Hidden fields:
Name
Value
Add...
Modify...
Remove
OK
Cancel
Help

CHAPTER 15

The Form Handlers (page 220)

After creating a form, select the handler that will take the information and use it in some manner:

Custom ISAPI, NSAPI, or CGI Script The handler sends the information to a script.

WebBot Discussion Component The handler adds the information to an online discussion; other users can view the message and respond.

WebBot Registration Component The handler takes the information from the form and adds it to an authentication database, so the user can log into the Web site later.

WebBot Save Results Component The handler saves the information in a text file or Web page.

Internet Database Connector The handler works with Microsoft Internet Information Server to connect a database to your Web site.

Defining Where to Save Data (page 220)

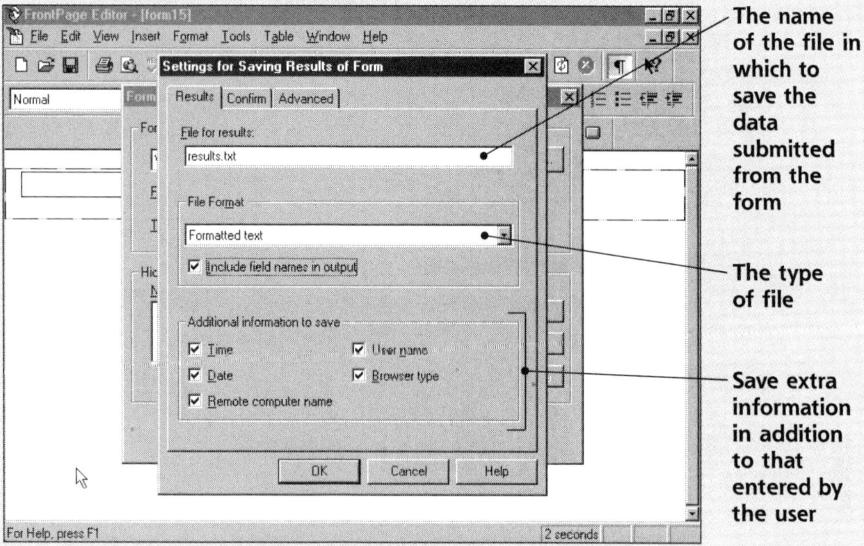

To Add a Customized Confirmation Page (page 222)

1. Select **File** → **New**, and in the New Page dialog box select Confirmation Form and click OK.
2. The text shown in [ ] brackets was placed there using the Confirmation Field WebBot. Double-click between [and] to open the dialog box shown in Figure 15-2.

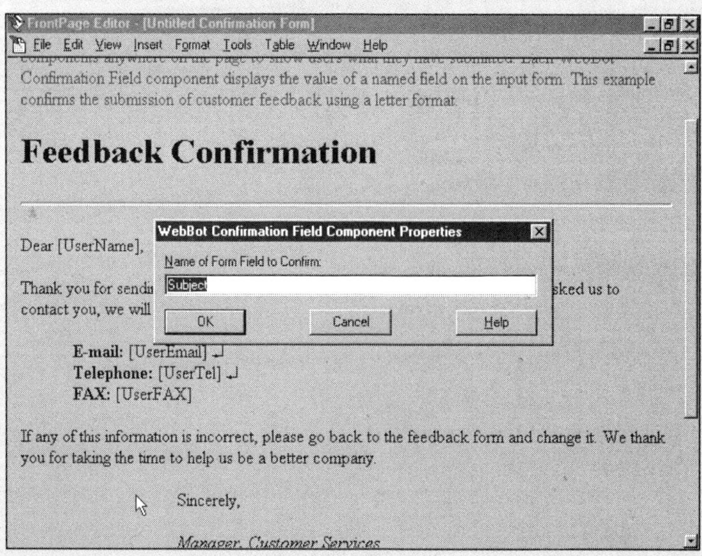

3. Double-click each of the WebBot text blocks in turn, and enter the name of the field, in the form in which the user will enter data, that you wish to use to provide data. For instance, if your form has a field called Email in which the user types his or her e-mail address, you'd double-click *[UserEmail]*, type **Email**, and click OK.

4. Remove any of the blocks that are not appropriate, along with any introductory text. Add any new entries you need. (Select Insert → WebBot Component to add new fields.)

5. Save and close the form.

6. You should return to the original form and open the Form Properties dialog box (right-click in the form and select Form Properties), click the Settings button, then click the Confirm tab.

7. Place the name of the confirmation-page file into the first text box.

To Send Form Data to CGI Scripts (page 232)

1. Select the Custom ISAPI, NSAPI, or CGI Script handler in the Form Properties dialog box.

2. If the CGI script requires any hidden fields, enter them by clicking the Add button.

3. Click the Settings button.

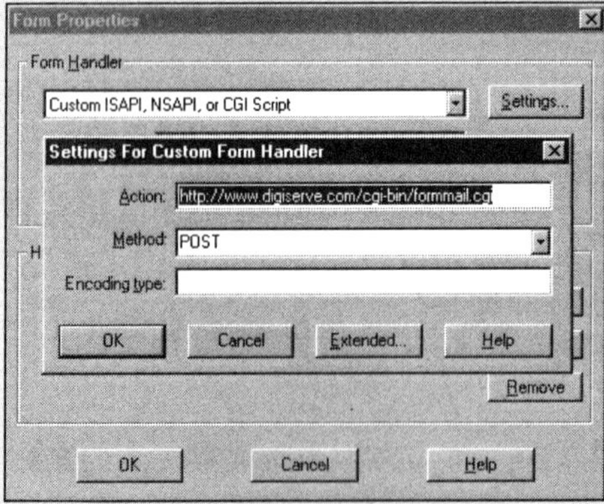

4. Type the URL of the CGI script into the Action text box.

5. Select the method (generally POST).

6. Click OK.

CHAPTER 16

The FrontPage Form Templates and Wizards (page 237)

- **Confirmation Form** — Displayed when a user submits data from a form.
- **Feedback Form** — Used to gather information from users.
- **Form Page Wizard** — Used to create all sorts of customized forms.
- **Guest Book** — Users enter information that is then placed in a Web page.
- **Product or Event Registration** — Users provide information when registering a product or for an event.
- **Search Page** — Lets users search the text of your Web site's pages.
- **Survey Form** — Gathers information from users; like the Feedback Form but more extensive.
- **User Registration** — Users can register themselves at a Web site, then log in when they return.
- **Discussion Web Wizard** — Creates a complex series of Web pages used for a discussion group.

To Use a Form Template or Wizard (page 184)

In FrontPage Editor, select File → New, then choose the template or wizard from the list.

The Discussion Web wizard is opened from the FrontPage Explorer: select File → New → FrontPage Web and select it from the list.

Creating a Search Page (page 239)

You can use the Search Page template, or insert a Search Component using the WebBot (Insert → WebBot Component, then select Search).

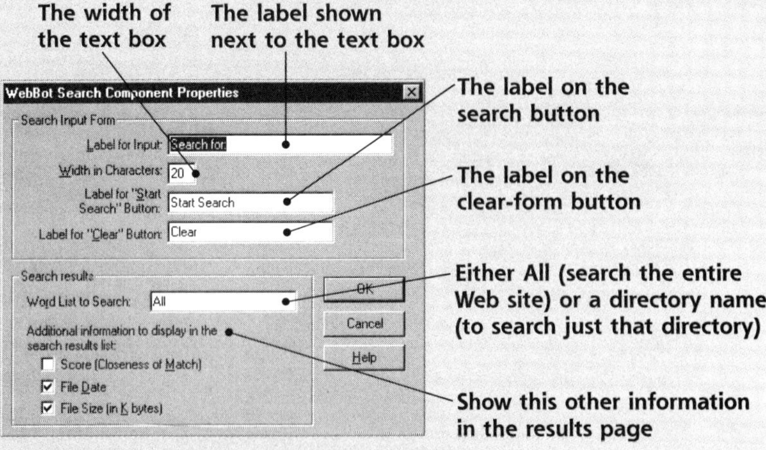

To Create a Discussion Group (page 241)

1. In FrontPage Explorer select File → New → FrontPage Web, select Discussion Web Wizard from the list, and click OK.
2. Click Next.

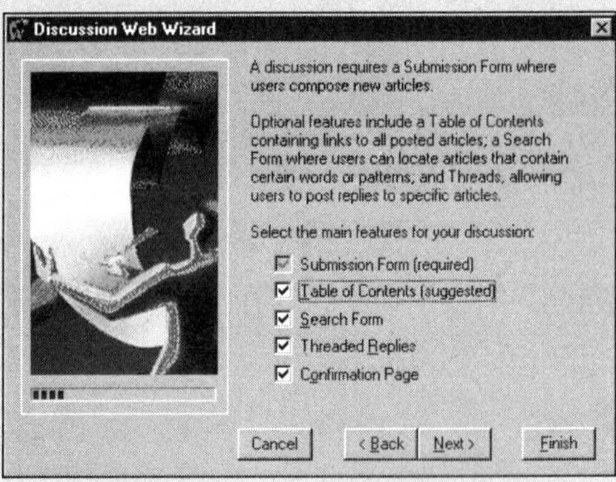

3. Select the features you want in the group and click Next.
4. Type a name for the discussion group, and the name of the directory in which the message files will be stored, and click Next.
5. Select the form fields that the user will work with when entering a message, and click Next.
6. Specify whether the web should be a registration-only web, or open to anyone, and click Next.

7. Define which way the messages will be listed in the message list — the table of contents — the oldest at the top or the newest at the top. Then click Next.
8. Tell the wizard if you want the discussion group's main page to be the web's home page (in which case the current index.htm is overwritten). Then click Next.
9. If you told the wizard you wanted a search page, define which columns appear in the results table when the user does a search. Then click Next.
10. Modify the template used by the discussion group to format the text and backgrounds in all the pages. Then click Next.
11. Select the frames option you want to use, and click Next.
12. Note the titles given to the important pages in the discussion group, then click Next.
13. Click Finish and the wizard completes its work, creating all the pages you need. If you are creating a registration-only web, a registration form is opened in FrontPage Editor; modify this form.
14. Go to FrontPage Explorer and open the root web.
15. Return to FrontPage Editor and save the registration document into the root web. Remember, registration forms must be saved in the root (see Chapter 15).

CHAPTER 17

To Copy Your Web to Another Server (page 253)

1. In FrontPage Explorer open the web that you want to copy.
2. Select File → Publish FrontPage Web.
3. Enter the name of the server you're copying the file to.
4. Enter a name into the Name of Destination FrontPage Web: the name of an existing web at the specified server (if modifying that web) or a new name (if creating a new web at that server). Or leave it blank to publish to your root web.
5. You'll normally leave the Copy Changed Pages Only check box selected. If you are creating a new web it has no effect; if you are modifying one it speeds up the process.
6. If the Add to an Existing FrontPage Web check box is checked, FrontPage transfers the files to the named web. If this box is cleared, FrontPage creates a new web (if you are creating a new web, you may have to inform the server administrator).

7. If transferring the root web, you can select Copy Child Webs (For Root Web Only) to copy the root web *and* all the subwebs stored in the root web.
8. Click OK and the process begins.

The Best Way to Transfer to a Non-FrontPage Server (page 256)

1. Select **Start** → **Programs** → **Accessories** → **Internet Tools** → **Web Publishing Wizard**.
2. Use the first Browse button to find the directory containing the files you want to transfer.
3. Check Include Subfolders if you want to transfer subdirectories within the selected directory. (However, the wizard will include the directories containing files that will be used by the FrontPage server extensions, which you won't need transferred, *and* subwebs.) Click Next.
4. Select the Web site to which you plan to transfer this information from the drop-down list box. If this is the first time you've used the wizard, click New.

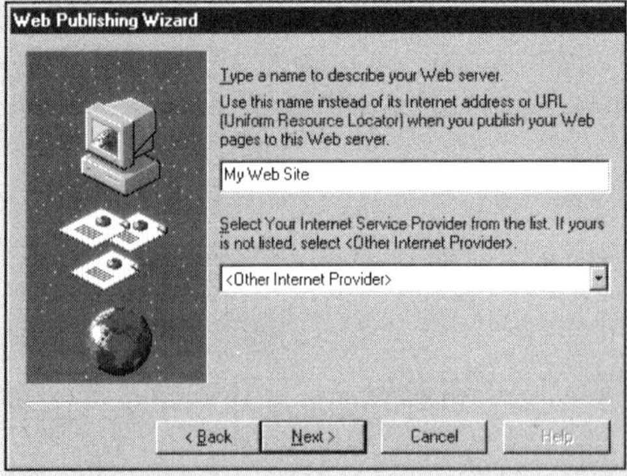

5. Type a name for this Web site.
6. Open the Select Your Internet Service Provider drop-down list box and see if your service provider is listed. If so, select it. If not, select <Other Internet Provider>. (When you click Next the information you see depends on your choice here. I'm going to use the <Other Internet Provider> as the example.)
7. Type the full URL of the directory in which you have to store your Web pages. Not the FTP directory that the system administrator may have given you, but the actual Web URL. Click Next.

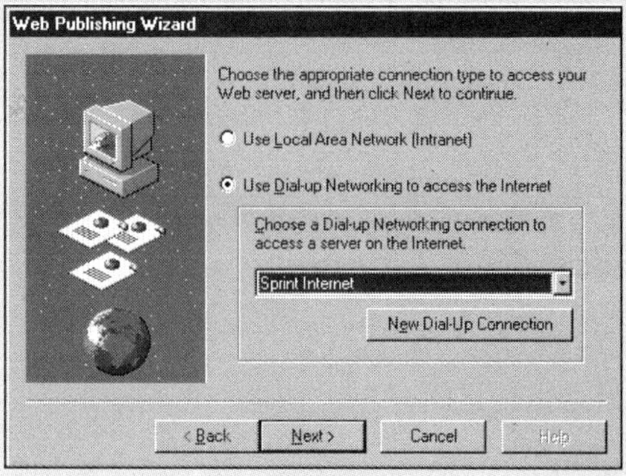

8. Select the first option if you are working on a network, the second if you are using Dial-Up Networking to connect to the Internet — select the Dial-Up Networking connection you use from the drop-down list box. Click Next in this box.
9. If you are using Dial-Up Networking, enter a user name and password, click Next, and the transfer begins.

If you chose the Use Local Area Network option, you'll have to click another Next button and the wizard then tries to connect to the Web server.

Providing Access for Other Web Authors (page 260)

1. In FrontPage Explorer select Tools → Permissions. If you are working in a subweb of the root web, you'll see the Settings pane (otherwise skip to Step 4).

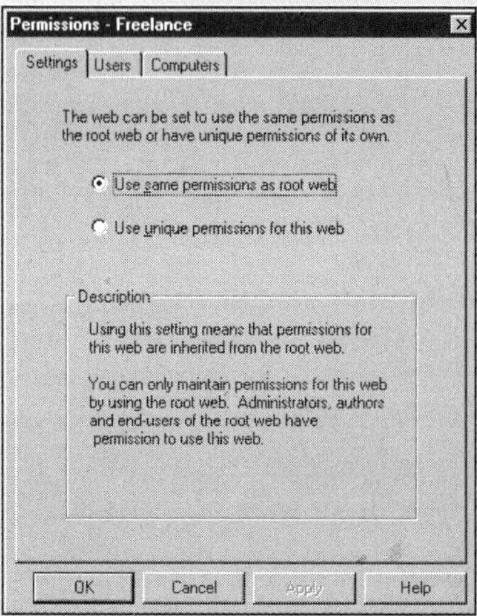

2. If you want to modify this web's permissions, click Use Unique Permissions For This Web and then click the Apply button.

3. Click the Users tab.
4. To create a new administrator or author account, click Add and the Add Users box opens.
5. Enter an account name, and then type a password in both password boxes.
6. Select the type of access (Browse This Web; Author and Browse This Web; Administer, Author, and Browse This Web).
7. Click OK and the new account is created.

VISUAL INDEX

FrontPage Explorer

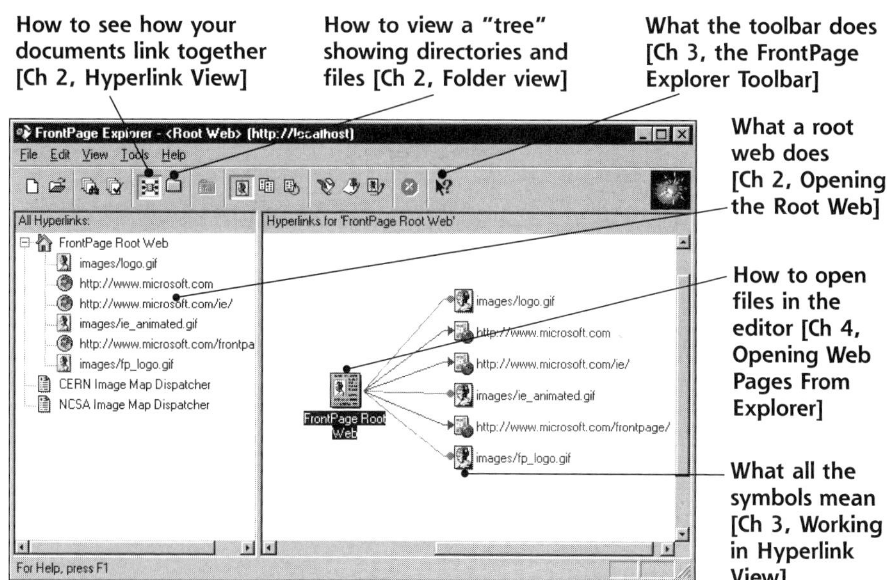

FrontPage Editor

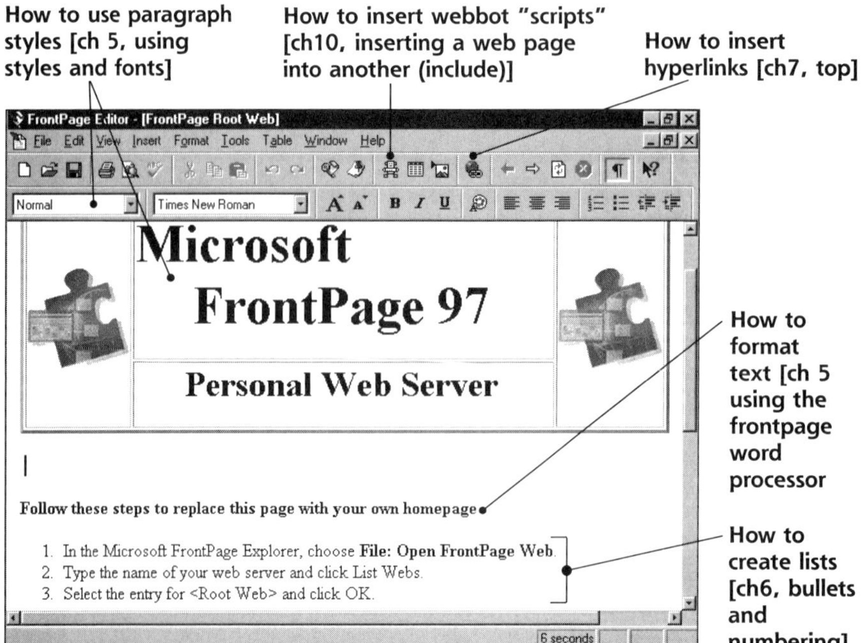

Creating Pages

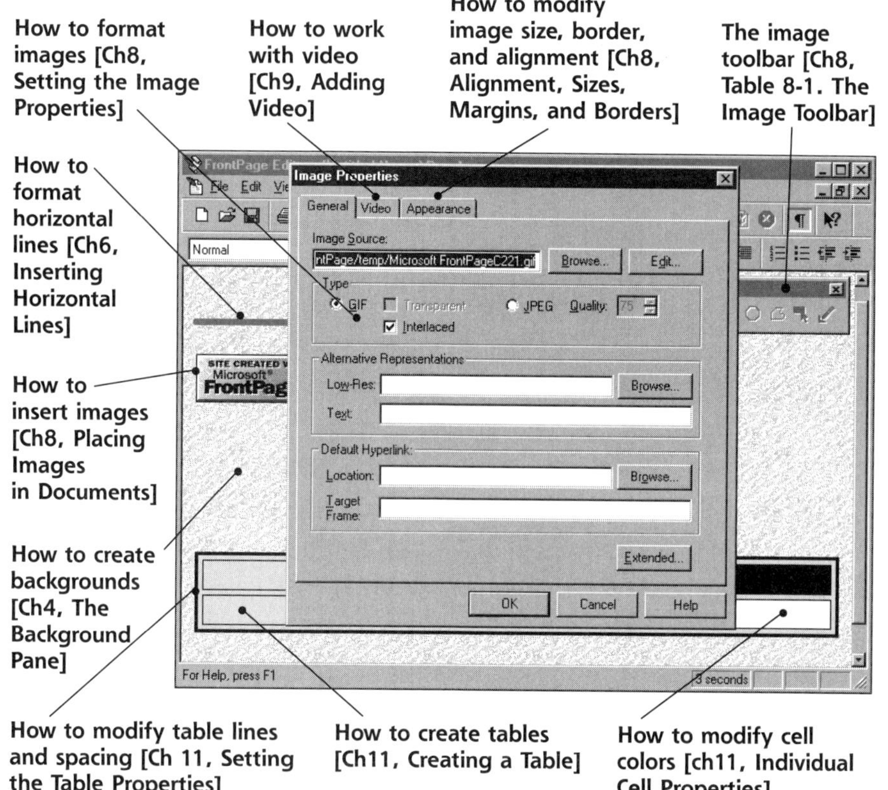
How to format images [Ch8, Setting the Image Properties]
How to work with video [Ch9, Adding Video]
How to modify image size, border, and alignment [Ch8, Alignment, Sizes, Margins, and Borders]
The image toolbar [Ch8, Table 8-1. The Image Toolbar]
How to format horizontal lines [Ch6, Inserting Horizontal Lines]
How to insert images [Ch8, Placing Images in Documents]
How to create backgrounds [Ch4, The Background Pane]
Image Properties
General
Video
Appearance
Image Source:
ntPage/temp/Microsoft FrontPageC221.gif
Browse...
Edit...
Type
GIF
Transparent
JPEG
Quality:
75
Interlaced
Alternative Representations
Low-Res:
Browse...
Text:
Default Hyperlink:
Location:
Browse...
Target Frame:
Extended...
OK
Cancel
Help
Normal
For Help, press F1
3 seconds
How to modify table lines and spacing [Ch 11, Setting the Table Properties]
How to create tables [Ch11, Creating a Table]
How to modify cell colors [ch11, Individual Cell Properties]

Creating Links

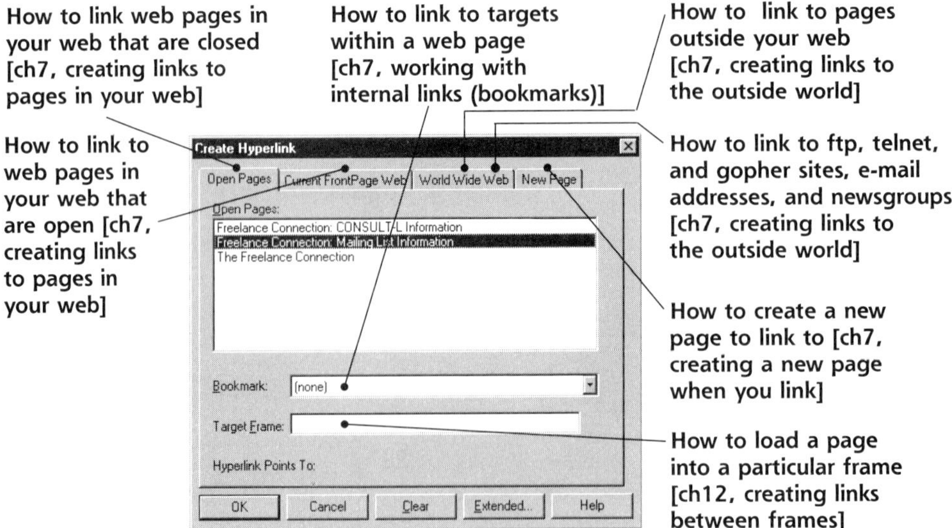

Working With Forms

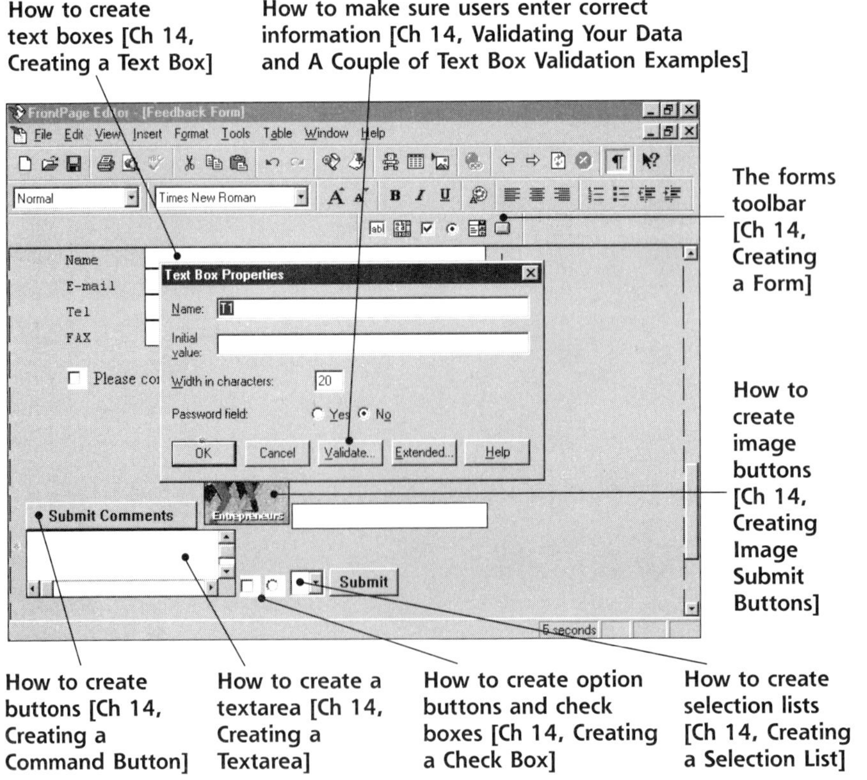

Making Forms Work

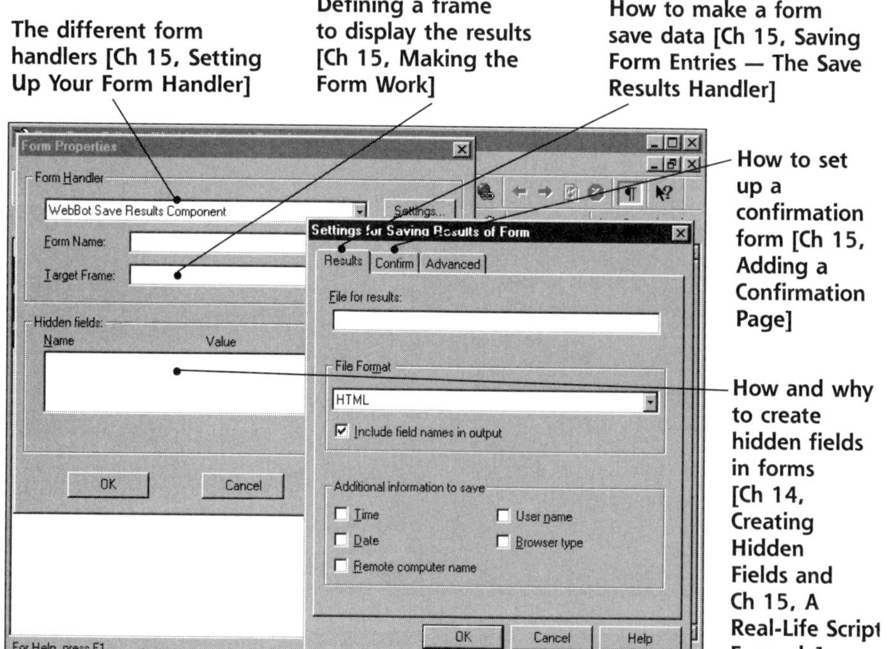

APPENDIX A

TROUBLESHOOTING GUIDE

Finding More Help

Many great places on the Internet provide help with problems you may encounter using FrontPage 97. These are free and contain a wealth of information. In some cases, you can ask other FrontPage users for help, and get real-world solutions to your problems.

Support Pages

Dave's Unauthorized FrontPage Support Site: `http://infomatique.iol.ie:8080/dave/`

Links to FrontPage Resources on the WWW (probably the best place to find FrontPage resources): `http://www.frontpage97.com/links.htm`

Microsoft's FrontPage Support: `http://www.microsoft.com/frontpagesupport/`

Microsoft's FrontPage Wish List: `http://www.microsoft.com/support/feedback/mswish.htm`

Microsoft's KnowledgeBase: `http://www.microsoft.com/kb/`

PMP Computer Solutions FrontPage Support: `http://www.pmpcs.com/support/frontpage.htm`

www.FrontPage97.com On-Line Users Group: `http://www.frontpage97.com/`

Chats and Discussion Groups

Akorn Access FrontPage Mailing List: `http://205.217.100.14/FrontPage/FPMailRef.html`

Chats by Jerry Haygood & Associates: `http://www.jhas.com/chat.asp`

FrontPage Users Forum, Italy: `http://www.bns.it/frontpage/`

GRM's FrontPage Users Forum: `http://www.grm.com/frontpage/`

Microsoft's FrontPage newsgroup: microsoft.public.frontpage.client at the msnews.microsoft.com news server.

Okanagan Online's Microsoft FrontPage Discussion Group: http://www.okonline.com/frontpage/

PMP Computer Solutions—Links to FrontPage Discussion Groups: http://www.pmpcs.com/support/fp/discussions.htm

VMT FrontPage Live Chat: http://www.thevmtbuilding.com/lobby.htm

Frequently Asked Questions Pages

Akorn Access: http://205.217.100.14/FrontPage/FPfaq.html

C. Demetrio: http://www.xerox.francoudi.com.cy/frontpage/index.html

Microsoft's FrontPage 97 FAQ: http://www.microsoft.com/frontpage/97beta/faq/readme_english.htm

Microsoft's FrontPage Support FAQ: http://www.microsoft.com/FrontPageSupport/content/faq/

Okanagan OnLine Computer Services Ltd: http://www.okonline.com/topten/fpfaq.htm

A Few Problems

Here are solutions to a few common problems you may run into.

No Server Extensions Installed

When you first start work after installing or reinstalling FrontPage, you may see a message telling you that there are no server extensions installed on port 80. This happens if, for some reason, the installation program has not installed the extensions properly on the FrontPage Personal Web Server; improper installation may have occurred if you told the FrontPage installation program to use an existing \FrontPage Webs\ directory, instead of the one the installation program wanted to create. Here's what to do:

1. Open the \Microsoft FrontPage\ directory in Windows Explorer. Look for the file named FrontPage Server Administrator (this is actually a shortcut to the fpsrvwin.exe file in the \Microsoft FrontPage\bin\ directory).
2. Double-click the shortcut to open the FrontPage Server Administrator. Look for the Server Configuration File and Content Directory lines near the top of the window (see figure on next page). These lines show you the current configuration. The Server Configuration File shows you the name of the file used to configure the server you are using. The Content Directory shows where your FrontPage webs are installed. As you can see in the illustration, there is no information shown on these lines, because the server extensions have not been installed correctly.
3. Click Install and you'll see the Configure Server Type dialog box. This contains a drop-down list box.

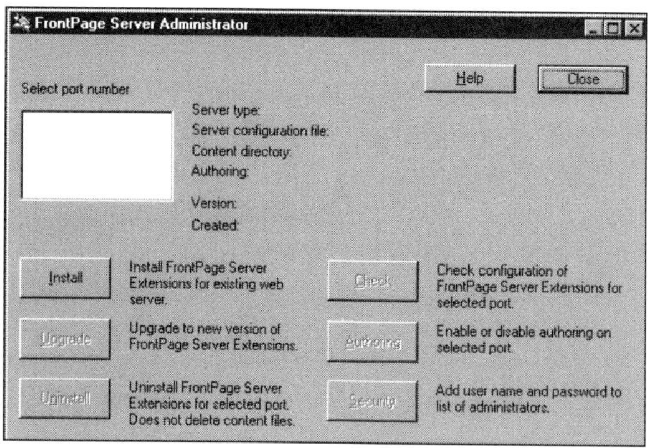

4. Select FrontPage Personal Web Server (I'm assuming that's the one you're working with) and click OK. The Server Configuration dialog box opens.
5. Click Browse and find the httpd.cnf file. It's in the \FrontPage Webs\server\conf\ directory. Click this file, then the Open button.
6. Click OK in the Server Configuration dialog box, then click OK in the Confirmation dialog box, and the server extensions will be installed.

Webs Don't Match

If you work on a web on your computer's hard drive and periodically transfer that web to a remote Web server, you'll probably discover eventually that the webs don't match; the remote web may contain files that used to be in your hard-drive web, but which you've removed or moved.

When you publish a FrontPage web using File → Publish, FrontPage transfers files, but it *doesn't* confirm that both webs are exact copies of each other. In order to fix this problem, keep track of files that you have renamed, moved, or deleted. When you publish to the remote server, the new files — that is, the ones that have been renamed or moved — will appear in the web correctly. But the original files will be there, too — the ones that you renamed, moved, or deleted in the local web. Consult the list and delete those files from the remote web.

FrontPage Editor Changed My URLs!

I think of FrontPage as an all-or-nothing tool. You should use it either to do virtually everything to your Web pages or nothing at all. You can, in theory, use the FrontPage Editor to open pages and save them outside a web. But if you do so, you'll find that the Editor renames your links when you save the file. For instance, what starts out as a link pointing to this URL

```
2-5.htm
```

ends up pointing to this URL

```
file:///E:/FrontPage%20Webs/Content/JavaScript/2-5.htm
```

FrontPage Changed My HTML Formatting!

Again, it's an all-or-nothing situation. If the HTML format is very important to you for a particular web, you may find you have to do without FrontPage for that web. FrontPage is very particular about the sort of HTML it accepts. It may take the HTML you've given it and reformat it a little, adding spaces and line breaks, for instance. That really doesn't matter in most cases, but in some it may.

I have a Web site in which I demonstrate several JavaScript examples (`http://www.netscapepress.com/support/javascript/`). I need complete control over how the HTML is formatted. For instance, I use the <XMP> tags to display the contents of a script on the face of the page. FrontPage, however, changes spacing, line breaks, and other formatting. In the end I had to stop using FrontPage for that web. I love working with FrontPage, but I've just had to do without in that case.

All My Links are Broken!

If you use Verify Hyperlinks and test your external hyperlinks, you may find that *all* were broken! What's going on? It may be that there was a problem with your Internet connection at that point. Try reconnecting, then try going to a few Web sites with your Web browser. Click the Reload or Restore button to make sure you're getting a Web page from the Web, not from your cache. Once you're sure the connection is working properly, try the Verify Hyperlinks procedure again.

Broken Links are Not Broken

When you use the Verify Links command, FrontPage may find that some of your links are broken, even if you know for sure they're not. This could happen for a couple of reasons. It may be that the server to which the link points is currently not working. Or perhaps it's simply working very slowly. FrontPage tries each link fairly quickly, and if it can't get through, it moves on to the next one. Sometimes it checks more quickly than the server is able to respond.

Broken Links Weren't Broken Before

In some cases, you may need to create links using a complete (absolute) URL, rather than a relative URL. (For instance, `http://www.myhost.com/mydirectory/thisfile.htm`, rather than simply `thisfile.htm`.) You may want to do this if you know that some of the pages in your web will be copied to other sites; perhaps they'll be used as part of an e-mail newsletter. If you use the absolute URL, a link will still work when moved to another site; if you use the relative URL, it won't.

If you use an absolute URL, FrontPage regards it as a link to the outside world, even if it's really a link to a site within your web. It has no way of knowing that it's really an internal link. Now, suppose you change the name of the file that is referred to by this link. All the relative links that point to this file are automatically modified by FrontPage to use the new filename... but your absolute link will *not* be changed. You'll have to change it by hand.

Opening the Clip Art Takes Too Long

When you click on the Clip Art tab in the Image dialog box, FrontPage loads the contents of the first subdirectory in the \Program Files\Microsoft FrontPage\clipart\ directory. This is the Animations directory, so you have to sit and wait while the animations are loaded into the box, even if you don't plan to choose an animation. This can be irritating on a slow computer. If you want to speed things up, create a new — empty — subdirectory called _ (underscore). This will appear at the top of the list and will load instantly because it's empty.

Microsoft Image Composer Doesn't Run

Microsoft Image Composer, the image-editing program that comes with FrontPage 97, sometimes has problems running. You need at the very least 16MB of RAM, preferably 32 MB. You must also be running in a 256-color video mode, though Super VGA mode, using 2MB video memory, is recommended.

Can't View _Private Files

If you try to view files that are stored in the _private directory directly from your Web browser, you'll find that the browser prompts you to enter an account name and password.

Imported Files Don't Work

Windows 95 and Windows NT allow you to create file and directory names using both uppercase and lowercase characters. You can call a file *thisfile, ThisFile,* or *THISFILE,* for instance. However, these operating systems don't actually regard names with the same characters but different case as different names. As far as Windows 95 and Windows NT are concerned, each of these three sample names are actually the same name.

Remember, though, that most operating systems that are used to run Web servers do regard case as important in file and directory names. In UNIX, for instance, *thisfile, ThisFile,* and *THISFILE* would be three different files.

This normally does not create problems. When you create files and links, rename files and links, or transfer a web across to a remote Web server, FrontPage will make sure that all case matches correctly. However, you might run into a problem in a few odd circumstances. Let's say, for instance, that you've created a web and transferred it to the remote server. Later, you modify an image on your hard disk; then, instead of importing it into your local web and transferring it using the File → Publish FrontPage Web command, you open the remote web and import the file into that web. You might find that the document using that image can't load the image; the case is no longer correct. There are a couple of ways around this problem. First, ensure that you never import from your hard disk onto a remote web. Always import into the local web and then transfer to the remote web. Or simply check that the case of the file is correct before importing it into the remote web.

Can't Delete Files and Folders

If you try to delete a file or folder in a web on a remote server, and you find that FrontPage is unable to delete the item, it may be because the server is using an old version of the FrontPage server extensions. With the latest extensions you *should* be able to delete things, so if you can't, contact the system administrator.

A More Recent Version?

Have you seen this message while trying to save a file?

```
A more recent version of <page> has been saved to the server by
   <username> on <date time>.
   Do you want to replace this with your file?
```

There's a bug in FrontPage that causes this message to appear inappropriately (this happens in Windows 95, but probably not in Windows NT). You try to save a file you've been working on, perhaps one that nobody else has ever worked on, and you see this message. I've found that if I avoid switching to another application while FrontPage Editor is saving, this normally won't happen. Anyway, if you do see this problem, click Yes and FrontPage should continue. (I usually then save again, just to make sure!)

Rename a Web, Lose Permissions

With some Web servers (Microsoft Internet Information Server, Microsoft Peer Web Services for NT 4.0, and the Microsoft Personal Web Server), if you rename a web, the permissions are set back to those of the root web. There's no solution but to reapply the permissions after renaming the web (or avoid renaming webs!).

HTML Attributes are Thrown Away

If you add special HTML attributes to some tags, FrontPage saves those attributes. But in other cases FrontPage cannot save them; it discards the attributes that it doesn't recognize. It will do that for these tags:

```
AREA, B, BASE, BASEFONT, BGSOUND, BIG, BLINK, CENTER, CITE, CODE,
  DFN, DIV, EM, FONT, HEAD, HTML, MAP, META, NEXTID, NOFRAMES,
  OPTION, SAMP, SCRIPT, SMALL, STRIKE, S, STRONG, SUB, SUP,
  TITLE, TT, U, VAR, NOEMBED, PARAM.
```

If you add extended attributes to any of these tags, you'll lose them. You can, however, create the entire tag, including the extended attributes, using the **Insert** → **HTML Markup** command.

APPENDIX B

WEB AND PAGE TEMPLATES AND WIZARDS

This appendix contains a quick description of each of the FrontPage templates and wizards.

Web Templates and Wizards

The web templates and wizards are created from the New FrontPage Web dialog box in FrontPage Explorer; select File → New → Front Page Web.

Normal Web Creates a new Web site containing a single blank index.htm Web page.

Corporate Presence Web Wizard Helps you create an integrated Web site with your choice of sections: What's New, Products/Services, Table of Contents, Feedback Form, and Search Form. (These are described below, under "Web Page Templates and Wizards.") Also enables you to select a look — Plain, Conservative, Flashy, Cool — choose default colors, and so on. A quick way to create an extensive and sophisticated Web site.

Customer Support Web Creates a customer support Web site, with Download, Suggestions, and Search pages, Frequently Asked Questions, and so on.

Discussion Web Wizard Creates a discussion group in which users can post questions and comments, and read and reply to others' postings.

Empty Web Creates a new Web site containing *no* Web pages or images, just the directory structure.

Import Web Wizard Used to import an existing Web site that was created with another HTML authoring tool, and used to create a new web.

Learning FrontPage Used by FrontPage's tutorial in the Getting Started book.

Personal Web Creates a personal Web site, with a single page that has personal information, a response form, and suggested external links.

Project Web A project-oriented Web site with an included header and footer that links to a variety of documents: Home, Members, Schedule, Status, Archive, Search, Discussions.

Web Page Templates and Wizards

The Web page templates and wizards are created from the New Page dialog box in FrontPage Editor; select File → New.

Normal Page A blank page; used to start a Web page from scratch.

Bibliography A list of reference sources.

Confirmation Form Use this in conjunction with another form page; this one displays a message thanking the user for the submission (see Chapter 15). You can use the Confirmation WebBot to show the user what he or she submitted.

Database Connector Wizard This is used to set up a connection from your web to an SQL database. See Chapter 9.

Database Results A blank form in which you can place database result fields. For use with the Database Connector wizard.

Directory of Press Releases Links at the top of the document to sections lower down, in which you can list press releases and link from this document to the press release documents.

Employee Directory An alphabetical list of employees at the top of the page with links to each employee's data lower down (photo, title, phone number, e-mail address, and so on).

Employment Opportunities A list of job openings at the top links down to descriptions of the jobs. A form at the bottom lets the user apply for a position.

Feedback Form A form collecting information from the user and saving it in a text file. However, you can modify the form to modify what is done with this information. See Chapter 13.

Form Page Wizard Helps you create a form. You pick the information that you want to collect, format the form, and then define how you want to save the information that the user enters into the form. The data may be saved in a Web page, saved as a text file, or sent to a CGI script. See Chapter 14.

Frames Wizard Helps you create a frameset, into which you can place the HTML documents you specify. See Chapter 12.

Frequently Asked Questions A page with a series of questions at the top, linked to answers lower down. Links after each answer take the user back to the top.

Glossary of Terms Letters of the alphabet at the top are linked to sections of the glossary below (A is linked to the A entries, and so on).

Guest Book More correctly termed a Comments Book, though it could be modified to also collect names and e-mail addresses. The user types a comment, which is added to the bottom of the Web page using the Include WebBot. You could also modify the page to do something different with the information submitted. See Chapter 16.

Hot List Category names at the top of the page link down to categories below, beneath which you can enter links to other Web pages.

HyperDocument Page A portion of a large hyperlinked manual. Replace the document name, section name, page name, section icons, and section titles, then insert the appropriate text.

Lecture Abstract A simple page with a title at the top, some speaker information, and a list of topics.

Meeting Agenda Another simple page; a list of topics and a list of attendees.

Office Directory A region list at the top of the page links down to specific regions, under which subregions are listed. You can add links to particular pages. I've seen this format used often by professional societies to link to Web sites maintained by local chapters.

Personal Home Page Wizard Helps you set up a personal Web page. You choose from categories such as Employee Information, Current Projects, Biographical Information, Contact Information, and so on. Then for each category you are prompted to enter the appropriate information. Also enables you to create a feedback form, the contents of which can be stored in a Web page or in a data file, or e-mailed to you.

Press Release A page formatted in typical press release style.

Product Description Categories at the top of the page (Product Summary, Key Features, and so on) link down to the appropriate sections.

Product or Event Registration The user enters registration information, selects from a list of options, chooses an option button, and submits the data.

Search Page A simple text-search form that will search the Web site, along with instructions on how to enter a search query. See Chapter 16.

Seminar Schedule A list of seminar sessions at the top links down to more information about each session.

Software Data Sheet A picture of a program window at the top, followed by sections describing benefits, features, system requirements, pricing, and so on.

Survey Form A form split into four sections. Responses are saved in a text document. See Chapter 16.

Table of Contents Uses the Table of Contents WebBot to create a table of contents page for your Web site. You choose a starting point, and the WebBot creates a list of all the documents downstream from the chosen one. The titles are then inserted into the Web page. See Chapter 10.

User Registration Creates a self-registration form. The user enters a name and password. This information can be used to confirm users' identities when they access the site later. See Chapter 15.

What's New A simple, manually entered list of changes to your Web site.

GLOSSARY

absolute URL — A *URL* that is complete, containing all the information required to find the referenced object on the *World Wide Web* or corporate *intranet.* See also *relative URL.*

anchor — The term given to an <A></A> *HTML tag* pair. These tags are used to create *links* between and within documents.

background image — An *image* displayed in a *Web* document. The image appears to be in the background, behind the text and images.

bookmark — 1. A reference to a *Web page* on the *World Wide Web* or on an *intranet.* Virtually all *browsers* have some kind of bookmark system that lets users keep a list of Web pages that they may want to return to. Some browsers refer to this as a bookmark system; others call it a *hotlist;* Microsoft Internet Explorer calls it the *Favorites.* 2. Term used by FrontPage to refer to what is often called a *target.* This is an *HTML tag* that refers to a particular position in the page. The *Web author* can then create a *link* from somewhere else in the document to the *tag.*

Boolean algebra — A system that uses two truth values (True and False) and several functions (AND, OR, NOT), to make decisions.

bot — See *WebBot.*

browser — A program that reads *HTML* files and displays the result. Browsers are used to work on the *World Wide Web.*

CGI — Common gateway interface, a system used to run programs linked to *Web pages.* CGI *scripts* are used to take information from a Web page and carry out some kind of procedure based on that information.

child web — A FrontPage *web* created at a domain, within the *root web.*

Client-side image map — An *image map* that does not require any input from the *Web server.* Rather, the *browser* can obtain all the required information from the *Web page* itself. Most older browsers cannot use client-side image maps, so they must use *server-side image maps.*

domain name — On the *Internet,* almost synonymous with *hostname,* though strictly speaking the domain name refers to a group of computers that share a common suffix. However, many domain names are not used as suffixes, but are used to identify a single host. Domain names may be *mapped* to a particular directory within a host, so a *Web server* can manage multiple domains on a single computer.

Editor, FrontPage — An *HTML editor,* the program that FrontPage uses for creating and editing *Web pages.*

Explorer, FrontPage — A program used by FrontPage for managing *webs*. Explorer is used to create, open, and move webs, and for a variety of other operations.

external image — An *image* that is not embedded into a *Web page*. Rather, the image alone is loaded when the user clicks a *link* that references the image.

Favorites — The term used by Microsoft for Internet Explorer's *bookmark* system.

frame — A portion of the *browser* window. The browser window may be split into two or more frames, with each frame containing a different document. Frames can be linked: a table of contents frame may contain *links* that load different documents into one of the other frames, for instance. Frames are often known as panes in other *hypertext* systems. See also *frameset*.

frame-definition document — The *Web* document that contains instructions on how to create a *frameset* or multiple framesets. The document is read by the *browser*, which then creates the specified framesets and places the specified documents into the appropriate *frames*.

frameset — A group of *frames* in a *browser* window. A browser may contain one or more framesets, each frameset containing two or more frames.

FrontPage Editor — See *Editor, FrontPage*.

FrontPage Explorer — See *Explorer, FrontPage*.

FrontPage Personal Web Server — The *Web server* that comes with FrontPage. FrontPage can't work without a Web server, so if you don't have one you can use FrontPage Personal Web Server. (Also known as the *Microsoft FrontPage Personal Web Server*.) See also *Microsoft Personal Web Server*.

FrontPage Server Extensions — See *server extensions*.

FTP — File Transfer Protocol, a system used for transferring files across the *Internet*.

generated HTML — *HTML* created by a program rather than by a *Web author*. For instance, a user may search for information at a *Web site*. A program finds the information the user wants, then creates a *Web page* by generating HTML.

gopher — A menu system that predates the *World Wide Web*. *Web authors* can create gopher:// *links* from *Web pages* to gopher sites. Most *browsers* can display gopher menus and documents stored at gopher sites.

home page — 1. Originally used to refer to the page that appears in a *browser* when the user starts the browser or uses some kind of Home command (a button, keyboard sequence, or menu option). 2. Now commonly used (and used by FrontPage) to refer to a *Web site*'s main page. When you visit CNN, for instance, going to `http://www.cnn.com/` takes you to CNN's home page. Linked to that home page are many other Web pages.

host computer — A computer connected to a network.

hostname — The unique name given to a computer on a network, to identify the computer to other computers that wish to communicate with it. A computer may actually have several hostnames. See also *domain name* and *multihoming*.

hotlist — Another term for *bookmark system*.

hot spot — An area of an *image map* that acts as a *link*; when the user clicks the hot spot, some action is carried out. For instance, another *Web page* may be loaded.

HTML — HyperText Markup Language, the formatting system used to create *Web pages*. FrontPage creates HTML files.

HTML editor — A program, such as *FrontPage Editor*, that creates *HTML* files.

HTML tag — See *tag*.

HTTP — Hypertext Transfer Protocol, the networking *protocol* used by the *World Wide Web*.

hyperlink — See *link*.

hypertext — A type of document (displayed in some kind of electronic device, such as a *browser*) that contains *links* that act as cross-references. When a link is activated — generally by clicking it — another, related, document is loaded. The *World Wide Web* is a giant hypertext system.

IIS — The Microsoft Internet Information Server.

image — A picture. Images may be *inline images* or *external images*.

image map — A picture in a *Web page* that contains multiple *hot spots*. There are two main types of image maps: *server-side image maps* and *client-side image maps*.

Inline image — An *image* that is embedded into a *Web page*.

Internet Assistant — A Microsoft Word add-in program that allows Word to create *Web pages*.

Internet Database Connector — A system used to link an *SQL* database to a *Web page*. This is used in conjunction with the Microsoft Internet Information Server and the Microsoft Personal Web Server.

Internet, the — A public, international system of interconnected computers. Literally tens of millions of computers are permanently or periodically connected to the Internet.

intranet — A private *Internet* — a private network that uses *HTTP*. An intranet works like the Internet; users can view *Web pages* through *browsers*, for instance. See also *PPTP*.

LAN — A local area network, a small network that connects computers and other devices (such as printers, modems, and faxes). See also *intranet*; an intranet may run on a LAN.

link — An area in a *hypertext* document that can be used to load a referenced document, *image*, sound, video, another part of the current document, and so on. In the *World Wide Web*, users viewing a document in a *browser* generally click links to activate them. With some older browsers, users must activate links using the keyboard.

mailto: link — A *link* that contains an e-mail address. When the user clicks the link (most *browsers* these days work with mailto: links) the user's e-mail program opens, and the e-mail address is placed into the appropriate part of an e-mail message.

manual-restart server — A *Web server* that must be restarted in order to read configuration files. When FrontPage creates a new *web* at a manual-restart server, the server must be restarted before the user can work with the new web.

mapped — A *URL* is mapped to a particular directory. The server reads the URL, then grabs information from the directory that the URL has been mapped to. This system enables *Web servers* to manage multiple domains, each domain being mapped to a different directory on the Web server computer.

META tag — A special *HTML tag* that contains instructions, to the *Web server* or other program reading the *Web page*, that are not directly related to formatting the Web page. For instance, the META tags may contain information identifying the *Web author*, the purpose of the Web page, the program used to create the page, and so on.

Microsoft Personal Web Server — A *Web server* distributed in the FrontPage Bonus Pack. A more advanced server than the basic *FrontPage Personal Web Server.*

multihoming — The process by which multiple *virtual hosts* are set up on one *Web server.*

password object — A form component in a *Web page*. A password object is a text box that, when the user types inside it, displays asterisks rather than the actual characters that were typed.

point-to-point protocol — See *PPP*.

point-to-point tunneling protocol — See *PPTP*.

PPP — Point-to-point protocol, a *protocol* used to connect computers to the *Internet*.

PPTP — Point-to-point tunneling protocol. A modification of *PPP* that allows *intranets* to be set up over the *Internet*. Using PPTP a company's employees can connect to the Internet, then connect to *Web sites* that are available only to authorized users of the PPTP network. Although connected to a public system, it appears to be an independent and private system.

production server — Part of a three-stage publishing system. A *Web site* is created using FrontPage on a personal computer, then transferred to a *staging server*. The system administrator can then transfer the Web site from the staging server to the *production server*, a computer running a *Web server* that is accessible to the Web site's intended audience.

protocol — A language used by computers and other devices on a network to communicate with one another.

relative URL — An incomplete *URL*, one that provides enough information to find any object as long as the *browser* knows where the *Web page* containing the URL is. The URL may simply name the referenced file, or perhaps a directory and the file. It doesn't include the *hostname* and may not include the entire directory path.

root web — The main FrontPage *web* at a particular domain.

script — A bit of programming code, written in a *script language*.

script language — A form of programming language that can be run by an interpreter (a program that reads the script and carries out instructions). For instance, JavaScript and VBScript are script languages that run within interpreters built into the Netscape Navigator and (in the case of VBScript) Internet Explorer *browsers*.

select object — A form component in a *Web page*. A select object may be in the form of a list box, a drop-down list box, or a text box with an arrow that lets you scroll through the options.

server extensions, FrontPage — Special programs installed at a *Web server*. They carry out a variety of tasks that might be carried out by *CGI scripts* if the server extensions were not available. For instance, they enable the *Web author* to set up a search page, create a discussion group, and so on.

server-side image map — An *image map* that requires the assistance of the *Web server*. Older *browsers* cannot use *client-side image maps*. With server-side image maps, when the user clicks an *image* information is sent to the server, which, based on the position of the mouse-click, decides which *Web page* or other object should be sent to the browser.

SQL — Structured Query Language, a programming language that is a de facto standard for obtaining information from, and updating, databases. Often pronounced "sequel."

staging server — A computer on which *Web sites* may be placed by *Web authors* prior to having the sites transferred to the *production server*.

tag — An *HTML* code that provides instructions to a *browser* on how to format a particular object (text or an *image*, for instance) within the *Web page*.

target — A *tag* in a *Web page* that marks a position within the page. The *Web author* can then create a *link* from somewhere else in the document to the target. FrontPage calls this a *bookmark*.

TCP/IP — Transmission control protocol/Internet protocol. A *protocol* used on the *Internet*.

telnet — A system by which computers can connect and log on to other computers across the *Internet*. *Web authors* may use telnet:// *URLs* in their *links*; when the user clicks such a link, a telnet program opens and connects to the referenced telnet site.

textarea object — A form component in a *Web page*. A textarea is a multiline text box.

To Do List — A FrontPage program that keeps track of tasks that the *Web author* has added to To Do List.

transmission control protocol/Internet protocol — See *TCP/IP*.

URL — Uniform resource locator, a *Web* address used to specify the position of computer files on the *World Wide Web* or *intranet*. There are both *absolute URLs* and *relative URLs*.

virtual host — A single *host computer* may have multiple *hostnames*. This is known as *multihoming*. For instance, a *Web-hosting company* can sell services to many customers, each of which has its own hostname. The hostnames are directed to the single Web-hosting computer. Each of these multiple hostnames is known as a virtual host.

watermark — A special type of *background image*. When the user scrolls through the text and *images* in the page, the watermark image remains static. Normal *background images* scroll with the page.

web — The term used by FrontPage to refer to a collection of *Web pages* and related files. This is not the same as a *Web site*. A Web site may contain several FrontPage webs, or it may be created from a single web. FrontPage can open only one web at a time. See also *root web* and *child web*.

Web author — Someone who uses *HTML* or a *WYSIWYG HTML editor* to create *Web pages*.

Web page — A document created using *HTML* and designed to be displayed in a Web *browser*.

Web presence provider — See *Web-hosting company*.

Web server — 1. A program used to administer a *Web site* or collection of Web sites, receiving requests for computer files from *browsers* and transmitting the files back to the browser. 2. A computer running Web server software. 3. The entire system, hardware and software.

Web site — A collection of related *Web pages* and other files on the *World Wide Web* or on an *intranet*. A *Web server* may manage one or more *Web sites*. See also *Web-hosting company*.

Web, the — Another term for the *World Wide Web*.

WebBot — A special utility in FrontPage used to create a *script* in a *Web page*. The script works in conjunction with the FrontPage *server extensions* to carry out some kind of task, such as inserting a particular *image* or file into the page at a specified time.

Web-hosting company — A company that sells the services of a *Web server*. You can buy space at the Web server for your Web site. Sometimes known as a *Web presence provider*.

webtop publishing — Microsoft regards FrontPage as a *webtop publishing* system. In the same way that a desktop publishing system is designed to make it easy for people without a great deal of technical expertise to produce books, brochures, manuals, and so on, webtop publishing systems enable people with little *HTML* knowledge to create *Web sites*.

winsock — Short for Windows sockets, a sort of *Internet* driver. In the same way that Microsoft Windows programs use printer drivers to connect to printers, Windows programs that need to work with the Internet or an *intranet* use winsock to connect to the network.

wizard — A program that leads the user through a series of steps in order to make a complicated procedure easy. For instance, FrontPage has a wizard that helps users create a discussion group, a very complicated procedure without the wizard.

World Wide Web — A software system running over the *Internet*. The World Wide Web is an enormous *hypertext* system containing tens of millions of documents linked together in a complex web.

WYSIWYG — An acronym, pronounced "wizzywig," that stands for "what you see is what you get." It's used to refer to word processing and desktop publishing programs and *HTML editors* that show you what the finished product actually looks like, rather than forcing you to use arcane codes and formatting characters. *FrontPage Editor* is a WYSIWYG editor because you don't have to create *HTML tags* — it creates them for you.

INDEX

SYMBOLS

A

B

C

(continued)

D

(*continued*)

E

F

G

H

(*continued*)

I

(*continued*)

J

K

L

M

N

O

P

Q

T

(continued)

U

V

W

X

Y

IDG
BOOKS
WORLDWIDE

IDG BOOKS WORLDWIDE REGISTRATION CARD

RETURN THIS REGISTRATION CARD FOR FREE CATALOG

Title of this book: Discover FrontPage™ 97

My overall rating of this book: ❑ Very good [1] ❑ Good [2] ❑ Satisfactory [3] ❑ Fair [4] ❑ Poor [5]

How I first heard about this book:

❑ Found in bookstore; name: [6] ❑ Book review: [7]

❑ Advertisement: [8] ❑ Catalog: [9]

❑ Word of mouth; heard about book from friend, co-worker, etc.: [10] ❑ Other: [11]

What I liked most about this book:

What I would change, add, delete, etc., in future editions of this book:

Other comments:

Number of computer books I purchase in a year: ❑ 1 [12] ❑ 2-5 [13] ❑ 6-10 [14] ❑ More than 10 [15]

I would characterize my computer skills as: ❑ Beginner [16] ❑ Intermediate [17] ❑ Advanced [18] ❑ Professional [19]

I use ❑ DOS [20] ❑ Windows [21] ❑ OS/2 [22] ❑ Unix [23] ❑ Macintosh [24] ❑ Other: [25] ____________ (please specify)

I would be interested in new books on the following subjects:
(please check all that apply, and use the spaces provided to identify specific software)

❑ Word processing: [26] ❑ Spreadsheets: [27]

❑ Data bases: [28] ❑ Desktop publishing: [29]

❑ File Utilities: [30] ❑ Money management: [31]

❑ Networking: [32] ❑ Programming languages: [33]

❑ Other: [34]

I use a PC at (please check all that apply): ❑ home [35] ❑ work [36] ❑ school [37] ❑ other: [38] ____________

The disks I prefer to use are ❑ 5.25 [39] ❑ 3.5 [40] ❑ other: [41] ____________

I have a CD ROM: ❑ yes [42] ❑ no [43]

I plan to buy or upgrade computer hardware this year: ❑ yes [44] ❑ no [45]

I plan to buy or upgrade computer software this year: ❑ yes [46] ❑ no [47]

Name: Business title: [48] Type of Business: [49]

Address (❑ home [50] ❑ work [51]/Company name:)

Street/Suite#

City [52]/State [53]/Zipcode [54]: Country [55]

❑ **I liked this book!** You may quote me by name in future IDG Books Worldwide promotional materials.

My daytime phone number is ____________

IDG BOOKS®
THE WORLD OF COMPUTER KNOWLEDGE

Please keep me informed about IDG's World of Computer Knowledge. Send me the latest IDG Books catalog.

NO POSTAGE NECESSARY IF MAILED IN THE UNITED STATES

BUSINESS REPLY MAIL

FIRST CLASS MAIL PERMIT NO. 2605 FOSTER CITY, CALIFORNIA

IDG Books Worldwide
919 E Hillsdale Blvd, STE 400
Foster City, CA 94404-9691